The Structure
and Dynamics of
Theories

Wolfgang Stegmüller

The Structure
and Dynamics of
Theories

SPRINGER-VERLAG

New York Heidelberg Berlin

1976

Wolfgang Stegmüller
Seminar für Philosophie, Logik und Wissenschaftstheorie
8 München 22,
Kaulbachstrasse 31, West Germany

Translated from the German
by Dr. William Wohlhueter.

Library of Congress Cataloging in Publication Data

Stegmüller, Wolfgang.
    The structure and dynamics of theories.

    Translation of Theorienstrukturen und Theoriendynamik, originally published as
v. 2, pt. 2 of the author's Probleme und Resultate der Wissenschaftstheorie und
analytischen Philosophie.
    Bibliography: p. 273
    Includes indexes.
    1. Science — Methodology. 2. Science — Philosophy. I. Title.
Q175.S762   501   75-28364

No part of this book may be translated or reproduced in any form without written
permission from Springer-Verlag.

© 1976 by Springer-Verlag New York Inc.

Printed in the United States of America.

ISBN 0-387-07493-7   Springer-Verlag   New York

ISBN 3-540-07493-7   Springer-Verlag   Berlin   Heidelberg

I have found that most scientists and philosophers are willing to discuss
a new assertion, if it is formulated in the customary conceptual framework;
but it seems very difficult to most of them even to consider and discuss
new concepts.

RUDOLF CARNAP, "Intellectual autobiography," in: Schilpp, P.A., *The Philosophy of Rudolf Carnap*, p. 77.

The man who takes historic fact seriously must suspect that science does
not tend toward the ideal that our image of its cumulativeness has suggested.
Perhaps it is another sort of enterprise.

THOMAS S. KUHN, *The Structure of Scientific Revolutions*, 2nd ed., p. 96.

Preface

The first part of this book, Part I, can be read from two quite distinct points of view: one, as an attempt to develop and defend the important aspects of an *entirely new approach to the analysis of the structure of scientific theories;* and second, as the source of the conceptual apparatus needed for the analysis of theory dynamics and the *metascientific reconstruction* of T. S. Kuhn's *notions of 'normal science' and 'scientific revolutions.'*

In the last few years a great deal has been written about Kuhnian 'irrationalism' and 'relativism.' Most writers felt that they must combat it; a few thought that they must develop it further and deploy it propagandistically against a 'logic of science.' According to the view developed in Part II of this book, both parties are on the wrong track.

As far as irrationalism is concerned, it must be said that Kuhn's position itself cannot be characterized as 'irrational' in any reasonable sense of the word. His language is much too clear, and his examples are historically too well founded. (He is thoroughly aware of his frequent use of metaphorical language which, as can also be shown, is his prerogative.) Without precedent in his work is the fact that *he appears to impute irrational behavior to the practioners of the exact natural sciences (of all people!).* And indeed he appears to impute it to *both* of the forms of scientific practice distinguished by him. Anyone engaged in *normal science* is a narrow-minded dogmatist clinging uncritically to his theory. Those engaged in *extraordinary research* leading to *scientific revolutions* are religious fanatics under the spell of conversion, trying by all the means of persuasion and propaganda to convert others to the 'new paradigm' as revealed to themselves.

Both pictures are erroneous. On the basis of the *nonstatement view* of theories developed in Part I and Chapter 15, both types of science may be interpreted as *rational* behavior. Since a theory in Kuhn's sense is not a system of sentences, but rather *a relatively complicated conceptual instrument,* the characteristic way it is held by 'normal' scientists is not a dogmatic embrace of certain assumptions or convictions; it amounts to employing this 'conceptual instrument' for solving certain problems (Kuhn's metaphorical comparison with the carpenter who, having botched the job, blames his tools, is a quite proper analogy.) *Holding one and the same theory is consistent with convictions or hypothetical assumptions which differ from person to person and from time to time.*

Theory dynamics as Kuhn understands it, i.e., the fact that a theory is never *rejected on the basis of 'falsifying data'* but always *dislodged by another theory,* also loses the appearance of irrationality in light of the nonstatement view. But here there do remain two rationality gaps. The first is summed up in the question: "Why is it that in times of crises when a theory is confronted with more and more anomalies this theory is not rejected even though no new one has been found?" This 'rationality gap' *cannot* be closed. One can, however, understand why this is not possible. No more is needed than a simple *psychological truism:* a leaky roof is better than none at all; for the shipwrecked a broken oar is better than none.

The second rationality gap is exposed by the question: "In what sense does theory dislodgement mean *scientific progress?*" This gap actually remains open for Kuhn. It can, however, be closed with the help of a macrological reduction concept. That Kuhn, and likewise P. Feyerabend, believe this gap is not to be closed, rests on the paradox that while searching for *logical arguments* to support the belief, they fall back entirely into the conceptual world of their opponents, namely, into the statement view of theories. Instead of concluding that in 'scientific revolutions' the dislodged and the dislodging theories are incommensurable *'because the theorems of the first cannot be inferred from those of the latter,'* one must conclude that *'thinking in terms of inference relations between sentences' is a fully inadequate method of comparing competing theories.*

Closing this rationality gap also provides a rebuttal to the charge of relativism leveled at Kuhn. Here we must again differentiate. Whether or not Kuhn himself embraces something like an 'epistemological relativism' is an *irrelevant* question as long as this position does not find its way into his historical analysis. What could be a *real cause for concern* is the circumstance that *epistemological relativism appears to follow from* his statements about scientific revolutions. Many critics have assumed this. Thus, the dispute with Kuhn focused on the alternative: "either epistemological relativism or vindication of 'cumulative scientific progress'." But with this alternative Kuhn's opponents maneuvered themselves into a hopeless position. In order to avoid relativism they either had to challenge Kuhn's historical competence—which cannot be done in good conscience—or they had to concede that most scientists are indeed guilty of irrational behavior in their research. In Popper's words, normal scientists are people "for whom you must feel sorry." And scientists' behavior in times of scientific revolution seems like that of the masses caught in political upheaval or religious wars. To use Lakatos' words, Kuhn's analysis of scientific revolutions is "applied mob psychology"; i.e., mob psychology applied to the irrational, unreasonable masses mustered under the notion of 'science pursuing human beings.'

Yet this alternative collapses with the closure of the second rationality gap. The phenomenon of one theory being dislodged by another need not be contested. It can be reconstructed in such a way as to yield a 'sensible' concept of scientific progress. *Relinquishing the thesis of an accumulation of knowledge, as Kuhn does, is entirely compatible with a nonrelativistic position.*

The internal difficulties besetting the works of Kuhn and Feyerabend, as detected by their critics, together with the historical plausibility of many of their claims, creates a situation virtually crying to be clarified in some way other than that afforded by traditional logical analysis. Something else adds to this chorus too: the discussions in *Criticism and the Growth of Knowledge,* edited by I. Lakatos and A. Musgrave, which have surely contributed more toward widening than toward narrowing the gulf between 'Kuhnians' and 'anti-Kuhnians.' Without claiming to be a futurologist I believe I can say that *at this intuitive level* the discussion can be carried on forever without the slightest chance of reaching any consensus. To achieve that, one must 'assume the burden of the concept.'

As a by-product, the reconstructions in Part II will show that points of departure and lines of thought which are *prima facie* quite different do in the end 'lead to the same thing.' This applies, e.g., to Lakatos' 'sophisticated falsification concept' vis-à-vis the reduction concept originated by E. W. Adams and developed and improved by J. D. Sneed.

Although it is likely that to many this book will appear polemical and provocative both in form and content, it should be remembered that *it is entirely dedicated to reconciling* the logic-oriented proponents and the 'rebellious' opponents of the philosophy of science. Whether or not this reconciliation comes off depends, among other things, on whether or not both sides are prepared to make concessions. Elegant expositions, justified critiques, and reckless exaggerations are at present divided about equally between both parties. One side must learn to see that they make it too easy for themselves in criticizing the 'irrationalism and relativism of Kuhn and Feyerabend' (on the basis of the statement view, i.e., a false presupposition, this is not at all difficult). On the other hand, Feyerabend in particular must acknowledge that it is a *non sequitur* to reject and discard a 'logic of science' because too strong a tendency to imitate proof theory has led the philosophy of science to misuse its instrument, logic.

Thus, the standpoint adopted in this book is that the works of T. S. Kuhn, too, have given us *a new metascientific conception.* Instead of assaulting his position on the basis of a preconceived stereotype of what rational scientific behavior should be, we will try to *reconstruct his conception systematically,* and are prepared to make more or less fundamental revisions concerning the notion of *'rational scientific behavior.'* This systematic reconstruction is missing in his own writings. He is, of course, primarily a historian, not a logician, and thus confines himself to numerous historical illustrations and a psychological, sociological description of his new conception. In itself there is nothing wrong with a psychological description. I, too, would have no qualms in depicting my own change of attitude toward Kuhn in the following language: "In the last two years my thinking has undergone a miniature revolution. I was caught in a deep intellectual crisis while studying his works when suddenly in the middle of the night the scales fell from my eyes and my 'paradigm' of *theory* underwent a change." Such a description does not, of course, preclude my being able to give *reasons* for the new outlook *too*. And that is what this book is about, including the reason why I am not very fond of the Kuhnian expression "paradigm."

The reconstruction of Kuhn's conception of science would not have been possible without the epochal work of Sneed who first created the conceptual framework needed for such a reconstruction. Unfortunately, Sneed's work, *The Logical Structure of Mathematical Physics,* is so difficult that I fear the number of those who really absorb his ideas cannot be very great.

Therefore, Part I strives to *present* Sneed's *ideas in the clearest way possible.* This involves simplifying, modifying, and supplementing them to some extent. Furthermore, the material is rearranged, including a much more detailed breakdown into subtopics. Finally, care is taken to embed his work in the context of those problems raised in my book [Theoretische Begriffe].

The treatment of classical particle mechanics in Chapter 6 is unfortunately too brief. Together with some of my colleagues and students I am planning *a separate publication on this theme.* In it further improvements are aimed at and open problems discussed.

The changes and simplifications vis-à-vis Sneed's text involve above all the following points: (1) the definition and discussion of the *criterion for T-theoretical;* (2) the formulation of the *central empirical claims* in Chapter 5; (3) the introduction of an additional concept of (strong) *theory proposition* in Section 7.2 which permits us to assign a propositional content to the central empirical claim of a theory; (4) the definition of the *expanded core* concept (especially concerning the *application relation α*); (5) the definition of the *reduction concepts;* (6) a discussion of the *paradigm* concepts of Wittgenstein and Kuhn, respectively; (7) the formulation of a *rule of autodetermination;* and (8) the way in which the *Kuhnian concept of holding a theory* is introduced. The *discussion of the rationality concept* in relation to Kuhn and his critics, especially in Chapter 11, is entirely new, as is the discussion of the latest works of Lakatos and Feyerabend.

I should like to thank Dr. A. Ḳamlah and Messrs. R. Kleinknecht, C. U. Moulines, W. Wolze, and E. Wüst for many valuable suggestions offered in the course of numerous discussions. The simplified version of claims (V) and (VI) was proposed by Messrs. Kleinknecht and Wüst. The discussions with Dr. Kamlah and Messrs. Wolze and Moulines served to clear up various problems concerning Sneed's concept of theory-dependent measurement, classical particle mechanics, and the set-theoretic apparatus. I must also thank Dr. Carlos-Ulisses Moulines for three especially important suggestions: a simplification in the reduction concepts; an improvement in the concept of the Kuhnian sense of holding a theory, which purged it of the last Platonic remnants left by Sneed; and the idea that theory reduction is an essential part of Lakatos' 'sophisticated falsification' concept.

Ms. G. Ullrich, Ms. K. Lüddeke, and Ms. E. Weinberg are due many thanks for the painstaking work invested in typing the manuscript. I should also like to thank all my colleagues and students who helped proofread, as well as Dr. U. Blau and Dr. A. Kamlah for preparing the index. Concerning the English edition I want to thank Dr. Wohlhueter for producing a careful meticulous translation.

To Springer-Verlag I again owe a debt of gratitude for having complied with all my wishes.

Wolfgang Stegmüller

Table of Contents

Part II

Theory Dynamics: The Course of 'Normal Science' and the Dislodging of Theories During 'Scientific Revolutions'

Introduction

Big brother—The wrong orientation?

Asked about the subject matter of the philosophy of science, one might reply: "Nobody knows." This reminds us of the way B. Russell once characterized mathematics. But while he intended in this, his typical droll manner, to point out the problem of mathematical knowledge, in the present context this answer could be meant quite seriously, i.e., maliciously.

A comparison with the situation in the philosophy of mathematics supports this claim. The development of the philosophy of mathematics into an exact science called *metamathematics* was prompted by the foundational crisis in mathematics. And since this crisis was spawned by the discovery of the antinomies in set theory, it is often thought to represent *a tragic event in modern mathematics.* Judging from the consequences, however, one might sooner arrive at the opposite conclusion: the discovery of antinomies was a most *fortunate event*, for it forcefully urged the formalization and precise articulation of the objects with which the philosophy of mathematics deals. Intuitive ideas about mathematical thinking were replaced by objects capable of being exactly described, and the philosophy of mathematics evolved into mathematical foundational studies which in all branches led to disciplines no less precise than mathematics itself—disciplines which today are considered a part of mathematics.

Unfortunately, empirical sciences have not undergone a foundational crisis of this sort, and thus there has been no compelling reason to transform conceptual and theoretical constructions in these disciplines into objects suitable for exact metatheoretical study. One simply went ahead *as if* such objects existed. Confronted with details, it was thought that primitive models formulated in a fragment of first-order language or a reference to 'what scientists actually do' would take care of the matter. The first alternative, however, produces results which can, of course, be no more representative of modern science than can positive sentential logic produce an adequate portrait of modern mathematical argumentation. Against the second alternative it may be objected that it scarcely offers more exact results than did the pre-Flood philosophy of mathematics, if that fortunate event mentioned above may be metaphorically thought of as the mathematical Flood.

Thus, there remained only a *philosophy-of-the-as-if* patterned after big brother *metamathematics*. What proved so extraordinarily fruitful there, *must* prove fruitful here too.

Now, the idea that *theories are certain systems or classes of sentences* is one of the most fundamental notions of modern logic and mathematics. And research concentrates on *logical inference relations obtaining between elements of these classes.* I will refer to this way of looking at things as the *micrological aspect* and the conception of theories as classes of sentences as the *statement view of theories.*

It cannot be denied that these two perspectives accounted for great successes in the foundational studies of mathematics. Yet this was no foregone conclusion; it was a consequence of the types of problems investigated there. Whenever we deal with questions like whether or not an axiom system is consistent, whether its axioms are independent of one another, whether it is complete or contains undecidable sentences, whether its decision problem is solvable or not, we are dealing with questions concerning the provability of sentences or their deducibility from other sentences.

One can well understand that, in view of the progress in metamathematics, philosophers of science tended unconsiously, but irresistibly, to adopt the statement view and micrological analysis. Philosophical *lingualism*, fashionable today as was psychologism at the turn of the last century, served to reinforce this tendency.

It is nevertheless nothing but prejudicial to suppose that modes of thinking and methods which have proved to be fruitful in an area *A must* also be so in another area *B*. Such a conviction can even produce a myth. Does the belief in the statement view and the success of micrological analysis perhaps constitute such a myth—one which could aptly be called the Hilbert–Gödel–Tarski myth, were it not for the false associations this might engender?

Some philosophers appear to have felt so. Yet instead of seeking better methods they rejected everything and rebelled against the philosophy of science.

Rebellion against or revolution within the philosophy of science?

The battle began about 1961. It was directed against all aspects of what might summarily be called the *logical-empiricist analysis* employed in modern philosophy of science. Its tools, methods, content, and presuppositions were all brought under fire.

The *tool* of today's philosopher of science, like the logician's and the metamathematician's, is modern logic. His *method* is the logical analysis and reconstruction of scientific languages, conceptual systems, and theories. Even if the philosophy of science were successful—which (because of its false presuppositions) it cannot be according to the rebels—its results would have little informative value. Since all logical analysis concerns only *'form,'* not *'content,'* one can, with logical methods, only arrive at statements about what holds *for all possible* sciences: the logical form *of all possible* scientific explanation, the logical character *of all possible* laws, the logical structure *of all possible* theories, the logical relationship between *any hypotheses whatever* and *any* data supporting them. But it is precisely specifics which are of real informative value and, therefore, philosophically interesting: *special* scientific explanations, *certain particular* laws and theories, and the methods of argumentation characteristic of *certain* disciplines.

The analogy between metatheoretical, logical, and metascientific concepts seems to support this claim, if not necessarily the alleged lack of interest thought to derive from it. As *metatheoretician* the logician bends his efforts toward explicating concepts such as "is true," "is logically valid," "is provable," "is deducible from," and further "is a deduction" and "is a proof" as well as "is consistent," "is complete," "is recursively undecidable," all of which have to do with sentences, sequences of sentences, and systems of sentences, respectively. Similarly, the philosopher of science *qua* metatheoretician attempts to explicate notions like "is an observational report," "is a law," "is meaningless," "is supporting (confirming, corroborating) data for," and further "is a causal explanation" and "is a statistical explanation" as well as "is a theory," all of which are also predicated of sentences, sequences of sentences, and systems of sentences, respectively.

Even if the philosophy of science were to specialize and thus succeed in arriving at a detailed understanding of notions like *historical* explanation, *anglistic* argumentation, *quantum-physical* law, or *biological* theory, it would still be damned to perpetual sterility according to the rebels, because it must be satisfied with the *static* aspect of science, i.e., with 'cross sections' of scientific systems at certain stages of development. But what is really interesting or important about the various disciplines is their evolution and development, i.e., the *dynamic* aspect which completely eludes logical analysis. In order to research this aspect, the logical method must be replaced by the *historical method.* Thus, it is no accident that the four outstanding critics of traditional philosophy of science, N. R. Hanson, S. Toulmin, T. S. Kuhn, and P. Feyerabend, command an extensive knowledge of the history of science and endeavor to support their criticism of traditional notions with *historical arguments.*

Criticism is, however, directed not only at logic as a tool and the analogy to metalogical concepts pervading metascientific studies. Various *empiricist assumptions* also came under heavy fire. The idea that all disciplines having anything to do with reality are empirically anchored became, according to these critics, a stereotype which led the philosophy of science astray. Two examples illustrate this. *Scientific language* was divided into a theoretical and an observational language. The task of explaining how theoretical terms can be interpreted with the help of the observational language, whose terms alone are fully understandable, belonged to the empiricist program of the philosophy of science in the wider sense. But ever since Hanson came up with the phrase 'the theory-ladenness of all observational data,' this dual-level conception of scientific language has come under ever-increasing criticism, the last stage of which holds this whole conception to be based on an untenable fiction: *there is no such thing as the neutral observer* who does not interpret his observations in the light of a theory; this is a philosophical pipe dream. A second example is to be found in the rival theories of *inductive confirmation* and *deductive corroboration*. According to the critics this altercation does not merely idealize factual occurrences in the various disciplines; it *imputes methods of argumentation to scientists, not even traces of which may actually be found*. As we will see, according to Kuhn there exists for example, not one single known procedure in the history of the exact natural sciences approximating the 'stereotype of falsification' of a theory by experience.

Thus, a number of philosophers were convinced that *the philosophy of science must take a brand new approach*. What first looked like an esoteric rebellion *against* the philosophy of science appeared to become a revolution *in* the philosophy of science. The best-known and presumably most important contribution as yet to the 'new approach' is contained in T. S. Kuhn's work, *The Structure of Scientific Revolutions*, which will be discussed in Part II. There are a number of additional reasons for singling out Kuhn. First, a discussion of all the works of the authors named would take us too far afield. A selection is imperative. Kuhn's book recommends itself here because in it the divergence from traditional modes of thought is particularly easy to discern, being distinctly accentuated by the author himself. Second, Kuhn is presumably one of the most competent contemporary historians of science. Thus, the ploy of shrugging off his historical theses as simply the ' speculations of an obscurant' is blocked. Third, this author uses language which, although often metaphoric, is nevertheless plain, clear, and to the point. The main reason is, however, the fourth: Kuhn's thinking does not exhaust itself in negative criticism. With the exception of occasional polemic remarks, it makes a series of positive constructive contributions.

The view that Kuhn's contributions are only significant for the history of science is, indeed, well represented.[1] Yet what follows should show that behind them there is a *novel new metatheoretic conception*. Kuhn himself was only able to expose the psychological-sociological side of this new conception—something which he never denied since he regards himself as a historian and does not claim to have made a new logical analysis. It is J. D. Sneed's book, *The Logical Structure of Mathematical Physics*, that first provides a conceptual foundation suitable for articulating the *logical*

---

[1] For a long time I, too, shared this view and thus, considered from the present standpoint, made a number of unjustified remarks about Kuhn in [Induktion].

aspects of some of Kuhn's new ideas, or for that matter even lets us know that there are such logical aspects.

In the context of a rebellion of various thinkers against the traditional philosophy of science, Kuhn's explicitly announced goal sounds quite modest. He emphasizes that he wants only to contest the idea of a linear development of science via a gradual accumulation of knowledge and replace it with a different theory of scientific development. That this goal implies a great deal more than the reader may first suppose will become plain, for example, when Kuhn blames the prefaces and introductions of scientific textbooks for the distorted picture of the evolution of science and simultaneously discerns in them the roots of modern positivism and empiricism. In the end, the conclusion—and a more radical one it could not be—seems to be that *the philosophy of science ought not to be pursued any more* because the particular kind of rationality which the philosophers of science imputed to science simply does not exist.

Kuhn's work, along with the writings of the other authors of the 'new approach' just mentioned, has elicited sharp criticism, especially from D. Shapere, I. Scheffler, and the 'critical rationalists.' But even if one holds all these critiques to be just—which we will not—there still remains a very unsatisfactory state of affairs. One would be forced to say: "Here the *theory* of science, there the *history* of science, and *never* the twain shall meet." This is most unsatisfactory, because the analysis of the structure of the sciences also includes the analysis of their developmental structure. And when the two types of analysis *cannot in any way* be combined into a single portrait of science, when in particular the results of the historian appear to entail a philosophical relativism, then *this must be a symptom that 'something is wrong.'*

The unsatisfactory state of affairs has not been altered by the discussion between Kuhn and his 'Popperian opponents.' Since a dispute of this sort— in this inexact, intuitive, figurative language—could be carried on forever without the slightest chance of overcoming the differences, once again logical analysis offers the only means of clarification, perhaps even reconciliation. Leaving aside partial truths on both sides, the whole debate fits exactly into the Kuhnian mold of a discussion between the advocates of different paradigms. Genuine communication is not really being sought.

We do not want to make the mistake of *using a faulty application of logic as a reason for rejecting logic as a tool altogether,* or of *confusing a just criticism of the statement view with a criticism of metalogical analysis.* If the reconstruction in Part II has any merit at all, it must be recognized that the Kuhn–Popper–Lakatos debate *represents one of the worst examples of talking right past one another by advocates of different views.* And it might be added that it is difficult to imagine a better proof of the potential of the *method of rational reconstruction* than the fact that with its help the roots of misunderstanding can be laid bare and a clarification achieved. First, however, we must learn to appreciate that, and why, the 'paradigms' of *theory* held by Kuhn and his opponents are not merely incompatible, but ' incommensurable.' For all of Kuhn's opponents a theory is something that can be construed as a system of statements in one way or another, whereas Kuhn's theory concept precludes this sort of interpretation. Sneed provides the model-theoretic means for making some sense of the ideas that a group of scientists *hold one and the same theory* despite changing and varying opinions, and that *a theory is immune to falsification* and need not be 'immunized' ('normal science'). It will also *become clear why a theory is not abandoned because of 'refuting experience,' but can only be dislodged by another theory* (revolutionary theory dislodgement instead of falsification in times of extraordinary research). At the same time the rational reconstruction will make it possible to cut down Kuhn's exaggerations, to point out the relative merits of repressed aspects, and above all *to close the rationality gap* which presumably causes Kuhn's opponents so much discomfort.

The second level of rationality

The initial appearance of scientific knowledge, itself a very puzzling phenomenon, we will call *the first level of rationality*. All attempts to explain the nature of this knowledge will be called *the second level of rationality*. The split is purely methodological. It is neither claimed that both processes were always separate, nor that they should remain so. Presumably research in the particular disciplines is often accompanied by methodological reflections, whereby the success of the former certainly can go hand in hand with the success of the latter. All metascientific endeavors, in trying to find out 'what's up with scientific knowledge,' belong to the second rationality level.

The first rationality level may presumably be traced back to the times when man first began to argue, whether for the sake of attaining knowledge or for recreational, magical, or yet other motives. Aristotelian logic offers one of the most impressive examples of second level rationality. That people in saying "therefore. . . ." appeal to rules which can be brought to light and explicitly formulated, belongs to one of the more astonishing and admirable discoveries of Occidental intellectual history, comparable with the most significant discoveries achieved in the natural sciences. That this discovery was followed by more than two thousand years of stagnation ought to be a warning that discoveries in this area do not just fall into our laps.

Today it is generally acknowledged that logical investigations are important and difficult. In the area of nonmathematical knowledge it is a different story. Here, efforts bent toward second level rationality are thought to be superfluous or simple.

The first thesis, implicit in Feyerabend's work, is ambiguous. It may mean that metatheoretical investigations are not necessary for the sciences. But even if this were so, it would not mean anything, since it might be added that the first rationality level is not necessary either. Perhaps it means, though, that the one interferes with the other: whoever is always reflecting about his own activity never achieves anything worthwhile. But this psychological difficulty would serve at best to force a practical division of labor. Finally, it might be meant that efforts toward clarity are damaging because they lead to 'mental arteriosclerosis' (Feyerabend).[2] It is scarcely conceivable how something like this can be substantiated. I assume that such concern for the mental well-being of certain compatriots is groundless since it presumably stems from an incorrect notion of clarity.

That the second rationality level is a simple matter is obviously the position of the *critical rationalists*. Otherwise their disinclination to precision and its necessary concomitant, formalization, can hardly be explained. The difference in my own position can best be illustrated with a paradigmatic example.

The demand for *strict testability* is, according to a fundamental rule of this philosophical theory, constantly violated by 'normal' scientists in Kuhn's sense because they never question the 'paradigm theory' which they hold. Such behavior appears to be *irrational* and, hence, something *which ought not to be*.[3]

But how do they know this? Do they command the infallible insight of metaphysical rationalists which tells them what kind of scientific behavior alone is sensible and permissible? Since the scientist should always be ready to change his beliefs, why does this dictum not also apply to the philosophers reflecting about them?

As Part II should show, the behavior of the normal scientist need contain ' no trace of irrationality.' His theories *are* immune to refractory experience and need not be immunized by conventionalistic tricks. One can do no more here than propagate *the insight that, and why, this is so*. But such insight can come only if the same intellectual mobility is granted at the metalevel as one believes must be required at the object level.

Our notions about rational scientific behavior are still quite blurred in many respects, and in any case still quite incomplete. Thus, I read those of Kuhn's passages which *seem* to contain a rebellion against the philosophy of science differently. For me Kuhn has *revealed new and different dimensions of rationality* which really could lead to a 'small revolution' in thinking about rationality. These dimensions are not to be denied, but *cleared up*. But in order to do so, one must be prepared to admit 'paradigm shifts' at the metalevel too, and, if necessary, make one. Like the physicist, the philosopher does not have all the right answers.

---

[2] [Empiricist], p. 322.

[3] Cf. Chapter 11, where the criticisms of Kuhn are presented.

Moreover, there is the detail work connected with the philosophy of science which, just like the 'puzzle solving' of normal science, can be unspeakably laborious. Even a small contribution toward clearing up the nature of *scientific rationality* can involve extremely difficult and time-consuming analyses. Here, too, the philosopher of science has no head start over a man like Kepler who, according to his own words, calculated until nearly mad for twelve years before obtaining Mars' trajectory, nor over a man like Hilbert who struggled in vain for decades pursuing a constructive consistency proof for number theory.

But why bother? Feyerabend calls on us to do it differently. Alas, the alternative is only an apparent one, because the goals are also different. Feyerabend is not concerned with *clarity about science*, but with *taking pleasure in science*. I should hate to have to play judge here and decide which of these two 'values' is the higher in case of a conflict. And neither do I want to be a kill-joy. But *if* we are after clarity, then—unfortunately—we cannot follow Feyerabend's call for the greatest possible "sloppiness in semantics," but must take as examples logicians like Aristotle, Frege, or Gödel.[4]

But this was a digression from the original theme. Had I a tendency to malicious exaggeration, I would say that critical rationalism is not critical at all. At the metalevel it is *naive metaphysical rationalism* and at the object level *extravagant rationalism*. (The exaggeration lies especially in the last label because Kuhn's formulation does contain a 'rationality gap' which should be closed. But this gap involves only scientific revolutions, not normal science.)

But why should a philosopher of science let himself be so strongly influenced— 'empiricists' and 'critical rationalists' would say infected— by a *historian* of science like T. S. Kuhn? This has its special reasons.

A fivefold feedback

Often one finds an entirely false picture of the philosopher's task of explicating concepts. It is thought that there is *a rectilinear progression from the given intuitive point of departure to the explication* in the course of which the vague intuitive notions are successively replaced by precise stipulations. As we have emphasized elsewhere,[5] it would be better to compare concept explication with the cybernetic model of a *feedback process*. It is necessary to refer back to the intuitive basis repeatedly, because it often first becomes apparent in the course of the explication attempt itself that certain intuitive notions are incompatible with each other, or ambiguous, so that differentiations are necessary which were originally overlooked.

---

[4] [Empiricist], p. 322.

[5] W. Stegmüller, [Statistik], p. 25f.

> One of the various possible interpretations of the so-called *hermeneutic circle* is to take this phrase as a rather unlikely label for a case of feedback between an explicandum, which is 'antecedently understood,' and the explication itself.[6]

This is not, however, the only kind of feedback to which metascientific analyses are obligated. There is a second kind of feedback between the philosophy of science and *logic*. Although the philosopher of science in the narrower sense does not need to aim at productive achievements in the area of mathematical logic, results there can be of great metascientific relevance. This book will offer an illustration. Without recourse to the method of axiomatization via the introduction of set-theoretic predicates, and still more to the instrumentarium provided by modern model theory, the precise articulation of the nonstatement view of physical theories would not have been possible.

This is also true of the relationship between the philosophies of science and of *language* (taking the latter in the widest sense of the word so as to include not only language philosophy, but linguistic philosophy as well[7]). Although this book will give us reasons to suppose that model-theoretic analyses will have greater metascientific relevance in the future than logico-linguistic investigations, the latter will continue to have considerable significance for many questions. The persistent controversy around the problem of delineating empirical from nonempirical sciences offers an example. Another may be found in the problem of the dependence of the meaning of scientific, especially theoretical, terms on the context of the whole theory. Some aspects of the problem will be discussed in Part II.

> One *essential difference* between the philosophies of language and science is that the philosopher of language can, for purposes of justification, always claim to be a *competent speaker*. The philosopher of science, on the other hand, is always exposed to the potential charge of being an *incompetent scientist*.

A fourth kind of feedback is found between the philosophy of science and the *various sciences themselves*. It has two different aspects. Results in the various scientific disciplines may prove relevant for basic metascientific assumptions. For example, a physiological theory of perception can shake presuppositions on which a certain variant of a theory of the observational language rests, as Feyerabend among others has pointed out. But more important still is the second aspect. The various sciences are the subject of metascientific investigations. Better knowledge of them will influence the

---

[6] For further interpretations of the so-called hermeneutic circle, cf. W. Stegmüller, "Walther von der Vogelweides Lied von der Traumliebe (74, 20) und Quasar 3 C 273. Einige Gedanken über den 'Zirkel des Verstehens'" (in preparation).

[7] Concerning this distinction, cf., e.g., J. R. Searle, *Speech Acts*, p. 3f.

philosophy of science, again a 'reciprocal' effect. So-called 'knowledge about various scientific disciplines' will *also* be influenced by the metatheoretic conception of its author.

The realization that the contemporary form of scientific practice does not represent the only way of practicing science brings us to the last sort of feedback: the one between the philosophy and the *history* of science. T. S. Kuhn's historical analyses of those epochs in which scientists held fast to one and the same theory, as well as of those periods in which a fundamental theory was dislodged by another, are not only relevant for confirmation theory and theory construction, *they are indeed incompatible with most metascientific results in these areas*. Every philosopher of science who even takes Kuhn's work seriously as *history*—as I do—must either get the feeling that something is fundamentally wrong in certain areas of traditional philosophy of science, or he must claim that Kuhn is blind to certain aspects of the historical dynamics of science. The least that should follow a decision in favor of this second alternative is a feeling of uncertainty and a bad conscience.

Just like normal science, which according to Kuhn is buoyed up at the beginning of a new epoch not by a real but only by *a promise of* success based on isolated, incomplete examples, the philosophy of science as metatheory of the various disciplines is based in the beginning *more on hope than on certified results*. Yet this hope goes further here, inasmuch as at the metalevel comparisons of theories are possible which at the object level cannot be carried out. Besides, the shift from one 'paradigm' to another is less difficult here than in the various disciplines, as will also be demonstrated below.

Some reasons for deviating from the standard model: Nonstatement view; Macrologic; Holism

We would now like to mention a few fundamental concepts and points of view of special relevance for the discussion to follow. In the end they will force us to deviate from traditional notions. The reader should not, however, expect to gain more than a vague clue from what are more on the order of announcements than expositions. Nonetheless, it is advisable to return here occasionally while reading the book to determine whether the connection between the points listed has been correctly grasped.

(1) We will adopt that variant of modern axiomatics according to which the axiomatization of a theory consists in *introducing a set-theoretic predicate*. The empirical claims of a theory are then sentences of the form "*c* is an *S*," whereby the predicate "*S*" represents the fundamental mathematical structure of the theory in question.

(2) A *strong concept of theoreticity* will prove to be the basis of many subsequent considerations. The dichotomy theoretical–nontheoretical relates not to a language, but *to a theory*. Since the definition of *T-theoretical* refers to a given theory *T*, this concept can only spawn empirical hypotheses. Should the corresponding empirical hypothesis for classical particle mechanics be correct, the position function is *CPM*-nontheoretical[8] despite the strong mathematical idealizations it contains, while *force* and *mass* are *CPM*-theoretical. Thus, in one sense the dichotomy is *absolute*.

(3) The criterion for *T-theoretical* leads to a paradox which is presumably not to be resolved within the confines of the statement view, or at best means putting up with considerable complications. This motivates the transition to the Ramsey formulation of a theory.

Newton's second law affords a very good illustration of this paradox. Traditional thinking presents the alternative: "Either this law is not a definition but an empirical claim, in which case there must be methods for measuring force independent of it, or there are no such methods, in which case this so-called law is in reality a definition."

But this line of thought must run much differently: "(1) Of course the second Newtonian law is *not* a definition. (2) Of course there is *no* method of measuring force independent of this law. Therefore. . . ." Therefore what? The logician will be inclined to say: "Therefore I give up." This is exactly *what we want* here, because the sooner one 'gives up,' the sooner one will learn to grasp 'what's up with theoretical quantities,' in particular what logical problems they create.

(4) The original variant of the Ramsey formulation proves to be in need of modification in three respects concerning aspects of theory, structure, and application usually neglected. First, the fiction of a 'universal application,' according to which a physical theory 'is talking about the entire universe,' must be discarded in favor of *several intended applications*. Second, there are, besides the fundamental law of the theory, *special laws* holding for certain applications. And finally, *additional constraints* hold *between* the different applications. (Thus the term "law," which usually covers constraints too, proves to be misleading and ambiguous.)

(5) Taking all of these factors into account forces us to replace the Ramsey sentence with the *central empirical claim* of a theory which is irreducible and expresses the entire empirical content of a theory at a given time. And so we have the first step toward a clarification of the *nonstatement view*.

(6) The attempt to isolate the conceptual elements used in a central empirical claim leads to *set-theoretic stipulations* for the characteristic mathematical structure of a theory. In particular, the *frame*, the *core*, and the *expanded cores* of a theory are specified. The last of these may vary with time while the theory remains stable. This is the second step toward a precise articulation of the nonstatement view.

---

[8] "*CPM*" stands for "classical particle mechanics." For details cf. Chapter 6.

(**7**) The *micrological perspective* is earmarked by the fact that it takes sentences as the (micrological) atoms and the inference relation between sentences as the basic (micrological) relation. *Macrologic*, on the other hand, uses labels for model-theoretic entities as 'letters,' e.g., labels for the class of *partial* possible models (i.e., physical systems 'about which the theory is talking'), the class of *possible* models (i.e., physical systems *enriched* by T-theoretical functions), the class of *models* (i.e., entities satisfying the basic mathematical structure of the theory), the class of *special laws*, the class of *constraints*, etc.

(**8**) The propositional content of a central empirical claim can be rendered in the linguistically independent macrological symbolism as $I_t \in \mathbb{A}_e(E)$. Such a *strong theory proposition* contains all that the theory in question has to say at time t. "I_t" designates the entire set of intended applications of the theory known at time t. "E" designates an expanded core of the theory (i.e., a certain 8-tuple whose members are entities of the sort mentioned in 7). And the application operation $\lambda_x \mathbb{A}_e(x)$ is designed to generate a certain *class of sets of possible intended applications* out of an expanded core.

(**9**) Another important macrological concept is that of *reduction*. It permits us to speak of the reducibility of one theory to another even when the theories are 'formulated in different conceptual languages.' Thus, it becomes possible to *close the rationality gap* opened by Kuhn's incommensurability thesis and Feyerabend's matching thesis of nonconsistency. (Both of these authors fall back into the micrological habits of their opponents at crucial places in their critique, i.e., into 'thinking in terms of sentences, classes of sentences, and inference relations between sentences and classes of sentences.')

(**10**) Talk of the *theory-ladenness of all observations* (Hanson, Toulmin, Kuhn, Feyerabend) can be made precise. This phrase, however, proves to be ambiguous—a point which appears to be overlooked most of the time. On the one hand, describing the partial possible models of one theory requires the use of *some other theory*. On the other hand, the description of the theoretically enriched possible models of a theory refers *to this theory itself* (creating the problem of theoretical terms).

(**11**) A certain clarification of Wittgenstein's *paradigm* concept is indispensible for a correct reconstruction of theory dynamics in Kuhn's sense. It permits us to make *precise statements* about the *kind of vagueness* which adheres to the determination of a set via paradigmatic examples.

(**12**) Only an 'infinitesimal part' of Kuhn's use of the expression "paradigm" will be taken over. But it will be enough to topple a good many traditional ideas. In contrast to the cases treated by mathematical logic for which the individual domains are *extensionally given*, both the set I of intended applications of the theory and the individual domain of each single application are, as a rule, only *intensionally given by means of a set of paradigm examples*.

(**13**) The precise articulation of the nonstatement view comes to a provisional end with the introduction of the concept of *holding a theory in the Kuhnian sense*. Both the temporally stable mathematical structures of a theory and its temporally varying expansions find their way into this concept. It also receives a realistic touch through a reference to the theory's creator and the set of paradigm examples I_0 of intended applications laid down by him. Precise notions of corroborated success, fulfilled promise of success, and belief in progress constitute further components of this concept.

(**14**) The concept of holding a theory permits an extensive exposition of the notion of *normal science*. People can hold one and the same theory and nevertheless differ a great deal in their empirical beliefs (constancy of the theory in the presence of varying and incompatible central empirical claims or theory propositions).

(**15**) The thesis of a *theory's immunity* or *nonfalsifiability* is a trivial consequence of the nonstatement view. A theory is not protected against ' refutation by observation' because it has been 'immunized,' but because it is the sort of entity of which 'falsified' cannot sensibly be predicated.

Kuhn's observation that in the course of normal science an empirical falsification discredits not the theory but merely the scientist holding it, is fully correct, as is the analogy conjured by the proverb: "It's a poor carpenter who blames his tools." 'Critical rationalism's' allegation that the normal scientist is a narrow-minded dogmatist is totally unfounded.

Instead of accusing the researchers holding a theory of irrational behavior, the harmony between metatheory and experience must be reestablished by *replacing the stereotype of rational behavior in scientists with an adequate concept of rationality*.

(**16**) A theory is not only immune to the failure of certain of its special laws. The *rule of autodetermination*, according to which a theory determines its own applications, even grants a theory *full immunity* in the face of *complete failure* in an 'intended application.'

(**17**) A further achievement of the nonstatement view lies in the clarification not only of the course of normal science (14–16), but also of *revolutionary change*. A physical theory is not eliminated 'by confronting it with contrary experience.' *It is dislodged by another theory*. Despite the beguiling assurances of Kuhn and Feyerabend, nothing irrational underlies this process either.

Whoever sees an irrational process in holding a theory in the sense of Kuhn (the course of normal science) or theory dislodgement (scientific revolution) is paying homage to a *stereotype*—in any case not to a *critical* but to an *extravagant (inhuman) rationalism*.

(**18**) The nonstatement view, supported by certain macrological concepts, *construes the evolutionary structures of science* in a way which disposes of the *appearance* of irrationality in the behavior of 'normal scientists,' as well as those involved in 'paradigm battles' in the sense of Kuhn. As soon as this perspective is achieved, the philosopher of science can turn over the reins to the historians, psychologists, and sociologists of research.

(19) Thus, the *normative methodology* with which Lakatos feels constrained to take to the field against the consequences of Kuhn's picture of science proves to be *superfluous because it rests on a false presupposition.* 'Kuhn's irrationalism' is but a pseudoirrationalism.

(20) Holism does not follow Hegel in claiming that "the truth is the whole," but *like* Hegel it does claim that "only the whole can be subjected to a test." This thesis can be reconstructed and *justified* not only in its weak version ('Duhem–Quine thesis'), but even in the strong version which contains two additional claims stemming from Kuhn and Feyerabend: namely, that one cannot sharply distinguish between the empirical content of a theory and the empirical data supporting the theory, and that the meaning of certain terms of a theory are themselves theory-dependent.

(21) As opposed to the critique to date, we can adopt a more differentiated position regarding the 'revolt against traditional philosophy of science,' especially as represented by Kuhn and Feyerabend. The rebellion against the (exaggerated) *imitation of metamathematics* in the philosophy of science is not only understandable, but *justified*. Therefore, only the conclusion that a 'logic of science' is ruled out altogether remains somewhat hasty.

(22) The alternative, "either *constant meaning and accumulation of knowledge* or *meaning shift and noncumulative substitution of theories,*" as well as its equation with "either *objective knowledge* or *relativism,*" are false. The failure of micrological comparisons between dislodged and dislodging theories bears the main responsibility for this. A 'relativistic conclusion' of total incomparability is drawn from micrological incomparability, and with it emerges mere change instead of progress. Despite micrological incomparability (because totally different conceptual apparatus precludes inferring sentences of the one theory from those of the other), a macrological comparison is possible *which permits us to differentiate between theory dislodgement with progress and theory dislodgement without progress.*

Summary of contents

Part I presents in partly simplified, partly modified form, J. D. Sneed's new method for analyzing the structure of scientific theories which has proved especially successful as applied to theories of mathematical physics. Sneed has opened up new paths in *four directions*. The dual-level conception of scientific language is replaced by a nonlinguistic *criterion for "theoretical" which is relativized to theories.* Using this criterion *the empirical content of a theory* is given a precise new treatment by picking up and emending Ramsey's approach. In contrast to the statement view, a *theory* itself is interpreted as a composite mathematical structure together with a class of intended applications. This also provides the conceptual framework for analyzing a phenomenon which until now seems to have defied metatheoretic reconstruction, namely, *theory dynamics*. This framework permits in particular a precise articulation of T. S. Kuhn's distinction between the course followed by *normal science* and the *dislodging of theories* in times of scientific revolution.

As a preliminary step in describing Sneed's methods, the *criticisms of the dual-level conception of scientific language* are discussed in an introductory chapter. These are grouped under the motto 'theory-ladenness of all observations.' Further, H. Putnam's challenge concerning the concept "theoretical," which cannot be adequately met within the confines of this linguistic theory, is introduced.

Since subsequent chapters make extensive use of a certain form of axiomatization of scientific theories, the *five different meanings of the concept of axiomatization of a theory* are discussed in a separate chapter. The method of axiomatization then used is the *informal set-theoretic axiomatization* via the introduction of a set-theoretic predicate. This method is illustrated with the help of a miniature theory which also appears in subsequent chapters of Part I for purposes of illustration. Furthermore, it is shown that on the basis of this method of axiomatization the empirical claims of a theory have the form "c is an S," whereby "S" designates the mathematical structure characteristic of the theory and "c" designates a model of the theory.

With his *functionalistic criterion for* "*T-theoretical*," Sneed answers Putnam's challenge. Those quantities are labeled *T-theoretical* whose values can be calculated only by 'recourse to a successful application of T.' When, for example, T is understood to be classical particle mechanics, *mass* and *force* are *T*-theoretical *functions* while the *position* function is a *T*-nontheoretical quantity. Since Sneed's criterion can cause a good deal of misunderstanding, various alternative articulations are formulated. Furthermore, some salient features of this criterion are pointed out, and various possible objections discussed.

The traditional idea concerning the empirical claims of a theory leads to a difficulty in all cases in which such claims contain theoretical terms. In order to substantiate a claim of the form "c_i is an S," one must always refer back to a statement "c_j is an S," i.e., to a statement *of exactly this form*. This difficulty is called *the problem of theoretical terms*. Its only known solution is the *Ramsey solution*, which consists of formulating the empirical content of a theory by means of its Ramsey sentence. Instead of Ramsey sentence (as in Stegmüller [Theoretische Begriffe], Chapter 7), we will speak here of the *Ramsey formulation* of a theory. When it is possible to find a predicate which is extensionally equal to the predicate of the Ramsey formulation of a theory, and which makes no reference to theoretical terms, we will say the theoretical terms in question are *Ramsey eliminable*. Where Ramsey eliminability does not hold, the theoretical terms demonstrably accomplish what cannot otherwise be achieved in determining empirical content: with their help possible observable states of affairs are precluded which cannot be eliminated by conditions formulated in the language of

T-nontheoretical terms ('observational language') alone (representing a situation analogous to that of Gödel's theorem in one important respect).

The Ramsey method is modified and improved in three respects. In the first place the fiction of a 'universal (cosmic) application' for a physical theory is laid aside. *Various 'intended applications of a theory'* are differentiated. The individual domains of different applications are different, but may overlap. (For example, the solar system as well as various parts of it are applications for classical particle mechanics.) A second generalization of the Ramsey formulation occurs with the imposition of *constraints* on the theoretical functions. Figuratively speaking, these establish 'cross-connections' between the various intended applications. Even the simplest such constraint, requiring only that the same individual always have the same function value (symbolically abbreviated by "$\langle \approx, = \rangle$"), has an extraordinarily strong inhibiting effect, as is shown using the example of the miniature theory. These two modifications of the Ramsey method *increase the achievement capacity of theoretical functions in an essential respect.* With their help prognoses can be made which were otherwise impossible because the domain in question had not yet been empirically explored (verification of the Braithwaite–Ramsey supposition). A third generalization of the Ramsey formulation follows when *special laws* are formulated for *certain applications* of the theory with the help of restrictions of the primary predicate characterizing the mathematical structure ('fundamental law').

Finally, the empirical content of a theory is given by a single irreducible statement called the *central empirical claim* or Ramsey–Sneed claim of the theory (sentences (5) and (6) above).

This procedure is illustrated in a separate chapter using classical particle mechanics as an example. Whoever prefers having the *abstract* line of thought leading to the central empirical claim of a theory illustrated by the *concrete* example of an 'actual physical theory' should have a look at Chapter 6 shortly after beginning Chapter 3.

With the specification of a schema for the central empirical claim *the first step toward overcoming the 'statement view,'* according to which theories are classes of sentences, has been taken. Not that the class of sentences has simply been replaced by a single sentence. There are good reasons for *not* identifying a theory with the central empirical claim.

In Chapter 7 all of the important conceptual components incorporated into a central empirical claim are characterized purely *model-theoretically.* The mathematical structure of a theory is analyzed into a *frame, core,* and *expanded core.* A *theory* itself is characterized as a nonlinguistic entity: namely, as an ordered pair consisting of a core *K* and the class of intended applications *I*. For practical reasons the question of how the class *I* is 'given to a physicist' is reserved for Part II.

The mathematical structure used in a central empirical claim is an expanded core. Augmenting Sneed's procedure we will, with the help of this model-theoretic apparatus, assign any given central empirical claim a propositional content called a *strong theory proposition*. The core of a theory (a certain quintuple) is a relatively stable component characteristic of the theory. The additional components of the expanded core (a certain 8-tuple) are, on the other hand, unstable. They change with the hypothetical additions to a theory made for the purpose of producing central empirical claims. In the difference between these two structures lies the conceptual basis for introducing the concept of holding a theory in Kuhn's sense in Part II. According to it physicists may hold one and the same theory although they attach entirely different beliefs and suppositions to it among themselves and in the course of time.

Within the framework of the nonstatement view, which is provisionally completed with the identification of a theory as a pair $\langle K, I \rangle$, various *equivalence concepts for mathematical component structures and for theories* can be introduced. In particular, the equivalence of theories which are 'totally different' in the sense that they work with entirely different theoretical concepts can be proved. More important still are the model-theoretic *reduction concepts*. The concept of the strict reduction of one theory to another is also applicable in cases where the conceptual systems of the theories are fully different. This concept also plays an important role in Part II inasmuch as it serves to close the rationality gap opened up by the Kuhnian incommensurability thesis.

Besides the supplement mentioned above, Part I also contains various technical simplifications and improvements vis-à-vis Sneed's work, in particular, for the symbolic formulation of central empirical claims and the definition of the reduction concepts.

The greatest service rendered by Sneed's work consists presumably in facilitating a new and better understanding of T. S. Kuhn's conception of science. In order to show this, Kuhn's theory will receive two exposures in Part II. First we will offer a purely intuitive sketch of his ideas, whereby those segments of his work which have been felt to be especially provocative, and were correspondingly heavily criticized, will be sharply accentuated. Then in the next chapter the most important criticisms from Kuhn's 'rationalistic' opponents will be sketched—albeit to show in the end that, and why, they are unsatisfactory at decisive points.

The unprecedented part of the Kuhnian challenge *seems* to be that if his basic theses are correct, *they render all species of the philosophy of science senseless*, and indeed for a very elementary reason: without exception, metatheories of science rest on a false presupposition. No matter how far apart philosophers of science may stand regarding other particulars, they all agree that the exact natural sciences represent a *rational* enterprise. But Kuhn appears to contest this assumption. Talk of 'Kuhnian irrationalism' is, however, misleading. It is not Kuhn *himself* who stands for irrationalism or obscurantism; *he appears to impute an irrational attitude*

17

to scientists, maintaining that only in this way can the development of the sciences be adequately understood. In particular, the quarrel between 'inductivists' and 'deductivists' concerning the form in which scientific theories are 'empirically substantiated' or 'empirically tested' appears to be *groundless* because there simply is no such testing.

And indeed it does seem to be alien to both forms of scientific enterprise delineated by Kuhn. In *normal science* theories are not subjected to criticism at all. They are *used as instruments* in solving scientific puzzles. And in times of *extraordinary research* theories are sometimes cast aside, not, however, because they 'have failed the test of experience,' but because they are *dislodged by other theories*. We will call this 'theory dislodging theory' instead of 'theory rejection on the basis of falsifying experience.'

Initially Kuhn set himself a quite unpretentious goal—namely, to show that traditional notions of scientific progress as a gradual growth process, an 'accumulation of knowledge,' are false and must be replaced by a different sort of description of scientific dynamics. Nevertheless, the result of his historical, sociological, and psychological research appears to produce a consequence of unparalleled radicalism, at least in the eyes of his critics; namely, the *normal scientist* is a narrow-minded dogmatist who clings uncritically to his theories. And the *revolutionary scientist* is a young religious fanatic attempting to convince others of the correctness of his new 'paradigm,' not, however, with arguments. Instead he uses his powers of persuasion and the propaganda drums to win others for his paradigm, to *convert* them to it. And in the end he is victorious when he has found enough believers and waits until those not letting themselves be converted simply die out.

Beginning with Chapter 12 this 'primary picture' of Kuhn's conception, which is already *a reflection in the mirror of his critics*, will be replaced by an entirely different one. We will maintain that Kuhn actually has not only a new historical, but also *a new metatheoretical conception*. In order to understand it one does not need to impute to scientists an irrational attitude, as his critics would have us think. Instead *one must free oneself of various 'inductivistic' and 'deductivistic' rationality cliches*.

The reconstruction of the concept of normal science will proceed, following Sneed, via the explication of the concept of *holding a theory*. As a first step the abstract logical theory concept of Part I will be expanded to the concept of a physical theory by the addition of three further stipulations and a weak concept of holding a theory (the Sneedian sense of holding a theory) will be introduced. The subsequent introduction of a strong concept of holding a theory (*the Kuhnian sense of holding a theory*) consists of making the weak concept sharper *and 'more realistic'* by adding further pragmatic concepts.

It turns out that on the basis of these concepts the entire Kuhn–Popper–Lakatos controversy represents one of the worst examples of people talking right past one another, comparable with the 'paradigm debates' in Kuhn's sense. All of Kuhn's opponents presuppose the statement view of theories as a matter of course, i.e., the idea that theories are classes of sentences (propositions). But such an idea is not compatible with Kuhn's conception. This point will become clear through the explication of the concept of holding a theory. According to it, holding a theory means *having a complicated conceptual apparatus* (and *not* sentences or propositions) *at hand*; namely, a *core* which one *knows* has already been used successfully a few times in core expansions and which one *hopes* can be used in the future for still better expansions ('normal scientific belief in progress'). *This attitude contains ' not a trace of irrationality.'* The 'immunity of theories to falsifying experience,' which is felt by many to be especially offensive, also finds here an entirely natural, unforced explanation. No matter how often attempts to expand a core (and thus to formulate theory propositions or central empirical claims) fail, this cannot be seen as proof that the core is worthless. *A theory is not the sort of entity of which it can sensibly be said that it has been falsified (or verified).* Even Kuhn's just (!) remark that in the course of normal science ' recalcitrant unmanageable experience' discredits not the theory but *only the scientist* can be naturally and simply interpreted here.

What still remains to be said in relation to the concept of holding a theory is something about the way in which the set *I* of intended applications of the theory is given. This set is almost never extensionally given as a fixed domain, but as a rule only intensionally, and indeed then only via *paradigmatic examples.* (This is the only—albeit very important—point of contact between the paradigm concepts of Kuhn and Wittgenstein.) The same also holds at a lower level for the individual domains of the various applications. These, too, are as a rule only intensionally given. In this way the theory receives an additional 'immunity against recalcitrant experience': if the theory fails completely with respect to an element of *I*, this element is simply removed from the set *I*. Whoever spies an 'immunization strategy' here is paying homage to an *extravagant*, not a *critical*, rationalism. (Can, e.g., anyone seriously maintain that with the appearance of the wave theory of light the observation that light "doesn't consist of particles after all" represents an 'immunization of the Newtonian theory'?)

Using the concept of holding a theory one can *distinguish precisely between two sorts of normal scientific progress.* One can also say exactly what may be called "normal scientific progress" and what may be called "normal scientific setback."

Some precise statements can also be made concerning *theory dislodgement* (the second form of theory dynamics). The most important thing here is to locate exactly where a rationality gap is to be found. All of those reproaches to the effect that Kuhn should have set a 'critical level' at which a theory must be rejected are *unjust.* One can do nothing here other than *create insight into why this demand cannot be met.* This insight is based on the nonstatement view along with an elementary psychological truth (namely, that a poor tool is better than none at all). On the other hand, those criticisms are *justified* which point out that Kuhn cannot lend any sense to the notion of scientific progress (other than that of power politics according to which the victors are simply *per definitionem* those who have brought progress). He can only speak of *upheavals.* This is a consequence of his thesis that the dislodging and the dislodged theories are *incomparable* (*incommensurable*). Here we find a *genuine rationality gap.*

Paradoxically both Kuhn and Feyerabend fall completely back into their opponents' way of thinking, i.e., into the statement view, in their attempts to substantiate the incommensurability thesis. Instead of concluding that dislodging and dislodged theories are incomparable "because the concepts of the one cannot be defined with the concepts of the other and the sentences of the one cannot be inferred from those of the other," one should argue as follows: "If a theory is dislodged by another which has *another core,* then 'thinking in terms of inference relations between sentences' is not suitable for comparing the theories."

Popper's concept of *verisimilitude* is also unfit for closing *this* rationality gap because truth is at best the goal of a scientific theory, but cannot be *the criterion by which we humans compare theories.*

On the other hand, the macrological concepts of Part I provide an adequate means for comparing theories—even in cases of 'complete hetero-geneity.' *Neither* the identity *nor* the similarity of the conceptual linguistic apparatus is presupposed there for either the equivalence or the reduction concepts. If, and how, these concepts must be modified in order to explicate the concept of 'revolutionary *progress*' is in any case a *logical* task. The historian of science oversteps his competence when he maintains that such an explication is impossible. (The historian of mathematics would be guilty of a similar breach of competence were he to maintain that a constructive consistency proof for a system of classical mathematics is impossible. This claim *may* be right, but it can only be grounded with *proof-theoretic,* not *historical* methods.)

Our position in relation to Lakatos' theoretical approach is split. His concept of a *research programme* does not come into conflict with Kuhn's ideas. Depending on interpretation, this concept is either identical with, or a special case of, the concept of normal science in Kuhn's sense (the special case being that of normal scientific progress without setbacks). Lakatos' *falsification concept* for '*sophisticated falsificationism*' represents in its precise form a method for closing the rationality gap, but only *because* it 'essentially' amounts to *a concept of theory reduction* despite a misleading context.

We regard Lakatos' *normative methodology,* on the other hand, in much the same way as does Feyerabend's 'epistemological anarchy.' But while Feyerabend came to his conclusions on the basis of (presumably fitting) reflections on the *disadvantageous consequences* of such a methodology, we contest the *presupposition* on which it rests: namely, the alleged irrationality of the 'Kuhnian scientist.' As soon as one recognizes that neither in epochs of 'normal research' nor in times of 'extraordinary research' and 'scientific revolution' is the behavior of the scientist irrational, the necessity of 'putting the scientific world in order' by way of a normative methodology disappears.

Part I
The Structure of
Mature Physical Theories
According to Sneed

1 Objections to the Dual-Level
Conception of Scientific Language
and to Carnap's Linguistic Theory

1.1 Criticisms of the concept of an observational language by Kuhn, Feyerabend, and Hempel

Part I deals with the entirely new approach of J. D. Sneed. To facilitate an easier understanding of the later chapters, we will, however, start with a *critical account of the dual-level conception of scientific language*. Such criticism must be sharply distinguished from the discussion in Chapter 5 of Stegmüller's [Theoretische Begriffe]. *Carnap's significance criterion for theoretical terms* was the sole object of investigation there and, as it turned out, of a hefty polemic. But Carnap's criterion is a very special case. The dual-level conception itself was left unscathed. Indeed, it constituted the tacitly accepted framework for all the analyses there.

It is, however, this persistent presupposition, this framework of the last three chapters of Stegmüller's [Theoretische Begriffe], which for some time now has been the target of an ever-increasing barrage of questions from an ever-increasing number of philosophers. These polemics go under different names. For the most part they are directed against the notion of an *observational language*. But there have also been questions raised concerning the *dichotomy* 'observable–theoretical,' or at least its *unequivocalness*, while still other philosophers take aim at the problematic notion of '*theoretical terms*' or try to direct attention to obscurities in the notion of the '*partial interpretation*' of theoretical terms.

A number of these criticisms, especially a number of those directed against the observational language, have already been laid to rest in Section 2 of

Chapter 3 of Stegmüller's [Theoretische Begriffe], namely, those imputing to the dual-level theory a notion of observability quite foreign to it. This includes all objections to the effect that the observational language is intended to be a 'sense data language,' that the statements of the observational language are supposed to be 'absolutely certain,' that the predications of the observational language are supposed to be 'decidable by observation,' etc. What has already been said there must suffice as protection against polemics of *this* sort. There remain, however, other objections and we want to have a look at the most important of these.

> A systematic exposition of all the criticisms of the dual-level conception would make a suitable topic for a separate monograph. Writing it would not be without its interesting moments—the more so because of the curious situations one occasionally encounters. In 'the fight against the concept of observability' one observes for example, how sometimes even prominent authors struggle to set up a straw man and then have to resort to even greater exertions to keep from being knocked over by their own creations.

By questioning the dual-level theory of scientific language in general we do appear to be headed for an unavoidable conflict with the arguments of Chapter 4 of Stegmüller's [Theoretische Begriffe]. For even if one does *not* find *all* of the arguments there convincing, *in toto* they seem to urge the dual-level conception rather forcefully.

But do they really? Again we must draw an important distinction; we must differentiate between reasons for *introducing theoretical concepts* into science and reasons for doing this *in the special way* in which Carnap and his followers did it. That these do *not* necessarily amount to one and the same thing will become quite clear to us as soon as we become acquainted with an entirely different procedure for characterizing theoretical concepts. But inasmuch as we have not yet arrived at such 'constructive alternative suggestions,' we will turn first to the aforementioned critique.

Metaphorically we could speak of the '*thesis of the theory-ladenness of all observational statements*' or of the '*thesis of the nonexistence of a neutral, theory-free observational language.*' Various authors have argued this thesis in various forms, whereby the particular form that they gave it was often influenced by their other theoretical convictions. According to T. S. Kuhn, for example, the way in which scientists observe the world and report their observations depends upon the theories, the 'paradigms,' they assume to be valid. Should such an assumption be revised because of a 'scientific revolution,' this revision amounts to ". . . a displacement of the conceptual network through which scientists view the world."[1] But then their experiential reports can obviously not be 'theory-independent' as it is presumed the statements of the 'observational language' must be.

---

[1] [Revolutions], p. 102.

Along the same lines, Feyerabend emphasizes: "We reinterpret ... our 'experience' in the light of the theories we possess—there is no 'neutral' experience."[2] And Putnam too takes a similarly critical stance in [Not].

What exactly is meant by these criticisms is probably expressed most clearly and tersely by Hempel in [Theoretical Terms]. When one speaks of observability, one must always consider *by whom* the observation is made; i.e., "observable" suggests not a one-place predicate of the metalanguage— "Term *t* is an observational predicate"—but rather a two-place predicate of the form "Term *t* is an observational predicate for the person *p*." The reason necessitating the introduction of a relation here lies in the fact that that which in *scientific discussion* qualifies as observable is not only a matter of *biological* characteristics possessed by 'every normal healthy human,' but is, to a great extent, dependent upon *the linguistic and scientific abilities which the 'person doing the observing' has acquired in the past.* When, for example, experimental physicists intersubjectively agree *that something ' has been verified by direct observation,'* this in *no way* means that such a verification 'by direct observation' could also be made by the man in the street *commanding neither the special knowledge nor abilities of the physicist.* But precisely this assumption is tacitly made in the *standard construction* of the observational language.

We can also look at the situation from the standpoint of the relation just mentioned. Why, then, does the traditional view of the observational language assume that it is a matter of a one-place predicate? The answer is that the explicit reference to a person *p* appears superfluous *because any* (and therefore *any other*) *member of the species homo sapiens can be substituted for p.* Aside from the very questionable proposition of whether this argument even yields a predicate suitable for the purposes of everyday usage, one can certainly say that a concept of observability suitable for a reconstruction of the scientific usage of this expression is out of the question on this basis, because in *all* scientific contexts the correct usage of "is observable" rests *on past learning experiences.* And in no single branch of science is this merely a matter of 'experience in handling instruments,' but most certainly also a matter of 'experience in handling theories.'

If, then, the intuitive idea of the difference between the 'language of the experimenter' and the 'language of the theoretician' is taken as the basis of the dichotomy *observational language–theoretical language,* it must be pointed out that it is an inadmissible simplification to think of the experimenter as a *scientifically unsophisticated* person *into whose experiential data theoretical considerations do not enter.*

Hempel suggests, therefore, giving up the concept of an observational language, and using instead the *historic-pragmatically relativized concept of an "antecedently available vocabulary."* Furthermore, this concept must

---

[2] "Wir deuten ... unsere 'Erfahrungen' im Lichte der Theorien um, die wir besitzen—es gibt keine 'neutrale' Erfahrung." [Theoretische Entitäten], p. 71.

also be hitched *to a specific theory being introduced at a specific time.* That is, when a new theory *T* is introduced in which expressions such as "the unconscious," "introverted," or "electrically charged" appear for the first time, these expressions of the new theory are 'theoretical' in the sense that they are not a part of the vocabulary already available to trained specialists. This does not preclude, however, that such expressions be incorporated into the available vocabulary *on the basis of sufficient familiarity with the new theory,* so that, with the introduction of a still later theory, *they belong to the antecedently available vocabulary relative to this latest theory.*

One can decide thus not to give up the *dichotomy* completely, but rather to take it in a new sense: The 'fixed' and 'temporally invariant' observational language may be replaced by that *pragmatic-historically relativized* part of a scientific language whose descriptive symbols are antecedently available terms. We will call such a part of the language a *basic empiricist language.* Its counterpart may, as before, be called the *theoretical language.* The boundary between the two languages is not inflexible, but depends rather on the *persons, points of time,* and *theory* to which one refers when making the comparison.

The reasons and motives for introducing the dichotomy given in Chapter 4 of Stegmüller's [Theoretische Begriffe] are, *mutatis mutandis,* applicable to this pragmatically relativized dichotomy.

For the discussion to follow, in Part I at least, this new concept is dispensable because later we will be working with a substantially stronger concept of *theoretical* for which the entire epistemological problem underlying the differentiation between observational or, as the case may be, basic empiricist language on the one hand and theoretical language on the other, has no relevance. This concept, stemming from Sneed, may well be the first concept of theoreticity to escape an objection raised by Putnam, an objection to which we now want to turn our attention for a moment.

1.2 Putnam's challenge

All attempts to date at delineating the concept *theoretical* are, we may say, characterized by their *negativity.* That is, when a term *τ* of a theory *T* is labeled *theoretical,* the reason given for this sort of qualification does not take the form "because *τ* plays such and such a role in *T* (holds a 'key position' in *T*, which is to be characterized as follows . . .)"; the reason given is rather: "because *τ* does *not* belong to the observational vocabulary," or "because *τ* does *not* belong to the antecedentally available vocabulary relative to the theory *T* for the person *p* at time *t*," depending on whether one has the original concept of an observational language in mind or, respectively, is using the pragmatically relativized concept of a basic empiricist language. The governing idea is in both cases the same: that which one already 'understands' can, *because it is perfectly understood,* be reckoned as part of the basic language; on the other hand, that which is not fully understood must (for the present) be distinguished as theoretical.

Actually, though, it appears that in many instances something substantially stronger is intended, namely, that a term τ is *theoretical* relative to a theory *T because within the framework of the theory T* (or, *within the framework of the applications of the theory T*) *it serves a very particular purpose distinguishing it sharply from those terms not serving this purpose.*

Putnam's reproach to the effect that as yet no one has attempted to clear up the specific role played by the theoretical terms within a theory we will call *Putnam's challenge*. Its substance is contained in the following sentence: "A theoretical term, properly so-called, is one which comes from a scientific *theory* (and the almost untouched problem, in thirty years of writing about 'theoretical terms' is what is *really* distinctive about such terms)."[3]

Let us now try to make clear to ourselves why there is no chance of finding an answer to this challenge within the framework of Carnap's theory, which, for reasons soon to become apparent, we will call the *linguistic theory of theoretical terms*. The following considerations will also show that the question in Section 1.1 (at the beginning of the sixth paragraph) was warranted; the dual-level conception of scientific language is not a direct consequence of the reasons urging the introduction of theoretical terms, for this conception represents only *one very special type of approach* for introducing them.

We will first ask ourselves how Carnap tried to achieve a precise distinction between theoretical and nontheoretical terms. There is but *one* answer: *by imitating the procedure used by logicians when constructing a scientific language.*

By this we mean that when a logician constructs a formal language, one of his first steps consists of *classifying the symbols* of this language. He must divide the vocabulary V exhaustively into two disjunct subclasses: the *logical symbols* and the *descriptive symbols*. The logical vocabulary V_L consists of the logical symbols, the descriptive vocabulary V_D of the descriptive symbols. Since the concept of logical consequence is determined by the meanings of the logical symbols, the fundamental decision as to what may be counted as basic logical apparatus and what belongs to the extralogical, 'empirical' part of a scientific language is made by this partitioning. Carnap, now, picks up this partitioning *and takes it one step further*. On the basis of considerations of the type presented in Chapter 4 of Stegmüller's [Theoretische Begriffe], the vocabulary V_D itself is further divided exhaustively into two disjunct subclasses V_O and V_T, the first consisting of the 'observational terms,' the second of the 'theoretical terms.' We may, therefore, designate as *linguistic* Carnap's method for realizing the dual-level concept. The disposition of symbols therein is given schematically in Fig. 1-1.

---

[3] H. Putnam, [Not], p. 243.

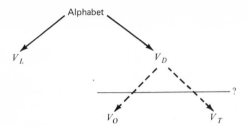

Figure 1-1

The horizontal line with a question mark across the broken lines representing the second division *should indicate the dubiousness of this step.* It is, namely, *in principle impossible to come up with an adequate answer to Putnam's question in this way,* if indeed one really feels this question to be a genuine challenge. The reason is simple: if the classification of symbols is a vital part of constructing the language, *then this classification must be completed before any particular theory is formulated.* The introduction of a *concept of "theoretical" relative to a particular theory* is, then, no longer possible.

Against this argument it might be objected that one could, from the very beginning, tailor the construction of the language to fit the theory in question. Relativizing the theoreticity concept to a particular theory would not, then, require a distinct stipulation to this effect; it would instead be a part of the historical connection of language to theory formulation. In what way theoretical terms 'are related to the theory *T*' would, then, be answered *in terms of the motivation cited for the construction of the language.*

So far as one is convinced that the concept *theoretical* must be relativized to a particular theory, it becomes immediately apparent that this escape is *closed* when one realizes *that various theories can be formulated in one and the same language* (and must be, if scientific language should, for example, allow for the formulation of all of modern physics, or at least enough of it so that two theories, e.g., mechanics and electrodynamics, can be formulated in it). One and the same term can be *theoretical with respect to one of these theories, but nontheoretical with respect to some other*!

These drawbacks concerning Carnap's procedure remain unchanged when the original concept of an 'inflexible observational language' is traded for a pragmatically relativized basic empiricist language. (Which is also the reason why an answer to the question, "Absolute observational language or pragmatically relativized basic empiricist language?" is irrelevant for the discussion to follow.)

In Chapter 3 we will become acquainted with Sneed's new procedure for introducing a concept of "theoretical." With this procedure we find for the first time an attempt to come up with a satisfactory answer to Putnam's challenge. This procedure does not simply and absolutely differentiate between theoretical and nontheoretical terms; the concept *theoretical* is relativized to a particular theory *T*, so that the new predicate reads "*x* is a *T*-theoretical term," and not "*x* is a theoretical term." From what has already been said, it should be clear that the introduction of such a relativized theoreticity concept means giving up Carnap's linguistic theory. Actually, the dichotomy is introduced in Sneed's work not *per fiat* (be it during construction of the language or later), but by means of a *criterion* which is first applicable 'when the theory is given,' when, that is, strictly speaking, the construction of a language and the formulation of the theory in this language is completed. (That the reference here is not to *formalized* languages or *formalized* theories, but rather to the 'usual *nonformalized versions* of theories,' is a consequence of the necessarily *pragmatic* aspect of Sneed's criterion.)

Inasmuch as we have just spoken of the necessity of relativizing the concept *theoretical* to a theory, and, in Section 1.1, spoke briefly of the thesis of ' the theory-ladenness of the observational language,' this seems also to be the proper place to direct attention to a confusion pervading a great deal of the literature pertinent to both the dual-level conception and the problem of theoretical terms. When on the one hand the '*theory-ladenness' of the experiential data*, which is formulated in the observational language and is relevant for a particular theory, is pointed out, and on the other hand the necessity of *relativizing* the concept of theoretical *to a theory* is spoken of, it appears that the two ideas add up to something quite similar. But one must distinguish sharply between the two lines of thought. The necessity of this becomes apparent if we ask how many theories are involved in each case, one or more? The answer will in each case be entirely different. In the first case we have the thesis *that what is experiential data for one theory is determined by another theory* (and not by the first theory itself!). Deliberations along these lines, stemming from Feyerabend and others, will first be broached in Chapter 16, where theory dynamics are treated. In the case before us now it is a matter of something entirely different: when terms are designated as *T*-theoretical, *the reference is to the very same theory T in which they themselves appear*. More specifically, the reference is to a role, still to be characterized, which they play in *T*.

The part played by theoretical terms according to Sneed *appears* to be an 'absurd' one. In order to ascertain the values of theoretical functions one must refer to *some successful application of precisely that theory in which they make their appearance*. Inasmuch as determining whether an application of a theory is successful or not involves computing the values of its functions, *including the values of the theoretical functions*, Sneed's criterion *appears* to give the theoretical functions a 'circular character'; i.e., in order to ascertain the values of such functions one must already know values of these functions. That this '*problem of theoretical terms*' is a serious one is not to be denied. As we will see, its solution will compel us initially to cast the empirical content of a theory in the form of a refined Ramsey sentence the ultimate consequence of which will be the *abandonment of the 'statement view of theories.'*

At those places where it comes to a 'confrontation' between Sneed's concept of *theoretical* on the one hand and the theoreticity concept suggested by our earlier discussion (with the pragmatically relativized basic empiricist language instead of the 'unchangeable' observational language) on the other, we will refer to Sneed's *T*-theoretical functions as *theoretical in the strong sense*, and to those terms not belonging to the basic empiricist language as *theoretical in the weak sense*. That the concept of a basic empiricist language mentioned above is irrelevant for Part I is simply a consequence of the fact that we will be discussing only the concept of theoreticity in the strong sense.

---

2   Axiomatic Theories

2.1 The axiomatic method; Five meanings of "axiomatization of a theory"

Later we will be taking axiomatized theories as a point of departure. This makes it imperative to consider initially the question of what is meant by the "axiomatization of a theory." It turns out that this can be understood in five different ways.

The first two meanings have a common *formal* feature: they regard an axiomatic system as a class of statements which are logical consequences of a finite subclass of this class. We will call Σ a *Euclidean axiomatic system* if and only if Σ is a class of statements and there is a finite subclass Δ of Σ whose elements are self-evident, and thus true, such that each statement of the difference class $\Sigma - \Delta$ is a logical consequence of Δ. The elements of Δ are the axioms of the system Σ.

> Because we are, for the moment, concerned only with drawing a comparison with the Hilbertian notion of an axiom system, we could just as well have spoken of the *concept of an axiomatic system in the Aristotelian sense*. Historically, though, various differentiations would have to be made that, for the most part, remain neglected in philosophical discussions of this topic. *Existential quantification*, for instance, plays a different role for Euclid than it does for Aristotle. Furthermore, *axioms in the strict sense* (relation sentences)

would have to be distinguished from *postulates* (construction sentences)—an undertaking which presented considerable difficulties even in ancient times. For a very penetrating and concise discussion of these and a number of other details, cf. K. v. Fritz, [Antike Wissenschaft], especially p. 206ff., 372f., 378ff., and 438ff.

Underlying the evidence postulate, according to which the truth of all axioms must be directly apprehensible, is the idea that the fundamental notions employed in the axioms be derived from intuition so that the evidence takes on the form of an 'insight emanating from these notions.'

Modern axiomatics was completely and systematically exhibited for the first time in 1899 in Hilbert's *Die Grundlagen der Geometrie*. Hilbert's efforts were bent toward freeing geometry from recourse to uncertain intuition. One could, therefore, also regard such axiomatics as *abstract axiomatics* in contrast to Euclidean, i.e., *graphic axiomatics*. According to Hilbert the axioms of geometry are merely assumptions about the mutual relations obtaining between the elements of three classes of things. The elements of these three classes are indeed called '*points*,' '*straight lines*,' and '*planes*' in accord with presystematic intuitive ideas; and similarly, the expressions '*lies between*,' '*coincides with*,' and '*is congruent with*,' suggestive of intuitive spatial relations, are used for the three fundamental relations. But the question as to what sorts of things and which relations are involved here is explicitly left open. The usual intuitive ideas should *not* be associated with the fundamental notions.

Because in Hilbert's view the axioms are free of intuitive spatial components, there can be, besides the *normal model* based on the original intuitive interpretation, still *other models* for them—some intuitive, some not. It is, then, entirely possible that a nonnormal model be found within the same 'regions of the intuition' which originally yielded the notions for the intuitively perspicuous model of the axiom system. An example of this within the framework of Euclidean geometry would be the so-called *sphere-bundle*. Here, the axiomatic concept *point* is to be understood as an arbitrary space with the exception of a single particular point. *Line* in the axiomatic sense may be any circle that passes through the point in question. And by *plane* in the axiomatic sense is to be understood a spatial sphere touching the point in question. The geometric relations mentioned above are accordingly relations between these new geometric elements. Despite its 'geometric perspicuity,' this model for Euclidean geometry has naturally little, if anything, to do with that model which furnished the intuitive basis for Euclid's axiomatization of geometry. That this and other models are admitted within the framework of Hilbertian axiomatics illustrates how the transition from Euclidean to modern axiomatics increased the *latitude of interpretation*. Instead of admitting only a single 'normal interpretation,' infinitely many 'models which make the axioms true' are now in principle possible.

31

We will call Σ a *Hilbertian axiomatic system* if and only if there is a Δ and an Ω such that Δ is a finite class of statements in a natural language over certain relations between the elements of one or more classes of objects, Ω represents the class of all statements that are logical consequences of Δ, and Σ = Δ ∪ Ω. As before, the elements of Δ will be called the axioms of the system Σ.

Hilbert portrayed the emancipation of his axiomatics from intuition with the remark that the basic notions of his axiomatic system—in the case of geometry the six concepts mentioned—*are defined* solely by requiring that the axioms should be thought to hold for them. This formulation brought a lively protest from Frege, who pointed out that these 'definitions ' are circular. In order to distinguish it from the usual method of defining new concepts, M. Schlick coined the phrase "*implicit definition*" for this Hilbertian method of 'partially specifying the meaning' of the basic concepts of a system.[4] But this was not a very fortunate expression either. For indeed, if someone inquires what "implicitly defined" means, the only answer must well be: "'*implicitly defined*' is defined as '*undefined.*'" The implicitly defined expressions are, namely, none other than the *undefined* basic terms. In the formal construction of a theory they act as *variables*. A theorem with respect to Hilbertian axiomatics is not to be thought of as an isolated statement ' deducible from the axioms.' It represents instead merely a statement-form with free variables, as do the axioms themselves. One first obtains a statement by constructing a conditional (if . . . then . . .) statement-form with the con-junction of the axioms as antecedent and the theorem in question, itself regarded as a statement-form, as consequence, and then placing before this conditional a universal quantifier, stretching over the entire statement-form, for each free variable. Maintaining that a theorem is correctly proved amounts, then, to asserting that the statement constructed in this way is *logically valid*.

Thus the transition from Euclidean to Hilbertian axiomatics has the epistemological consequence, not to be underestimated, of reinterpreting the nature of mathematical proof. The mathematician no longer proves categoric statements, but *general conditionals*.

By assigning to the individual terms in the axioms definite objects and to the property and relation predicates properties and relations, one obtains an *interpretation* of the axiom system. If as the result of an interpretation the axioms become true statements, i.e., if the assigned objects exhibit the properties and relations as described by the axioms, then we say that this system of things, properties, and relations represents a *model* of Σ. In a model all theorems are then also true because the logical consequences of true statements must themselves be true.

---

[4] The expression "implicit definition" is often attributed to Hilbert himself. It is not, however, to be found in his writings. I do not know who really used it for the first time, but in any case it seems to have made its first appearance in the works of Schlick.

Up to this point we have sketched only one sort of Hilbertian axiomatics. It could more exactly be called *informal Hilbertian axiomatics.* The qualification "informal" should remind us that the axioms are formulated in the language of ordinary discourse. The next-to-last paragraph already contains, however, an 'implicit' allusion to *formal Hilbertian axiomatics.* The difference between these two forms of Hilbertian axiomatics consists of the fact that whereas the former is formulated in a language of ordinary discourse, the latter is formulated in a formal language. *The construction of a formal language* must in this latter case precede the formulation of the axiom system Σ. Initially this formal language is constructed simply as a *syntactical system S.* Following the introduction of an alphabet, the well-formed formulas of *S* are defined in the metalanguage and from these a subclass *A* is selected representing the *axioms* of Σ. Finally, a class *R* of inference rules is stipulated, which permit one to infer further formulas from given formulas. These inference rules are also formulated purely syntactically; i.e., they concern only the outer form of the formulas, not their 'meaning.' Through these rules the notion of a direct inference of a formula from others is defined. The axiomatic system Σ may be identified with the triple $\langle S, A, R \rangle$. A *proof* in Σ is a finite sequence of formulas such that each member of the sequence is either an axiom or is, through the application of one of the inference rules of *R*, a direct inference from preceding members of the sequence. The last member of a proof is called a *theorem.*

Formal axiomatic systems are also called *calculi.* The process of constructing a mathematical theory as an axiomatic system within the framework of a formal language no longer containing any expressions of ordinary discourse is sometime called the *calculization of this theory.*

Besides informal, Hilbert himself also had need of formal axiomatics, not, however, to axiomatize geometry—on the contrary, this was done using a purely informal basis—but rather to pave the way for the realization of his projected *proof theory.*

> The notion of axiomatization is usually applied only if a number of further conditions are fulfilled; namely, both the class of the well-formed formulas and of the axioms must be *decidable*, and the inference rules must be *effective.* If these conditions are met, the question of whether a sequence of formulas is a proof (but not of whether a formula is *provable!*) can be decided in a purely mechanical way.
>
> A brief and precise definition of the notion of a formal axiom system is given in W. S. Hatcher, [Foundations], p. 12ff. For a formal system of set theory see Fraenkel and Bar-Hillel, [Set Theory], p. 270ff. A general description of the syntactical characterization of formal languages is given in Carnap's works on semantics; cf. also Stegmüller, [Semantik], Chapter 9.

The concept of a *model* can be introduced within the framework of formal axiomatics by transforming the syntactically characterized formal language *S* into a *semantic system* through the introduction of an interpretation *I.*

An interpretation I of S over a nonempty set ω can thereby be understood as a function assigning elements of ω to the individual symbols of S, sets of elements of ω to the unary predicates of S, and n-place relations between elements of ω to the n-ary predicates. Using this function one can then define what it means to say that a formula of S holds in an interpretation I. A *model of* Σ *over* ω is an interpretation I of S in which all the axioms of Σ hold.

Problems concerning the *dependence* and *independence* of axioms already appeared in connection with Euclid's axiomatic system as witnessed by the long discussion over the possibility of inferring the parallel postulate from the rest of the axioms of Euclidean geometry. Other demands made of an axiom system such as *completeness* and *consistency* first drew attention with the appearance of formal axiomatics. Before the question of the completeness of an axiom system can be exactly formulated, one must have semantic concepts with whose help a precise notion of validity can be defined. And as far as the question of consistency is concerned, it could never appear so long as the conviction persisted that the axioms were evident truths. That Hilbert's proof theory (within the metatheory of which a 'constructive' proof of the consistency of classical mathematics was to be realized using only such steps in the argument as were thought to be 'harmless') depended upon a calculization of classical mathematics, reflects the fact that only a calculus itself can be *the object of precise mathematical study.*

A fourth type of axiomatization is the *informal set-theoretic axiomatization* or the *informal axiomatization by definition of a set-theoretic predicate.* When, in connection with the discussion of informal Hilbertian axiomatics above, the expression "implicit definition" came up, it was pointed out that this did not involve definitions at all, but rather, that the concepts in question represent the basic undefined concepts of the axiom system. When, however, these basic concepts are thought of as variables, the conjunction of the axioms becomes a statement-form of which it actually can be said that it *explicitly defines* a concept—albeit a concept of 'higher order' than the concepts which themselves appear in connection with an interpretation of the axiom system. In the case of an axiom system for Euclidean geometry, the explicitly defined concept could be called a *Euclidean structure.* In the case of number theory the concept in question is that of a *progression.* All the concepts appearing in such a definition can be introduced as set-theoretic concepts.

In a bold generalization characteristic of logicians and mathematicians, the expressions "*axiomatization of a theory*" and "*introduction of a set-theoretic predicate*" are held to be synonymous. Here again we must speak of an *informal* axiomatization because the set-theoretic predicates are not introduced within the confines of a formal system of set theory, but rather in a *language of ordinary discourse* on a purely intuitive level. In mathematics this method is very frequently used. An informal set-theoretic axiomatization of the theory of groups may serve as an illustration. The following

34

is one of the many possibilities of introducing the set-theoretic predicate "is a group":

X is a group iff there exists a B and a $\otimes$ such that:

(1) $X = \langle B, \otimes \rangle$;
(2) B is a nonempty set;
(3) $\otimes$ is a function with $D_I(\otimes) = B \times B$ and $D_{II}(\otimes) \subseteq B$;
(4) for all $a, b, c \in B$: $a \otimes (b \otimes c) = (a \otimes b) \otimes c$;
(5) for all $a, b \in B$ there is a $c \in B$, so that $a = b \otimes c$;
(6) for all $a, b \in B$ there is a $c \in B$, so that $a = c \otimes b$.

B is, intuitively speaking, the nonempty set of elements of a group stipulated by (2); $\otimes$ is a binary group operation. (3) demands that the application of $\otimes$ to any two elements of a group yield in turn an element of the group. The conditions (5) and (6) guarantee the possibility of a reciprocal inverse operation, which may also be called division when the group operation is called multiplication.

The six stipulations of this definition are sometimes called *axioms*. This can easily lead to confusion when the various sorts of axiomatization are compared with each other. "Axioms" in the present sense of the word must be sharply differentiated from that which is called "axiom" in the other forms of axiomatization. There, axioms were either statements (the first sort), statement-forms (the second sort), or formulas (the third sort). Here, however, an axiom is a *part of the definition* of a newly introduced set-theoretic predicate.

One of the advantages of this fourth type of axiomatization is that the concept of a model of an axiom system can be introduced without recourse to complicated technical apparatus. A *model* is understood here simply as *an entity fulfilling the set-theoretic predicate*. If, therefore, an axiomatization of group theory is understood as the introduction of the set-theoretic predicate "X is a group," and everything fulfilling this predicate is called a group, then the amazingly simple statement, "all groups and only groups are models of the axiomatization of group theory," is not some kind of circular claim, but rather *an absolutely precise specification of the models of axiomatized group theory*—assuming, of course, that the fourth type of axiomatization has been chosen.

This fourth type of axiomatization has still another advantage, which for our purposes will play an important part. The axioms describe a *mathematical structure* manifested in the sum total of the relations expressed in them. *Interesting structures*, with which various scientific disciplines work, are more or less awkward to handle when such a structure must be described by a whole set of sentences or formulas. Their use is facilitated considerably when one can refer to the structure through a single set-theoretic predicate.

Therefore, in what follows we will make use of this method of axiomatization by definition of a set-theoretic predicate. This method is not restricted only to those cases employing an algebraic or mathematical structure in the narrow sense. Rather, it can be said that *any* axiom system, especially any axiom system for a particular branch of physics, describes a certain particular mathematical structure. The structure, for example, described by axiomatizing classical particle mechanics is captured by the set-theoretic predicate "*x* is a classical particle mechanics." This predicate, defined in Chapter 6, will form an important illustration for the abstract discussion of Sneed's refinement of the Ramsey method in Chapter 5. A considerably more primitive set-theoretic predicate, used occasionally for purposes of illustration before then, will be introduced in Section 2.2.

For the sake of completeness still another, fifth type of axiomatization should be mentioned. Carnap speaks of the introduction of an *explicit predicate* or an *explicit concept* for an axiom system. This is none other than the formal counterpart of an informal set-theoretic axiomatization. The relationship between the introduction of an explicit predicate and the informal definition of a corresponding set-theoretic predicate is entirely analogous to the relationship between a formal Hilbertian axiomatic system and the corresponding informal Hilbertian axiomatic system. While the fourth type of axiomatization uses the language of set theory in a purely intuitive way, that is, as a nonformalized 'naive set theory,' an explicit predicate is introduced within the confines of a *formal* system (or subsystem) of set theory. Exactly as was the case with the third type of axiomatization, a formal language is employed in which the extralogical axioms are set-theoretic (supplemented by so-called definition axioms).

Inasmuch as the following discussion will not be based on a formal language, we will always be making use of *informal* set-theoretic axiomatization.

> As the reader will already have conjectured, there is a close connection between the third and the fifth type of axiomatization. As a matter of fact, any formal axiomatization in the Hilbertian sense can be transformed into the definition of an explicit predicate provided that there is a formal system of set theory available. For a short description of this method cf. Carnap, [Logik], p. 176f. For a detailed description of a formal system of set theory cf. the work of Fraenkel and Bar-Hillel quoted above.

The traditional view of *empirical scientific theories* can be split into two separate claims:

(1) Empirical scientific theories are *classes of statements*, some of which can be established as true or as false only by empirical means.
(2) The logical relations between the statements of an empirical scientific theory can be exhibited by an *axiomatic system*.

We will stick by the second assumption here. We have already decided on the fourth type of axiomatization. The first assumption amounts to the

' statement view' of theories. *Prima facie* it is a very plausible assumption, the more so because an analogous conception of theories as classes of statements—not of course *empirically testable* statements—has proved exceptionally viable in researching the foundations of logic and mathematics. One of the most important results of Sneed's investigations has been, though, to *jar this first assumption*. It turns out that from the beginning there are ' internal' logical, systematic grounds militating against it. Second, we will see that only by giving up (1) is it possible to bridge the gap between two apparently incompatible lines of thought within the contemporary philosophy of science.

> This bridge is made possible, however, only by *adding still other structures* to the logical structure mentioned in (2). In the language of model theory a set *M* of models may be said to correspond to the mathematical structure of an axiomatic theory designated by the basic set-theoretic predicate. In Chapter 7 *seven further structural characteristics* will be added to this set. The eight characteristics constitute the so-called expanded core *E* of a theory. Together with the set *I* of 'intended applications,' the possible descriptions of which are discussed systematically in Chapter 14, *this forms a vocabulary suitable for introducing macrological concepts*. With these macrological concepts it will be possible to formulate precisely various notions which heretofore appeared to be inaccessible to exact definition. Among these in particular are T. S. Kuhn's concept of *normal science*; one aspect of I. Lakatos' concept of a *research programme*; the *reduction relation between theories* obtaining when, in the case of a 'scientific revolution' in Kuhn's sense,[5] one theory dislodges the other; as well as the *concept of falsification* in Lakatos' 'sophisticated falsificationism.'

Before beginning the discussion of systematic problems we will, however, investigate the question of how a set-theoretic predicate, introduced in the course of the fourth type of axiomatization of a theory, may be used to formulate an *empirical statement*.

2.2 The traditional conception of the empirical claims of a theory; The example of a miniature theory *m*

We take as a basis that form of axiomatization which we called the *informal axiomatization by definition of a set-theoretic predicate*. We use informally "is an *S*" for an arbitrary set-theoretic predicate. In the case of a theory of physics this predicate characterizes *the entire mathematical structure* of the theory in question. (This is not an observation, but rather a linguistic convention on the use of the expression "mathematical structure.") How can one use such a predicate (such a mathematical structure) in formulating

[5] This reconstruction involves, however, rejecting Kuhn's incommensurability thesis.

an *empirical claim*? The most obvious suggestion is also the simplest: make a simple predication, i.e., a statement of the form

(I)   *c* is an *S*,

where *c* is a name or a definite description of some entity. In order to use (I) as an empirical statement one must, of course, make sure that this sentence is not already 'true on purely logical grounds.' The circumstances under which this could happen can best be illustrated with an example. We will return to this example a number of times in Part I for purposes of illustration. It is 'abstract' in the sense that (for the time being) it is not interpreted intuitively. In the example a miniature theory, designated by "*m*," is characterized by a set-theoretic predicate.

D1   *x* is a *V* iff there exists a *D*, an *n*, and a *t* such that

(1) $x = \langle D, n, t \rangle$;
(2) *D* is a finite nonempty set;
(3) *n* and *t* are functions from *D* into $\mathbb{R}$;
(4) for all $y \in D$: $t(y) > 0$;
(5) if $r = |D|$ and $D = \{y_1, \ldots, y_r\}$,[6] then $\sum_{i=1}^{r} n(y_i) \cdot t(y_i) = 0$.

In the context of the usual axiomatic construction only (4) and (5) would be thought of as 'actual axioms'; the first three conditions serve merely to characterize formally those entities and their parts of which it 'makes sense' to ask whether they fulfill the predicate "is a *V*" or not. Such entities may be called *possible models of V*. The *models of V* are, then, those entities for which the predicate "is a *V*" actually holds. It will prove useful to characterize the possible models with a distinct predicate:

D2   *x* is a V_p iff there exists a *D*, an *n*, and a *t* such that

(1) $x = \langle D, n, t \rangle$;
(2) *D* is a finite nonempty set;
(3) *n* and *t* are functions from *D* into $\mathbb{R}$.

The possible models of *V* are, therefore, exactly the models of V_p. This example may again serve to illustrate the general case. We can also introduce the class terms $\hat{V} = \{x \mid x \text{ is a } V\}$ and $\hat{V}_p = \{x \mid x \text{ is a } V_p\}$. The statement "*d* is a *V*" can then be symbolized by "$d \in \hat{V}$." Analogously (I) can be given as

(I*) $c \in \hat{S}$.

Now let "*d*" be an abbreviation for the triple $\langle \{1, 2\}, \{\langle 1, 2 \rangle, \langle 2, -4 \rangle\}, \{\langle 1, 6 \rangle, \langle 2, 3 \rangle\}\rangle$. Inasmuch as $d \in \hat{V}_p$, *d* is a possible model of *V*. Could we,

---

[6] "$|D|$" designates the cardinal number of the elements of *D*.

with the help of the predicate "is a V" or, respectively, the corresponding class term "$\hat{V}$," formulate an empirical statement of the form

(a) $\qquad\qquad\qquad\qquad d \in \hat{V}$?

Certainly not. One need make no empirical investigation to ascertain that (a) holds. (4) is directly fulfilled because the individuals 1 and 2 have the positive t-values 6 and 3, and with the corresponding n-values, namely 2 and -4, one can check out condition (5): $2 \cdot 6 + (-4) \cdot 3 = 0$.

We can therefore say it is a necessary condition that the term c not specify all three members in the form of lists if (I) is to represent an empirical claim. We will express this by forbidding an *explicitly extensional* specification of the members of the entity designated by c.

This condition is certainly met when the set D is introduced not by the specification of a list, but rather *intensionally* through the specification of a property. When there are functions things become a bit more complicated. Here, the intensional characterization consists of a description of a system of relations. As long as it is a matter of *extensive quantities*, three attributes must be given: a property G defining the domain of the system of relations, a binary relation R, and a tertiary relation o (i.e., the combining operation in the sense of Chapter 2, Section 4b of Stegmüller's [Theoretische Begriffe], p. 51ff.). The intensional characterization of a function f, which expresses an extensive quantity of the sort stipulated by D1(3), consists of describing an extensive system of relations $\langle G, R, \text{o} \rangle$ with $D \subseteqq G$ and effectively specifying one value for the function f. This capitalizes on the fact that every extensive system is homomorphic to a numerical extensive system $\langle N, \leqq, + \rangle$, which itself is unique save for similarity transformations.[7]

The condition which must be fulfilled in order that sentences of the form of (I) may be used to make *empirical claims* can now be concisely formulated as follows: the term c must characterize a possible model of V, indeed, by specifying D, n, and t, not all of which are to consist of lists, i.e., not all of which are given in an explicitly extensional form. This does not, however, suffice to make (I) an empirical statement. We require additionally that the statements attributing the defining property of D to particular objects and the statements attributing the relational properties R and o to pairs or triplets of elements of D, or eventually other objects, be *empirical statements*.

What has just been illustrated by this example holds in general. We may for now, though, spare ourselves a critical examination of the problem of whether the statement-schema (I) really represents *the* adequate method of formulating the empirical sentences of a theory because Sneed's treatment of the theme "theoretical concepts" will supply a sufficient reason *not* to pursue this path any further, but rather to fall back upon a modified Ramsey sentence for formulating the empirical content of a theory.

[7] For technical details cf. Stegmüller, [Personelle Wahrscheinlichkeit], Appendix III; Sneed, [Mathematical Physics], p. 18ff.; or Suppes and Zinnes, [Measurement].

3 Sneed's New Criterion for Theoreticity

3.1 The criterion for the concept "*T*-theoretical"

The replacement of the concept of an observational language in favor of that of a *basic empiricist language* took a justified *epistemological* criticism into account. Where the former was built around the fiction of a 'pure observer' whose psychophysical characteristics and abilities could be extracted from a general description of the species *Homo sapiens*, the latter substitutes a group of researchers armed with linguistic and scientific skills acquired over a more or less extended period of training.

Nevertheless, in spite of this *historic-pragmatic* relativization endemic to the concept of a basic empiricist language, it retains in common with its predecessor, the observational language, a *positive characterization* of the 'fully understandable' basic language and its conceptual inventory, while the rest, the 'theoretical superstructure,' of whose key concepts even the most well-equipped specialist can gain (at first) only the most indirect and partial understanding, remains *negatively characterized*.

With this negative characterization of the theoretical domain Putnam's challenge had to go unanswered, because the evidence that certain quantities are theoretical in the sense that they 'stem from a theory' can obviously be produced only when one commands a criterion which in the first place *makes reference to a theory* and, second, characterizes *positively* some feature peculiar to these theoretical concepts.

Sneed feels that with his criterion, which we will call *functionalistic*, he has found an adequate answer to Putnam's challenge. In order to get a preliminary feel for the new dichotomy to which this criterion leads, and in order to better discern the relationship between the epistemological distinction "observable–nonobservable" and the new functional distinction "theoretical–nontheoretical," we will pick up an interesting remark made by Bar-Hillel in [Neo-Pseudo Issue].[8] In his opinion the dichotomy "observational–theoretical" is *the result of a confusion*, namely, that of getting the dichotomies "observable–nonobservable" and "theoretical–nontheoretical" mixed up. And in fact one can distinguish *two dichotomies* even after making the suggested historic-pragmatic relativization. In contrast to Carnap's 'conventionalistic' conception, also accepted by Bar-Hillel in [Neo-Pseudo

---

[8] [Language], p. 267.

Issue], according to which the distinction between theoretical and non-theoretical is the result of an arbitrary ". . . slice in a continuum,"[9] Sneed's criterion leads in all concrete cases to an *objective distinction which cannot be changed per fiat.* In anticipation we can more specifically say that *if* Sneed's criterion proves adequate, and *if* his conjecture about the role of the position, force, and mass functions in classical particle mechanics is right, *then mass and force are theoretical* quantities while the *position function* represents a *nontheoretical* quantity. *No decree can change that!* In particular, it is not possible to take different pairings of this trio, e.g., the functions of force and position or of mass and position, as theoretical and regard the remaining one as nontheoretical. Thus, despite the fact that Sneed's criterion for theoreticity is *pragmatically relativized*, it is in one sense, still to be described, an '*absolute criterion.*'

Logicians tend to scratch their heads as soon as they even attempt to come to grips intuitively with the basic idea of Sneed's criterion. For in every instance in which it has been successfully applied it appears to lead inevitably to a logical circle or an infinite regression depending on the circumstances of the case. Nevertheless, this does not constitute an objection to the criterion; it offers rather a *psychological explanation as to why no one in forty years of discussing 'the riddle of theoretical concepts' got the idea of formulating the criterion in this way long before Sneed did.* This paradox, which appears with every successful application of the criterion, and which we, following Sneed, call *the problem of theoretical terms*, casts the Ramsey sentence of a theory in a brand new light. It is, namely, inconceivable that the problem can be mastered without recourse to it. The Ramsey sentence—albeit in a threefold refined form—represents not merely a *conceivable possibility* of exhibiting the empirical content of a theory; it proves itself *indispensable.*

> To avoid any misunderstanding, though, one should be forewarned that "theory" is *not* to be identified with "empirical content of a theory." As one of its most important results, Sneed's analysis involves abandoning the ' statement view of theories.' Accordingly, *a theory may not be identified with a system or class of sentences.*
>
> The new theory concept will prove to be extraordinarily important in two respects: first, as a means of rationally reconstructing and 'demythologizing ' the *holistic position*, including the extreme versions advanced by Kuhn and Feyerabend; secondly, as providing a logical framework for the systematic treatment of *theory dynamics.*

Sneed's basic idea is roughly this: exactly *those quantities or functions whose values cannot be calculated without recourse to a theory T* (more specifically, *to the successfully applied theory T) are theoretical* in relation

[9] [Language], p. 268.

to this theory *T*. In order to introduce the concept *T-theoretical*, being *relativized to a theory T* as it is, the concept of *T-dependent measurability* must be introduced as a preliminary step.

A precise formulation of the criterion involves a certain difficulty stemming from the fact that two different kinds of concepts are required. To the first class belong the presystematic notions which are not replaced at a later point by an exact explication. Among these is in particular the fundamental notion of the "*existing expositions of a theory.*" To the second class belong such notions as are subsequently explicated more exactly. Because various subsequent explications rest on the differentiation between theoretical and nontheoretical, only such notions may be used here whose explication would not involve this differentiation if a circle is to be avoided. In order to attain both maximal intuitive clarity and maximal precision, we will depart considerably from Sneed's procedure and give three versions of the first definition. The first uses only intuitive notions; in the third as many systematic concepts as possible are anticipated; the second falls roughly in the middle. To help understand these definitions, the important differentiations employed are listed in a table followed by some explanatory comments. The

Presystematic	Systematic
Abstract:[a]	
Theory *T*	The mathematical structure *S* corresponding to the theory *T*
Concrete:	
Applications of $T: T_1, T_2, \ldots, T_i, \ldots$	The empirical statements of the form: $c_k \in S$ for $k = 1, 2, \ldots, i, \ldots$ corresponding to the applications of the theory
Abstract:	
The 'abstract function *f*' occurs in *T*	The bound variable ϕ corresponding to *f* occurs in *S*
Concrete:	
The concrete function f_i subsumed under *f* occurs in T_i	The function constant ϕ_i, subsumed under ϕ, occurs in c_i, where c_i is the term occurring in front of the $\in$ in the empirical statement $c_i \in S$ corresponding to the *i*th application of *T*; and indeed as exactly the *j*th function of c_i, when ϕ is the *j*th bound variable of *S*

[a] To avoid any misunderstanding it must be pointed out that even in presystematic usage the expression "theory" represents in a certain sense an abstraction. It does not necessarily mean the same as that which an 'innocent physicist' might call a theory. He would perhaps be more inclined to label as a "theory" that which we in Part II call *holding a theory*.

intuitive or presystematic concepts are given in the left column, their systematic counterparts in the right.

> *Remark.* As before, we use the symbols "$\in$," "c_i," and "S" both as symbols of the object language and as metatheoretical names of themselves, i.e., autonymically. On the right side of the table the symbols are used exclusively as metatheoretical names.

> *Explanatory comments.* (1) The relation between the presystematic notions and their explications is expressed by the verb forms "correspond to" or "corresponding to." The correspondence relation holds, therefore, for the elements of the same line. We will say that concrete concepts proceeding out of abstract concepts as specializations for a particular application of the theory were obtained from the respective abstract concept by subsumption.[10] This relation holds between the first and second, and again between the third and fourth lines.
>
> (2) It is not assumed that a theory has only a single 'universal' application. The same abstract theory will as a rule have *various different applications*. It is assumed, though, that even at the intuitive level the set of empirical sentences of a theory can be divided into subsets each of which belongs to exactly one application—or indeed constitutes one such application. We think of the applications as being consecutively numbered in such a way as to enable us to speak of the first, of the second, of the ith application. It is *not*, however, assumed that the individual domains of different applications are disjunct. The most interesting cases will prove to be just those where different applications have a nonempty intersection. For the sake of simplicity, at the intuitive level we will already speak as if each separate application were exhibited by a single sentence (and not by a set of sentences).
>
> (3) A general or abstract theory T (e.g., classical particle mechanics) is for presystematic purposes best thought of as a *class of statement-forms* in which the basic concepts occur as *free variables*. In passing from T to a concrete application T_i (e.g., the application of classical particle mechanics to the solar system or the system of Jupiter and its moons) these free variables become *function constants* and the statement-forms become *sentences*.
>
> (4) For systematic considerations the situation is entirely different. At the abstract level neither a system of sentences (statement-forms) nor a single sentence corresponds to the theory, but

---

[10] In order to avoid an overdose of technical pedantry we will dispense with an exact definition of the subsumption concept. On the 'linguistic level' it is always a matter of substituting a function constant for a function variable or a schematic function symbol.

rather to a *concept exhibited by that set-theoretic predicate S through whose introduction the theory was axiomatized*. Inasmuch as the purpose of axiomatizing a theory is to expose its mathematical structure, we can call the concept designated by S its *mathematical structure*. (This allusion to the purely conceptual nature of an abstract theory vaguely anticipates the subsequent rejection of the ' statement view' of theories in favor of a purely set-theoretic characterization of the key concepts such as frame, core, and expanded core of a theory.)

(5) To each individual application T_i of T there corresponds only a single statement of the form $c_i \in S$. We speak of *the ith empirical claim of the theory T*. This statement is, therefore, no one particular sentence taken from the set T_i but rather that systematic statement corresponding *to the entire set T_i itself.*

(6) In the left-hand column of the table metaphorical quotes are used when speaking of the functions occurring in the abstract theory. The reason for this is that while a function symbol "f" is treated as a function variable at the abstract level, its specialization for two different applications i and j with intersecting domains D_i and D_j can yield an f_i and an f_j each of which is indeed a function in its own right, but whose union does not represent a function on $D_i \cup D_j$ because $f_i(x) \neq f_j(x)$ for at least one element from $D_i \cap D_j$. (Eliminating this eventuality requires, as will be shown later, building special *constraints* into the empirical statements of the theory.)

(7) In order to obtain a unique invertible correspondence for functions, both a bijection between functions f and bound function variables ϕ and a bijection between functions f_i and function constants ϕ_i must be assumed. The latter must be such that exactly that function constant ϕ_i subsumed under the bound function variable ϕ corresponding to f corresponds to the concrete function f_i subsumed under f.

(8) It must also be assumed even at the intuitive level that we command an *identity criterion for theories* sufficiently sharp to enable us to decide unambiguously if a given statement belongs to one theory or another.

(9) Finally, it is assumed that in all existing expositions of a theory *the methods* by which the values of the functions are to be calculated can be unambiguously recognized. Should these methods make use of physical laws, then this assumption includes the further supposition that one can unambiguously recognize these laws.

We are now ready to begin with the first definition:

D3   (a) The concrete function f_i occurring in the ith application T_i of the theory T is *measured in a T-dependent way* iff there is an

$x_0 \in D_i \cap D_{\mathrm{I}}(f_i)$ (i.e., an element x_0 belonging both to the domain of the ith application of the theory T and to the domain of f_i) such that in each existing exposition of T_i the descriptions of a method of measuring $f_i(x_0)$ presuppose the existence of a j such that T_j holds.

(**b**) . . . iff there is an $x_0 \in D_i \cap D_{\mathrm{I}}(f_i)$ such that in each existing exposition of T_i the descriptions of a method of measuring $f_i(x_0)$ contain a sentence of the form $c_j \in S$.

(**c**) . . . iff there is an $x_0 \in D_i \cap D_{\mathrm{I}}(f_i)$ such that in each existing exposition of T_i the descriptions of a method of measuring $f_i(x_0)$ are such that from the sentences representing a specialization of this method for measuring $f_i(x_0)$ a sentence can be logically inferred which, for some j, L-implies the sentence $c_j \in S$, where S is the mathematical structure of the theory T.

The last phrase could also be rendered as: "... are such that the sentences representing a specialization of this method for measuring $f_i(x_0)$ contain as a logically necessary condition a sentence of the form $c_j \in S$ for some j."

The second and third versions offer alternatives for defining Sneed's basic idea, namely, that for a function measured in a theory-dependent way there exists for each known application of the theory in which this function occurs at least one object in its domain the calculation of whose value *presupposes some successful application of this theory*. The intuitive phrase "presupposes," or more exactly "*A* presupposes *B*," is taken here to mean that *B* is a logical consequence of *A* (and not vice versa, cf. Section 3.2.11 below).

It should be noted that the predicate introduced in this first definition applies only to concrete functions, whereas the predicate "*T*-theoretical" is, at first, reserved for abstract functions.

D4   The function f (occurring in the abstract theory T) is *theoretical with respect to T* (or simply *T-theoretical*) iff in every application T_i of T the concrete function f_i subsumed under f is measured in a T-dependent way.

If a function f occurring in T is not T-theoretical, then we will say that f is *T-nontheoretical*.

The general concept *T-theoretical* for abstract functions can also be carried over to the concrete functions subsumable under them. "f_i is *T-theoretical*" means then that this concrete function f_i (e.g., the force function *in a particular application* or *in a particular 'real model'* of classical particle mechanics) is subsumable under an abstract T-theoretical function (e.g., under the force function of classical particle mechanics). It should not be overlooked, however, that "f_i is T-theoretical" represents as a rule a *substantially stronger* statement than "f_i is measured in a T-dependent way." For whereas the latter concept concerns only that measuring process involved in the ith application of the theory, the concept T-theoretical appeals to the measuring processes in *all* the applications of T. If, in particular, the function f_i subsumable under the abstract function f is indeed T-dependently measured, but is not T-theoretical, then there must be an application T_j of T such that the concrete function f_j occurs in T_j, is subsumable under f, and is measured in a T-independent way.

These concepts can also be applied to function terms at the systematic level. In particular, a bound *function variable* ϕ will be called *T-theoretical* if there is a T-theoretical function f such that ϕ is the function variable corresponding to f. And a *function constant* ϕ_i is T-theoretical if it is subsumable under a T-theoretical function variable ϕ. On the basis of the preceeding stipulations this means that ϕ is a T-theoretical function variable occurring as the nth member function in the definiens of S, and ϕ_i is the nth member function of c_i in the empirical statement $c_i \in S$ corresponding to the ith application of T.

3.2 Some conspicuous characteristics of Sneed's concept "T-theoretical"; farewell to the observational language and to correspondence rules?

The following remarks are intended as a further preliminary clarification.

3.2.1 Relativity to a theory

Relativizing the concept "theoretical" *to a particular given theory T* constitutes an essential departure from that procedure which we called Carnap's *linguistic theory*. Only by appealing to this linguistic theory can one speak of a *dual-level conception of scientific language*. For only then is the descriptive vocabulary divided into two subclasses, V_O (the class of the observational terms) and V_T (the class of theoretical terms), in such a way that the distinction is already a part of the scientific language. For this division is built into the language in formal analogy to the division of the symbols into logical and nonlogical. Inasmuch as it is made *before any theory is formulated*, it remains unaffected by any theory which may subsequently be formulated in the language.

Sneed's procedure, on the other hand, implicitly recommends that *this practice of the logicians not be imitated in the philosophy of science*. His criterion is first applicable when not only the rules of the scientific language are known, but *the theory itself* is given too. We can then get different results for *one and the same* concept depending on which theory we relate it to. For example, the concept *pressure* could be a *theoretical* concept *with respect to classical particle mechanics* while being *nontheoretical with respect to thermodynamics*. The scientific language can be the same in both cases as long as it is rich enough to allow for the formulation of both theories.

3.2.2 A strong and a weak stipulation in the criterion

A *very strong stipulation* is made at one place in D4; at another, a *very weak one*.

The *strong stipulation* which must be met if a function may properly be called *T*-theoretical lies in the phrase "in *every* application." It would, for example, be a mistake to invoke Sneed's criterion in support of the contention that *position* and *spatial length* are theoretical quantities on the grounds that in many of the usual applications of classical particle mechanics these quantities would be *determined by mechanical methods*. In order to classify these concepts as nontheoretical in relation to classical particle mechanics it is *not* necessary that *all methods* for determining position be independent of classical particle mechanics. It is enough if there are *certain* applications of this theory in which it is possible to determine position by entirely different means, e.g., by optical methods. Formally speaking, *it is possible that in a particular application a function is measured in a T-dependent way and is nevertheless a T-nontheoretical function.*

The existential quantification in the definiens of "measured in a *T*-dependent way" is, on the other hand, a weak stipulation. In most cases a stronger one is actually met. Sneed's conjecture that indeed for *all* individuals any methods of measuring force assume Newton's second law to hold in a physical system in addition to some particular force law may well be right.[11] Perhaps such a stronger stipulation is met in all, or at least most, of the known cases where Sneed's conditions for "*T*-theoretical" are filled (so that in each application *recourse to a successful application of the theory* is not only necessary in at least one instance, but *always*). Seen from this angle, one could consider Sneed's existential quantification to be a *minimal condition* for *T*-theoreticity.

3.2.3 The pragmatic character of the criterion

The definiens of "*T*-dependent measurability" contains the *pragmatic notion* of an existing exposition of a theory. As with all pragmatic notions, this one too has no sharply delineated extension. It must suffice to point out that not only 'original scientific treatises' are included but also the expositions of theories and their applications in textbooks and lecture notes as well as oral presentations.

The reference to *existing expositions* disturbs many. The chief reason for this 'pragmatic restriction' of the theoreticity concept may be found in the goal of the next chapter, which aims at reconstructing various ideas

[11] Sneed, [Mathematical Physics], p. 117.

47

connected with Kuhn's conception of science. We should, therefore, as far as possible avoid introducing concepts which could be reproached as 'Platonistic.'

One can quickly recognize the respective advantages and disadvantages of an absolute versus a relativized criterion by drawing the following comparison:

That part of the definiens of D3(a) beginning with "such that in each" could be shortened to: "such that *each hitherto known (empirical[12]) method* of measuring $f_i(x_0)$ presupposes an application T_j of T." We will call this the *(temporally) relativized criterion*. It yields an *absolute criterion* by dropping the two words "hitherto known" so that it now reads: "such that *each (empirical) method* of measuring $f_i(x_0)$ presupposes an application T_j of T."

The relativized criterion has the advantage of leading in each instance to a hypothesis which is in principle *verifiable*. (One needs only to examine carefully every known method.) The absolute criterion has the corresponding disadvantage. For according to it the allegation that f_i is measured in a T-dependent way is in principle an unverifiable hypothesis that could be falsified sometime in the future. On the other hand, the relativized criterion has the disadvantage of *incorporating the store of knowledge at a certain point of time into the logical structure of the theory*. Perhaps a 'Kuhnian' would see no disadvantage in this, but rather support for the view that every theory contains temporally relativized components. Those who share this view would thus prefer the relativized criterion; those to whom this seems implausible can at any time choose the absolute criterion.

> C. U. Moulines proposed a stronger criterion (indeed for *nontheoreticity*). It uses the idea of an *underlying theory* (e.g., a prephysicalistic theory of measurement) and may possibly avoid both of the disadvantages just mentioned.

Sneed's criterion can be called a *functional criterion* or an *implemental criterion* for *theoreticity*, because *the way in which the functions occurring in a theory are implemented* is the decisive factor in the "theoretical–nontheoretical" polarization.

3.2.4 The 'absolute' character of the criterion

This pragmatic restriction notwithstanding, the criterion is *absolute* in the following sense: it *determines objectively* whether a function is T-theoretical or T-nontheoretical. A comparison with the earlier notions of observational or basic empiricist language indicates an essential difference in this respect. How the line between the observable and the 'theoretical' in the sense of the nonobservable is to be drawn, or, alternatively, where full

---

[12] Naturally the expression "empirical" is not used here in the sense of "theory-independent." It is used parenthetically only to distinguish from purely *computable* methods. The same holds for the next example.

comprehension should end and 'partial comprehension' begin is, for them, *optional*. Furthermore, it seems sensible to let this option be dictated by *expediency* and, as does Hempel, *extend the line further and further* in the course of ensuing developments, because again and again in scientific discourse concepts and contexts once thought to be 'more or less theoretical' are subsequently added to those thought to be fully comprehensible.

Sneed's concept of *T*-theoretical, on the other hand, draws an objective line. No one can exercise an option in determining what falls under this concept; one can only express (true or false) *opinions*. The extension of this concept is, in concrete application, *no* longer a matter of *fiat*, but rather of *metascientific hypothesis*.

It is, for example, Sneed's metascientific hypothesis that *force* and *mass* are *T*-theoretical concepts whereas the position function is *T*-nontheoretical so far as *T* is understood to be classical particle mechanics. Sneed's hypothesis may be wrong. *But if it should prove to be right, then nothing can change this.* It is, then, no longer simply *expedient*, but on the contrary *necessary* to maintain that classical particle mechanics contains the two theoretical quantities *force* and *mass* and the nontheoretical quantity *position*.

This example also directs attention to a certain innate preference for Sneed's criterion as opposed to previous attempts. As far as classical mechanics is concerned, most philosophers of science would accept Sneed's hypothesis. *But why?* If, e.g., one recalls all the arguments which Carnap and Hempel have adduced in favor of the 'theoretical' character of dispositions, in particular metric dispositions, *it must appear the most natural thing in the world to call the (doubly differentiable!) position function a theoretical quantity.* When nevertheless only *force* and *mass* are used as examples of theoretical functions by many philosophers of science, is this not symptomatic of an instinctive appeal to *another* theoreticity criterion, namely, to the one Sneed formulated explicitly for the first time?

3.2.5 The superiority of Sneed's criterion to the dual-level conception

Three further points demonstrating the superiority of Sneed's criterion are the following:

(1) The disadvantages, discussed earlier, adhering to the notion of an observational language fade away; for it is *not* claimed *that the nontheoretical functions must be thought of as observable in some—always still to be defined— epistemologically important sense of the word.*

(2) The unresolved problem of the adequacy of correspondence rules involved in the dual-level conception disappears. It too is not solved but 'dissolved.' Only when the observable is taken as the sole starting point of comprehension must one take it upon oneself to formulate rules which pump 'meaning' from the observational language into the 'syntactical superstructure' of the purely theoretical. The critical discussion in

Stegmüller, [Theoretische Begriffe], Chapter 5.9, shows that this is no trivial problem *for the dual-level conception*. (The discussion of *this particular point* in Chapter 5 of that work concerns *not only* Carnap's significance definition, but a difficulty *germane to the dual-level conception as such*.)

(3) Putnam's *complaint* to the effect that no one has ever shown if, and in what sense, theoretical concepts 'stem from theories' *is finally silenced*. In Sneed's criterion one might plainly see *the first attempt at an adequate reply to Putnam's challenge*.

The last point is the most important. The disadvantage mentioned in (1) might disappear as soon as the observational language is replaced by a pragmatically relativized, temporally variable basic empiricist language in Hempel's sense. And as far as the problem of correspondence rules is concerned, it is at least *conceivable* that a solution be forthcoming, for instance, by formulating more precise criteria which would guarantee the elimination of the absurd examples depicted in Stegmüller, [Theoretische Begriffe], Chapter 5.9. An adequate solution of the problem posed by Putnam's challenge, on the other hand, is, as we have already made clear to ourselves in Section 1.2, unthinkable without *a criterion for "theoretical" which is both 'positive' and relativized to a theory* (whether this be Sneed's criterion or some other).

3.2.6 Farewell to the observational language?

The following two notions are introduced for terminological convenience. By *strong empiricist basis conception* we mean the original form of the dual-level theory of scientific language. Hempel's concept of a pragmatically relativized basic empiricist language we will call the *liberalized empiricist basis conception*. Our question now is this: *in order to do justice to the nature of theoretical concepts, is it at all necessary to retain the empiricist basis conception, be it the strong or the liberalized version*?

The answer is definitely "*no*." It is typical of *all* versions of the empiricist basis conception that the nontheoretical (the 'observable,' the 'fully comprehensible,' etc.) is *positively*, the theoretical on the other hand *negatively* characterized; indeed, as that which cannot be counted to the observational (basic empiricist) language, is *not* fully comprehended, etc. Sneed proceeds in exactly the opposite direction. *The theoretical is distinguished positively, the nontheoretical negatively as that which does not meet the criterion for T-theoretical.*

Of course this does not exclude the possibility of retaining, for other reasons, some version of the empiricist basis conception *too*. Carnap's critique of Bridgeman's method of introducing disposition and metric concepts shows that *for certain purposes* it may seem advisable to hang on to such an additional dichotomy. Assume that one wants to introduce concepts of this sort. Assume further that one finds Carnap's objections to Bridgeman's requirement of 'full definability' convincing. One will then, at least provisionally, think of the newly introduced concepts *as being only partially interpreted* and not want to count them as part of the basic empiricist language—at least not until such time as 'competent specialists' have acquired 'sufficient routine' in using them.

As long as only a single theory is involved these two dichotomies can be displayed schematically as in Figure 3-1. It is assumed here that *T*-theoretical

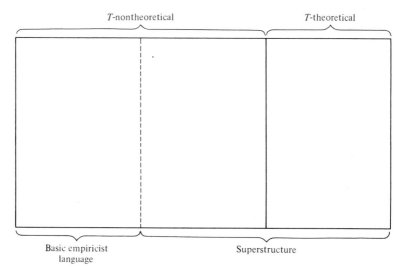

Figure 3-1

concepts are a part of the superstructure when there is one, but not that all concepts belonging to the superstructure are *T*-theoretical.

It should, however, be taken into account that several theories may be formulated in the same language, so that Figure 3-2 would offer the more appropriate schema. (Whether or not a nonempty intersection of the three

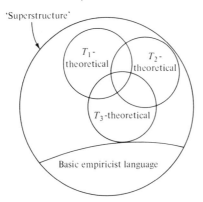

Figure 3-2

small circles is a serious possibility can presumably not be determined before more is known about the hierarchical organization of various theories.)

If the epistemological concept of a basic empiricist language is adopted, the problems inherent in it appear again. Sneed's method offers no solution to the 'semantic problem' of the comprehensibility of the terms belonging to the 'superstructure.' This sort of problem has no analogue *within his conception* as the subsequent Ramsey solution for the problem of theoretical terms will show. His procedure is, therefore, not semantically deficient so long as we confine ourselves to those questions occasioned by his criterion for " *T*-theoretical."

3.2.7 A potential objection: The criterion is too strong

We must now discuss a likely objection to Sneed's criterion. It consists of the allegation that the criterion is much too strong because it seldom, if ever, is necessary when determining the value of a function to take *an entire theory* into consideration as is required in the definiens of *T*-theoretical. On the contrary, all that one needs are *special laws* occurring in the theory.

Such an objection rests on a misunderstanding which overlooks the way that Sneed treats axiomatic theories. For him the axiomatization of a theory consists of introducing a set-theoretic predicate. This sets up in each concrete instance a general framework which is then filled in by the particular laws in various ways. Hence, in the formal treatment of theories special laws are not obtained by weakening this basic set-theoretic predicate characteristic of the theory, but rather by placing additional *restrictions* on it. Illustrations of this may be found in Chapter 6. There, only Newton's second law finds its way into the set-theoretic predicate "*x* is a classical particle mechanics" in addition, of course, to a logical-mathematical characterization of the formal properties of the members of a quintuplet fulfilling this predicate. A special law of mechanics is obtained by restricting this predicate. For example, Hooke's law is obtained through two such additional stipulations: first, "classical particle mechanics" is restricted to "Newtonian classical particle mechanics" (which amounts to adding Newton's third axiom), and then this latter predicate is in turn restricted by the addition of *what is usually known as Hooke's law.*

> Had Sneed adopted the traditional view, i.e., the 'statement view' of theories, according to which theories are to be thought of *as classes of sentences*, he would have had to formulate his criterion somewhat differently. The concept " *f* is theoretical with respect to classical particle mechanics" would then, for example, have to be characterized by the fact that in each concrete application of this theory certain values of *f* could only be obtained by assuming that Newton's second law, or indeed this law and at least one further force law hold.

3.2.8 A second potential objection: The process is circular

This objection runs as follows: on one hand Sneed rejects the statement view solely because of the difficulty connected with his notion of theoretical concepts; on the other hand the concept *T-theoretical* is itself formulated in a way already presupposing the rejection of the statement view.

To this may be replied that the second half of the objection is not correct. Indeed, first the adoption of the refined Ramsey sentence and then the rejection of the statement view is based on the problem of theoretical concepts. But the definition of *T-theoretical* in the 'language of set-theoretic predicates' is entirely a matter of convenience. As was just indicated, the translation into the traditional idiom would indeed be more awkward but is always possible.

3.2.9 Application of the criterion to nonphysical theories

The definition of "*T*-theoretical" is *confined to functions* because Sneed is concerned exclusively with physical theories whose basic concepts are always metric. This theoreticity criterion *could*, however, also prove fruitful for other theories whose conceptual apparatus has still not reached the stage of quantitative concepts. In these cases the concept of *T*-dependent measurability would be replaced by that of *T*-dependent determination of truth value, or briefly, *T*-dependent determination. On the basis of a distinction paralleling that for functions, namely, between the abstract relation R and the concrete relations R_i subsumed under it, the definitions for binary relations would run roughly as follows:

(1) The *truth value* of the class of R_i sentences is *determined in a T-dependent way* iff there exists at least one pair of objects $\langle a, b \rangle$ in the domain of the ith application of the theory such that in each existing exposition of T_i the validity of $\langle a, b \rangle \in R_i$ presupposes that an application T_j of T holds.

(2) The relation R is *T-theoretical* iff in each application T_i the truth value of the class of R_i sentences is determined in a *T*-dependent way.

The other versions of formulating the first of these concepts can be, *mutatis mutandis*, taken over from the foregoing.

3.2.10 Theory hierarchies

It has already been pointed out that because the concept *theoretical* is relativized to a theory, T_1-theoretical concepts are as a rule T_2-nontheoretical when T_2 is a 'later' theory in the sense that T_2 utilizes concepts from T_1 while T_1 manages without concepts from T_2. In this respect classical particle mechanics must be thought of as a particularly fundamental theory. Yet the impression that it represents the most elementary of theories in relation to which theoretical concepts are defined would presumably be mistaken.

All physical theories are based on theories of measurement (or, more exactly, *of metrics*). When the logical reconstruction of these latter theories, especially geometry and temporal metrics, is further developed than is currently the case, concepts such as *length* will presumably prove to be *theoretical relative to some metric theory*. Will this characteristic carry over in relation to those physical theories incorporating such concepts? That is, will they prove to be theoretical relative to these theories too? The initial spontaneous negative reaction could easily do an about-face as soon as one considers spatial and temporal measurement procedures more closely. For instance, the majority of traditional procedures for measuring spatial distance, including the more exact methods for testing the rigidity of measuring rods, depend on mechanics. All known clocks, with the exception of the atomic clock, which first came into use only a short time ago, are also mechanical systems.

Such considerations appear to cast some doubt on Sneed's hypothesis that the position function is a nontheoretical function in relation to classical particle mechanics. Against such doubts it may nevertheless be maintained that spatiotemporal metric theories underlie *various different* theories of physics, in particular some which are independent of each other in the sense that one is not reducible to the other. Let T^1 and T^2 be two such theories (e.g., mechanics and optics). One can assume that there are applications of T^1 in which, for example, the methods of measuring length rest at the most on laws of T^2 (e.g., on the laws of optics), and applications of T^2 in which the methods of measuring length presuppose T^1. According to the definition of *T-theoretical*, length would then be *neither a T^1-theoretical nor a T^2-theoretical quantity*. The supposition that no primary concept of spatiotemporal metrics has the status of a *T*-theoretical quantity in relation to a *special physical* theory *T* is, therefore, presumably sound. This, of course, is perfectly compatible with the hypothesis that these concepts are theoretical in relation to a theory which adequately reconstructs the metrics of spatial and temporal relations.

> The *correction factors* for measurement procedures which presuppose special theories, present, however, a special class of problems. An exact logical analysis of these correction methods *could* lead to a revision of the supposition just mentioned. To me, though, it seems that an appropriate reconstruction of both the 'corrective process' and the process of successive approximation would do better to *work with the idea of a feedback between theories* according to which entire theories may be reciprocally adjusted on the basis of results and precision achieved in other theories.

3.2.11 Presupposition in the
transcendental-analytical sense

The definition of *T*-dependent measurability of a function f_i given by Sneed in [Mathematical Physics], p. 31, stipulates that there must be an individual *x* in D_i such that the existing expositions of the application *i* of theory *T* contain no description of a method of measuring $f_i(x)$ which does not presuppose a successful application of *T*.

The term "presuppose" as used here reminds us of the notorious difficulty of correctly interpreting Kant's curious phrase "condition of the possibility of." When, for example, Kant describes the 'metaphysical presuppositions of experience,' i.e., the synthetic *a priori* principles which he tried to establish in the Transcendental Analytic, as being conditions of the possibility of (both scientific and prescientific) experience, the difficulty can be succinctly formulated as follows: in accordance with standard scientific usage a *condition* can be understood to be either a *necessary condition* or a *sufficient condition* or a *necessary and sufficient condition*. But all three interpretations seem to be inadequate here. The first would force Kant to allege that his metaphysics of experience is a logical consequence of Newton's physics; the second, that Newtonian physics can be inferred from his metaphysics of experience; and in the third instance, that his metaphysics of experience is logically equivalent with the Newtonian theory. Viewed in the light of Kant's intention all of these alternatives seem equally absurd.

In principle the solution of this difficulty must well be the one I suggested in [Kant's Metaphysik der Erfahrung], p. 27ff. (The additional complications arising from the fact that Kant had two different arguments, a 'regressive' and a 'progressive,' running in 'contrary directions' cannot, however, be entered into here. The following remarks are simplified accordingly.) It runs: *transcendental-analytical conditions of possibility are necessary conditions for a certain metatheoretical statement*: namely, for the statement "there exists an empirical science," briefly (*E*). Thus the apparent paradox disappears by shifting from the level of the object language to that of the metalanguage. The principles belonging to the metaphysics of experience are accordingly to be thought of *as logical consequences of* (*E*). Hence, a transcendental-analytical presupposition ('condition of possibility') is actually to be reconstructed as a *logical consequence*.

By analogy, Sneed's phrase "to presuppose" is taken in the sense of a transcendental-analytical presupposition. This is specifically recognized in the third version of the first definition by rendering the (schematized) phrase "*A* presupposes *B*" as "'*B*' is a logical consequence of '*A*.'" The reader is urged to keep in mind that a *presupposition* is not a *premise*, but a *logical consequence*.

We can again make use of the miniature theory *m* from Section 2.2 as an illustration by giving it a graphic interpretation. It involves a quite simple

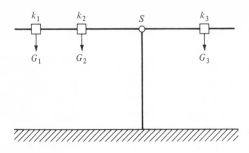

Figure 3-3

static application of classical mechanics whose mathematical structure is given by the set-theoretic predicate V. Consider a beam scale as depicted schematically in Figure 3-3 at some place on the earth's surface for which the field of gravity may be supposed to be 'quasiconstant.' The beam pivots at the center of gravity S. Three movable bodies k_1, k_2, and k_3 are suspended from the arms of the beam so that the scale is in balance and at rest.

> Strictly speaking, this system is a system of *rigid body mechanics* that may first be described in terms of particle mechanics when the beam has been resolved into sufficiently small parts (particles). This means incorporating the law of gravity and the support force f_s which is of the same direction as, and equal to the total weight of the system, but is of opposite orientation from the sum of the weights.

Because the beam is supported at the center of gravity, its torque disappears. When, therefore, G_i is the weight of body k_i and l_i its distance from the fulcrum, the system can be described as follows with the lever law deducible from mechanics:

$$G_3 \cdot l_3 = G_1 \cdot l_1 + G_2 \cdot l_2.$$

For r bodies from $D = \{k_1, \ldots, k_r\}$ the functions

(1) $$n(k_i) = \begin{cases} +l_i, & \text{if } k_i \text{ lies to the right of } S; \\ -l_i, & \text{if } k_i \text{ lies to the left of } S; \end{cases}$$

and

(2) $$t(k_i) = G_i$$

yield the statements:

(3) $$t(k_i) > 0$$

(4) $$\sum_{i=1}^{r} n(k_i) \cdot t(k_i) = 0,$$

that is, precisely the stipulations (4) and (5) of D1.

Further, it may already be pointed out that both constraints discussed below,[13] $\langle \approx, \ => \rangle$ as well as the additivity, or respectively, extensivity condition, are fulfilled for the function t.

---

4 "Theoretical Term": A Paradoxical Concept?

4.1 The problem of theoretical terms

Let T be an arbitrary theory having the mathematical structure S, i.e., the structure described by the set-theoretic predicate "x is an S." We will now sketch a difficulty connected with *the traditional view of the empirical content of a theory*, which *need* not, but nevertheless always *can* appear if the theory contains T-theoretical terms. The vague phrase "a difficulty . . . which . . . can appear" is unavoidable, because strictly speaking the difficulty appears in the *context of testing* or *of confirming* hypotheses, and no detailed account of the nature of testing or confirmation will be given here.

Two facts about testing (the applications of) theories containing only metric concepts will suffice for formulating this problem:

(1) To convince oneself that the ith application T_i of a theory T is correct, one must ascertain the values for *certain* arguments (i.e., elements of D_i) of the functions occurring in T_i, and then check whether these values meet the conditions set out in the definition of S.

(2) If the domain D_i of the ith application of the theory is not finite, this cannot be done for all arguments. (Nonverifiability of the application of a theory for an infinite domain.)

Let us assume now that an investigation (of the existing expositions) of T reveals that this theory contains the (abstract) T-theoretical function t, while the rest of the functions in T are T-nontheoretical. Let us also assume that the empirical content of the applications of a theory are expressed in the traditional way. If, then, we select the kth application of T, the empirical claim that T was correctly applied is a sentence of the form "c_k is an S," where c_k designates a possible model of S. What happens now when we try to convince ourselves that a sentence of this sort is correct? According to (1) we must ascertain values of the functions occurring in T_k, and check to see whether they fulfill the axioms (i.e., whether they satisfy the mathematical structure described by S). How is this possible? For the T-nontheoretical functions this presents no problem in principle; but ascertaining the values

---

[13] Concerning this notion, cf. Sections 5.3 and 5.4.

for the *T*-theoretical function *t* might require presupposing *certain physical laws to hold*.

> We might, of course, be lucky and not come up against any arguments of *t* involving such a 'presupposition.' But we have absolutely no guarantee that establishing the 'empirical basis of confirmation' for the assumption of "c_k is an *S*" does *not* involve such arguments. And we must admit that the question of the corresponding values 'cannot be dodged simply by ignoring it.'
>
> Besides, we must remember that in the definition of *T*-theoretical only the weakest condition was formulated. Where the stronger condition, namely that the measurement of *every* value presupposes some successful application of the theory ('that certain laws of the theory hold'), is met—as is presumably the case for the force function in classical particle mechanics—even the lucky chance just mentioned disappears.

According to the traditional method, though, each assumption to the effect that a law holds is to be exhibited by a sentence of the form "*c* is an *S*." *Thus, the justification for presuming that "c_k is an S" holds can only be complete when we are able to show that for some j a statement of the form "c_j is an S" holds.* In other words, we can present no empirical data to support the claim that c_k is an *S* unless we have empirical data to support the claim that c_j is an *S*; or again: the answer to the question of whether the *k*th application of the theory is successful depends on the answer to the question of whether some application of this theory is successful.

When the number of applications of a theory is finite, we are confronted with a *circulus vitiosus*; where it is infinite, we land in an *infinite regress*.

4.2 The Ramsey solution to the problem of theoretical terms

To begin with we can refer back to the miniature theory *m* from Section 2.2, which consisted of introducing the predicate "*x* is a *V*." We will assume the function *t* to be *m*-theoretical. In addition to the notion of a possible model V_p of *V*, it will prove useful to introduce that of a partial possible model V_{pp} as well:

D5   *x* is a V_{pp} iff there exists a *D* and an *n* such that

(1) $x = \langle D, n \rangle$;
(2) *D* is a finite nonempty set;
(3) *n* is a function from *D* into $\mathbb{R}$.

As before, we introduce here too the abstraction term $\hat{V}_{pp}$ as an abbreviation for $\{x \,|\, x \text{ is a } V_{pp}\}$. And as we called the models of $\hat{V}_p$ possible models of *V*, so too will we refer to the models of V_{pp} as the *partial possible models* of V. This terminology holds in general. Intuitively speaking, the point of departure is in each instance some theory in axiomatic form. If the axiomatization has the 'usual form' we rewrite it in the form of a definition of a set-theoretic predicate S.[14] The *models* of the axiomatized theory are the entities fulfilling this predicate. A much weaker condition requires only that it *makes sense* to ask of an entity whether it is an S. Those entities x meeting this condition we will call *possible models* of S. They will be characterized by a predicate S_p. (This transition was illustrated for the miniature theory by weakening the D1 predicate V, which exhibits the mathematical structure of the theory in the form of a set-theoretic predicate, to obtain the predicate V_p of D2.) The *partial possible models* are obtained from this latter predicate by still another weakening. They are, roughly speaking, what remains after the theoretical functions have been 'chopped off.' A partial possible model is an 'observable fact,' i.e., something which can be described by means of T-nontheoretical terms alone, and should be 'explained' with the help of the partly T-theoretical apparatus of the theory. The set-theoretic predicate characterizing the partial possible models of S will be called S_{pp}. (A comparison of V_p with the D5 predicate V_{pp} illustrates the second weakening within the minitheory.)

We turn now to the method of solving the problem of theoretical concepts which Sneed calls the *Ramsey solution*.

As an auxiliary concept we introduce the binary relation "xEy," which may be read as "x *is an enrichment of* y." In order to avoid the technical complications involved in the exact formulation of a general definition, this notion will only be defined for our minitheory. The reader should, however, have no trouble abstracting the generalized schema from it. The relation E should be introduced in such a way that the first member is a possible model and the second member a partial possible model obtained from the first by 'dropping' the theoretical functions. The precise definition runs:

D6 xEy (to be read: "x *is an enrichment of* y" or "y *is enriched by* x"[15]) iff there exists a D and an n such that

(1) $y = \langle D, n \rangle$;
(2) $y \in \hat{V}_{pp}$;
(3) There exists a function t from D into $\mathbb{R}$ such that $x = \langle D, n, t \rangle$.

Sentence (I) (or, respectively, (I*)) will now be replaced by the following existential quantification:

(II) $\vee x(xEa \wedge x$ is an $S)$

---

[14] Here, as in many other places, we employ the autonymic idiom. The predicate "S" is used as a name for itself; thus, the quotation marks are left out.

[15] More exactly, one must speak of *theoretical* enrichment. Sneed's expression "extension" is avoided here, because in logic it is usually associated with the *extension–intension* dichotomy.

or

(II*) $\vee x (xEa \wedge x \in \hat{S})$.

(In our minitheory $\hat{V}$ replaces $\hat{S}$ and b replaces a.)

Notice that due to the definition of enrichment the statement "a is a partial possible model of S" is already contained in (II). Thus, (II*) is logically equivalent to:

$$\vee x(a \in \hat{S}_{pp} \wedge xEa \wedge x \in \hat{S})$$

("There exists an enrichment of the partial possible model a of S which is an S").

The relationship between (II) and (I) becomes clearer if we use the set-theoretic idiom and, as was just done, again write out the superfluous part, with $\hat{S}_{pp}$. We then have the sets:

$$K_1 = \{y \,|\, y \in \hat{S}_{pp}\},$$
$$K_2 = \{y \,|\, y \in \hat{S}_{pp} \wedge \vee x(xEy \wedge x \in \hat{S})\}.$$

(II) says that

$$a \in K_2,$$

i.e., that a is an element of the class of those partial possible models of S which can be enriched to models of S. When, looking at our minitheory again, we substitute V for S and b for a, we can interpret the substance of this statement as follows: *b is one of those 'observable' facts* (i.e., facts describable without using theoretical functions) *which can, by the addition of a T-theoretical function, be enriched to a model of the theory* whose mathematical structure is exhibited by the set-theoretic predicate "x is a V."

Is a sentence of form (II) a more likely candidate for making the empirical claims of a theory than the sentence (I)? This involves two questions: first, can (II) be used at all for the purpose of making empirical claims? And second, does the problem of theoretical terms raise its head here too?

In principle, the first question may be answered affirmatively. For certain predicates S, however, it may be *provable* that a statement of form (II) holds for *every* a which is an S_{pp}, or for *no* $a \in \hat{S}_{pp}$. In such cases (II) can obviously not be used to make an empirical claim. For our minitheory, though, one can formulate precisely the conditions under which (II) leads to an empirically verifiable or falsifiable claim. To this end we start with the following theorem, whose proof is trivial:

Theorem 1
Let $\langle D_i, n_i \rangle \in \hat{V}_{pp}$. There is then an $x \in \hat{V}$ which is an enrichment of $\langle D_i, n_i \rangle$ iff either $n_i(z) = 0$ for all $z \in D_i$ or there are $y, z \in D_i$ such that $n_i(y) > 0$ and $n_i(z) < 0$.

Hint: In the first case choose a t fulfilling condition (4) of D1; i.e., one whose values are always positive. In all other respects t can be chosen completely at random. In the second case make use of the fact that under the assumption a solution of equation (5) can always be found which fulfills condition (4) for t. Should y and z be the *only* elements of D_i, then indeed not the t-values themselves, but, nevertheless, their *ratios* are determined by the ratios of the n_i-values. For in this case

$$\frac{t(y)}{t(z)} = - \frac{n_i(z)}{n_i(y)}$$

holds. If D_i contains other elements, then not even the ratios of the t-values are determined by the n_i-values, although certain ratios of t-values are precluded by n_i-values.

Suppose now that by empirical means two objects x and y have been found in D_i such that $n_i(x) > 0$ and $n_i(y) < 0$. By virtue of Theorem 1 one could then say that (II) is *empirically verified*. If, on the other hand, an investigation of *all the objects* in D_i should reveal that their n-values are uniformly positive or negative, we would have an *empirical falsification* of (II). (Naturally we must not forget that the expressions "verification" and "falsification" are to be used with caution inasmuch as the n-values are calculated with the help of *hypothetical* assumptions.)

> In many instances we will have to be satisfied with a *prima facie confirmation* of (II). This consists of the *failure* of a 'sufficient number' of empirical attempts to find n-values[16] which would preclude enriching the partial possible model $\langle D, n \rangle$ to a model of S. In this connection Sneed also notes a *purely calculational aspect* of theoretical functions: no matter how the empirical search aimed at discovering the truth value of (II) turns out, *it will not involve anything that could properly be called a measurement of t-values*, because in relation to such investigations the t-functions only come into play '*after all the empirical work has been done.*'

For the present, though, neither the problem of testing statements of this form nor the question of whether (II) perhaps has some disadvantages not accruing to (I) will concern us further. For inasmuch as Sneed's criterion for T-theoretical leads to the problem of theoretical terms, our main concern centers around the following proposition:

> *Sentences of type (II) present a possible solution to the problem of theoretical terms.*

This problem arose when we attempted to formulate the empirical content of a theory with the help of sentences like (I). For if one wants to convince oneself that the sentence "c is an S" is true, one must, in the presence

---

[16] Naturally we are not confining ourselves to our minitheory here. In general remarks of this kind n-values always represent values of any T-nontheoretical function and t-functions stand for any T-theoretical functions.

of T-theoretical functions, first establish the truth of some sentence *of exactly this form. This sort of difficulty does not confront sentences of the form of* (II), because there is no need to calculate the values of any theoretical function in order to check out the truth value of (II). The investigation is conducted *at a purely empirical level*, whereby we call any investigation working with nontheoretical functions empirical. In the case of our minitheory, for example, three things are involved. First, it must be *empirically* established whether or not certain objects are elements of D. Second, one must find the n-values for these individuals—again by *empirical* means. Third, one must see if (II) holds for these values. *And this, too, is possible without having to calculate the values of any theoretical functions, because the claim (II) is equivalent to a condition imposed upon the empirical n-values.*

This primitive example illustrates the general case. Determining whether or not (II), or its set-theoretic version

$$a \in K_2,$$

holds, involves *two separate tasks*. The one is *purely empirical*: it is concerned with the question of membership in an empirical domain and the values of empirical functions. The other is *pure computation*. This serves well to emphasize the metascientific import of the two model concepts. The first task involves the question of *whether something is a partial possible model of a theory*. The second concerns the problem of *whether a given partial possible model can be enriched so as to yield a model of the theory*. The 'theory' is represented by its mathematical structure S (and the partial possible models are those entities satisfying a substantially weaker predicate, namely, the one left after the 'axioms proper' and the theoretical terms have been dropped from S).

Sneed calls the idea of using sentences of form (II) (instead of sentences of form (I)) to exhibit the empirical content of a theory *the Ramsey solution to the problem of theoretical terms (theoretical concepts)*.

This label could, however, cause a misunderstanding. It is *not* meant to designate *the solution* to the problem of theoretical terms *suggested by Ramsey*. Ramsey was never confronted with the problem in its present form, because he never used Sneed's theoreticity criterion (although he may have had some form of it in mind). It must be understood as an abbreviation for "*that solution to the problem of theoretical terms obtained by using the Ramsey substitute to exhibit the empirical content of a theory instead of a statement of the form* (I)."

We will also call a statement of form (II) a *Ramsey formulation of the empirical content of a theory*, or simply, *Ramsey formulation of a theory*. We should, however, call attention to a minor technical difference from the description of the Ramsey sentence presented in Chapter 7 of Stegmüller, [Theoretische Begriffe]. The existential quantification in (II) is *over entire enrichments* of possible partial models, *not just over theoretical concepts*.

This modification is negligible though, because implicitly it includes the existential quantification over the theoretical concepts, as may be seen directly from the definition of the enrichment relation xEy.

Exhibiting the empirical content of a theory in a sentence of form (II) may well offer a promising start toward a solution to the problem of theoretical terms, yet this alone does not guarantee that the defining characteristic of theoretical terms, namely, that their measurement presupposes the truth of some empirical laws of T, will be *intelligibly* reflected within the framework of this different sort of reconstruction. The latter would require that at least certain statements of form (II)—those corresponding to the laws in question—provide a basis or justification for calculating T-theoretical functions with the help of 'observed measurements.' But this is actually the case. For whenever a measuring device is used which we have good reason to believe is *a model of S*, it is always possible (in the language of the minitheory), given the n-function values, to calculate the t-function values which make it a model. In this case, though, uniqueness of the actual t-values is not even required (cf. the example above of a two-member domain for which only the *t-ratios* are reflected by the *n-ratios*).

Despite all this, it will later be shown that the Ramsey method leads to inadequate results *if it is adopted without modification.*

4.3 Ramsey formulation and Ramsey eliminability; The real achievement of theoretical concepts in the absence of Ramsey eliminability

Let us again compare the predicating formulation of the empirical content of a theory (I) with the corresponding Ramsey formulation (II), i.e., "c is an S" with "there exists an x such that x is an enrichment of the partial possible model a of S and x is an S." The relationship between these two statements becomes clearer if we investigate the relationship which the term "c" in the first sentence bears to the term "a" in the second.[17]

To this end let us once again assume that the applications of the theory in question are suitably numbered. Both statements should serve to formulate the ith application of the theory. The term "c" designates an entity which can also be designated by "$\langle D_i, n_i, t_i \rangle$," because according to the claim (I) this entity is a model of S (indeed the ith model of S). On the other hand, the term "a" designates that entity which results from deleting the theoretical function t_i from c, i.e., that entity which, according to our assumption (II), claims to be the ith partial possible model of S which can be enriched to a model of S. Hence, instead of "a" we can write "$\langle D_i, n_i \rangle$." Both sentences then run as follows:

(I') $\langle D_i, n_i, t_i \rangle$ is an S,

[17] Sneed's text is confusing in that he uses the same symbol "Q" for both constants.

and

(II′)   there is an x such that x is an enrichment of $\langle D_i, n_i \rangle$ and x is an S.

(II′) corresponds roughly to what we called the Ramsey sentence of a theory in Chapter 7 of Stegmüller, [Theoretische Begriffe].

> The word "roughly" is inserted because (II′) diverges in two respects. First, as already mentioned, it quantifies over enrichments and not simply over theoretical terms. Second, it does not claim to exhibit the empirical content of the entire theory T, but only that of the *i*th application T_i of this theory.

We are continually speaking of *one and the same theory* on the one hand and of *different applications* of this theory on the other. This is not a case of exaggerated pedantry. The distinction between various applications of a theory will prove to be extraordinarily important in connection with modifying the Ramsey method and in settling definitively the question of just what a theory is.

In Chapter 7 of Stegmüller, [Theoretische Begriffe], the Ramsey method was described as the quantificational procedure for eliminating theoretical concepts. An inquiry into the 'ontological status' of the Ramsey sentence revealed, though, that the theoretical entities as such are not eliminated. Sneed, however, understands something entirely different under the *Ramsey elimination of theoretical concepts*,[18] and it is his notion of Ramsey elimination which we want to adopt from now on. To clarify this notion we will again make use of set-theoretic symbolism.[19] The defining statement-form "$y \in \hat{S}_{pp} \wedge \vee x(xEy \wedge x \in \hat{S})$" of the class K_2 we will call $\Phi(y)$. K_2 can then be written as $\{y \mid \Phi(y)\}$. In the present context, but *only* in the present context, we will also call $\Phi(y)$ the *Ramsey predicate of the theory*. One can now ask if it is possible to delineate the extension of K_2 *without resorting to T-theoretical terms*. The question can also be put as follows: K_2 is a subset of K_1 (namely, the set of those partial possible models that can be enriched so as to yield the set of models). Can *this same subset* of K_1 be delineated without using predicates containing T-theoretical terms? In short: can this subset of K_1 be delineated in a T-nontheoretical way? A positive answer means being able to produce a predicate meeting the following two conditions: first, it must contain only T-nontheoretical terms; second, it must be extensionally identical with K_2.

Assume $\Psi(y)$ to be such a predicate with $K_2 = \{y \mid \Psi(y)\}$. We will call this new predicate an *empirical predicate*. It is empirical in the sense that it is 'constructed entirely out of T-nontheoretical concepts.' We may also call it an *empirical equivalent* of the partly T-theoretical Ramsey predicate, i.e.,

---

[18] Cf. Sneed, [Mathematical Physics], p. 49f. and p. 52f.

[19] Cf. p. 60 above.

of that predicate originally used to delineate the extension of K_2. The expression "empirical equivalent" will also be used to designate the statement-forms constructed by means of this predicate. Whenever such an empirical equivalent can be found, it may be said that *a Ramsey elimination of the theoretical terms has been found*. This carries over, then, to the empirical claims of the theory. In place of the sentence "$a \in \{y \,|\, \Phi(y)\}$," we now have *the unalloyed empirical statement* "$\Psi(a)$."

> The notion of Ramsey elimination with the help of an empirical equivalent can be conveniently illustrated with our minitheory. As we saw in Section 4.2, the claim
>
> **(II^m)** $\qquad\qquad\qquad \lor x(xEb \wedge x \in \hat{V})$
>
> is, for a given intended application b, logically equivalent with the statement that the second member n_1 of b has the value 0 for all elements of the domain, or some with positive and some with negative values. If D_1 is the domain, the definition of the predicate "$\langle D_1, n_1 \rangle$ is a P_1," will be "for all $y \in D_1$: either $n_1(y) = 0$ or, if $n_1(y) > 0 \, (n_1(y) < 0)$, then there exists a $z \in D_1$ such that $n_1(z) < 0(n_1(z) > 0)$." In view of Theorem 1, this predicate is demonstrably an empirical equivalent of the predicate resulting from the substitution of "$\langle D_1, n_1 \rangle$" for "b" in (II^m). The m-theoretical function is, therefore, demonstrably Ramsey-eliminable. (II^m) *can be completely replaced by the purely empirical statement* "b is a P_1." This latter statement is entirely empirical because our hypothesis was that n_1 is an empirical, i.e., an m-nontheoretical quantity.

In order to describe the situation more exactly we must make a further distinction. It will be worthwhile noting this complication now, because the concept of Ramsey eliminability will serve to give us a clearer picture of the job done by theoretical concepts than we had before Sneed arrived upon the scene. For *the work done by theoretical concepts emerges very plainly when Ramsey eliminability demonstrably does not hold.*

Until now we have tacitly simplified the situation when we spoke of different applications of a theory. We have spoken as if the set-theoretic predicate S were simply applied to various entities while itself remaining unchanged. But this is not generally the case. As a rule the application of a theory to a domain involves considering special laws *holding in this domain alone*. This is reflected in our set-theoretic idiom by the fact that although the point of departure is indeed always one and the same basic predicate S (representing the mathematical structure of the theory), nevertheless, *from application to application various restrictions* are imposed on this predicate.[20] If we mark these restrictions with upper indices, each being identical with the number of the application in question, then the predicate

---

[20] It will pay the reader to begin getting used to *the idea of thinking of special laws as attributes distinguished by restrictions on the set-theoretic predicate characterizing the mathematical structure of the theory.*

S^j is used in the jth application and the predicate S^k in the kth application, etc. What is, then, the *statement-form* used to construct the sentence (II′) (which, as we remember, corresponds to the ith application of the theory)? Obviously:

$$(\mathbf{II}^i) \qquad\qquad \vee x(xEy \wedge x \text{ is an } S^i).$$

When we have found an empirical equivalent for the statement-form $\Phi^i(y)$, we say that *the theoretical terms in the ith application of the theory have proved to be Ramsey-eliminable*. In our minitheory this would mean the Ramsey elimination of the t-function from the ith application.

As long as we are considering only individual applications, we will speak of Ramsey eliminability *in the weak sense*. Theoretical terms can, of course, be Ramsey-eliminable for *certain* empirical claims, i.e., from certain applications, and not for others. On the other hand, where it is possible to devise a *general* method for generating empirical predicates, permitting the construction of an empirical equivalent for *each* application of a theory, we will speak of *Ramsey eliminability in the strong sense*. Where N is the number of applications of a theory, a Ramsey elimination of the T-theoretical functions is first realized when, for each i ($i = 1, 2, \ldots, N$) an empirical equivalent to $\Phi^i(y)$ has been found. The differentiation under discussion emerges from the fact that we must assign different Ramsey predicates to different applications of a theory. When, and only when, an empirical equivalent has been found for *at least one* of these Ramsey predicates, do we have weak Ramsey elimination. If, though, an empirical equivalent can be produced *for all* the Ramsey predicates of a theory, we have a strong Ramsey elimination.

Assume now that it can be proved that the T-theoretical terms for a certain, let us say the kth, application of a theory are not Ramsey-eliminable. It can then be rightfully maintained that the *'empirical content' of the theory in question T includes more than can be expressed by the 'observational'* (*i.e., nontheoretical*) *part of the theory*. This contention is based on the knowledge that the theoretical terms perform *an actual, indispensible task: namely, that of helping to preclude possible observable states of affairs* (i.e., states of affairs describable in T-nontheoretical terms alone) *which cannot be precluded with the help of conditions formulated exclusively in the 'language of the observational vocabulary'* (i.e., in the language of T-nontheoretical terms).

This does not, of course, allow us to conclude that theoretical terms *serve no purpose at all* when they actually are Ramsey-eliminable. Even when nothing prevents their Ramsey elimination, they can serve to simplify a theory considerably. The important point, though, is that the contribution of theoretical terms, when not Ramsey-eliminable, *is not confined solely to the question of the economy of the empirical applications of a theory*. (The ' nature of economic contributions,' present even in the case of Ramsey elimination, is discussed in greater detail later.)

In [Mathematical Physics], p. 52ff., Sneed sketches a procedure of investigating for Ramsey eliminability in deductive theories formulated in a first-order language with identity. As an example he takes a theory T having a single extralogical axiom containing a T-theoretical term τ which is not Ramsey-eliminable if the domain is infinite. For a finite domain, on the other hand, Ramsey eliminability can always be proved, as follows from a theorem of Craig and Vaught.[21]

Let us for the moment call the sentence which, in the presence of Ramsey eliminability, is built by means of the empirical equivalent to (II) a *Ramsey reduction* of the ith application of the theory. Another of Sneed's results then says that *the Craigian Ersatz theory* or 'replacement theory' (in the sense of Stegmüller, [Theoretische Begriffe], Chapter 6, p. 348) *cannot serve as a Ramsey reduction of the original theory*, because Ramsey eliminability is something stronger than Craig eliminability. (Cf. Sneed, *op. cit.*, pp. 56 and 57. We have just used the earlier terminology; strictly speaking one must now say "application of a theory" instead of "theory.")

A final question concerns *the relationship of Ramsey eliminability and explicit definition.* From an intuitive standpoint it would seem that the former implies the latter, because a successful Ramsey elimination is tantamount ' *to reducing the theoretical superstructure to an empirical foundation* ' which may be described entirely by T-nontheoretical terms. Nevertheless this is not the case. This circumstance is, in terms of our minitheory, connected with the problem of the extent to which n-functions *uniquely determine* the t-functions. Only when a *unique* determination holds for *every* application can one assume that the t-function may be *explicitly defined* by means of the n-function. In all other cases such a conclusion is unwarranted. In particular, explicit definability certainly does not hold in the mere presence of weak Ramsey elimination. And even in the presence of strong Ramsey elimination definability cannot be taken for granted, because the condition of uniqueness need not be fulfilled.

Thus the explicit empirical definability of T-theoretical terms and Ramsey eliminability are *not* equivalent. This is an important point, for it means that *besides the explicit definition of theoretical terms Ramsey elimination offers, as a rule, a different but very real possibility of reducing theoretical superstructure to an empirical (nontheoretical) fundament.*

Concerning this theme, Sneed discusses an interesting historical example (*op. cit.*, p. 59f., and Chapter 6) which had already been mentioned in Stegmüller, [Theoretische Begriffe], Chapter 2, p. 135ff. Using our present terminology it could be said that Mach made the mistake *of inferring the explicit definability of the mass function by means of the position function from the weak Ramsey eliminability of the mass function* in a two-element domain.

[21] Cf. Craig and Vaught, [Finite Axiomatizability].

5 A Threefold Refinement of the Ramsey Method

5.1 The limitations of the Ramsey formulation

Can the Ramsey substitute for an empirical application of a theory be used to make predictions? The answer is "sometimes yes, sometimes no." Our minitheory will once again serve to illustrate. We had the statement

(**II^m**) $\qquad\qquad\qquad \forall x(xEb \wedge x \in \hat{V})$,

which, as we remember, implicitly contains the statement "$b \in \hat{V}_{pp}$." b is the partial possible model $\langle D_1, n_1 \rangle$. We will assume that (II^m) is sufficiently well grounded empirically to warrant believing that it is true.

Sneed tenders two types of prediction which can be made under these circumstances:

(1) If all known elements of D_1 have n_1-values which do not allow $\langle D_1, n_1 \rangle$ to be enriched to a model for S, then one can *predict* that there are still undiscovered elements of D_1.

(2) If one has good reasons for assuming that D_1 has exactly r elements and l n_1-values are known, then one can make certain *predictions* about the n_1-values for the remaining $r - l$ elements of D_1.

> Both (1) and (2) follow from Theorem 1, p. 60. Depending on whether or not anything is assumed about the number of objects in D_1, (1) or (2) are fulfilled when, for example, k objects of D_1 have been observed with the result that all have positive n_1-values or all have negative n_1-values.

A historical example of type (1) was the prediction of the existence of the planet Neptune on the basis of the known paths of all planets discovered prior to 1846 and the assumption that a statement like (II) must hold for a certain form of Newtonian mechanics.[22] Here D_1 is the class of objects belonging to the solar system. It proved impossible to enrich this system as it was known in 1846 to a model for the Newtonian mechanics mentioned.

Examples of type (2) are provided by all those applications of classical mechanics in which the subsequent positions of particles are predicted from their initial positions. In this case the initial positions of all the particles correspond to the l known elements of D_1, while the subsequent positions correspond to the $r - l$ *unknown* n_1-values.

[22] For details see Chapter 6; cf. also Section 14.2.

These examples of the prognostic powers of the Ramsey formulation are, however, somewhat meager. This is no mere accident. It can easily be shown that most *nontrivial* uses of known measurements of theoretical functions *cannot* be realized with the help of statements of form (II). Such nontrivial uses appear in three contexts: namely, when *testing* hypotheses, when using them for *explanation*, and when using them to make *predictions*.

For the present it will suffice to point out one thing common to all these contexts which cannot be reconciled with (II). In all nontrivial cases of this sort the values of *T*-theoretical functions obtained *in certain applications* are relevant *for other applications* of the same theory. In the case of classical particle mechanics these are the values for masses and forces. Notice that we have already passed from one application to another when the values determined by means of a measuring device are used *outside of this apparatus itself*, when, for example, the mass ratio of two bodies as determined by a scale is used to predict their behavior as members of a compound pendulum system. We will speak here of *the problem of transition from one application of a theory to another*.

It should be clear that *this problem of transition from one application to another cannot be solved within the present conceptual framework*. Assume, for instance, that a statement of the form (II) is used to calculate t_i-values from 'observable' n_i-values as described at the end of Section 4.2. None of these results gives us the slightest clue about the value of the nontheoretical function n_k or the theoretical function t_k of the kth application, when $k \neq i$. This is the case even if we assume D_i and D_k to overlap. For there is no guarantee that the concrete nontheoretical functions n_i and n_k or the concrete theoretical functions t_i and t_k must have the same value for one and the same argument $x \in D_i \cap D_k$; i.e., it may well be that $n_i(x) \neq n_k(x)$ or $t_i(x) \neq t_k(x)$. Thus, even when we have reason to believe a claim like (II) holds, this can, at best, be assessed as a very limited partial representation of the empirical content of the theory, since all the important and interesting applications of scientific knowledge are frustrated at the point where one tries to *bring the measurements* obtained in certain situations *to bear on other situations*, be it for purposes of explanation or prediction, or to test the hypothesis that 'the theory holds in these other situations, too.'

5.2 First generalization of the Ramsey formulation: The introduction of several 'intended applications' of a theory

One handy way to avoid the difficulties mentioned would be to drop the idea of different applications of one and the same theory in favor of a single '*universal domain of application*' for the theory. Some such assumption has probably dominated to a great extent the analysis of the theory concept to date. It is an especially tempting idea where classical particle mechanics is concerned which, after all, seems to be applicable 'to everything.' The governing intuitive idea here may be roughly characterised as follows: "Given the paths of all material bodies in the universe for all time, there are mass and force functions which, together with the position function determined by these paths and appropriate force laws, produce a model for an adequate axiomatization of classical particle mechanics. Hence, there is but a single domain of application for this theory: namely, the cosmos in its entire spatiotemporal magnitude."

Various reasons, however, speak against this *'cosmic aspect of theory application.'* The most important of these may well be that *we have not the faintest notion of how to formulate it precisely.* A radical departure from the actual practices of physicists would be inevitable, creating in turn the danger of slipping into an unrealistic metascience of science fiction. And even if this program could in principle be realized, one would presumably encounter intractable difficulties *when one wanted to use the theory to make relatively simple explanations or predictions,* e.g., to explain the paths of the planets or, to take something still more banal, to predict the behavior of two elastic balls upon colliding on a level table top. Finally, *elucidating the distinguishing feature of theoretical functions,* namely, that the determination of their values requires the help of empirical laws, would seem to be impossible on this basis. It does not seem possible to clear up this point by using a 'universal' claim of the form (II) either, since *the idea of a transition from one application of the theory to another* forms an indispensable part of the analysis for such a clarification.

Troubles of this sort are likely to provoke the radical suggestion of giving up the Ramsey method completely and shopping around for something entirely new. But this amounts to throwing out the baby with the bath water. The advantages of this method, some of which have not even been mentioned, are too great to acquiesce in such a proposal, particularly as there seems to be no other method known for disposing of the problem of theoretical terms.

Thus, it seems advisable, following Sneed, to modify the Ramsey method *in several essential respects* rather than reject it. The results of our investigations so far can be summed up as follows: *the unmodified Ramsey method solves only half of the problem.* It shows how 'uninterpreted' theoretical terms can be used in the empirical claims of a theory (and indeed not only to improve the 'economy' but, where Ramsey elimination fails, even to preclude possible 'observable situations' which demonstrably could *not* be ruled out with the help of nontheoretical concepts alone). *On the other hand, this method fails to account for the role of theoretical terms in all those sentences involving explanation, prediction, and the testing of hypotheses.*

Sneed's procedure will be easier to follow if split into three different components—one could say three different suggestions for refining the Ramsey method—each to be treated separately. The first modification consists of getting really serious about the idea of *different applications of one and the same theory* and incorporating a precise form of it into the Ramsey method.

Typical of all the remarks about the different applications of a theory made so far is an intuitive vagueness which must now be redressed. The basic idea is as follows: instead of beginning with *one* domain of individuals, we begin with a *set* of such domains. The theoretical and nontheoretical functions will also be replaced by *sets* of such, and likewise for the partial possible, the possible, and the models themselves. In contrast to the 'simple' Ramsey sentence (II), the *expanded Ramsey sentence* (III$_a$) says not merely that a certain partial possible model can be enriched so as to yield a model of the theory, but indeed that *for the elements of a set of partial possible models there exists a whole set of enrichments each of which yields a model of the theory.* Briefly, a given set of partial possible models can be enriched so as to yield a set of models. For the sake of clarity Gothic letters will be used for sets of entities, with the latin counterparts of the Gothic letters denoting the entities themselves, i.e., the elements of the sets. The 'fictitious' pragmatic starting point is an arbitrary physical theory with its applications. For the sake of simplicity the following concepts will only be introduced for our minitheory. The general procedure can be directly extrapolated from these.

Let D_i be the domain of individuals of the ith application of the theory, and

$$\mathfrak{D} = \{D_1, D_2, \ldots, D_i, \ldots\}$$

be the set of domains of all the applications.

This class may be finite *or infinite*. It is *not* assumed that the sets D_i are disjunct. An example of three nondisjunct sets belonging to different applications of classical particle mechanics are the solar system, Jupiter with its moons, and the earth-moon system. Only the second and third of these sets are disjunct; the first and second have as a common element Jupiter; the first and third, the planet earth.

We also introduce the union

$$\Delta = \cup D_i, \qquad D_i \in \mathfrak{D}$$

for later use. $\Delta \in \mathfrak{D}$ can, but need not, be the case; i.e., the *possibility* of a 'universal' domain of application should not be excluded *a priori*.

The index set of $\mathfrak{D}$ (i.e., the set of lower indices of elements of $\mathfrak{D}$) will be called $Ix(\mathfrak{D})$. For each $i \in Ix(\mathfrak{D})$ let t_i be a function from D_i into $\mathbb{R}$. Then we let

$$t = \{t_1, t_2, \ldots, t_i, \ldots\}.$$

Here, too, it will be convenient to introduce the union

$$\tau = \cup t_i, \qquad t_i \in t.$$

The domain of τ is Δ. But it should be noted that τ *need not be a function.* An analogous stipulation holds for the nontheoretical functions

$$\mathfrak{n} = \{n_1, n_2, \ldots, n_i, \ldots\}.$$

Finally, we will need the class

$$\{\langle D_1, n_1 \rangle, \langle D_2, n_2 \rangle, \ldots, \langle D_i, n_i \rangle, \ldots\}.$$

We will call the elements of this class *the intended applications of the theory.*

In analogy to **D6** we introduce now a *generalized* concept of enrichment as follows:

D7 $\mathfrak{x}\mathfrak{E}\mathfrak{y}$ ("$\mathfrak{x}$ is an enrichment set for $\mathfrak{y}$") iff there is a $\mathfrak{D} = \{D_1, D_2, \ldots, D_i, \ldots\}$ and an $\mathfrak{n} = \{n_1, n_2, \ldots, n_i, \ldots\}$ such that

     (1) $\mathfrak{y} = \{\langle D_1, n_1 \rangle, \langle D_2, n_2 \rangle, \ldots, \langle D_i, n_i \rangle, \ldots\}$;

     (2) for all $y \in \mathfrak{y}$: $y \in \hat{V}_{pp}$;[23]

     (3) there is a class $\mathfrak{t} = \{t_1, t_2, \ldots, t_i, \ldots\}$ such that for all $i \in Ix(\mathfrak{t})$: t_i is a function from D_i into $\mathbb{R}$;

     (4) $\mathfrak{x} = \{\langle D_1, n_1, t_1 \rangle, \langle D_2, n_2, t_2 \rangle, \ldots, \langle D_i, n_i, t_i \rangle, \ldots\}$.

Intuitively this definition says that $\mathfrak{x}$ is a set of enrichments for the set $\mathfrak{y}$ of partial possible models of V (so that $\mathfrak{y}$, therefore, is a set of possible models for this predicate).

For the sake of clarity we will introduce the following relation per (by itself superfluous) definition:

D8 $\mathfrak{x} \subseteqq \hat{V}$ iff there are three classes $\mathfrak{D}, \mathfrak{n}, \mathfrak{t}$ with

$$\mathfrak{D} = \{D_1, D_2, \ldots, D_i, \ldots\},$$
$$\mathfrak{t} = \{t_1, t_2, \ldots, t_i, \ldots\}$$

     and

$$\mathfrak{n} = \{n_1, n_2, \ldots, n_i, \ldots\}$$

     such that

     (1) $\mathfrak{x} = \{\langle D_1, n_1, t_1 \rangle, \langle D_2, n_2, t_2 \rangle, \ldots, \langle D_i, n_i, t_i \rangle, \ldots\}$;

     (2) for all $x \in \mathfrak{x}$, x is a V (i.e., $x \in \hat{V}$).

For the generalized case, V is replaced by S, $\hat{V}$ by $\hat{S}$, V_{pp} by S_{pp}, etc. The first version of the *generalized Ramsey sentence* is

(III$_a^m$) $\vee \mathfrak{x}(\mathfrak{x}\mathfrak{E}\mathfrak{b} \wedge \mathfrak{x} \subseteqq \hat{V})$

or, for the abstract case,

(III$_a$) $\vee \mathfrak{x}(\mathfrak{x}\mathfrak{E}\mathfrak{a} \wedge \mathfrak{x} \subseteqq \hat{S})$.

---

[23] Instead of (2) we could also write $\mathfrak{y} \subseteqq \hat{V}_{pp}$.

(III$_a$) makes the following claim: "For the set a (in the minitheory b) of partial possible models of that theory whose mathematical structure is described by the set-theoretic predicate $S(V)$, there exists a set of enrichments, one for each partial possible model in a (b), such that every single one of these enrichments is a model for $S(V)$."

5.3 Second generalization of the Ramsey formulation: Constraints as 'restraining cross-connections' on the intended applications of a theory

As it stands the modification of the Ramsey formulation represented by (III$_a$) is immediately subject to a fundamental objection. It is, namely, a complete mystery why (III$_a$) should qualify as an application *of one theory*. When, for example, the number of applications is finite, say N, then (III$_a$) comprises nothing other than *a symbolic compilation of the applications of N different theories*—albeit theories with isomorphic mathematical structures. According to this objection the generalization effected by (III$_a$) is merely a pseudogeneralization consisting of nothing more than a symbolic abbreviation.

This objection is justified at this point. It can only be disposed of after introducing the other two modifications of the Ramsey formulation still to be discussed.

A second modification of the Ramsey formulation consists of *establishing certain kinds of cross-connections between the different intended applications* (i.e., partial possible models[24]) which from the outset considerably reduce the number of partial possible models of the theory that can be enriched to models. These cross-connections we will call *restraining conditions* or *constraints*. We can illustrate this concept with the help of two important examples. An especially simple constraint consists of requiring that

(a) $\qquad \tau = \cup\, t$ be a function from Δ into $\mathbb{R}$.

The import of this condition becomes clear if we remember that even when x belongs to the intersection $D_i \cap D_k$ of the domains of the ith and kth applications the original Ramsey formulation did not imply $t_i(x) = t_k(x)$. This eventuality is now ruled out. For *(a)* means that 'the same' theoretical function assigns to *any one individual the same value should this individual occur in different applications of the theory*. (Only by virtue of this additional condition we are justified in speaking of 'the same' theoretical function.

---

[24] In [Mathematical Physics], at the bottom of p. 66, Sneed remarks that he will refer to the particular individual domains D_1, D_2, ... as *intended applications of the theory*. This is misleading because later he *never* actually uses the expression "intended application" in this sense. On the contrary, he always takes it to mean "individual domain *plus nontheoretical functions*." Cf. particularly p. 180ff. of his book.

For it requires that the different *concrete functions* proceeding out of the same abstract function yield the same value for the same individual.) If one takes the mass function of classical particle mechanics, this means that in our example above the first and third applications of classical particle mechanics assign the planet Earth, and the first and second applications the planet Jupiter, the same mass. When (*a*) is fulfilled one occasionally says that the function in question characterizes an '*intrinsic property*' (*constant property* or *conservative quantity*) of the individual. Constraints on *theoretical* functions are indeed the most important and interesting cases, but this is, of course, not the only possibility; constraints may also be imposed on nontheoretical functions.

Still other kinds of constraints result *when limitations are imposed on the values of the function* τ. One of the more important limitations of this sort, which can also be nicely illustrated with the mass function, is the requirement *that this theoretical function yield an extensive quantity*. In this case it is essential that one consider not the single *concrete* theoretical functions but their *union* τ for which (*a*) holds, i.e., the stipulation that it is indeed a function.

Let o be a mode of combination (in the sense of Stegmüller, [Theoretische Begriffe], Chapter 1, 4.b) defined on Δ, i.e., on the union of all $D_i \in \mathfrak{D}$. For any two $x, y \in \Delta$ (*not* necessarily elements of the same application D_i !),

(*b*) $$\tau(x \text{ o } y) = \tau(x) + \tau(y)$$

should hold.

With the help of these two constraints it is possible to modify the generalized Ramsey sentence (III_a) in such a way that intuitively it says roughly the following: "Assume a set of domains and of nontheoretical functions on each domain which together form a set $\mathfrak{a}$ of partial possible models for a theory T whose mathematical structure is described by the predicate S. There is then a class t of theoretical functions on the domains of these partial possible models whose union τ characterizes an *intrinsic property* of the individuals of these domains (i.e., is a function on the union Δ of $\mathfrak{D}$), is *extensive* for o (i.e., fulfills the condition (*b*)), and is such that for the elements $t_i \in t$ each triplet $\langle D_i, n_i, t_i \rangle$ is a model of S."

The functional character and extensivity of τ are just examples of constraints. Before we explicitly formulate the *modified form of the generalized Ramsey sentence* we will define the *general* notion of constraint. Strictly speaking it will be a definition *schema* in which the variable R can be replaced by an actual constraint as required by the situation. Note that in contrast to the intuitive exposition above, the order of indices makes a difference here. Thus, $\mathfrak{D}$ and t must be construed *as sequences* instead of classes. This guarantees that each D_i is assigned one particular t_i.[25]

---

[25] Without this stipulation a 'higher-order' function would have to be introduced which assigns each element D of $\mathfrak{D}$ a function from D into $\mathbb{R}$. This would be an unnecessary complication. For each $k \in Ix(\mathfrak{D}) \cap Ix(\mathfrak{t})$ we say that the function t_k is *assigned* to the domain D_k.

D9   Assume that

(a) $\mathfrak{D}$ is a sequence $\langle D_1, D_2, \ldots, D_i, \ldots \rangle$;[26]
(b) $\Delta = \cup \mathfrak{D}$;
(c) t is a sequence $\langle t_1, t_2, \ldots, t_i, \ldots \rangle$ such that each $t_k \in t$ is a function from D_k into $\mathbb{R}$;
(d) $Ix(\mathfrak{D}) = Ix(t)$ and for every k in this index set the member t_k is assigned to the member D_k of $\mathfrak{D}$.

Then t *is constrained by* $\langle R, \rho \rangle$ iff

(1) R is an n-ary relation on Δ;
(2) ρ is an n-ary relation on $\mathbb{R}$;
(3) for all $x_1, \ldots, x_n \in \Delta$ and all $D_{i1}, \ldots, D_{in} \in \mathfrak{D}$ such that $x_j \in D_{ij} (1 \leq j \leq n)$: if $R(x_1, \ldots, x_n)$, then $\rho(t_{i1}(x_1), \ldots, t_{in}(x_n))$.[27]

The two constraints mentioned so far afford an illustration of the definition. The identity of individuals in Δ will be symbolized by "$\approx$" so as not to be mistaken for numerical identity which will be symbolized by "$=$." The constraint guaranteeing that $\tau = \cup t$ is a function on Δ may be expressed as follows: "t *is constrained by* $\langle \approx, = \rangle$" (since $y_1 = y_2$ follows from $\tau(x) = y_1$ and $\tau(x) = y_2$). In the case of mass this would mean that when some one individual is included in the domains of different applications, the two concrete mass functions assigned to these domains must yield the same real number as value. Briefly, the same objects retain the same mass independent of the application in which they are included.

That τ be extensive with respect to o is guaranteed by requiring that t *be constrained by* $\langle R_1, \rho_1 \rangle$, whereby R_1 is a tertiary relation on Δ which, for all $x, y, z \in \Delta$, satisfies the condition that $R_1(x, y, z)$ iff x o $y \approx z$, and ρ_1 is a tertiary relation on $\mathbb{R}$ satisfying the condition $\rho_1(u, v, w)$ iff $u + v = w$.

As a rule *several* constraints are imposed upon theoretical functions as shown by these examples. To prevent the symbolism from becoming unmanageable, the phrases "$\langle R, \rho \rangle$ is a constraint on t" and "t satisfies the constraint $\langle R, \rho \rangle$" will be used as equivalent 'stenographic abbreviations' for a statement to the effect that several constraints are imposed on t. This one pair functions as 'symbolic representative' for all these constraints. Another abbreviation would be the following: Assume that $\mathfrak{x} \mathfrak{E} \mathfrak{y}$. Then

$$C(\mathfrak{x}, R, \rho)$$

means: "the set t of t-functions, namely, the set of the third members of the elements of $\mathfrak{x}$, is constrained by $\langle R, \rho \rangle$."[28] (In this last phrase the abbreviation just introduced is used.)

---

[26] In the following $D_i \in \mathfrak{D}$ abbreviates the proposition that D_i is an element of that class whose elements are exactly the members of $\mathfrak{D}$; a similar convention holds for $t_i \in t$.

[27] Note that for each k with $1 \leq k \leq n$ exactly the function t_{ik} is assigned to the domain D_{ik}.

[28] Thus, "is constrained by" is shortened to "C."

As shown by $\langle \approx, = \rangle$, the constraints are, strictly speaking, not on functions, but on *sets* of functions. For example, in the special case of $\langle \approx, = \rangle$ the constraint says that the set of concrete functions obtained from a certain abstract function through specialization can be '*combined*' *into a single concrete function* defined on the union of individual domains.

As a second modified version of the generalized Ramsey sentence we have:

$(\mathbf{III}_b)$ $\qquad\qquad \vee x(x \mathfrak{E} \mathfrak{a} \wedge C(x, R, \rho) \wedge x \subseteq \hat{S})$

We have already anticipated its intuitive content above (for the special constraint discussed there). $\mathfrak{a}$ is again a given class of partial possible models of the theory, and $C(x, R, \rho)$ a compendium of the required constraints in the sense just mentioned.

We introduced the tertiary relation C with a conditional definition. We could have instead introduced the four-place relation $C(x, \eta, R, \rho)$ with an *unconditional definition* whose definiens runs as follows: "x is an enrichment set of η, and the set of those t, for which there is a D and an n such that $\langle D, n, t \rangle \in x$, is constrained by $\langle R, p \rangle$." Using this relation the first member of the conjunction in the above formulation could be left out so that the generalized Ramsey sentence would take the following form:

$(\mathbf{III}_b)$ $\qquad\qquad \vee x(C(x, \mathfrak{a}, R, \rho) \wedge x \subseteq \hat{S})$.

Later we will use C as either a three- or four-place relation as befits the situation.

Sneed points out that it would be a mistake to think we have *discovered* that the mass function is an extensive quantity. Nay, we *postulate* this to be the case. Moreover, if we consider this postulate in the present context of the reconstruction of theory applications, the situation is substantially more abstract than in traditional discussions. What we are postulating is, roughly, the existence of an 'intrinsic' quantitative property of physical objects called "mass." It is extensive in relation to the o operation, and it enables us to enrich the motions in physical systems so as to obtain models for classical particle mechanics. This aspect is 'abstract' insofar as *one cannot*, as Sneed emphasizes, *imagine an* experimentum crucis *which would provide an airtight proof that mass is not an extensive quantity*. Only *after making a great number of unsuccessful attempts* to find a mass function meeting the conditions just laid down might we come to the conclusion that our assumption of its existence is false.

> The last remark is also relevant for the theme "testing and confirmation." It turns out that for t-theoretical concepts in Sneed's sense a situation similar to that of statistical hypotheses holds.[29] There is, namely, no asymmetry between verifiability and falsifiability, *but symmetry with respect to nonverifi-*

---

[29] Cf. Stegmüller, [Statistik], Part III, 1.d.

ability and nonfalsifiability. In relation to 'accepted experiental data' there are no 'definitive refutations.' This fact will be discussed in detail in Chapters 16 and 17, where it should become somewhat more evident.

When the generalized Ramsey sentence contains constraints, that is, has the form (III$_b$), not (III$_a$), *the objection that it represents nothing more than a symbolized compilation of N theories disappears.* The different intended applications of a theory are no longer isolated from each other, but *are bound together by "cross-connections" established by the constraints.*

> Later, in the model-theoretic treatment (cf. Chapter 7), it will become still more obvious that constraints reduce—as a rule considerably—the class of partial possible models which can be enriched to models, indeed, in a way *impossible to achieve by imposing conditions on the intended domains of application taken separately.*

With the notion of constraint one can, moreover, recognize an ambiguity in the expression "*natural law.*" Natural laws in the usual sense of the word will be discussed in the following Section 5.3. *But the demands made by constraints could also be thought of as natural laws.* The extensivity of the mass function again serves as a good illustration. As already mentioned, it would be a mistake to suppose that *by empirical means we discover mass to be an extensive quantity.* "Hence," one is inclined to think, "it can only be *a hypothetically assumed natural law.*" As such, one cannot object to this formulation. But one must not forget that this 'natural law' has *a completely different logical status* than, e.g., special force laws. While the latter *hold in certain intended applications* of a theory *but not in others*, i.e., describe ' specific features' of certain partial possible models, the former does not *represent a feature of some one intended application, but rather a certain kind of connection obtaining between all intended applications.* Therefore such 'natural laws' must be characterized by means of the notion of constraint. On the other hand, natural laws such as special force laws (e.g., the law of gravity, Hooke's law, etc.) can, in our present mode of formal exposition, be introduced *by restrictions on the basic predicate characterizing the mathematical structure of the theory.*

Disposing of the special objection directed against (III$_a$) does not, of course, mean that the basic doubts concerning the 'primeval formulation ' (II) of the Ramsey sentence which motivated the generalization of the Ramsey method disappear too. But one can easily convince oneself that a *generalized Ramsey sentence of form (III$_b$) can be used to infer function values for one application of a theory from those already known in a different application of this theory.*

Such a *nontrivial* use of the values of theoretical functions is already possible when a class of T-theoretical functions is constrained by nothing more than $\langle \approx, = \rangle$. The function values obtained in one application may under this constraint be transferred to all those individuals in *other* applications belonging to the intersection of the domains of the original and the new application. Because of the connection with *T*-nontheoretical functions, these results can then be used for *predicting* 'observable' values, and in some cases for *testing*.

5.4 Discussion of the doubly modified Ramsey formulation using the example of the miniature theory *m*

This can be illustrated using again our minitheory from Section 2.2 as an example. Let $\mathfrak{D}$ have a finite number q of elements $D_1, D_2, \ldots, D_q$. Thus we are dealing with q applications. Let $\langle \approx, = \rangle$ be the only constraint; i.e., the t function serves to measure a constant property of the individuals. Let "b" designate the class of intended applications of the theory, i.e., the class $\{\langle D_1, n_1 \rangle, \ldots, \langle D_q, n_q \rangle\}$ of partial possible models (hence, $b \subseteq \hat{V}_{pp}$). This yields:

$(\mathbf{III}_F^m)$ $\qquad\qquad \forall x (x \mathfrak{E} b \wedge C(x, \approx, =) \wedge x \subseteq \hat{V}).$[30]

The question now is *whether or not we can envisage this statement as expressing the complete empirical content of the theory.*

Let $t = \langle t_1, \ldots, t_q \rangle$ be the sequence of t-functions used for the construction of the enrichments. The constraint stipulates that $t = \bigcup t$ be a *function on* $\Delta = \bigcup \mathfrak{D}$. Let the number of individuals in Δ be N. The validity of D1(4) and (5) (cf. p. 38) for t in *each* element D_i of $\mathfrak{D}$ is necessary and sufficient to guarantee that the function t on Δ take values fulfilling $(\mathbf{III}_F^m)$. If we designate the given n-functions defined on D_i with n_i, we obtain, on the basis of stipulation (5) of this definition, q homogeneous linear equations with unknown $t(x)$:

$$\sum_{[x \in D_1]} n_1(x)t(x) = 0 \qquad [31]$$

$$\vdots \qquad \vdots \qquad \vdots$$

(G) $$\sum_{[x \in D_i]} n_i(x)t(x) = 0$$

$$\vdots \qquad \vdots \qquad \vdots$$

$$\sum_{[x \in D_q]} n_q(x)t(x) = 0$$

---

[30] The addition of the upper index "*m*" to "**III**" should remind us that we are dealing with our minitheory, the lower index "*F*" that the 'functional condition' is the *only* constraint.

[31] The number of individuals in the various domains has not been fixed. That is why the summation over a domain is given as it is. Note that these domains are not necessarily numerically equal. Thus, the number of individuals in each cannot simply be given as N/q.

Since the number of individuals in Δ is exactly N, N is also the number of unknowns. (One must not forget that for $i \neq j$, $n_i(x) = n_j(x)$ need *not* hold; for *we have imposed no constraint on the n-functions like that for the functions* t_i.) Condition (4) of the definition stipulates that the t-values are all positive. This amounts to requiring *a nontrivial solution for the equation system* (G). According to the theory of linear equations it is then necessary and sufficient that *the rank s of the coefficient matrix be smaller than* N (condition A). (This matrix consists of, besides the values $n_i(x)$, zeros, because in the ith equation the argument x does not run over *all* N individuals, *but only over those which are elements of* D_i. Independent of the special condition just formulated, $s \leq q$ and $s \leq N$ must, of course, hold in any case for the rank s. This is exploited later for classifying the cases.)

The condition just formulated for the rank of the matrix is a *necessary* condition if (III_F^m) is to be made true. Because of condition (4) of D1 another, likewise *necessary* condition for the truth of (III_F^m) stipulates that for a given $D_j \in \mathfrak{D}$ the n_j-values cannot have the same sign for all the individuals of D_j (condition B). (The uninteresting case where all n-values are 0 is not considered.)

While in (G) *each element* of $\mathfrak{D}$, i.e., each individual domain of the various intended applications, has its own equation, the conditions A *and* B contain statements over *each subclass* of $\mathfrak{D}$. (This latter fact would suggest an analogous treatment of the minitheory for an infinite number of applications. In this case one needs only to require that these two conditions hold for each finite subset of $\mathfrak{D}$.)

In order to infer further consequences from these two conditions the relationship of the two numbers N (number of individuals) and q (number of applications) must be examined. The three logically possible cases are

$$(a) \ N > q; \quad (b) \ N = q; \quad (c) \ N < q.$$

In case (a), condition A is always fulfilled[32] so that for the values of the nontheoretical n_i-functions only condition B is relevant, which already holds for (II^m). For (b) and (c) condition A amounts to requiring that certain arithmetic relations hold between the values of the n_i-functions. The reason for this difference between (a) on the one hand and (b) and (c) on the other is easy to see. With (a) the domains *could* be mutually disjunct, in which case the expanded Ramsey formulation is nothing more than a conjunction of simple Ramsey formulations of the form (II), one for each domain, and the constraint is empty. The domains *could*, however, overlap for (a), in which case our constraint is too weak to impose limitations on the values of the n-functions. With (b) and (c) it is an entirely different story. Here the domains *must* overlap. (This holds for (b) because the conditions (4) and (5) from D1 cannot be fulfilled in domains of only one element. The product of two

---

[32] $s \leq q$ holds in *all* cases.

positive numbers cannot be 0, since the body of real numbers is free of zero divisors.[33]) The constraint $\langle \approx, = \rangle$, which is indeed addressed only to the theoretical functions, in these cases imposes limitations on the n_i-functions, too, thus permitting predictions which would otherwise be impossible. However, before we make this somewhat vague remark quantitatively precise, we want to take up the question of Ramsey elimination again.

> Sneed points out (*op. cit.*, p. 77) still another difference between (II) and (III$_b$) which can also be illustrated by our minitheory. (II) could happen to be trivially true in the sense that *each* partial possible model can be enriched to a model of S. But (III$_b$) need *not* hold in the same trivial way because the constraints could preclude the possibility of finding *t*-functions for certain models of S_{pp} such that (III$_b$) could be satisfied.

5.5 The problem of Ramsey eliminability for the generalized Ramsey formulation

For the simple Ramsey formulation, a Ramsey elimination of the theoretical terms had per definition been found as soon as someone had the good fortune to find an empirical equivalent of the Ramsey predicate. It seems natural to take a similar route in the case of the generalized Ramsey formulation. For the sake of a terminological distinction we will, from now on, call the original form of Ramsey eliminability, including its two subspecies, connected with sentences of form (II) *Ramsey$_1$ eliminability*.

For our example, the minitheory m, the analogue for (*a*), i.e., $N > q$, is obvious. One need only remember that the conditions A and B are not only necessary for the truth of (III$_F^m$), but, taken together, also sufficient. Since, as we have seen, condition A must automatically be fulfilled in case (*a*), the *wholly empirical condition B* is equivalent to this Ramsey claim. *One can, therefore, take this condition as the empirical equivalent of* (III$_F^m$). But Ramsey eliminability holds in the other two cases as well, because condition A, $s < N$, is also verifiable without the help of theoretical terms.

In precise terms, *Ramsey eliminability* of m-theoretical functions obtains because an *empirical equivalent* to the Ramsey predicate

$$\bigvee \mathfrak{x}(\mathfrak{x}\mathfrak{E}\mathfrak{y} \wedge C(\mathfrak{x}, \approx, =) \wedge \mathfrak{x} \subseteq \hat{V})$$

can be given. It is *equivalent* in the sense that it holds for exactly the same class (or sequence) of partial possible models as does this Ramsey predicate. It is *empirical* in the sense that it involves only properties of the nontheoretical n-functions; in particular, the constraints it imposes concern only nontheoretical functions.

This concept can be extrapolated from the special instance just considered to the general case (III$_b$). We will speak then of *Ramsey$_2$ eliminability*.

---

[33] We again ignore the trivial case where *all* n-values are 0.

It is easily seen that with the admission of constraints on theoretical functions, Ramsey eliminability of the theoretical terms in (III_b) becomes *a stronger concept* than Ramsey eliminability of the theoretical terms in (II). Ramsey eliminability in sentences of form (II) does *not* imply Ramsey eliminability in sentences of form (III_b) using the same set-theoretic predicate.

5.6 Three achievements of theoretical functions: Economy, empirical focus, prognosis; 'Conditional verification' of the Braithwaite–Ramsey thesis for the generalized Ramsey formulation

The analyses up to this point suggest that theoretical functions have three kinds of achievements to their credit. The first includes all the *simplifications* of a theory made possible with their help. We may call this an *economic achievement*. In order to distinguish it clearly from the other two, it will be useful to consider only those cases where Ramsey eliminability holds, i.e., *where these terms are in principle not necessary*.

This kind of achievement can readily be illustrated by the empirical claim (III_F^m) of the minitheory m—indeed *without using a precise notion of simplicity*. As we saw, the theoretical terms can be Ramsey-eliminated in this case. But from the practical point of view there is a world of difference between the case where the empirical sentence of the theory is formulated with the help of the m-theoretical function t and the case where the empirical equivalent is asserted using only the nontheoretical functions n_i. In the first case the simplest constraint imaginable is used: namely, $\langle \approx, = \rangle$ which stipulates that the union of the functions t_i represents a function on the union of the domains. In the second case, however, rather complicated constraints must be placed on the nontheoretical functions n_i requiring in concrete situations a more or less tiresome, time-consuming investigation if one is to convince oneself that they are fulfilled. One must calculate the rank of a coefficient matrix built with n_i-values, and check that for each domain D_i there are two n_i-values having different signs. (In this last instance the investigation must be continued until one runs across a measurement having a different sign than all the foregoing values, which is tough when this happens to be the last individual of the domain to be investigated.)

Concerning the tasks which can *only* be performed by theoretical terms, we have already met *one type* in Section 4.3 while discussing empirical claims of the form (II). Where there is no Ramsey$_1$ eliminability (and thus *a fortiori* no Ramsey$_2$ eliminability), some 'conceivable observable states of affairs' can be ruled out with the help of theoretical terms which otherwise could not.

This bears a certain formal resemblance to Gödel's incompleteness theorem for elementary arithmetic. The achievement of the theoretical terms can be compared to that of Tarski's notion of truth as applied to elementary arithmetic, while the nontheoretical terms correspond to the axiomatic calculi. Just as Gödel's theorem shows that it is impossible to draw a line between arithmetic truth and arithmetic falsity by axiomatic means, it is, in those cases where the Ramsey formulation has no empirical equivalent, impossible to ' rule out' exactly those *conceivable* empirical states of affairs by means of nontheoretical concepts which can be eliminated by the Ramsey formulation incorporating theoretical terms. *Every empirical predicate with which one tries to approximate the Ramsey predicate proves to be too liberal or too narrow*; either the statement constructed with its help excludes less than the Ramsey sentence—hence *too little* compared with the intended force of the empirical claim of the theory—or it excludes more—hence *too much* when one takes the intended force of the theory's claim as the standard.

Thus, this first kind of genuine, i.e., exclusive achievement of theoretical terms, represents a sort of *empirical focus* otherwise unobtainable. The focusing pertains to the predicate defining the class of partial possible models of the theory.

In order to clarify a *second*, perhaps even more important *type of exclusive achievement* of theoretical terms, we will again pick up the line of thought from the end of Section 5.4; i.e., we will take another look at the minitheory *m* and its corresponding generalized Ramsey formulation (III$_F^m$). To obtain numerical results we will follow Sneed and assume that $\mathfrak{D}$ contains the three domains $D_1 = \{x, y\}$, $D_2 = \{x, z\}$, and $D_3 = \{y, z\}$. Thus $q = N = 3$. Since for each single domain a corresponding statement of form (II) follows from each statement of form (III), we can make use of the earlier results obtained for domains with two elements (cf. the remark following Theorem 1 in Section 4.2). Hence we get:

(a)
$$\frac{n_1(x)}{n_1(y)} = -\frac{t_1(y)}{t_1(x)}; \qquad \frac{n_2(x)}{n_2(z)} = -\frac{t_2(z)}{t_2(x)}; \qquad \frac{n_3(y)}{n_3(z)} = -\frac{t_3(z)}{t_3(y)}.$$

With the constraint $\langle \approx, = \rangle$ holding for *m*-theoretical functions t_i we get the special cases:

(b)
$$t_1(x) = t_2(x); \qquad t_1(y) = t_3(y); \quad t_2(z) = t_3(z).$$

From (b) follows:

(c)
$$\frac{t_1(y)}{t_1(x)} \cdot \frac{t_3(z)}{t_3(y)} = \frac{t_2(z)}{t_2(x)},$$

and on account of (a), (c) yields:

(d)
$$\frac{n_1(x)}{n_1(y)} \cdot \frac{n_3(y)}{n_3(z)} = -\frac{n_2(x)}{n_2(z)}. \quad {}_{34}$$

---

[34] This last equation also follows from condition *A* for the equation system (*G*) together with our present stipulation $q = N = 3$; it is nothing other than the result of taking zero as the coefficient determinant.

Assume now that we are dealing at first with the domains D_1 and D_3. In both cases we check to see whether the domain D_i ($i = 1, 3$) together with n_i, i.e., the partial possible model $\langle D_i, n_i \rangle$ of V, can be enriched to a model $\langle D_i, n_i, t_i \rangle$ of V by choosing a suitable function t_i. (This test is an elementary task. The functions n_i are assumed to be nontheoretical. We can, therefore, obtain their values by *empirical means* and then only have to see whether both n_i values are 0 or have opposite signs.)

By means of (c) one can calculate the ratio of the t values for the remaining domain D_2, namely $t_2(z)/t_2(x)$. *This can be thought of as a prognosis of the ratios of the theoretical values in this remaining domain.* That this prognosis is possible is due solely to the fact that the constraint $\langle \approx, = \rangle$ holds, since it is needed to obtain (c).

> Instead of prognoses we could, of course, have taken other instances of 'systematizing,' such as certain types of explanations or retrodictions. The 'prognostic achievement of theoretical terms' is for us simply the 'paradigm' for all such systemizations.

Finally, along with (a) we can calculate the ratio of the empirical n-values for the domain D_2 by means of the results just obtained, namely, $n_2(x)/n_2(z)$. *This gives us an empirical prognosis.* The n_2 values are indeed 'observable'; they were, however, assumed by us to be *unknown*, since by hypothesis D_1 and D_3 were the only domains subjected to empirical observation.

It is obvious that the Ramsey claims of form (II) associated with these two domains could never succeed in this prognostic endeavor. They would relate exclusively to their respective domains as their only application. D_2 would be a 'wholly foreign' domain about which they could say absolutely nothing (just as they would stand in no relation to each other either).

In the present case the prognostic achievement must be credited *entirely to the constraint on the theoretical functions.* For (b) follows from this constraint and in turn yields (c) which, in its turn, yields the 'actual' *empirical prognosis* of the value on the right side of (d).

In this way the Braithwaite–Ramsey thesis (cf. Stegmüller, [Theoretische Begriffe], Section 5.5) is in a certain sense *verified*, albeit only for the case where the empirical content of a theory is exhibited by the *generalized* Ramsey formulation. For we have just seen that the prognostic power— and with it naturally the power of testing a hypothesis—depends on two conditions: first, one must be able to distinguish several only partly overlapping 'intended applications' (partial possible models) of the theory T, and second, there must be at least one constraint imposed on the T-theoretical functions which serves to bind these 'intended applications' to each other. Only under these conditions is it possible for values *actually observed* in one domain to become relevant for *observable* values in *other* domains which have never been subjected to an empirical investigation.

The qualification "in a certain sense" is added because in the case at hand the *T*-theoretical functions are *not* the *only* means available for making a prediction. This strong claim could first be made when no Ramsey eliminability obtained, a condition which according to our earlier results is not fulfilled here. But where no Ramsey eliminability obtains one can, in view of the present analysis, indeed speak of an exclusive achievement of theoretical terms: *they enable us to predict, explain, and test hypotheses in ways which would otherwise not be possible.*[35]

Thus we can credit three kinds of achievement to theoretical terms. In many cases they enable us to present the *empirical content* of a theory in a *substantially simpler form* than is possible without them. In some cases—namely, where Ramsey$_1$ eliminability does not hold—it is only with their help that we can prune this empirical content in such a way that exactly the intended applications become models of the theory. And in those cases where not even Ramsey$_2$ eliminability holds they often provide the means for making *predictions* which could not otherwise be made.[36]

All of these results are obtained under the weakest condition imaginable, namely, that *the only* constraint placed on the *T*-theoretical functions is $\langle \approx, = \rangle$. This condition is so weak that its explicit formulation may even appear superfluous. But this is certainly not the case. It is only our usual way of speaking together with a less than fully rational intuition which might create this impression. *Language habits* foster the notion that when one obtains concrete functions (e.g., gravity, mass of planets, etc.) from abstract functions (*force, mass*) by specialization it goes without saying that 'nothing other than functions' can result. But this can by no means be taken for granted; i.e., it is not *logically certain*. And as for *intuition*: when the earth is considered as part of the solar system in *one* application of particle mechanics and as part of the earth–moon system in a *different* application, our 'intuitive grasp' of these two applications of one and the same theory is liable to feign the nonexistent logical necessity of having to assign the earth the same mass in both cases.

Additional nontrivial calculations are obtained when the theory contains other constraints besides this elementary one, for example, the requirement that the theoretical function represents an extensive quantity. Using the symbolism of D9 we give the constraint as $\langle R_1, \rho_1 \rangle$. $C(\mathfrak{x}, R_1, \rho_1)$ would then be inserted conjunctively into the Ramsey formula for the minitheory m. We will call the resulting formula (III_{FE}^m) (where "F" again indicates the

---

[35] Cf. Sneed, *op. cit.*, p. 79f., for a prognostic use of theoretical functions within *one and the same domain* which must, however, route itself through *other* domains. This is a special case in which the domain in question includes the others as subdomains.

[36] There is a vagueness adhering to all of these intuitive formulations which can be removed either by referring back to the exact conditions and the exact context of the previous discussions or by substituting for the intuitive notions involved the model-theoretic counterparts from Chapter 7.

functional constraint, and "*E*" the extensivity constraint). As an example we will take $\mathfrak{D} = \{D_1, D_2, D_3\}$ with $D_1 = \{x, y\}$, $D_2 = \{x, z\}$, and $D_3 = \{x, y \circ z\}$. The constraints yield

(e)
$$\frac{n_3(x)}{n_3(y \circ z)} = \frac{n_1(x)}{n_1(y)} + \frac{n_2(x)}{n_2(z)}.$$

> *Proof.* Because of the analogy between the present D_3 and condition (*a*), the left side of (*e*) is identical with
>
> $$-\frac{t_3(y \circ z)}{t_3(x)}.$$
>
> Because of the constraint $\langle R_1, \rho_1 \rangle$ (extensivity), this is identical with
>
> $$-\frac{t_3(y)}{t_3(x)} - \frac{t_3(z)}{t_3(x)}.$$
>
> The constraint $\langle \approx, = \rangle$ allows for derivations analogous to (*b*) so that this last expression can be rewritten as
>
> $$-\frac{t_1(y)}{t_1(x)} - \frac{t_2(z)}{t_2(x)},$$
>
> which in turn yields the right side of (*e*) by the analogies to (*a*).

Thus, when the *given* domains are D_1 and D_2, the new constraint allows us *to predict* the ratios of the n_3-values in the third domain on the basis of the known values of n_1 and n_2. Without this constraint these two classes of values would have no connection with each other, and this isolation would remain unaffected were $\langle \approx, = \rangle$ the only constraint imposed on the t-functions.

In the general case involving n individuals the additional constraint $\langle R_1, \rho_1 \rangle$ would allow us to use the following equation for calculating t-values for all $m \leq n$:

$$t(\cdots(x_1 \circ x_2) \circ x_3) \cdots \circ x_m) = \sum_{i=1}^{m} t(x_i).$$

5.7 Third generalization of the Ramsey formulation: Introduction of special laws via restrictions on the basic predicate; The central empirical claim (Ramsey–Sneed claim) of a theory

The idea of exhibiting the empirical content of a theory T in a sentence of form (III$_b$) rests on the following line of thought. Let two predicates be given: one of comparatively little content, one substantially stronger. The first does nothing more than *delineate the possible intended applications of the theory*, i.e., the class of partial possible models. The second predicate, the *basic predicate*, describes *the mathematical structure of the theory T* itself. The empirical claim (III_b) attached to a theory alleges then that there is a subclass, designated by the singular term a, of the class of entities fulfilling the first predicate, i.e., the class of all partial possible models or all possible intended applications, the elements of which can be enriched in such a way as to yield a class x whose elements in turn satisfy the mathematical structure of T (are, that is, models for the basic predicate) whereby the T-theoretical functions occurring in the enrichments fulfill all constraints $C(x, R, \rho)$.

This reconstruction of "empirical content of a theory" still does not account for the fact that in the various particular applications of one single theory T *various special laws* may hold. This sort of law interests us insofar as it involves T-theoretical functions. A 'theoretical' law can be understood as an additional condition imposed on the T-theoretical functions. We must require then not only that the theoretical functions, together with the non-theoretical functions, fulfill the *basic predicate* in *all* applications, but that *in addition they take certain forms in certain applications which they do not retain in other applications*. Again, the Newtonian theory offers a good illustration. The solar system is a special application of classical particle mechanics. Newton postulated that in this *application* each 'particle' exerts a force on every other one. This force attracts, works along the straight line between the two particles, and is inversely proportional to the square of the distance.

How can one or more such *special laws* be expressed in our formalism? The answer is readily at hand: the basic predicate, determining the mathematical structure of the theory *for all applications* must be *restricted by adding to it conditions* for those applications whose presystematic formulations require special laws. Thus, the adequate treatment of special laws consists in the introduction of *restrictions on the basic predicate*. This, of course, still does not settle the other main question of how such restrictions may be used to modify a statement of the form (III_b).

To simplify the discussion we will use the following symbolic abbreviations: nonempty restrictions of set-theoretic predicates "P" will be designated by adding a superscript to "P." For example, S^i is a restriction of S. We will say then that S^i is a *predicate restriction* on S. Intuitively speaking, S^i is derived from S by adding at least one more axiom to the definiens of the latter. Different predicate restrictions may effect one another. This would be the case, for example, when S^i and S^j are both predicate restrictions on S and S^j is also a predicate restriction on S^i.

To keep things from getting too complicated we will assume that the special laws represented by the predicate restriction S^1 will apply only to a subclass a^1 of the class a of partial possible models.[37] Two alternatives now

---

[37] a^1 can, of course, be a *unit class*, in which case the special laws in question hold only for this one application.

present themselves. Should this presystematic notion be articulated by *adding* to the 'general empirical claim' (III_b) a special claim formulated with $\mathfrak{a}^1$ instead of $\mathfrak{a}$ and S^1 instead of S, i.e., by conjoining the special claim to the general? Or should the special claim be *built into* (III_b), i.e., used to *modify* the general claim itself? The first suggestion proposes a *conjunction* of

(III_b) $\qquad\qquad \vee x (x \mathfrak{E} \mathfrak{a} \wedge C(x, R, \rho) \wedge x \subseteq \hat{S})$

and

(III_c) $\qquad\qquad \vee \eta (\eta \mathfrak{E} \mathfrak{a}^1 \wedge C(\eta, R, \rho) \wedge \eta \subseteq \hat{S}^1)$

(In relation to our minitheory $C(\eta, R, \rho)$ means, of course, that the set t^1 of theoretical functions used to enrich the elements of $\mathfrak{a}^1$ to models of S^1 satisfy the constraints $\langle R, \rho \rangle$.)

The second suggestion proposes using the predicate restriction S^1 of S to construct a statement of the following form for some $\mathfrak{a}^1 \subset \mathfrak{a}$:

(IV) $\quad \vee x [x \mathfrak{E} \mathfrak{a} \wedge C(x, R, \rho) \wedge x \subseteq \hat{S} \wedge \{y | y \in x \wedge \vee z (z \in \mathfrak{a}^1 \wedge yEz)\} \subseteq \hat{S}^1].$

The objection to the first alternative is essentially the same as we have already used in our arguments against (III_a). There, *one* theory threatened to disintegrate into a set of *different* theories (having merely a common symbolic representative). Here we find ourselves confronted with *two* *applied theories* (III_b) and (III_c). Only with (IV) is one justified in speaking of *the* empirical claim coupled to *one and only one theory*.

Decisive, though, is the objection that the conjunction of (III_b) and (III_c) is too weak. This becomes clear when one realizes that (IV) *logically implies both (III_b) and (III_c), but not vice versa.* (IV) says, namely, that there is a class x of enrichments of the elements of $\mathfrak{a}$ all of whose elements are models of S; that, moreover, those elements of x which are enrichments of the elements of $\mathfrak{a}^1$ are not only models for S but even for S^1; and finally, that the T-theoretical functions used to generate this set x of enrichments satisfy the set of constraints $\langle R, \rho \rangle$.

By comparison the conjunction of (III_b) and (III_c) requires somewhat less. These two statements would be satisfied under the following three conditions. First, there is a set t of T-theoretical functions which enrich all the elements of $\mathfrak{a}$ to models of S and meet the constraints $\langle R, \rho \rangle$ (satisfaction of (III_b)). Second, there is a set t^1 of T-theoretical functions which enrich all the elements of $\mathfrak{a}^1$ to models of S^1 (and so automatically to models of S) and meet the constraints $\langle R, \rho \rangle$ (satisfaction of (III_c)). Third, t^1 *is not a subclass of* t. (IV) would, however, be *false* under this last condition, because it specifies that t^1 be a subclass of t. In other words, *(IV) contains, in addition to the conjunction of (III_b) and (III_c), the stipulation that the class of T-theoretical functions satisfying (III_c) be a subclass of those satisfying (III_b).* Only when (IV) is satisfied (and not merely the two other statements) can one begin with a set of T-theoretical functions enriching the elements of $\mathfrak{a}^1$ to models for S^1, *add to these still other T-theoretical functions*—defined on the elements of $\mathfrak{D} - \mathfrak{D}^1$—which enrich the elements of $\mathfrak{a} - \mathfrak{a}^1$ to models of S, and still have the guarantee that *all* of the T-theoretical functions chosen satisfy the constraints $\langle R, \rho \rangle$. The constraints could be such as to render this procedure ineffective when *nothing more* than (III$_b$) and (III$_c$) hold.

> The following situation using our minitheory illustrates this. Let $\mathfrak{D}^1 = \{D_1\}$, $\mathfrak{D} = \{D_1, D_2\}$ so that $D_2 \in \mathfrak{D} - \mathfrak{D}^1$, and $x \in D_1 \cap D_2$. S and S^1 are given. $\langle \approx, = \rangle$ is the only constraint. This last condition means that $t_1(x) = t_2(x)$. Now it might prove impossible to assign the individual x *one and the same* value for t_1 and t_2 such that $\langle D_1, n_1, t_1 \rangle$ is a model for S^1 and $\langle D_2, n_2, t_2 \rangle$ is a model for S. Should, however, the last two conditions hold for some $t_1(x) \neq t_2(x)$, then we have one of those situations satisfying the conjunction of (III$_b$) and (III$_c$), but not (IV).

Thus it is the additional content of (IV) which fuses the claims of two 'different empirical theories' (III$_b$) and (III$_c$) into *one* 'empirical theory' (IV). One can also easily see that the *predictive and testing powers* of (IV) are greater than those afforded by (III$_b$).[38]

A statement of form (IV) covers only the special case where the theoretical functions take on special forms for *one* set of intended applications. From this, though, the general case, whereby T-theoretical functions have different forms for different classes of intended applications may be constructed. We obtain a statement of the following form:

$$(\mathrm{V}) \quad \bigvee \mathfrak{x}[\mathfrak{x}\mathfrak{E}\mathfrak{a} \wedge C(\mathfrak{x}, R, \rho) \wedge \mathfrak{x} \subseteq \hat{S} \wedge \{y \mid y \in \mathfrak{x} \wedge \bigvee z(z \in \mathfrak{a}^1 \wedge yEz)\} \subseteq \hat{S}^1$$
$$\vdots$$
$$\wedge \{y \mid y \in \mathfrak{x} \wedge \bigvee z(z \in \mathfrak{a}^n \wedge yEz)\} \subseteq \hat{S}^n]$$

(This statement corresponds to sentence (5) in Sneed (*op. cit.*, p. 106). In the present formulation Sneed's multiple indexing of predicates is superfluous, as is the indexing of "$\mathfrak{x}$." This is because among other things we allow predicates S^i to be restrictions on one another, e.g., S^2 to be a restriction on S^1.)

The intuitive content of this statement can be given roughly as follows: "there exists a set of T-theoretical functions which fulfills a class of constraints and with whose help all the partial possible models ('physical systems') of a theory belonging to the set $\mathfrak{a}$ can be enriched to models of the basic predicate S in such a way that the elements of certain subsets $\mathfrak{a}^1, \ldots, \mathfrak{a}^n$ of $\mathfrak{a}$ can be enriched to models for suitable restrictions $S^1, \ldots, S^n$ of the basic predicate."

We will call (V) *the Ramsey–Sneed claim* of a theory or *the central empirical claim of a theory*. The label is justified in that the Ramsey method constitutes the basis of the entire approach, while Sneed modified and refined the method in three essential respects: he adopted *multiple domains of application*, he

---

[38] Cf. Sneed, [Mathematical Physics], p. 104.

introduced *constraints* imposed on the *T*-theoretical functions, and he incorporated *restrictions on the basic predicate* as a means of formulating special laws holding only for certain applications. The refinement lies in the fact that the Ramsey–Sneed claim, in contrast to the original Ramsey sentence (II), *permits nontrivial calculations of function values,* making of this sentence a suitable instrument for prediction and hypothesis testing.

Depending on circumstances, (III_b) or a sentence like (VI), yet to be described, can also serve as a central empirical claim of a theory.

> Strictly speaking, one must not use the definite article here because such a sentence can be formulated in infinitely many ways. Nevertheless, they are all *logically equivalent*, so that any one of them can be taken as representative of the whole equivalent set.

All the empirical claims made by a theory are expressed *by the single cohesive statement* (*V*). This is only the first step of the break with the 'statement view,' according to which theories are *classes* of sentences. *It is not, however, maintained here that the Ramsey–Sneed claim of a theory should stand for the entire theory itself.* We have not yet broached the question of what *a theory* is, or better, how it should be reconstructed. The *empirical content* of a theory can indeed be exhibited by (V) or a like statement. But, as we will see, *it would be extremely impractical to identify a theory with this empirical content itself.*

The reason for this, if we may anticipate for a moment, is roughly as follows: special laws holding only for certain applications might be found after the theory, characterized by the basic predicate *S*, has been around a long time. On the other hand, such special laws can appear and then later prove to be false. (Further changes which concern the intended applications will be discussed in Chapters 15 and 16.) In such cases it seems best to say that *the theory itself remains constant while its empirical contentions,* each represented by a central empirical claim, *are continuously changing.* Although at present we are still considering theories from the *static* standpoint, it will, in view of the subsequent notion of holding a theory (Chapters 12 and 15), do well to *supply the central empirical claim with a temporal index* indicating the time span during which this claim is maintained by a person or research group. In the event of a subsequent transition to some *other* central empirical claim a *new* time index is taken. The *theory itself* is not affected by this temporal flux as long as the same basic predicate *S* is used for the various incompatible central empirical claims. It remains the constant factor in the flux of appearances (claims). Later we will have occasion to use the temporal indices explicitly when working with the *propositional counterpart* of a central empirical claim. This notion, introduced in Chapter 7, is formulated entirely in the language of set theory, and has the advantage of presenting the content of such a claim in a most simple, transparent way.

(V) still does not represent the most general form that the empirical claim of a theory can take. Besides the *general* constraints on certain classes of functions, *additional constraints* may appear involving just *those theoretical functions occurring in special laws holding only for certain applications.* Here the possibility, introduced in Section 5.3 in connection with (III$_b$), of formulating constraints with the help of a *four-place* relation C recommends itself. It enables us to symbolize general and additional constraints in the same way. *General* constraints can be expressed by $C(x, a, R, \rho)$, while the presence of additional constraints or 'law constraints' $\langle R^i, \rho^i \rangle$ on the theoretical functions in enrichments $x^i \subset x$ of a^i (with $a^i \subset a$) can be analogously given by $C(x^i, a^i, R^i, \rho^i)$. Because there can be at most n such classes of additional constraints so far as there are n predicate restrictions $S^1, \ldots, S^n$ of S, we obtain the following generalization of (V) with $a^1, \ldots, a^n \subset a$:[39]

(VI) $\quad \forall x \{ x \subseteq \hat{S} \wedge C(x, a, R, \rho) \wedge \forall x^1 [x^1 \subseteq x \wedge x^1 \subseteq \hat{S}^1 \wedge C(x^1, a^1, R^1, \rho^1)]$

$$\vdots$$

$$\wedge \ \forall x^n [x^n \subseteq x \wedge x^n \subseteq \hat{S}^n \wedge C(x^n, a^n, R^n, \rho^n)]\}.$$

(This statement permits, as did (IV) and (V), some predicate restrictions to be restrictions on others. The x^i here correspond to the classes $\{y | y \in x \wedge \forall z(z \in a^i \wedge yEz)\}$ of (V). For those x^i in which special laws *but no additional constraints hold*, the definition of $\langle R^i, \rho^i \rangle$ must be constructed so that it is tautological and $C(x^i, a^i, R^i, \rho^i)$ effects no additional constraint.)

An intelligible paraphrase of the content of this statement in the natural idiom, be it ever so adumbrated, is scarcely possible without assuming (VI) to be already understood. Nevertheless we will have a go at it. Roughly (VI) says the following for a theory T with the *basic* mathematical *predicate* S: "There is a set of T-theoretical functions which fulfill a given class of constraints $\langle R, \rho \rangle$, and with whose help all those partial possible models of the theory belonging to the class a can be enriched to models of the basic predicate S, indeed in such a way that first, the elements of certain genuine subsets $a^1, \ldots, a^n$ of a are enriched to models for the predicate restrictions $S^1, \ldots, S^n$ of S, and second, if required, some of the subsets of T-theoretical functions used for these special enrichments fulfill the additional constraints $\langle R^i, \rho^i \rangle$."

> In anticipation of Chapter 6, statements of the form (V) or (VI) can be given special interpretations by taking as the basic predicate "is a classical particle mechanics." The partial possible models, in particular all those belonging to a, are then *particle kinematics* whose theoretical enrichments become *particle mechanics.* It is then claimed that a set of such enrichments exists,

---

[39] Remember that when using the four-place relation C, the relation xEy can be omitted because it is already built into the definition of C.

and that these are, moreover, *classical* particle mechanics (i.e., Newton's second law holds for them), whereby the theoretical functions *mass* and *force* used in these enrichments fulfill certain constraints. It is also claimed that there are genuine subsets of α which can be enriched to models of restrictions of classical particle mechanics. These restrictions consist in the incorporation of certain further laws, e.g., Newton's third law or Hooke's law. Finally, it can be required that the theoretical functions used in these enrichments of subsets of α satisfy certain additional constraints.

The subsequent set-theoretic analyses will be easier to understand if we note that α designates an element of the *power set* of the set of all partial possible models, and that likewise the bound variable *x* varies over the elements of the *power set* of the set of all models.

5.8 Remarks concerning the empirical content, testing, falsification, and corroboration of theories

The Ramsey–Sneed claim (VI) of a theory *T* is presumably the most adequate method for simultaneously *displaying the empirical content of T in its entirety and licking the problem of theoretical terms.*

As a rule the transition to ever more complex Ramsey formulations will be accompanied by *a tightening up of empirical content.* One can quickly convince oneself of this by considering *two 'detrivializing' steps.* As has already been mentioned, a sentence of form (II) could be trivially true in the sense that *every* partial possible model could be enriched to yield a model. But this does *not* mean that (III$_b$) must hold too; likewise (with slight modifications) in making the transition from (III$_b$) to (V) or (VI). (III$_b$) too *could* be trivially true in the sense that any subset of α (and eventually others) can be enriched to a set of models without doing violence to the constraints on theoretical functions, while at the same time (V) is *not* trivially true because it might be possible to come up with empirical *n*-values which make it impossible to find theoretical values satisfying it.

To prevent any premature conclusions on the part of the reader, it must again be expressly pointed out that we are *not* maintaining that *the theory T consists 'after all of nothing but' a sentence of form (VI).* Such is by no means our intention! On the contrary, as will be urged by the discussion in Chapter 7, *a theory should not be thought of as a linguistic entity at all, in particular, neither as a class of sentences nor as a cohesive sentence of the above form.* It is only alleged that (VI) *correctly* presents all the empirical claims of a theory at a given time in a concise and systematic fashion, and that this form of presentation is *necessary* in order to master the difficulty mentioned and in order to exhibit adequately the connection between various 'intended applications' for the theory as well as the validity of special laws.

91

This last point provides the conceptual basis for 'demythologizing holism' in Chapter 17. Therefore, it is worth dwelling briefly on it. The '*statement view of theories*' postulates that the empirical content of a theory, or indeed the theory itself, is to be construed as a *class or a conjunction of hypothetically assumed sentences*. In contrast to this the philosophical position underlying the Ramsey–Sneed claim of a theory is that the theory must *not* be thought of as such a class or conjunction of hypotheses, because this view can account neither for the interdependence of the hypotheses nor the connection between these temporally unstable hypotheses and the temporally stable core of the theory. As far as interdependence is concerned, it may be seen that the *constraints* imposed on theoretical functions serve to establish *cross-connections* between the various intended applications. These lateral connections prevent the empirical content of the theory from 'degenerating' into special hypotheses. The constraints also exonerate our intuitive idea that a theoretical function represents *but one quantity* in all the applications of the theory. And as for special laws, if they are rendered as *restrictions* on the predicate defining the mathematical structure of the theory, then it becomes possible *either to give up or to add special hypotheses and still retain the basic mathematical structure of the theory as is.*

In Chapter 7 the various concepts connected with theories will be characterized in a *purely set-theoretic* way. The results obtained have significance over and above the present context inasmuch as they provide for the first time a suitable conceptual framework for discussing precisely the *problem of theory dynamics*. One of the most important results of this discussion will be to provide a basis for effecting a 'reconciliation' between the 'Kuhnians ' and their 'rationalistic opponents.'

It can come as no surprise to the reader who has carefully followed the discussion so far that in the light of its developments various traditional ideas about the empirical testing, refuting, and corroborating (confirming) of theories will be in need of revision. But it is also important to see *in what respect* they need revision. The *kind of explication* given these notions is *not* the problem. (In the present context we have *nothing whatever* to say about this theme, which belongs to a different topic.) It is, rather, *the use* of such notions—whatever their explication may look like—*to arrive at metatheoretical conclusions over the presumed truth or falsity of empirical claims of the form* (*VI*) that needs revision.

Some aspects of the situation may already be discussed in relation to (III$_b$), which offers a considerably simpler milieu. The results can then be transferred *mutatis mutandis* to the more complex case (VI).

(1) One point concerns the question of membership in the set a. If this set is given extensionally, i.e., if its elements are explicitly listed, there is no problem. In most cases, however, the set of intended applications of a theory will be given by specifying a *property*. In this case it is conceivable that the membership of an entity x in a will be tested by an *experimentum crucis*.

Whether, and how, we can contrive such a critical test cannot be said *a priori*. Nevertheless, the example given for the minitheory *m* in Section 5.6 indicates the general structure of such a test. One must attempt 'with all deftness' to exploit the already known elements of $\mathfrak{a}$, the intersections of their domains, and the constraints on the theoretical functions in order to make an empirical prognosis for the partial possible model *x* whose candidacy for membership in $\mathfrak{a}$ we have before us. The truth of this prognosis must then be checked.

Note that a *negative result* of the test does not *constitute a falsification of the theory*. It only justifies concluding that *x must be excluded from that set of intended applications of the theory for which (III$_b$)* holds. (This point point will be further elaborated in Part II.)

(2) Is, though, the empirical claim (III$_b$) itself *empirically falsifiable?* Yes, *if* it has already been decided that certain entities do belong to $\mathfrak{a}$.[40] Since claims of form (II) can be inferred from this claim, the simplest way here is to deduce from the given generalized Ramsey formulation a suitable claim of form (II) which may be shown to be false. This means demonstrating that the partial possible model $a \in \mathfrak{a}$ named in the claim can *not* be enriched to a model for the predicate "is an *S*."

(3) A third possibility consists of using the procedure described in (1) with the exception that this time the test is applied to a physical system *a* known to belong to the set $\mathfrak{a}$. With this method one could, for example, *falsify* (III$_F^m$). Choose two suitable elements of $\mathfrak{D}$ with overlapping domains. *Assume hypothetically that (III$_F^m$) is true, in particular that the constraint* $\langle \approx, = \rangle$ *holds*, and calculate a relation between *t*-values *for a new, third domain a*. This can now be used to make a prediction about certain relations between empirical quantities (*n*-values). Should this prediction fail, (III$_F^m$) is 'empirically refuted.'

It must not be overlooked, however, that the refutation only holds relative to the assumption that *a* belongs to the intended applications of the theory. An adherent of the theory can, of course, decide to react as in case (1), i.e., to exclude *a* from the domain of applications of the theory. A radical proponent of 'falsificationism' would indeed immediately smell an 'immunization strategy' behind such a move. But this suspicion would be unfounded. Where the theory itself is concerned, such a suspicion is *always* unfounded, because *on the basis of Sneed's conception a theory is simply not that sort of entity of which it makes sense to say it has been falsified.*

(4) Something like '*definitive verification*' also appears to fall within the realm of possibility. One must but check out all elements of $\mathfrak{a}$ to see whether they fulfill the condition (II). Should these elements be finite in number and explicitly given, the finite number of tests *could* lead to the conclusion that the claim (III$_b$) is verified. For a primitive theory like *m* this may well be the case. *It would, however, be unrealistic to presume that such a situation holds*

---

[40] This is, of course, again a trivial decision if $\mathfrak{a}$ is given per list. But this is not normally the case; cf. Section 14.1.

for any really interesting physical theory. (Besides, it must be remembered that those *hypothetical* elements pointed out in Chapter 1 of Stegmüller, [Theoretische Begriffe], always find their way into so-called 'observations' of nontheoretical quantities.)

It is much more realistic to turn to Popper's idea of *repeated unsuccessful refutation attempts.* When tests like the ones described are made and *no refutation* results, one may say that *the empirical claim (III$_b$) has been corroborated.* One is apt to think that the more often such refutation attempts fail, the *better* the claim is *confirmed.* Whether this intuitive feeling concerning a gain in credibility for the assumption that (III$_b$) will continue to withstand all future tests can be adequately and precisely explicated, or whether it is an illusion, would be a question for a theory of confirmation.

---

6 The Example of Classical Particle Mechanics

6.1 Particle kinematics, particle mechanics, and classical particle mechanics

Up to this point the discussion has generally been on a quite abstract level. Occasionally the theory *m* was used for purposes of illustration, but this miniature theory has an extraordinarily primitive structure. Classical particle mechanics is the first 'real' physical theory to which the abstract ideas articulated so far must be applicable if they are to be adequate. We will for now ignore the fact that there are several equivalent versions of this theory. The question of just what may be understood by '*equivalent*' *formulations of one and the same theory* is itself a difficult problem which can be tackled only later in the set-theoretical discussion of the important concepts connected with the three kinds of models. For the present it must suffice to say that the following discussion will be based on Newton's version of particle mechanics as formulated by McKinsey et al. in [Particle Mechanics].

In this work physical theories were characterized by set-theoretic predicates for the first time. This will force us to deviate substantially from the presentation in Chapter 2 of Stegmüller, [Theoretische Begriffe].

In addition, the conceptual inventory employed in the various generalizations of the Ramsey formulation must be reproduced for the axiomatic treatment of particle mechanics. This includes the three kinds of model concept (models, possible models, and partial possible models), the restrictions on primary predicates facilitating the introduction of special laws, and finally the consideration of various kinds of constraints.

Corresponding to the three predicates S, S_p, and S_{pp} (in the minitheory, V, V_p, and V_{pp}) we now have in that order $CPM(x)$ ("x is a classical particle mechanics"), $PM(x)$ ("x is a particle mechanics"), and $PK(x)$ ("x is a particle kinematics"). The idea is, then, that the mathematical structure of those systems of particles moving in accord with Newton's second law will be characterized by the primary set-theoretic predicate, i.e., by the first predicate in the list. Thus, this second law will be the only axiom 'proper.'[41] Since all special laws will be introduced by restrictions on the primary predicate, the extension of this predicate itself will be called the *fundamental law of the theory*.

All systems of objects satisfying the primary predicate are *models* of the theory. The second predicate describes merely the formal structure of those entities of which it makes sense to ask whether or not they satisfy the predicate "x is a classical particle mechanics." Thus, a particle mechanics is a *possible model* of the theory. The last predicate retains what is left after ' deleting' both of the theoretical functions from particle mechanics, namely, the nontheoretical position function. Thus a particle kinematics is a *partial possible model* of that theory whose fundamental set-theoretic predicate is $CPM(x)$. In particular, the intended applications of the theory consist of those systems of moving bodies whose spatial extension can be neglected.

These concepts will be defined now starting with the last, the simplest, and progressing to the more complex.

D10 $PK(x) \leftrightarrow$ there exists a P, a T, and an s such that:

(1) $x = \langle P, T, s \rangle$;
(2) P is a nonempty finite set;
(3) T is an interval of real numbers;
(4) s is a function with $D_I(s) = P \times T$ and $D_{II}(s) \subseteq \mathbb{R}^3$. Further, s is twice differentiable wrt time in the open (sub)interval of T.[42]

If we start with a certain intended application of classical particle mechanics, P is the set of particles of this application, i.e., the set of objects whose motions should be explained by the theory. The use of the set T rests on the following idealization: it is assumed that any time interval can be isomorphically mapped onto a suitable interval of real numbers, and indeed so that the 'earlier-than' relation on the time interval corresponds to the ' smaller-than' relation on the assigned interval of real numbers. Under this assumption one can, for the application in question, identify T with some set of real numbers which is isomorphic with the time interval during which one investigates, and hopes to explain, the motion of the objects in P. Finally,

[41] Newton's third law will lead to a *restriction* of the primary predicate and thus to the special law concept of *Newtonian* particle mechanics.

[42] Under $\mathbb{R}^3$ we understand the triple Cartesian product of the set of real numbers with itself. An open time interval results by striking the endpoints of T if any were given.

$s(u, t)$ is the position vector of the particle u at time t with respect to some spatial coordinate system. Thus the numbers of T should correspond to time points, and each value $s(u, t)$ to the distance between the particle u and the coordinate origin at time t. In order to ensure this for every element of T and for every s-value, the theories of temporal metrics and geometry underlying classical particle mechanics would have to be logically reconstructed. This reconstruction will not be given here, but it is assumed. (For some hints concerning details cf. Sneed, [Mathematical Physics], p. 86ff. and p. 116. Attention should be called to the fact that the notion of length can be *theoretical with respect to the underlying metric theory*. This does *not* prevent us from holding the position function to be nontheoretical in the present context, since the theory to which "nontheoretical" must be relativized here is not the theory *underlying* particle mechanics, but *particle mechanics itself*. And relative to it spatial distances are certainly not theoretical quantities in Sneed's sense, because there are (e.g., optical) methods of measuring distance quite independent of mechanics.)

D11 $PM(x) \leftrightarrow$ there exist P, T, s, m, and f, such that

(1) $x = \langle P, T, s, m, f \rangle$;

(2) P is a nonempty, finite set;

(3) T is an interval of real numbers;

(4) s is a function with $D_I(s) = P \times T$ and $D_{II}(s) \subseteq \mathbb{R}^3$; Further, s is twice differentiable wrt time in the open subinterval of T;

(5) m is a function with $D_I(m) = P$ and $D_{II}(m) \subseteq \mathbb{R}$ such that $m(u) > 0$ for all $u \in P$;

(6) f is a function with $D_I(f) = P \times T \times \mathbb{N}$ and $D_{II}(f) \subseteq \mathbb{R}^3$ and $\sum_{i \in \mathbb{N}} f(u, t, i)$ is absolutely convergent for all $u \in P$ and $t \in T$.

In the predicate "x is a particle mechanics" the functions m and f are introduced in addition to the concepts already occurring in the previous definition. In an intended application of classical particle mechanics we will let $m(u)$ be the mass of the particle u and $f(u, t, i)$ the ith force acting on this particle at time t. The values are with respect to given measurement scales for mass and force. A particle mechanics is the sort of entity of which it makes sense to ask whether it satisfies the second law of Newton. On the formal side this law is expressed by restricting PM so as to obtain CPM.

In the next definition the following convention concerning the symbolic notation of derivatives will be used. If f is a function of one real variable whose values are real numbers or vectors of real numbers, the derivative of f at the place x will be denoted by $Df(x)$ ("D" for "derivative"). That function whose value is $Df(x)$ for every real number x for which $Df(x)$ exists will be called Df. Values of the form $DDf(x)$ and functions of the form DDf will be abbreviated by $D^2f(x)$ and D^2f, respectively. For any given $u \in P$, let s_u be the unary function whose value at time $t \in T$ is $s(u, t)$; i.e., $s_u = s(u, t)$. Then instead of $Ds_u(t)$, the derivative of this function at time t, we will write $Ds(u, t)$.

D12 $CPM(x) \leftrightarrow$ (1) $PM(x)$;
   (2) for all $u \in P$ and $t \in T$:
$$m(u) \cdot D^2 s(u, t) = \sum_{i \in \mathbb{N}} f(u, t, i).$$

We will follow Sneed now in assuming that it is correct to regard m and t as *CPM-theoretical* in the previously defined sense.

> For the force function this should be obvious. Sneed says, for example: "All means of measuring forces, known to me, appear to rest, in a quite straightforward way, on the assumption, that Newton's second law is true in some physical system, and indeed also on the assumption that some particular force law holds" (*op. cit.*, p. 117).
> For the mass function this may not be so obvious. Among other things it must be made clear that using a scale to determine the mass ratios of two bodies—regarded as 'particles'—assumes that *this scale together with both objects on its pans is a model for classical particle mechanics in which the force function has a certain form.*

Thus we can justifiably use the previous terminology and say that every particle kinematics is a *partial possible model*, and every particle mechanics a *possible model* for *CPM*. The models for *CPM* are exactly the classical particle mechanics themselves.

As was the case with our minitheory m, we can now define the enrichment relation to be used in the Ramsey formulation (cf. Section 3.2). The definition will be much simpler if, for each n, a projection function $\Pi_i (1 \leqq i \leqq n)$ is used which serves to isolate the ith member of the n-tuple $\langle v_1, \ldots, v_n \rangle$; i.e., $\Pi_i(\langle v_1, \ldots, v_n \rangle) = v_i$.

D13 xEy ("x is an enrichment of y") $\leftrightarrow PK(x) \wedge \bigvee m \bigvee f$
   $[x = \langle \Pi_1(y), \Pi_2(y), \Pi_3(y), m, f \rangle] \wedge PM(x).$

If a is a partial possible model of *CPM* and "*CPM*" is substituted for "S," the Ramsey sentence (II) for this object a is

(CPM-II) $\bigvee x(xEa \wedge CPM(x)).$

This statement cannot be used to formulate an empirical claim because it is trivially true. It can easily be shown that every particle kinematics can be enriched to a classical particle mechanics. Hence, the theoretical terms in (CPM-II) are Ramsey-eliminable in a trivial sense.[43] In our earlier terminology PK is an empirical equivalent of the Ramsey predicate which can

---

[43] As shown by the following remark, "in a trivial sense" means here that no effort is needed to find an empirical equivalent; PK is itself one.

be extracted from (CPM-II) (i.e., "*PK*(*y*)" has the same extension as the predicate which results from substituting "*y*" for "*a*" in this sentence).

> This sort of triviality is, however, not to be taken for granted. It has nothing to do with the fact, already noted, that the Ramsey formulation cannot be used for nontrivial predictions. This earlier situation did not hinder the theoretical terms from doing a 'real job,' namely, that of precluding possible observable states of affairs which cannot be ruled out by 'empirical' methods alone (cf. Sections 5.6 and 4.3), whereas in the present situation even this achievement is stifled because of Ramsey elimination. When this present situation is labeled *trivial* (cf. the last footnote), the expression "trivial" is being used in still another, third sense.

6.2 The introduction of constraints

Again it seems appropriate to take the same route in generalizing the Ramsey formulation as was taken in Section 5.3 at the abstract level, since this method seems to offer the only possibility of using a theory for nontrivial empirical applications while at the same time overcoming the problem of theoretical terms. Since a sentence of form (III$_a$) is nothing more than the symbolic representation of a conjunction of Ramsey formulations, we can pass directly to the analogue of (III$_b$). The various intermediate steps will only be sketched intuitively, not formally.

First, the set or sequence $\mathfrak{D}$ of possible applications D_i must be specified. Some of these applications consist, for example, of the solar system and its subsystems. (To what extent the elements D_i of $\mathfrak{D}$ must be '*given*' and to what extent $\mathfrak{D}$ can remain '*open*' will be discussed in Part II in connection with the notion *paradigm*.) In order to link the intended applications with one another by means of the 'cross-connections' we have called "constraints," it is essential that *one* particle appear in *several applications of the theory*, indeed, in *several at one time*. The two most important constraints on the mass function m are *independence of system* and *extensivity*. The first means that a particle u receives the same value $m(u)$ in each application where it appears. This is precisely the constraint $\langle \approx, = \rangle$. Thus, mass is declared to be a constant property of bodies. The second constraint requires that m be an *extensive quantity*.

> Sneed has some very interesting observations to make about this second feature which may well serve to jar traditional ideas concerning the difference between fundamental and derived measurement.[44] If, namely, mass may correctly be regarded as a theoretical quantity *in Sneed's sense*, it is by no means clear that there is a relational property of objects underlying this quantity (in the way in which such a relation is otherwise always used within fundamental measurement). Indeed, one can *subsequently* define a relation S such that $S(x, y)$ iff $[m(x)/m(y)] \leq 1$. But it is questionable if *any knowledge* is

---

[44] Cf. especially p. 84ff of his book.

gained this way. Considerations of this sort—only hinted at here—indicate the widespread intuitive idea that the *extensivity* of the mass function is an *empirical fact* to be fallacious. It is much more appropriate to regard it as *a theoretical working hypothesis* which must *prove itself* in the course of various kinds of applications of classical particle mechanics.

In accord with our previous notation these two constraints will be lumped under "$C_m(x, R_1, \rho_1)$," whereby x represents the set of possible models needed for the empirical claim to follow.

The constraint $\langle \approx, = \rangle$, symbolized by "$C_f(x, R_2, \rho_2)$," should hold for the force function too. But this constraint should only be applicable when the forces acting on particles are observed simultaneously; i.e., the force function should only be system-independent *for identical time spans.*[45] This limitation renders the constraint on force functions much less effective than its analogue on mass functions. We *always* assign the same particle the same mass regardless of application and time of observation. But we can say absolutely nothing about the forces acting on particles when we pass from one time interval to another. Nevertheless, even this weaker constraint $\langle \approx, = \rangle$ contains, as Sneed emphasizes, a *continuity requirement*, because for overlapping time intervals *the same* forces must be used for the intersection when dealing with the same sets of particles.

We are now in a position to formulate a sentence representing a specialization of (III$_b$) tailored to the present case. In it "x is an S" will be replaced by "x is a classical particle mechanics."

(CPM-III) $\quad \bigvee x[x \mathfrak{E} \mathfrak{a} \wedge C_m(x, R_1, \rho_1) \wedge C_f(x, R_2, \rho_2) \wedge x \subseteqq \widehat{CPM}]$

Intuitively the sentence says that $\mathfrak{a}$ is a set of partial possible models for the primary predicate "x is a classical particle mechanics," i.e., a set of models for "x is a particle kinematics"; further, that this set can be enriched to a set x of possible models of the fundamental predicate by adding for each element two functions, and this, indeed, in such a way that each of these possible models becomes a model for the fundamental predicate (for which per definition Newton's second law holds) and the constraints on the mass and force functions are satisfied, which means absolute system independence and extensivity for the mass function and system independence for the force function within the same time spans.

6.3 A theoretical concept of explanation

The generalized Ramsey sentence just formulated can, in contrast to the previous one, express a *nontrivial empirical statement*. Besides this it offers a possible explication for the phrase "to explain something with the help

---

[45] The different treatment accorded mass and force in relation to the constraint $\langle \approx, = \rangle$ could be handled formally by additional indices marking the temporal dependence. These would only be used for symbolizing forces, not masses.

of a theory." The *notion of explanation* to be considered here differs from the one discussed in Stegmüller, [Erklärung], in that the explanation is directed at *systems of particles in motion* and *not some one particular fact*. These systems are, when (CPM-III) is true, exactly the elements of α as formally described by the stipulations of the definition of the predicate "is a particle kinematics." (Where it should be remembered that these systems are not merely sets of particles, i.e., domains of individuals, but rather of 'particles with time-dependent position functions.') We can now define as follows: the motions in all of these systems are *explained* by making of them, the systems, *models of classical particle mechanics* in an appropriate way. "In an appropriate way" means here "such that the given constraints are satisfied."

This is a *model-theoretic notion of explanation*. It channels the explanation of certain phenomena (motions) in certain systems (particle kinematics) back to a complex empirical statement according to which these systems are enrichable to *models* for the primary predicate corresponding to a theory. This concept of explanation is, of course, also applicable *mutatis mutandis* when using the classical mechanical analogues to the still more complicated Ramsey formulations (V) or (VI) instead of (III$_b$).

6.4 Special force laws and predicate restrictions: Newton's third law, Hooke's law, the law of gravity

We will limit ourselves to some intuitive remarks concerning possible restrictions of the fundamental predicate.[46] These amount to requiring the force functions to take special forms in certain applications. This demand is formulated by means of special laws. *All of these laws will be expressed in the set-theoretic formulation by restrictions on the predicate CPM(x).* These restrictions are obtained by adding appropriate additional stipulations to the fundamental predicate.

Suppose that we want to require the forces to satisfy Newton's *third law* together with an additional condition. More exactly, the forces should appear only in pairs of which the partners are equal in magnitude, of opposite direction, and act precisely along the straight line connecting two particles.

First the pairing must be formally expressed. This can be realized by means of a binary one–one symmetric function ϕ defined on a subset of $P \times \mathbb{N}$ (where $\mathbb{N}$ is the set of natural numbers) and satisfying the condition that if $\langle v, j \rangle = \phi(\langle u, i \rangle)$, then $v \neq u$. This condition guarantees that no particle exerts a force *on itself*. When $\langle v, j \rangle = \phi(\langle u, i \rangle)$ the value of the force function

---

[46] For a much more detailed discussion cf. Sneed, [Mathematical Physics], pp. 129–144.

$f(u, t, i)$ is to be understood as one of the forces exerted by particle v at time t on particle u. The desired additional condition says then:

(a) for all u, v, i, j: if $\langle v, j \rangle = \phi(\langle u, i \rangle)$, then for all $t \in T$:

    (α) $f(u, t, i) = -f(v, t, j)$;
    (β) $s(u, t) \cdot f(u, t, i) = -s(v, t) \cdot f(v, t, j)$.

(α) stipulates that 'actio' and 'reactio' are identical except for sign; (β) guarantees that both forces work parallel to the line $s(u, t) - s(v, t)$ connecting the two particles.

The predicate $NCPM(x)$ ("x is a Newtonian classical particle mechanics") can now serve as an abbreviation for a classical particle mechanics x fulfilling condition (a). Two more restrictions of this predicate should be mentioned. The one guarantees that Hooke's law holds, the other does the same for the law of gravity.

The first can be realized by stipulating that each particle exerts at most one nonzero force on any other, and that this force is at any time a function of the distance between the two particles. This stipulation takes the form of a condition imposed on a function $h(u, v, z)$.[47] Hooke's law can then be formulated as follows:

(b) There exist functions K from $P \times P$ into $\mathbb{R}$ and d from $P \times P$ into $\mathbb{R}^3$ such that for all $u, v \in P$ and all $z \in \mathbb{R}^3$:

$$h(u, v, z) = K(u, v)(z - d(u, v)).$$

The 'Hookeian forces' h acting between two particles u and v are thus characterized as being proportional to the extent to which the distance vector between the two particles deviates from an equilibrium value $d(u, v)$. The addition of (b) to the predicate $NCPM(x)$ produces the predicate $HNCPM(x)$ ("x is a Newtonian classical particle mechanics *satisfying Hooke's law*").

Using the functions h, which may be characterized exactly as in the paragraph before (b), the *inverse-square law* can be expressed by the following condition:

(c) There exists a function K from $P \times P$ into $\mathbb{R}$ such that for all $u, v \in P$ and all $z \in \mathbb{R}^3$:

$$h(u, v, z) = K(u, v) \cdot \frac{z}{|z|^3}.$$

And the *law of gravity* can be expressed with the help of the one–one mapping ϕ described above by requiring of the force K introduced in (c) that

(d) If $\langle v, j \rangle = \phi(\langle u, i \rangle)$, then there exists a real number G such that

$$K(u, v) = G \cdot m(u) \cdot m(v).$$

---

[47] For an exact formulation of this condition, cf. Sneed, *op. cit.*, p. 140f. (D20).

Adding these last two conditions to the predicate $NCPM(x)$, we get the predicate $GNCPM(x)$, which says "x is a Newtonian classical particle mechanics satisfying the law of gravity."

The transition from CPM to $NCPM$ corresponds to the transition in Chapter 5 from the fundamental predicate S to a restriction S^i. The last two transitions correspond to two different restrictions on the predicate S^i at the abstract level.

It is now obvious how such predicates may be used to formulate a statement of form (V) from Section 5.7 for classical particle mechanics. It has just been shown how the predicate restrictions are to be used. The subclasses of α cover those intended applications in which Newton's third law, Hooke's law, or the law of gravity hold. If we further assume additional constraints for special force functions, i.e., constraints holding only for those domains where these force functions have the special form, we obtain the specialization of (VI) for classical mechanics.

No matter how many intended applications we start with, how many general and special constraints are required, or how many laws holding only for certain domains must be introduced, we can in every case say that the entire empirical content of a proposition intended to express all of this *may be formulated with the help of a single cohesive empirical statement— the Ramsey-Sneed claim of the theory*. The empirical content not only *can*, but *must* be rendered in this way, if at the same time the problem of theoretical terms is to be successfully dealt with.

6.5 Some further remarks about additional constraints, Galilean transformations, and Newton's second law

In order to round out the brief picture of a 'real physical theory' presented in this chapter and to facilitate the understanding of certain aspects of a physical theory, we will close this chapter with some further comments on three important points. The first concerns the notion of *additional constraints* which will be illustrated with a simple example. The second concerns *Galilean transformations*. The third concerns *the epistemological role of* Newton's *second law*, which we have taken as the fundamental law of classical particle mechanics.

6.5.1 *An example illustrating the part played by additional constraints*[48]

In this example we will use the predicate restrictions, introduced above, dealing with special force laws. For the sake of completeness we will explicitly formulate part of the condition described intuitively in Section 6.4 just before

---

[48] Cf. Sneed, *op. cit.*, p. 147.

Hooke's law was introduced. The predicate UNCPM(x) ("x is a unitary Newtonian classical particle mechanics") is intended to say that between two particles at most one nonzero force is at work. Using the one–one mapping ϕ (cf. the paragraph immediately preceding (a) in Section 6.4) this predicate can be defined as follows:

$UNCPM(x) \leftrightarrow$ there exists a P, a T, an s, an m, and an f such that

(1) $x = \langle P, T, s, m, f \rangle$;
(2) $NCPM(x)$;
(3) $\wedge i \wedge j \wedge m \wedge n \wedge p \wedge q$ $[(i, j, m, n \in \mathbb{N} \wedge p, q \in P \wedge \langle q, j \rangle$
$= \phi(\langle p, i \rangle) \wedge \langle q, n \rangle = \phi(\langle p, m \rangle)) \rightarrow i = m \wedge j = n].$

Consider now the system consisting of the earth, a spring fastened near the surface of the earth, and an object suspended from the spring. A natural way of applying the formalism of classical particle mechanics to this system is to regard it as a system of three particles: the support p_1, the object p_2 suspended from the spring, and the earth p_3. The paths of these three particles are observed to satisfy two conditions: they all move in the same straight line, and the distance between p_1 and p_3 remains constant. It is now claimed that this system is a partial possible model for $UNCPM$; i.e., by adding mass and force functions it can be enriched to a model of this predicate. The choice of functions is, however, *limited* because it must be possible to enrich subsystems of this system to models for *other* specializations of *CPM*. Thus, general constraints are imposed on the mass and force functions because they 'must allow' for enrichment in respect of these *other* set-theoretic predicates. The force f_{12} between the first and second particles is, in addition, required to be a Hooke's *law force*. The constraints $K_{12} = K(p_1, p_2)$ and $d_{12} = d(p_1, p_2)$ contained in Hooke's law are determined by the paths of the particles connected by this spring in applications which can be enriched to models for *HNCPM*. The *additional constraints* here are the quantities K_{12} and d_{12}. Note carefully that K and d are functions characteristic of the spring; i.e., one supposes them to be 'intrinsic' or 'constant' properties of *this spring*. Thus, for a given pair of particles they take certain values. The decisive factor here is not this last (trivial) fact, but the first. The spring, which in the present system does not even occur as a distinct entity, can be used in a legion of applications of the predicate "is a Newtonian classical particle mechanics satisfying Hooke's law." For *each* physical system which can be constructed with *this* spring and particles connected by it, we must take *these* quantities K and d characterizing the intrinsic properties of the spring in order to produce a model for *HNCPM*. As with the general constraints, one sees that *the additional constraints also impose their limiting effects by insisting on the identity of function values in different applications.* Since the additional constraints always appear in the context of special laws, they may also be called law constraints.

The same goes for the force f_{23} between the second and third particles. The choice is limited because it must be a *gravitational force*, i.e., equal to $m(p_2) \cdot g$, where g is the acceleration of a freely falling body near the earth's surface. g expresses an 'intrinsic property of the planet Earth.' The empirical claim (UNCPM-II) for this system together with the known additional constraints K_{12} and d_{12} enable us to calculate $m(p_2) \cdot g$, and, g being known, the mass $m(p_2)$ of the object suspended from the spring.

This shows that an exact analysis of even so elementary a system as the one under consideration must recognize that, besides the specialization of the theory's fundamental predicate to meet special laws holding for this system (here, from *CPM* to *UNCPM*), certain individuals of the system also appear in the applications of *other* specializations. The 'cross-connections' between these different applications are furnished by the general and additional constraints which take some of the arbitrariness out of the choice of theoretical functions.

6.5.2 *Invariance and Galilean transformations*

What is to be understood by the demand that the laws of mechanics be invariant under Galilean transformations? To begin with, physical systems which are partial possible models for *CPM* represent models for *PK* that may be enriched to models for *CPM* by the addition of force and mass functions. In order to describe the paths of particles in models of *PK*, one needs an inertial system. The invariance condition means, now, that a correct answer to the question of whether force and mass functions can be found which are suitable for enriching a given particle mechanics to a model (an appropriate restriction) of the predicate "is a classical particle mechanics" must not depend on the inertial system used to describe the paths of the particles in this particle mechanics. In terms of a Ramsey–Sneed claim[49] this means that when a certain model a of *PK* satisfies an empirical claim of form (II), formulated with the help of a suitable restriction of *CPM*, and when a' is obtained from a by means of a Galilean transformation, then (II) also holds for a'. Moreover, the mass functions needed to satisfy these two claims are identical, and the force functions differ only in that the force vectors are exhibited in different coordinate systems. A precise definition of the notion of Galilean transformation referred to here is given in J. C. C. McKinsey et al., [Particle Mechanics].

6.5.3 *The epistemological role of Newton's second law*

The fallaciousness of the common alternative "Newton's second law— definition or empirical hypothesis?" has already been pointed out in the introduction. In the above axiomatization "force" and "mass" are undefined primitive symbols. Applying Padoa's method, it can even be *proved that* Newton's *second law cannot be used as a definition of the force function in*

---

[49] For the sake of simplicity only a sentence of form (II) will be considered here.

any of these set-theoretic predicates.[50] The contrary opinion, held among others by Lorenzen, can be refuted.[51]

From the definition of the concept of *T*-theoreticity we also know that, and why, the impossibility of regarding Newton's second law as a definition does *not* permit us to conclude it to be a matter of '*empirical truth.*' We do *not* measure the values of mass, force, and position functions independently in order subsequently to convince ourselves of (or discover) the empirical fact that these quantities together satisfy Newton's second law. No proof (such as we had in the first case), but nevertheless a clear symptom for the faultiness of this assumption may be seen in the fact that one can conceive of no empirical fact which might be regarded *as refuting this law.*

Clearsightedness in this respect seems so extraordinarily difficult because the statement conception of theories fogs our vision. Yet the realization that this Newtonian law is not a definition (and this demonstrably so), and that on the other hand the fact that it cannot be empirically falsified does not suffice to give it a 'tautological character,' could constitute an important step toward ridding ourselves of that conception and establishing a new interpretation within the framework of a nonstatement view. The empirical content of classical particle mechanics does *not* disintegrate into a class of independent, isolated empirical claims. It is displayed *in toto* by a single cohesive statement of form (VI). And with this *one* statement, covering simultaneously all the applications of the theory, it is claimed that for all these intended applications mass and force functions can be found which without exception fulfill the second law, assume special forms in certain of these applications, and are linked to each other 'right across these applications' by constraints.

To speak of *the* empirical claim of this form is, however, somewhat misleading when one considers the pragmatic passage of time. For even though the second law must appear in *all* empirical claims of this kind—otherwise it would be an empirical claim made *with some other theory*—the form of the statement remains sufficiently variable—one could say sufficiently pliable—to allow for the most varied modifications in respect of special force laws, the constraints on force functions, yes even the domain of intended applications. Thus, with the passage of time the most varied, even incompatible empirical claims *of this theory* can be formulated. This reflects nothing other than the life of the theory—its empirical setbacks and advances. These setbacks and advances could be metaphorically construed as the metabolism of the theory.

[50] For details cf. J. C. C. McKinsey et al., [Particle Mechanics], p. 268ff. For a lucid exposition of the Padoa method cf. Essler, *Wissenschaftstheorie* I, p. 102ff.

[51] Cf. Lorenzen, *Methodisches Denken*, especially p. 147, where Newton's second law is taken as a definition of force. In Lorenzen's theory this incorrect assumption, along with an analogue postulating mass to be definable, is important, because the thesis of the existence of an '*a priori* protophysics' is built on it.

In Part II we will gain a better insight into this situation. The model-theoretic apparatus, to which we now turn, will prove to be an indispensable aid.

7 What Is a Physical Theory? Sketch of an Alternative to the Statement View of Theories

7.1 Theory as mathematical structure, as proposition, and as empirical sentence

Time and again we have spoken of a theory T without ever having characterized to any great extent the entity referred to. An intuitive vagueness surrounded talk about 'the' theory. Assuming now that this notion can be satisfactorily explicated—indeed so as to justify the use of the definite article—we can say that the relation between the linguistic formulation of the empirical content of a theory and the theory itself is a many–one relation.

Even when it is assumed that only *one single 'cohesive' central empirical claim* of form (V) or (VI) (and not a *class* of sentences) displays this content correctly, there exist as many possibilities for expressing this same content in one sentence as there are various axiomatizations of T—the word "axiom" taken here in its traditional sense. One has only to remember that various axiomatizations of *the same* theory lead to various extensionally identical predicates "is an S."

But we will meet an even stronger reason for construing this relation as a many–one relation. This characterization will retain its hold even then, when the central empirical claim is replaced by the equivalence class corresponding to it.

The first obvious suggestion for applying the expression "theory" without any reference whatever to the linguistic formulation of the empirical content of a theory, is to identify the theory with what we have occasionally called its mathematical structure. This identification would clearly enough dispose of the 'statement view' of theories. According to it a theory is a *conceptual*, not a *linguistic* entity.

But here we immediately run across the first complication: *how is this mathematical structure to be characterized*? Only while considering the traditional view of expressing the empirical content of a theory by means of sentences of form (I) could one have been tempted to identify the mathematical structure of the theory with that entity designated by the predicate "is an S." This structure was modified several times in making the transition

106

to the Ramsey formulation (II) and its three subsequent generalizations (III$_b$), (V), and (VI). Thus, we are faced with the task of describing the mathematical structure of a theory under the following strictures. First, *the difference between theoretical and nontheoretical functions* must be taken into account. Second, the *constraints* must be effectively represented. Finally, *all special laws*, which hold only in certain applications of the theory, and which were rendered in (V) and (VI) with the help of restrictions on the primary predicate, must be accounted for.

A second complication follows. Above we spoke only of the relationship between theory and linguistic expression. No less important is the *proposition* which a sentence of form (III$_b$), (V), or (VI) expresses. Since the theory itself is to be reconstructed as a conceptual structure, the proposition must be distinguished as a *third kind of entity*, and indeed in such a way that it remains *constant* when one linguistic rendition is exchanged for another, logically equivalent one.

Thus we arrive at the following provisional picture. *One and the same* mathematical structure, called a *theory*, can be used in the most diverse ways to express a *proposition*, or *theory proposition* as we will call it. Each of these theory propositions stands in a one–many correspondence to sentences of the form (V) and (VI). (This correspondence can be made one–one by replacing the sentences with equivalence classes.) We now have to explicate these three notions and their relationship to one another more exactly.

> *Remark.* By distinguishing three categories of entities we escape an objection which might easily arise when reading Chapter 7 of Sneed's book. Sneed concentrates entirely on the explication of what we have called the mathematical structure, i.e., on the explication of *a purely conceptual entity*. Only occasionally does he speak of propositional entities, and then only in an intuitive way. Thus, the reader might get the misleading impression that Sneed is advancing a thesis to the effect that theoretical physicists are concerned solely with constructing such conceptual entities while claims are, for them, something comparatively foreign and unimportant. The suspicion of such an absurd position can be avoided by differentiating between the two equally important concepts of *a theory as a logical mathematical structure* and *a theory proposition*.

7.2 Frame, core, and expanded core of a physical theory

The primary predicate "is an *S*" (for particle mechanics, "is a *CPM*") played a fundamental role in formulating the empirical claims (I) through (VI). The extension of this predicate can also be fixed with the help of other predicates. If we ignore the 'incidentals' of linguistic dress and of the kind of formulation, it appears expedient to regard the *set of models* of this predicate as the basic mathematical structure. Those objects of which it makes sense to ask if they are models, but which do not necessarily have to satisfy the 'axioms proper' in the definiens of "is an *S*," we called *possible models*. The corresponding predicate was "is an *S_p*." Finally, the *partial possible models* were those objects issuing from possible models when 'the theoretical functions were deleted.' They constituted the extension of the predicate "is an *S_{pp}*." The indices "*p*" and "*pp*" served purely mnemonic purposes. We want now to proceed analogously in considering the structures ' themselves' without reference to certain kinds of linguistic formulation. The set of models is called *M*, the set of possible models, *M_p*, and the set of partial possible models, *M_{pp}*.[52] (The lower indices are chosen for the same practical reason as before. We could just as well have taken three different class symbols.) In the following discussion we will as a rule assume that we are dealing with a theory having theoretical functions and nontautological axioms, i.e., axioms having a genuine limiting effect.

We recall that the elements of the sets named are systems of relations. The sets of entities *which may possibly have the basic mathematical structure* can be described abstractly without referring to this earlier convention. Following Sneed we will call such a set *a matrix for a theory of mathematical physics*.[53]

D14   *X* is an *n-matrix for a theory of mathematical physics* iff

(1) *X* is a set;
(2) for all β : $\beta \in X$ iff there exist $D, f_1, \ldots, f_n$ such that the following conditions are satisfied:
   (a) $\beta = \langle D, f_1, \ldots, f_n \rangle$;
   (b) *D* is a nonempty set;
   (c) for all $i(1 \leq i \leq n)$, f_i is a function with $D_I(f_i) \subseteq D$ and $D_{II}(f_i) \subseteq \mathbb{R}$.

Aside from the limitation mentioned in the last footnote there are three more respects in which this definition is too special to be a fully abstract characterization. As has already been shown by the example of particle mechanics, one would not always stipulate just *one* domain of individuals as the domain of all the functions; sometimes *several* are stipulated. Second, it will not always be practical, sometimes not even possible, to define all the functions f_i *on one and the same* domain (cf. the force function in particle mechanics, which is defined on a Cartesian product of three sets). Third, it will often be advisable to include additional stipulations about the nature of the functions in the

[52] Using the earlier symbolism we could also have written "*Ŝ*," "*Ŝ_p*," etc. In the present context, though, we specifically want to avoid any reference involving the predicate "is an *S*."

[53] Sneed introduced a somewhat more general concept than the one defined here in that he left the nature of the ranges of the *n* functions open; i.e., they may consist of complex numbers, vectors, and other mathematical objects. We limit ourselves, however, to real functions so as to keep the basis from which we start as simple as possible.

concept of *possible* models instead of reserving them for the model concept. Here, too, the predicate "is a *PM*" serves as an illustration.

Such potential generalizations should be kept in mind in the discussion which follows. It is not necessary to introduce the most general notion of frame covering *all* cases. It is enough to be clearly aware of the modifications one must make on a somewhat more special concept like the present one in order to obtain such a general notion of frame.

The difference between theoretical and nontheoretical functions can be represented by a function r mapping M_p into M_{pp}. To this end let us agree that from now on when k nontheoretical functions occur in an s-tuple of functions, the members of this s-tuple should be arranged so that the first k are nontheoretical while the theoretical take the last $s - k$ places.

The most fundamental and important mathematical entities for a theory will be introduced via the concept of the frame for a theory of mathematical physics. (The phrase "of mathematical physics" will always be omitted in the following definitions.)

D15 $F(X)$ ("*X is a frame for a theory*") iff an M_p, an M_{pp}, an r, an M, and two integers k and s with $k \leq s$ exist such that

(1) $X = \langle M_p, M_{pp}, r, M \rangle$;

(2) M_p is an s-matrix for a theory;

(3) $M_{pp} = \{y \mid \lor z \lor D \lor f_1 \cdots \lor f_k \cdots \lor f_s (z \in M_p \land z$
$= \langle D, f_1, \ldots, f_s \rangle \land y = \langle D, f_1, \ldots, f_k \rangle)\}$;

(4) r is a function with $D_I(r) = M_p$ and $D_{II}(r) \subseteq M_{pp}$ such that
$\langle D, f_1, \ldots, f_s \rangle \in M_p \to r(\langle D, f_1, \ldots, f_s \rangle) = \langle D, f_1, \ldots, f_k \rangle$;

(5) $M \subseteq M_p$.

Three components of this definition are especially important: the *matrix* M_p, the *fundamental mathematical structure M*, and the *differentiation between theoretical and nontheoretical functions* via the function r. Later, after the concept of a theory itself has been introduced, M will also be called the *fundamental law of a theory*. Intuitively M_{pp} contains the nontheoretical or 'empirical' functions used to describe *the intended applications of a theory*. M_{pp} itself includes 'the set of all conceivable applications of a theory' (hence, *more* than just the intended applications of the theory). In terms of our previous idiom it is the set of the *partial possible models* (the models for "is an S_{pp}" in the abstract instance; the models for "is a *PK*" where mechanics is concerned). M_p is the set of possible models. It is identified with the matrix of the theory (the models for "is an S_p" in the abstract instance; the models for "is a *PM*" where mechanics is concerned). The 'actual basic mathematical structure' is fixed by the set of models M which must always be a subset of the set of possible models. One can speak here of the *basic mathematical structure* because this structure is common to *all* the physical systems to which the theory may be applied. For this reason, and because of the fact that special laws are obtained by specializing this basic mathematical structure, the appelation 'fundamental law' is also appropriate. The function r is called the *restriction function*. It assigns to each element of the matrix, i.e., to each possible model, exactly that element of the conceivable applications, i.e., of the partial possible models, which is the result of deleting the theoretical functions from the matrix.

In *op. cit.*, p. 166, Sneed mentions an alternative for defining "frame." It is more abstract that D15 and has the advantage of deleting point (2) with its reference to the previously introduced notion of a matrix. One does not need, then, to commit oneself in this respect and avoids the complications already indicated. For the set M_p the only condition, besides (5), is

$$M_{pp} \cap M_p \neq \varnothing \quad \text{iff} \quad M_{pp} = M_p.$$

This permits the inclusion of theories having no theoretical functions at all. (M_p is identical with M_{pp} for such theories.) One further avoids here the explicit mention of functions by replacing condition (4) of D15 with: r is a function of M_p into M_{pp}, so that when $M_p = M_{pp}$, then $y = r(x)$ iff $y = x$. r is then to be understood as an identity mapping should there be no theoretical functions involved.

The foregoing model-theoretic concepts are sufficient for formulating the intuitive content of the simplest generalized Ramsey sentence (III$_a$). For this we use the predicate corresponding to this statement which is a result of replacing the constant a with the variable ŋ. ŋ varies over the subsets of M_{pp}. In general, though, we naturally do not arrive at a true statement for each of these subsets. Those subsets which do yield a true instance constitute then a select *subclass A* of the power set of the set of all partial possible models, i.e., of the power set of M_{pp}. A could be called the *class of the possible intended application sets*. This subclass A is characterized by the fact that its elements are such subsets of M_{pp} which become 'genuine' models, i.e., elements of M, through the addition of theoretical functions. It is maintained that the set of partial possible models designated by a, i.e., *the set of intended applications of the theory*, is an element of the select subset just described:[54]

$$\text{a} \in A \subseteq \mathscr{P}(M_{pp}).$$

If we decide to apply the notion of *enrichment* not only to partial possible models, but also to *sets of* such models in the sense that the elements of these sets are enriched to possible models, we can then express the content of (III$_a$) as follows: a certain subset of all conceivable applications M_{pp}, namely a, is selected, and it is asserted that *this set of intended applications* of the

---

[54] Sneed's intuitive expositions in *op. cit.*, p. 155 (top) and p. 167 (bottom), are not wholly correct. In the first one "subset" must be replaced by "element" at various places. On p. 167 the whole text must be changed in order to get a correct statement.

theory is *an element of that distinguished subclass of $\mathscr{P}(M_{pp})$ whose elements can be enriched to sets of models.* (We suggested above calling this distinguished subclass the "class of possible intended application sets.")

For the discussion which follows it will be helpful to introduce 'higher-order' analogues to the restriction function r along with the corresponding inverse functions. To simplify the symbolism we will make use of the iterated power function: $\mathscr{P}^n(X) = \mathscr{P}(\mathscr{P}^{n-1}(X))$ and $\mathscr{P}^0(X) = X$ for any set X. Let $\langle M_p, M_{pp}, r, M \rangle$ be a frame. Note that for condition (3) and beyond, r need not be reversible; i.e., there can be $y_1 \neq y_2$ such that $r(y_1) = r(y_2)$. Occasionally the equivalence $Y \in \mathscr{P}^n(X)$ iff $Y \subseteq \mathscr{P}^{n-1}(X)$ may be used to aid our intuition.

D16   (1) R is a function with $D_I(R) = \mathscr{P}(M_p)$ and $D_{II}(R) = \mathscr{P}(M_{pp})$ such that for all $X \in \mathscr{P}(M_p)$:

$$R(X) = \{z \mid z \in M_{pp} \wedge \vee x(x \in X \wedge r(x) = z)\};$$

(2) $\bar{R}$ is a function with $D_I(\bar{R}) = \mathscr{P}^2(M_p)$ and $D_{II}(\bar{R}) = \mathscr{P}^2(M_{pp})$ such that for all $\bar{X} \in \mathscr{P}^2(M_p)$:

$$\bar{R}(\bar{X}) = \{Z \mid Z \in \mathscr{P}(M_{pp}) \wedge \vee X(X \in \bar{X} \wedge R(X) = Z)\};$$

(3) e is a function with $D_I(e) = M_{pp}$ and $D_{II}(e) \subseteq \mathscr{P}(M_p)$ such that for all $y \in M_{pp}$:

$$e(y) = \{x \mid x \in M_p \wedge r(x) = y\};$$

(4) $\mathscr{E}$ is a function with $D_I(\mathscr{E}) = \mathscr{P}(M_{pp})$ and $D_{II}(\mathscr{E}) \subseteq \mathscr{P}^2(M_p)$ such that for all $Y \in \mathscr{P}(M_{pp})$:

$$\mathscr{E}(Y) = \{X \mid X \in \mathscr{P}(M_p) \wedge R(X) = Y\};$$

(5) $\bar{\mathscr{E}}$ is a function with $D_I(\bar{\mathscr{E}}) = \mathscr{P}^2(M_{pp})$ and $D_{II}(\bar{\mathscr{E}}) \subseteq \mathscr{P}^3(M_p)$ such that for all $\bar{Y} \in \mathscr{P}^2(M_{pp})$:

$$\bar{\mathscr{E}}(\bar{Y}) = \{\bar{X} \mid \bar{X} \in \mathscr{P}^2(M_p) \wedge \bar{R}(\bar{X}) = \bar{Y}\};$$

(6) E is a function with $D_I(E) = \mathscr{P}(M_{pp})$ and $D_{II}(E) \subseteq \mathscr{P}(M_p)$ such that for all $Y \in \mathscr{P}(M_{pp})$:

$$E(Y) = \{x \mid x \in M_p \wedge r(x) \in Y\};$$

(7) $\bar{E}$ is a function with $D_I(\bar{E}) = \mathscr{P}^2(M_{pp})$ and $D_{II}(\bar{E}) \subseteq \mathscr{P}^2(M_p)$ such that for all $\bar{Y} \in \mathscr{P}^2(M_{pp})$:

$$\bar{E}(\bar{Y}) = \{X \mid X \in \mathscr{P}(M_p) \wedge R(X) \in \bar{Y}\}.$$

Explanatory note. When x is an element of M_p, $r(x)$ is the corresponding element of M_{pp} obtained by 'lopping off the string of theoretical functions' from x. The functions R and $\bar{R}$ work analogously each at the next highest level. When y is an element of M_{pp}, $e(y)$ is the set of elements of M_p having the same configuration of nontheoretical functions as y. Analogous to R and $\bar{R}$, $\mathscr{E}$ and $\bar{\mathscr{E}}$ repeat this expansion procedure each at the next highest level. When, on the other hand, Y is a subset of M_{pp}, then $E(Y)$ is the set of those elements of M_p obtained by *adding all possible configurations of theoretical functions* to the elements of Y. $\bar{E}$ does likewise one step higher for given *classes* of subsets of M_{pp}.

The functions introduced in (3) and (5) of this definition suggest three precise versions of the enrichment notion. The same assumptions are made as for the last definition.

D17 (1) For every $y \in M_{pp}$, x is an enrichment of y iff $x \in e(y)$;
(2) For every $Y \subseteq M_{pp}$, X is an enrichment of Y iff $X \in \mathscr{E}(Y)$;
(3) For every $\bar{Y} \subseteq \mathscr{P}(M_{pp})$, $\bar{X}$ is an enrichment of $\bar{Y}$ iff $\bar{X} \in \bar{\mathscr{E}}(\bar{Y})$.

Until now we have oriented ourselves to the set-theoretic correlate of (III_a). In order to switch over to the first really interesting generalization of the Ramsey sentence, (III_b), we must find *a set-theoretic counterpart to the notion of constraint*. To this end we will, with the help of our present conceptual apparatus, characterize in an entirely abstract way the function which constraints must satisfy. It is designed to prevent a situation in which all sets of possible intended applications (*all* elements of the distinguished class A of sets of possible intended applications) can be enriched to sets of models for the predicate characterizing the basic mathematical structure. Certain of these intended applications will be ruled out by constraints. We can think of this process of 'exclusion per constraint' as already beginning with the *possible* models, not first with the models themselves.[55] Formally speaking, this means that a subclass is picked out of the set $\mathscr{P}(M_p)$, i.e., out of the power class of the set of all possible models, and indeed in such a way that no single unit set is affected. This last stipulation guarantees that only sets of at least two possible models will be 'thrown out' by the constraints; i.e., only *combinations of* possible models are excluded. The 'eliminative' task of the constraints proceeds by attempting to establish 'cross-connections' between possible models. Such sets of possible models whose elements cannot be made to conform to these cross-connections are then dropped. The possibility of enriching any particular possible model considered by itself is not affected by this.

As with (III_b), the symbol "C" will again be used for the constraint concept, this time, however, in a purely set-theoretic sense. In the previous linguistic context it designated as a rule a compendium of *several* different constraints. Since now, however, that set of linguistically formulated constraints is exhibited *as a single set*, we will use the singular and speak of *the* constraint.

---

[55] The 'axioms proper,' which reduce the set M_p to its subset M, are irrelevant as far as the constraints are concerned.

D18   If X is a set, then *C is a constraint for X* iff

(1) $C \subseteq \mathscr{P}(X)$;
(2) $\wedge x(x \in X \rightarrow \{x\} \in C)$.

This definition does *not* cover *all* aspects of the notion of constraint. The fact that constraints act on *sets of functions* (more exactly, on sets of function places[56]) by requiring that certain unions of functions yield functions will be dealt with below. But first we introduce the second important model-theoretic concept, the concept of the *core of a theory*.

D19 $K(X)$ ("*X is a core of a theory*") iff there exist M_p, M_{pp}, r, M, and C such that

(1) $X = \langle M_p, M_{pp}, r, M, C \rangle$;
(2) $\langle M_p, M_{pp}, r, M \rangle$ is a frame for a theory;
(3) C is a constraint for M_p.

A core is—excepting that aspect of constraints still to be dealt with—*that mathematical structure used in a generalized Ramsey sentence of form* (III$_b$) *to exhibit an empirical claim.*

Instead of modifying the concept of constraint again, the functions defined in D16 will now be pressed into service to differentiate the three cases where the constraints affect *only* the theoretical functions, only the nontheoretical functions, or *both* the theoretical and the nontheoretical functions.

D20   Let $X = \langle M_p, M_{pp}, r, M, C \rangle$ be a core of a theory. We then say:

(1) *X is only theoretically constrained* iff $\bar{R}(C) = \mathscr{P}(M_{pp})$;
(2) *X is only nontheoretically constrained* iff $\bar{E}(\bar{R}(C)) = C$;
(3) *X is vacuously constrained* iff $C = \mathscr{P}(M_p)$;
(4) *X is heterogeneously constrained* iff neither (1) nor (2) nor (3) is the case.

One could deal with that aspect of constraints neglected in D19 by adding to it as a fourth condition the adjunction of (1)–(4) from D20. When the constraints do an 'effective' job, the adjunction of (1), (2), and (4) from D20 would be the first, and the negation of (3) from D20 the second stipulation to be added.

Earlier we mentioned the distinguished class A of sets of possible intended applications of which the set designated in (III$_a$) by the term a is an element. Let us assume now that a class C of constraints is imposed on those sets of partial possible models occurring in A which are enrichable to models

---

[56] Cf. the convention above concerning the order of the theoretical and the nontheoretical functions occurring in an element of M.

of the theory. In other words, the class A is now determined on the basis of (III_b) instead of (III_a). Using the functions introduced in D16, this class can now be succinctly characterized as follows, where $\mathbb{A}$ is a function whose arguments are cores:

$$\mathbb{A}(K) = \bar{R}(\mathscr{P}(M) \cap C).$$

> Cf. Sneed, *op. cit.*, p. 169ff. for the derivation of theorems needed to prove several propositions in the next section. Sneed illustrates the three complicated relations introduced at p. 175 of his book with graphic drawings on pp. 176–178.

We turn now to the most formidable task of this section, namely, *the purely model-theoretic characterization of the mathematical structure used in the sentences (V) and (VI)*. For this we need above all the concept of *law*. As with the concept of constraint, this notion, too, can be characterized by an abstract property. At the linguistic level special laws were indeed introduced via restrictions of the fundamental predicate of the theory, and this would seem to suggest introducing them now as subclasses of M. Nevertheless it is advisable, as with constraints, to characterize the laws in such a fashion that they take effect on the set of *possible* models. In fact, the formulation of special laws involves only the general properties of those entities which must be known before the 'axioms proper' are formulated. Thus, *laws for a frame should be introduced as subsets of the first member of this frame* (i.e., as subsets of M_p). A law is nontheoretical when it imposes no strictures on filling the places for theoretical functions; in other words, when it contains *all enrichments* of configurations of such theoretical functions as occur in it. Theoretical laws can then be defined via negation. (Since only the formal features of those things which *may be chosen as laws* are given, it would be better to speak of law *candidates*.)

D21   Let $F = \langle M_p, M_{pp}, r, M \rangle$ be a frame for a theory. Then:

(1) *X is a law for F* iff $X \subseteq M_p$;
(2) *X is a nontheoretical law for F* iff X is a law for F and $E(R(X)) = X$;
(3) *X is a theoretical law for F* iff X is a law for F and is not a nontheoretical law.

A mathematical structure used in a sentence of form (V) or (VI) will be called an *expanded core*. It contains all the members occurring in the core and three more, namely:

(a) *A set L of laws* for the underlying frame. The possibility that in certain applications no special laws are required should be left open. Hence we require that M be an element of L.

(b) *A set C_L of special constraints* of the kind described in the intuitive exposition of (VI). This set is, just like C, a set of constraints *for M_p*. It is, however, in addition linked to the laws in L. If these laws are theoretical, C_L should constrain only the theoretical functions.

(c) *A binary relation α called the application relation*. This relation couples the special laws, the elements of L, to those intended applications for which they hold. The most important properties of this requirement are expressed in stipulation (5) (cf. the explanatory remarks which follow the definition).

D22   *EK(X)* (*"X is an expanded core of a theory"*) iff there exist M_p, M_{pp}, r, M, C, L, C_L, and α such that

(1) $X = \langle M_p, M_{pp}, r, M, C, L, C_L, \alpha \rangle$;
(2) $\langle M_p, M_{pp}, r, M, C \rangle$ is a core for a theory;
(3) L is a set such that
   (a) $M \in L$;
   (b) for all $x \in L$, x is a law for $\langle M_p, M_{pp}, r, M \rangle$;
(4) C_L is a constraint for M_p such that for all elements x of L which differ from M: if x is a theoretical law for $\langle M_p, M_{pp}, r, M \rangle$, then $\bar{R}(C_L) = \mathscr{P}(M_{pp})$;
(5) α is such that
   (a) $\alpha \in Rel \wedge D_I(\alpha) \in \bar{R}(\mathscr{P}(M) \cap C) \wedge D_{II}(\alpha) = L$;
   (b) $\wedge x \wedge g \wedge h[(x \in D_I(\alpha) \wedge g, h \in L \wedge \langle x, g \rangle \in \alpha \wedge g \subseteq h)$
      $\rightarrow \langle x, h \rangle \in \alpha]$;
   (c) $\wedge z \wedge x[\langle z, x \rangle \in \alpha \rightarrow \vee y(z = r(y) \wedge y \in x)]$.

The conjunction (5) is listed in three parts so that we may more quickly convince ourselves of the intuitive adequacy of the application relation α. (*a*) describes only the formal structure of α. Its domain must be a subset of M_{pp}, indeed, a set of possible applications, hence, an element of $A = \bar{R}(\mathscr{P}(M) \cap C)$. A *set of laws* comprises its range. α can only be construed as a many–many relation, not as a function, because one law can hold in *several* applications and as a rule *several* laws hold in the same application. Both of the other stipulations should serve to assign the laws to those intended applications in which they hold. (*b*) stipulates that any liberalization h of a law g holding in x also holds in x. (*c*) stipulates that $\langle z, x \rangle \in \alpha$ holds only if z is a restriction of a possible model y occurring in the law x. This extra stipulation guarantees that a law $g \in L$ actually 'holds' in those applications assigned to it on the basis of the relation α and prevents the construction of an 'absurd' application relation assigning laws to *other* applications as those in which they actually hold.[57]

---

[57] Sneed's stipulation (cf. *op. cit.*, p. 180), on the other hand, does *not* preclude such absurd assignments.

We will speak of a *theoretically expanded core* if and only if all the elements of L are theoretical laws for $\langle M_p, M_{pp}, r, M \rangle$. If a quintuple X is given so that $K(X)$, i.e., if X is a core, and there is a Y with $EK(Y)$, i.e., Y is an expanded core, such that X is identical with the first quintuple of Y, we will say that Y *is an expansion of* X. This is an abbreviation for: the expanded core Y represents an expansion of the core X.

We turn our attention now to a more exact analysis of the applications of a theory. The set of *intended applications* was designated in (III_b), (V), and (VI) by the constant $\mathfrak{a}$. If this constant is replaced by the variable $\mathfrak{y}$, each of these sentences becomes the corresponding Ramsey formula or Ramsey predicate *whose extension consists of the class of sets of possible intended applications of the theory*. Where the empirical content of the theory can be rendered with the simple statement (III_b), this class will again be called A. Where a more complex statement of the form (V) of (VI) is used, it will be called A^*. A and A^* are distinguished as including exactly the *truth cases* for the generalized Ramsey formula of these statements, i.e., that set of partial possible models which are enrichable to models and which at the same time satisfy the rest of the conditions formulated in the statements in question. Using the present model-theoretic conceptual apparatus to characterize these classes, we can give the extension of the Ramsey predicate for (III_b) as

(i) $$A = \bar{R}(\mathscr{P}(M) \cap C)$$

and the propositional content of (III_b) as

$$\mathfrak{a} \in A.$$

We must now ask if we can work with the analogous equation for the generalized Ramsey formula (VI), namely,

(ii) $$A^* = \bar{R}(\mathscr{P}(M) \cap C \cap C_L),$$

so that the propositional content of (VI) can be expressed as

$$\mathfrak{a} \in A^*.$$

The answer is unfortunately negative. In order to see that A^* cannot be characterized in this simple manner we have only to examine an arbitrary element from the class of sets of possible intended applications, e.g., that set designated in (VI) by $\mathfrak{a}$. This must be a set of possible applications whose elements can be enriched by adding theoretical functions satisfying the general and the special constraints C and C_L so as to yield models (elements of M) *which, moreover, must satisfy the additional special laws.*

Were it not for this last, italicized feature of the elements of A^*, (ii) would be correct; for it serves to meet all conditions up to—but not including—this one. Formulated positively, this means that still another stipulation is needed to guarantee that the laws from L hold in the special intended applications. This additional stipulation can be expressed with the help of α: "Every enrichment of an element x of the set $\mathfrak{a}$ is an element of all the elements of L which are assigned to x by α."[58] In this way we arrive at the definition D23b. Stipulation (c) of this definition expresses exactly what has been described by the last sentence in quotation marks. The definition D23a is stuck in to take care of an ambiguity in the intuitive exposition above. In describing the class A we referred back to the statement (III$_b$). It was tacitly assumed thereby that the appropriate model-theoretic entities of a core correspond to the linguistic entities of this sentence. Strictly speaking, though, we must start with the core itself. Besides, we must not use the as yet unexplicated notion of a theory.[59]

D23a   Let $K = \langle M_p, M_{pp}, r, M, C \rangle$ be the core of a theory. *The class* $\mathbb{A}(K)$ *of sets of possible intended applications* is then given by

$$\mathbb{A}(K) = A = \bar{R}(\mathscr{P}(M) \cap C).$$

D23b   Let $E = \langle M_p, M_{pp}, r, M, C, L, C_L, \alpha \rangle$ be an expanded core of a theory. *The class* $\mathbb{A}_e(E)$ *of sets of possible intended applications* is then given by

$$\mathbb{A}_e(E) = \left\{ X \middle| \begin{array}{l} X \subseteq M_{pp} \text{ and there is a } Y \text{ such that} \\[4pt] \text{(a) } Y \in (\mathscr{P}(M) \cap C \cap C_L); \\ \text{(b) } X = R(Y); \\ \text{(c) } \wedge y \wedge x[(y \in Y \wedge x \in X \wedge x = r(y)) \\ \qquad\qquad \to \wedge u(\langle x, u \rangle \in \alpha \to y \in u)] \end{array} \right\}$$

Note that both $\mathbb{A}$ and $\mathbb{A}_e$ are functions. The first has cores, the second, expanded cores as arguments, while the function values are the classes of sets of possible intended applications corresponding to the given argument. Using the projection function Π_i, the function $\mathbb{A}$ could, for example, be defined by

$$\lambda_x \mathbb{A}(x) = \{z \mid \vee u \vee v (z = \langle u, v \rangle \wedge K(u) \wedge v = \bar{R}(\mathscr{P}(\Pi_4(u)) \cap \Pi_5(u)))\}.$$

The function $\mathbb{A}_e$ could be defined analogously.

Stipulation (c) guarantees that the enrichment of each element x of X is an element *of all* laws (i.e., "x is subsumable under all laws") assigned to it by α.

[58] This formulation is so awkward because a law is a set of possible models while L represents the class of *all* laws; i.e., L is a class of sets of possible models. An enrichment of the element x mentioned above is, however, a certain particular model.

[59] This concept of a theory has not been explicated *in isolation*. In all the definitions so far a theory has only been spoken of *in certain definite contexts*, e.g., "frame of a theory," "core of a theory," etc.

It should also be pointed out that the word "possible" is inserted into the nomenclature of $\mathbb{A}(K)$ and $\mathbb{A}_e(E)$ to remind us that each such set *could* be picked as an intended application of the theory. The *actual* selection of such a set is made by choosing the constant $\mathfrak{a}$ when asserting a sentence of the form (III_b), (V), or (VI)—assuming, of course, that the claim is true.

7.3 Theories and theory propositions; The propositional content of a Ramsey–Sneed claim

In Section 7.2 we endeavored to develop a precise notion of the mathematical structure of a theory. In the process this concept was split into three components. If one likes, one can regard the mathematical structure of a theory as an ordered triple $\langle \mathcal{R}, \mathfrak{K}, \mathfrak{E} \rangle$ whose three members are a *frame*, a *core*, and an *expanded core* in that order.

A physicist does not, however, confine himself to the construction of conceptual entities. In his hands these are but *an instrument for formulating empirical claims.* If we assume now that depending on the situation one of the sentences (III_b), (V), or (VI) represents an adequate linguistic formulation of the *entire* empirical content of such a theory, we must then ask how the proposition expressed by such a statement can be abstractly characterized *without reference to the incidental linguistic trappings*, i.e., in a purely model-theoretic way. The propositional content of a central empirical claim will be known as a *theory proposition*.

Still another, as yet unanswered question asks what sort of entity a theory is; i.e., how is the notion of a theory to be reconstructed?

In principle, two answers could be given to each of these questions, because in each instance it is possible to differentiate between a strong and a weak concept. It will, however, prove useful not to make a symmetric choice, but rather to opt for the strong concept of theory proposition and the weak concept of a theory. But first let us introduce the various possibilities.

We will start with the notion of a theory. One can say that two components are essential for a theory: its *mathematical structure* and *a set of intended applications I*. Thus, one could identify a theory with an ordered pair consisting of a mathematical structure and this set I. We have not as yet made any detailed examination concerning the set I. It is best reserved for the discussion of theory dynamics in Part II. Thus, we will not yet attempt to give a fully adequate definition of "theory." Instead we will content ourselves with presenting *necessary conditions* for a theory in the following definition.

Depending on how the first component, the mathematical structure, is construed, different concepts result. A frame is certainly too meager to serve as the basis for a workable theory concept. Hence, there remain two possible candidates for the mathematical structure: cores and expanded cores. Accordingly, we can call an ordered pair $\langle K, I \rangle$ consisting of a core K and a set *I* of intended applications a *theory in the weak sense*, while a *theory in the strong sense* would be an ordered pair $\langle E, I \rangle$ consisting of an expanded core and such a set *I*. The first definition is given explicitly:

D24 *X* is a (*weak*) *theory of mathematical physics* only if there are M_p, M_{pp}, *r*, *M*, and *C* such that

(1) $Y = \langle M_p, M_{pp}, r, M, C \rangle$ with $K(Y)$;
(2) $X = \langle Y, I \rangle$;
(3) $I \subseteqq M_{pp}$ and $I \in \bar{R}(\mathscr{P}(M) \cap C)$.

Condition (3) represents a minimal common sense requirement. It would be patently absurd to consider a theory where intended applications were in part not even partial possible models, for these include all 'conceivable' applications.

We have enclosed "weak" in parentheses. The corresponding concept of a *strong theory* is the exact duplicate incorporating an expanded core instead of a core. The concept of a strong theory will, however, only be used in the next definition and then appears no more. The reason will become apparent in Part II when we take up Sneed's suggestion for explicating the dynamic concept of *normal science in the sense of* T. S. Kuhn. According to Kuhn it is characteristic of normal science that the theory remains constant while the convictions of the theoreticians constantly change. We will attempt to formulate this idea with the help of our present weak theory concept, because in the sort of situation described the core remains constant while special laws, additional constraints, and even the set of intended applications can be subjected to change.

For the *theory proposition* the situation is exactly reversed. As already mentioned, we want to assign propositions to claims of form (V) and (VI). Obviously this is possible only if we do not limit ourselves to the core alone but consider the special laws and additional constraints too, i.e., the *expansions* of such cores. Remember now that in those claims the constant $\mathfrak{a}$ designates a set of partial possible models and that *I* is just such a set. We also recall that all the mathematical structures used in those claims find their precise expression in expanded cores. Thus, the theory proposition corresponding to a theory must be identified with the assertion that the second member of a strong theory is an element of the class of possible intended applications determined by the first member. Since for a given expanded core this class can be precisely characterized with the help of the function $\mathbb{A}_e$, we obtain the following definition:

D25 Let $X = \langle E, I \rangle$ be a strong theory with the expanded core *E* and the set of intended applications *I*. Then the assertion

$$I \in \mathbb{A}_e(E)$$

will be understood as the theory proposition corresponding to *X*.

The phrases "theory belonging to an expanded core" and "theory proposition belonging to an expanded core" can now also be given a precise meaning. The exact definitions are left to the reader.

The reference to the theory concept, made here for the sake of simplicity, could of course be avoided. We could have directly pursued the following line of thought: the conceptual instrument employed in a central empirical claim of form (VI) is an expanded core E. This core determines the class $\mathbb{A}_e(E)$ of possible intended applications of the theory. (VI) claims that the set designated by α is an element of this class. If we call this set I we obtain the proposition $I \in \mathbb{A}_e(E)$.

> If we take an ordinary core K instead of an expanded core E and apply the operation $\mathbb{A}$ to it, we get the concept of a weak theory proposition: $I \in \mathbb{A}(K)$.
>
> The reason that in this instance the weak concept is less important to us lies in the fact that we are interested in an adequate rendition of the propositional content of the central empirical claim of a theory, and that *as a rule*[60] *this content represents something considerably stronger than a weak theory proposition.*

Theory propositions will subsequently play an important role. They cannot, however, be dealt with here, because that would require precise statements about the way in which I can be 'given.' This problem leads to the quite difficult discussion of paradigms which must also be reserved for Part II, since it too falls within the province of the discussion of the Kuhnian conception of science. One thing can be anticipated, though. As soon as this question of how I is to be given is cleared up, it will also be meaningful to say that a person *believes in* such a theory proposition, i.e., is *convinced of its truth*. This belief is none other than the *belief that $I \in \mathbb{A}_e(E)$*.

> To speak of the truth and falsity of a theory proposition is in principle no longer problematic, although the precise definition of this differentiation would in the present case require considerable technical effort. A Tarski semantic would have to be built into the metalanguage of an object language strong enough to formulate the set-theoretic apparatus we have used. The first requisite step would be to replace the intuitive set-theoretic conceptual apparatus with a formalized set theory. The definition of truth would then have to fulfill Tarski's well-known condition which intuitively speaking says that a proposition of the form $I \in \mathbb{A}_e(E)$ is true iff I is 'really' an element of the set generated by the operation $\mathbb{A}_e$ out of the expanded core E; otherwise it is false.

We will call a theory proposition *tenable* if $I \subseteq M_{pp}$; otherwise *untenable*. Thus, that such a proposition is untenable means that the set of 'given' intended applications does not consist entirely of partial possible models.

---

[60] "As a rule" means here "in all cases where the central empirical claim does not have the simple form (III$_b$)."

This accords well with the definition of "theory" given above. Finally, a theory proposition could be called *adequate* when I is a *maximal* set such that $I \in \mathbb{A}_e(E)$, i.e., when I is a set that cannot be increased without making the theory proposition false.

One last point must still be considered in detail; namely, *the relationship between a central empirical claim and a theory proposition.* Assuming the empirical content of a theory to be adequately expressed by a sentence of form (VI), our task is to establish the sort of connection between the various parts of this sentence and the theory proposition which will guarantee that a sentence of this form expresses exactly one theory proposition. In this respect we will content ourselves with some intuitive observations concerning the 'truth' case. We will again use symbols from Sections 5.2 and 7.2.

The set-theoretic predicate "is an S" must, obviously, describe the basic mathematical structure; i.e., the extension of this predicate must be identical with the set of models. Thus $M = \hat{S}$ must hold. Moreover, the enrichment relation $\mathfrak{E}$ of (VI) must be so defined that in each instance it enriches one element of M_{pp} to an element of M_p. $M_p = \hat{S}_p$ and $M_{pp} = \hat{S}_{pp}$. As soon as these sets are given, r can be introduced in accord with D15. α from (VI) must designate a set of possible intended applications, i.e., a set I such that $I \subseteqq M_{pp}$. Moreover, since we are considering the formulation of a *true* proposition, $I \in \mathbb{A}_e(E)$ must hold where E is the expanded core used in (VI). In order to give this last phrase a precise meaning, the members of $E = \langle M_p, M_{pp}, r, M,$ $C, L, C_L, \alpha \rangle$ must be stipulated. For the first four this has just been done. The set L must contain exactly those laws symbolized in (VI) by restrictions on the primary predicate "is an S." Thus, it must contain as elements exactly the extensions of these restrictions. The sets C and C_L must describe exactly the general and the special constraints. For the set-theoretic characterization of constraints, the supplementary stipulations mentioned immediately following D20 must be used. The properties of α are characterized partly in D22, (5), partly by the additional condition in the definition of the operation $\mathbb{A}_e$.

If all of these conditions are satisfied for a given sentence of form (VI), i.e., if we have identified all eight elements of the core E on the basis of the components contained in this sentence in the manner described, we say:

> *The content of this sentence is the (theory) proposition*
> $I \in \mathbb{A}_e(E)$.[61]

One could also say that this proposition is *the meaning* of the sentence of form (VI) without having to borrow surreptitiously from intensionalism.

Thus we have described all four sorts of entities, namely, *theory, mathematical structure, central empirical claim,* and *theory proposition,* and we have

---

[61] A *statement* is often understood as a sentence together with its meaning. In the present context a statement would then have to be construed as an ordered pair consisting of a Ramsey–Sneed claim and the proposition representing its content.

clarified the relationship obtaining between the last three of them excluding for the moment the concept of theory.

Concepts such as that of a theory proposition could be called *macrological concepts*. As we know, the entire empirical content of a theory of mathematical physics, including the special laws which at a given time are thought to hold, is expressed by one single sentence of the form mentioned. Provided that this sentence is adequately formulated, it contains everything that could normally be found in a comprehensive textbook. That we have been able to pack the content of this sentence into such an abbreviated form *containing all that there is to say*, is due to the fact that, besides "$\in$," we have employed quite complicated set-theoretic concepts as 'letters' of our macrological alphabet, namely, "I" as a name for the class of intended applications, "E" for designating an expanded core, and "$\mathbb{A}_e$" as a symbol for the application operation, and correctly fused these macroconcepts as letters into the proposition $I \in \mathbb{A}_e(E)$.

---

8 Identity and Equivalence of Theories

8.1 Weak and strong formal identity of theories

The concept of theory proposition was introduced specifically for the purpose of giving a precise explication to the idea that a Ramsey–Sneed claim of a theory is the means by which a certain expansion of the theory core may be utilized to exhibit the empirical content of the theory at a given time in an adequate manner. In this context the mathematical structure characteristic of the theory at that particular time was identified with the expanded core, and theory proposition so defined that it could be equated with the content of an appropriate Ramsey–Sneed claim. Nevertheless, the definiens remained free of any reference to linguistic entities. The concept of a theory-based theory proposition was to be introduced independent of linguistic contingencies as well as of the contingencies connected with the form of axiomatization. Such was the motive for the purely model-theoretic definition of the concept of theory proposition.

Had we, in analogy to this concept, introduced only the concept of a *strong* theory, various reasons could immediately be given why this concept is *too narrow*. Suppose, for example, that the class of domains of application were to change slightly. This change might take the form of an *increase*—new possible applications are discovered—or a *decrease*—tentative applications must be rejected as a result of 'inexplicable' phenomena, of 'contradictory data' so to say. In such cases it would be *unsatisfactory* to say that *the theory has been rejected*. The same holds when within the framework of certain intended applications special laws are added or deleted.

The desiderata emerging in the light of these possible changes could be summed up as follows: we need a theory concept which allows us to speak of an *unchanging* theory in the face of small, or even substantial changes in the special laws, special constraints, or intended applications. The strong theory concept obviously does not permit this. All changes of the kind just mentioned directly precipitate a change in at least one of the members of the expanded core, and thus per definitionem, a change in the strong theory.

Objections of this sort have already been anticipated and met by opting for the concept of a weak theory as the really important one. This will become more obvious in Part II, where it will be argued that it is *not* irrational *to hang on to a theory despite falsification of its special laws*; indeed, that it is not even necessarily irrational *to hang on to a theory when it has been 'falsified' for the entire spectrum of intended applications*, or better still, when it has seemingly proved itself to be unapplicable.

> In [Mathematical Physics], p. 183, Sneed defines the concept of *theory of mathematical physics* so that it corresponds to our concept of *tenable weak theory*. Sneed offers, however, no analogue to our concept of theory proposition.

Since we, in contrast to the statement view, do not understand a theory as a class of sentences, it is not immediately clear what we mean by phrases to the effect that two theories are identical or equivalent with each other or that one is reducible to the other.

The notion of identity is the simplest to introduce. Let $T_1 = \langle X_1, I_1 \rangle$ and $T_2 = \langle X_2, I_2 \rangle$ be weak theories. T_1 and T_2 will then be called *formally identical* iff $X_1 = X_2$. We speak here of *formal identity* since only the conceptual apparatus of the first member, not the class of intended applications, is involved. Thus, for two theories to be identical in the weak sense it is necessary and sufficient that both possess *the same mathematical structure*, maintain *the same distinction between theoretical and nontheoretical functions*, and *coincide fully with respect to general constraints*.[62]

A fully analogous concept of strong formal identity can be introduced. Taking two strong theories, we will call them *formally identical in the strong sense* if their first members, which in this case are *expanded* cores, coincide. Hence, the identity of all special laws and constraints is added here.

---

[62] In [Rigid Body Mechanics], E. W. Adams defines an even more liberal concept of formal identity, stipulating only *identity of basic mathematical structure*. Such an identity concept will, however, prove adequate only as long as the purely logical aspects of the theory are being studied without any attention whatever to considerations of application. Where *applied* physical theories are concerned, the differentiation between theoretical and nontheoretical functions as well as the general constraints are no less important than the basic mathematical structure.

For reasons already mentioned, the concept of weak formal identity is considerably more important.

> An objection could be raised against the formal identity criterion introduced here on grounds that it improperly neglects the *syntactic aspect* of the sentences exhibiting the empirical content of a theory. It might be that some of the relevant mathematical structure does not *explicitly* show itself as part of the entities satisfying the predicate, but is only *implicitly* manifest in the predicate. (For examples in which a part of the mathematical structure can be 'buried ' in a syntactical apparatus, cf. Sneed, *op. cit.*, p. 195.)
>
> This objection serves to point out nothing other than the fact that establishing an identity in either the weak or the strong sense can be a nontrivial task. The mathematical structure need not be 'written all over the face' of the linguistic formulation of a theory. This holds for theories in their presystematic form *as well as* their logical reconstructions.

8.2 Introduction of various equivalence concepts for theories

More important than identity concepts for theories is the explication of an adequate concept of the equivalence of two theories. Here, the intuitive basis, i.e., the explicandum, resides in those phrases often used by physicists when, for example, they maintain that the Lagrangian or the Hamiltonian formulation of mechanics is equivalent with the Newtonian, or that Schrödinger's formulation of quantum mechanics is equivalent with Heisenberg's.

Were we to retain the traditional view, whereby theories are understood to be *classes of sentences*, this task would be more or less trivial. The equivalence of theories would reduce to an equivalence relation between classes of sentences. It is the rejection of the statement view that makes the explication of workable concepts of theory equivalence a nontrivial task.

On the other hand, this task becomes *really interesting* for the first time, since the desired concept should function where 'thinking in terms of equivalent classes of sentences' fails. It should enable us to speak of the equivalence of *different* theories built on the basis of entirely *different* conceptual apparatus.

First it must be made clear that, and in what sense, the equivalence of theories is something entirely different from their formal identity. In the latter case the theories display an identical (basic or expanded) *mathematical structure* while the question of applications is fully irrelevant. For equivalence, on the other hand, the main intuitive idea is that two theories '*yield the same empirical consequences.*' We will content ourselves with elucidating the concepts without writing out the definitions in all their technical detail.

A *core* of a theory will be understood here either as a core or an expanded core. Two cores will be called *application-equivalent* if they have the same set of conceivable applications, that is, if the partial possible models are the same in both cases. If two cores K_1 and K_2 'say exactly the same thing about possible intended applications' before being expanded by the addition of special laws, they will be called *initially equivalent*. If we designate the members of the second core K_2 with symbols obtained by adding a prime to those used for K_1, initial equivalence can be defined by the following stipulations:

(a) $M_{pp} = M'_{pp}$;
(b) $\bar{R}(\mathcal{P}(M) \cap C) = \bar{R}'(\mathcal{P}(M') \cap C')$.

According to our previous terminology, the second stipulation says that the class of sets of possible intended applications for the one core is identical with that of the other core.

When for each expansion E_1 of K_1 there is an expansion E_2 of K_2 such that the class of sets of possible intended applications of E_1 is identical with its counterpart for E_2, K_1 and K_2 will be called *effect-equivalent*. In this case stipulation (a) remains unchanged while (b) must be replaced by

(b') For every expansion E_1 of K_1 there is an expansion E_2 of K_2 such that $\mathbb{A}_e(E_1) = \mathbb{A}_e(E_2)$ and vice versa.

If in this last instance the *cores are theoretically expanded*,[63] we will speak of *theoretical effect-equivalence*.

We list now some important theorems without proof (cf. Sneed, *op. cit.*, p. 190ff.):[64]

(1) *Initial equivalence and effect-equivalence are logically equivalent concepts.*
(2) *Theoretical effect-equivalence logically implies initial equivalence. The converse does not hold.*
(3) *Any core is initially equivalent to a core containing no theoretical functions.*
(4) *Nontheoretical constraints cannot be eliminated* (e.g., by introducing suitable functions).
(5) *Any core is initially equivalent with a core whose constraints are all of a theoretical nature.*

With the exception of (2), all of these results are somewhat surprising. The first theorem is especially important for inquiries concerning the equivalence of physical theories. It is sufficient to establish initial equivalence which is easier to prove formally. All results obtained can then be carried over to effect-equivalence. (3) has special import for a systematic investigation of the problem of Ramsey eliminability.

[63] That is, those expanded cores E whose sixth member L contains as elements, besides M, only theoretical laws in the sense of D21 (whereby the frame to which the law concept is relativized consists naturally of the first four members of E).

[64] The reader who has understood the concepts introduced up to now will have no difficulty giving a precise articulation to the somewhat inexact but unambiguous terminology used to formulate the theorems.

In toto, these results suggest differentiating two types of formal equivalence between theories: *weak formal equivalence* based on the concept of initial equivalence, and *strong formal equivalence* based on the concept of theoretical effect-equivalence.

In *op. cit.*, p. 206ff., Sneed implements this conceptual apparatus to compare classical particle mechanics in the Newtonian formulation as depicted in Chapter 6 with Lagrangian generalized mechanics. They are *different* theories; i.e., they are not even formally identical in the weak sense. This is a direct consequence of the fact that the theoretical functions in both theories are different. In the Newtonian they are *mass* and *force*; in the Lagrangian, *generalized forces* and *total kinetic energy of the system*. Using a suitable formulation of the Lagrangian version of classical particle mechanics,[65] it can be shown that the cores of both theories are initially and thus effect-equivalent; hence, that *weak formal equivalence most certainly obtains*. The question of theoretical effect-equivalence remains, however, open. (The difficulty here is the lack of any natural way of 'reproducing' theoretical expansions of the core of classical particle mechanics in the Lagrangian generalized mechanics, and vice versa.)

One might object to the extremely general concept of core as defined in D19 on the grounds that in all known physical theories constraints are placed only on theoretical functions. Thus, it would seem appropriate to strengthen this concept accordingly by adding stipulation (1) from D20. Further, it might be thought that since in all physical theories the core is only expanded with *theoretical laws*, the concept of expanded core, too, should from the beginning be limited to that of a *theoretically expanded* core. This latter idea is also supported by (2) above.

To both criticisms it might first be replied that they rest on empirical hypotheses (about actual theories) rather than logical, syntactical, or semantical grounds. From a logical point of view it is hard to see why physical theories with nontheoretical constraints or nontheoretical special laws should not be advanced at some time. To the first criticism it could, moreover, be replied that due to theorem (4), quoted above, the exclusion of constraints for nontheoretical functions would have the impossibility of eliminating theoretical functions as a logical consequence. This would amount to a trivial negative solution to the problem of Ramsey eliminability.

Pragmatic grounds do, however, urge that *theoretical* constraints and theoretical laws be given priority. In the case of constraints this priority may be argued for as follows. The values for nontheoretical functions can in principle always be ascertained independent of the theory. Thus, it is always possible that a comparison of empirically ascertained values in different applications would show that a constraint must be false. Empirical 'falsification' of constraints on nontheoretical functions is always possible. For theoretical functions this situation can as a matter of principle never arise.

---

[65] This version is based essentially on that of B. N. Jamison in [Lagrange's Equations].

They need no special 'immunization' against the danger of empirical falsification; they are immune in this respect. If we encounter incompatibilities here, we can, *due to the theory dependence of their measurements,* always allow that an error has been made in ascertaining certain values. Thus, only constraints on theoretical, not, however, on nontheoretical functions can be regarded as a permanent part of a theory and consequently be incorporated into its core in a rational reconstruction. This is perhaps the main reason that in practice constraints are imposed only on the theoretical functions.[66]

That priority be given to theoretical laws is dictated especially by the fact that only through such laws the theoretical concepts are delineated. Thus each increase in the class of theoretical laws is accompanied by an increase in the number of possibilities for obtaining values for theoretical functions.

9   The Reduction of One Theory to Another

We must distinguish sharply between *philosophical* and *specific scientific* reduction theses. By philosophical reduction theses we mean, for instance, statements asserting that platonic contexts are 'reducible' to nominalistic ones, that sentences and contexts from physicalistic languages can be 'translated' into phenomenalistic languages, or that the 'essential' part of classical mathematics is 'reducible' to a constructively established basis. Special scientific reduction theses were first expounded in physics. In contrast to philosophical reduction theses, most of which are seen to be either unclear, highly problematic, or refuted, these theses can be precisely formulated *and* well grounded. Typical are statements to the effect that rigid body mechanics is reducible to particle mechanics, that thermodynamics is reducible to statistical mechanics, that geometric optics is reducible to electromagnetic theory, and also that classical particle mechanics is reducible to relativistic mechanics when velocities are small in comparison to the velocity of light.

The first workable attempt at a precise formal account of the reduction relation is found in Adams [Rigid Body Mechanics]. Sneed also follows it. Additional complications arise because Adams considers only the basic mathematical structure of a theory. Thus all those elements characteristic of an expanded core, namely, the distinction between theoretical and nontheoretical functions, the general and special constraints, and the special laws holding only for certain intended applications, are missing.

We will begin with some intuitive preliminaries. Let T be that theory which is to be reduced to a 'basic theory' T'. T' will be called the *reducing theory*

[66] Cf. Sneed's interesting remarks on this subject, *op. cit.*, p. 201f.

relative to T. T will be called the *reduced* theory relative to T'. The reduction is to be realized via a *reduction relation* which 'transposes' the basic concepts of T into those of T', and indeed in such a way that the basic laws of T can then be 'mapped' onto those of T'.

One expects the reduction relation to map each intended application of T onto (at least) one intended application of T' in such a way that every explanation or other systematic achievement of T can be taken over by T'. If, then, an $x \in M_{pp}$ corresponds to an $x' \in M'_{pp}$,[67] it intuitively will be said that x and x' are '*the same*' *object*—albeit *described each time in a different way.*

The reducing theory may justifiably be regarded as the more fundamental because it allows for finer differentiations than the reduced theory, which is in this sense less complete, less precise. Linguistically this means that *to one particular description of a physical system* in terms of the vocabulary of the reduced theory there correspond, as a rule, *various descriptions of the same physical system* in the language of the reducing theory. Thus it appears appropriate to construe the reduction relation as a *one–many relation* with the domain M_{pp} and the range M'_{pp}. Its converse must then be a function.

In order that the second property of the reduction relation be satisfied, it must be possible to deduce the fundamental laws of T from the fundamental laws of T' and the reduction relation. For practical purposes this means that when S' is a sentence from T' describing a physical system and S the *corresponding* sentence from T, then S' is true *only if* S is true. For this it is not enough, in contrast to Adams' procedure, to require of the reduction relation that *each x have the basic mathematical structure of T so far as there is an x' corresponding to it which has the basic mathematical structure of T'.* Besides this 'formal' aspect of the reduction relation, the other factors in expanded cores which are characteristic of applications must be adequately reflected too.

We will now introduce step by step various reduction concepts and describe their essential attributes. E and E' in this context are always expanded cores whose members are designated in the usual way.

The first step will introduce a weak reduction relation ρ between E and E'. This is a one–many relation between elements of M_{pp} and M'_{pp}. On the basis of ρ a relation $\bar{\rho}$ between $\mathscr{P}(M_{pp})$ and $\mathscr{P}(M'_{pp})$ will then be introduced with whose help we will try to give a precise account of the idea that the reduction relation allows us to deduce what T says about a physical system from what T' says about the 'corresponding' physical system.

For the sake of simplifying the definition we will introduce two auxiliary concepts defining general logical properties common to all reduction relations. The second 'repeats' the first at the next highest level. (Consequently the dash used in designating the second relation takes on the role

---

[67] The members of an expanded core of T will be designated as before; those of an expanded core of T' will be distinguished from these by the addition of a prime.

of a logical operator applied to the first relation.) Because in this book we will not be making any systematic use of the reduction relations to treat logical mathematical problems, the definitions will not be numbered.

$rd(\rho, A, B)$ ("ρ *formally reduces A to B*") iff

$$St(A) \wedge St(B) \wedge A \neq \emptyset \wedge B \neq \emptyset \wedge Rel(\rho) \wedge D_I(\rho) = A$$
$$\wedge\ D_{II}(\rho) \subseteqq B \wedge Un(\rho^{-1}).$$

"*St*" is the predicate symbol for "is a set." The definiens says that the domain of the relation ρ is identical with the nonempty set A, its range is included in the nonempty set B, and its converse is indeed a function.

Assume $rd(\rho, A, B)$. Then the relation $\bar{\rho}$ of the next higher level fulfilling the conditions

$$Rel(\bar{\rho}) \wedge D_I(\bar{\rho}) = \mathscr{P}(A) \wedge D_{II}(\bar{\rho}) \subseteqq \mathscr{P}(B)$$
$$\wedge\ \wedge X\ \wedge X'[\langle X, X' \rangle \in \bar{\rho} \leftrightarrow \wedge x(x \in X \rightarrow \vee x'(x' \in X' \wedge \langle x, x' \rangle \in \rho))].$$

is uniquely assigned to ρ.

We will abbreviate this stipulation with $RD(\bar{\rho}, \mathscr{P}(A), \mathscr{P}(B))$ ("ρ *formally reduces the power set of A to the power set of B*").

The definition of the weak reduction relation is then as follows:

$WRED(\rho, E, E')$ ("ρ *weakly reduces E to E'*") iff

$$EK(E) \wedge EK(E') \wedge rd(\rho, M_{pp}, M'_{pp})$$
$$\wedge\ \wedge X\ \wedge X'[\langle X, X' \rangle \in \bar{\rho} \wedge X' \in \mathbb{A}_e(E') \rightarrow X \in \mathbb{A}_e(E)].$$

That E is weakly reducible to E' can now be expressed as $\vee \rho\ WRED(\rho, E, E')$.

In both instances it is assumed that E and E' are expanded cores of theories: $E = \langle M_p, M_{pp}, r, M, C, L, C_L, \alpha \rangle$ and $E' = \langle M'_p, M'_{pp}, r', M', C', L', C'_{L'}, \alpha' \rangle$. Note, too, that we *speak* of the reduction of one expanded core to another, but that the relation ρ is defined as a relation between *physical systems* (partial possible models).

The last part of the definition of the weak reduction relation is decisive. *It reproduces in Sneed's complex conceptual language precisely Adams' basic idea concerning the reduction concept as discussed above.* For one thing it is no longer *single* physical systems which are brought into relation with one another, but *sets of* such systems; thus, the transition from partial possible models x and x' to corresponding sets of them, X and X', between which the higher level relation $\bar{\rho}$, 'induced' by ρ, then holds. For another thing, we are no longer dealing with one single mathematical structure, as Adams did, but with Sneed's considerably more complicated structure which also involves the distinction between theoretical and nontheoretical functions, the general and special constraints, and the special laws of L as well as L'.

129

Thus, this part of the definition must be formulated with the help of strong theory propositions. It says roughly: "If there exists an $X' \subseteq M'_{pp}$ corresponding to a subset X of M_{pp} and X' is an element of the class $\mathbb{A}_e(E')$ of sets of possible intended applications (determined by the expanded core E'), then X is an element of the class $\mathbb{A}_e(E)$ of sets of possible intended applications (determined by the expanded core E)." (The reader is reminded that intuitively speaking the elements of $\mathbb{A}_e(E)$ are just those sets of partial possible models (i.e., those sets of physical systems) whose elements can be enriched by the addition of theoretical functions satisfying all constraints C and C_L to possible models which are models of the basic mathematical structure and which satisfy the special laws postulated by L.)

In one essential respect the weak reduction relation delivers far too little (hence its name). It says, namely, *absolutely nothing about how the theoretical functions of the reduced theory are related to the theoretical functions of the reducing theory*. Should the reduction concept be *adequate*, this cannot be left entirely to whim. *This* defect may be disposed of by introducing the concept of *incomplete reduction* which relates not physical systems, but their enrichments (possible models). (The reason for this particular designation will be given below.)

Again the definition is facilitated by introducing an auxiliary concept. For all subsets Y of M_p (i.e., for all $Y \in \mathcal{P}(M_p)$) let $\mathbb{M}(E)$ be the class $\{Y \mid R(Y) \in \mathbb{A}_e(E)\}$ so that $Y \in \mathbb{M}(E) \leftrightarrow R(Y) \in \mathbb{A}_e(E)$.

Hence the class $\mathbb{M}(E)$ contains those sets of possible models whose restrictions are elements of the application of the core E. According to the definition of the application operation, these sets fulfill the conditions (1) $Y \in (\mathcal{P}(M) \cap C \cap C_L)$ and (2) $\wedge y(y \in Y \rightarrow \langle r(y), y \rangle \in \alpha)$. Using this concept we obtain a simpler definition than Sneed's version (cf. his definition of "closely reduces to" on p. 224 of his work):

$IRED(\rho, E, E')$ ("ρ *incompletely reduces E to E'*") iff

$$EK(E) \wedge EK(E') \wedge rd(\rho, M_p, M'_p)$$
$$\wedge \wedge Y \wedge Y'[\langle Y, Y' \rangle \in \bar{\rho} \wedge Y' \in \mathbb{M}(E') \rightarrow Y \in \mathbb{M}(E)].$$

Here ρ is a one–many mapping from M_p onto M'_p so that the relation $\bar{\rho}$, 'induced' by ρ, maps subsets of M_p onto subsets of M'_p in such a way that *the subset Y of M_p fulfills the constraints and special laws of the expanded core E if the subset Y' of M'_p satisfies the constraints and special laws of E'.*

This mapping does not accomplish what we want either, but this time for an entirely different reason: the relation of incomplete reduction simply does not link those kinds of entities 'which physical theories are all about,' namely, physical systems (partial possible models as intended applications of theories), but rather their *enrichments*. The intended applications of a theory consist only of individuals plus nontheoretical functions. Here, however, possible models—things consisting of individuals plus non-theoretical *plus theoretical functions*—are being coupled with each other.

In the following sense, though, the incomplete reduction relation does induce a nontheoretical or empirical reduction relation ρ^*. If $x \in M_{pp}$ and $x' \in M'_{pp}$ have enrichments $y \in M_p$ and $y' \in M'_p$ such that $\langle y, y' \rangle \in \rho$ for the incomplete reduction relation ρ, then $\langle x, x' \rangle \in \rho^*$ should hold.

It would be nice if the ρ^* were a weak reduction relation. We would then have found our way back to the starting point and at the same time produced an adequate correspondence between the theoretical functions of the reducing and reduced theories. *Unfortunately, this is not the case.* The reason becomes clear when one compares the last components of the definitions for *WRED* and *IRED*. Let Y be a set of enrichments for the elements of X and Y' a set of enrichments for the elements of X'. If *this* set Y' guarantees that $X' \in \mathbb{A}_e(E')$, then the corresponding set Y guarantees that $X \in \mathbb{A}_e(E)$. (This follows directly from the definitions of *IRED* and $\mathbb{M}$.) Assume, though, that there is *but one* set Y' of enrichments for the elements of X' ensuring that $X' \in \mathbb{A}_e(E')$, and that *this one set* Y' does on the basis of the relation $\bar{\rho}$ from *IRED* not correspond to *any* set Y of enrichments for the elements of X although some *other* such set Y'_1 does. In this case $\langle X, X' \rangle \in \rho^*$ indeed holds, as does $X' \in \mathbb{A}_e(E')$. Nevertheless, the definition of *IRED* offers no guarantee that $X \in \mathbb{A}_e(E)$ holds too.

This deficiency can be remedied by tightening up the incomplete reduction relation through an additional stipulation which intuitively says: "if the ρ^* relation obtains between x and x', and x' has an enrichment in M', then on the basis of ρ this enrichment corresponds to at least one enrichment of x within M." The resulting relation we will call *strict reduction*. The definition runs as follows:

$RED(\rho, E, E')$ ("ρ *strictly reduces E to E'*") iff

$IRED(\rho, E, E') \wedge \wedge x \wedge x' \wedge y \wedge y'\{[x \in M_{pp} \wedge x' \in M'_{pp} \wedge y \in M_p \wedge y' \in M'_p \wedge x = r(y) \wedge x' = r'(y') \wedge \langle y, y' \rangle \in \rho] \rightarrow \wedge z'[(z' \in M'_p \wedge x' = r'(z')) \rightarrow \vee z(z \in M_p \wedge x = r(z) \wedge (\langle z, z' \rangle \in \rho)]\}$.

By 'amputating the theoretical enrichments' we can extract from this relation a relation ρ^* between partial possible models with the following stipulation:

$$\rho^* = \{\langle x, x' \rangle | \vee y \vee y'(\langle y, y' \rangle \in \rho \wedge x = r(y) \wedge x' = r'(y'))\}.$$

Thus, by way of a 'detour' which included relations between theoretical functions (definitions for *IRED* and *RED*), we have found our way back to a relation *between physical systems*. This detour should serve to remedy the deficiency, described above, in the weak reduction relation. And on the other hand, the defect mentioned in connection with the definition of *IRED*—which would be *unavoidable* if ρ^* were defined with the help of an incomplete reduction relation—in fact *no longer* exists as attested by the following theorem.

Theorem

Let E and E' be expanded cores for theories of mathematical physics of the kind described. Then, if RED(ρ, E, E') (i.e., if ρ strictly reduces E to E'), then WRED(ρ^*, E, E') (i.e., ρ^* weakly reduces E to E').

In the relation ρ^* appearing in this theorem we have thus found a reduction relation which accomplishes all that the first definition did (and is, therefore, at least as adequate as that one was), but which also satisfies those requirements not fulfilled by the first definition.

For the same reasons which made it desirable to introduce a theory concept, we now want a *reduction concept for theories*. As a preliminary step, the various reduction concepts for *expanded* cores must be transformed into reduction concepts for *plain* cores. This is most easily done with the help of an auxiliary concept, namely, the expansion of a core K. By this we mean any expanded core E obtained from the 5-tuple K by adding to it a class of laws, a class of special constraints, and an application relation α, thus producing an 8-tuple representing the expanded core. The technical definition, in which we use the projection function Π_i, runs as follows:

$EK(E, X)$ ("*E is an expanded core for X*") iff

$$K(X) \wedge EK(E) \wedge \overset{5}{\underset{i=1}{\wedge}} (\Pi_i(E) = \Pi_i(X)).$$

Now we can define: ρ reduces the core K to the core K' iff for every expanded core E for K there exists an expanded core E' for K' such that ρ reduces the expanded core E to the expanded core E'. By substituting in the definiens each of the three reduction concepts *WRED, IRED,* and *RED* for "reduces," we obtain three concepts of *core reduction* completely parallel to our former procedure.

Two things are now required if the relation of the *reduction of one theory to another* is to hold. The core comprising the first member of the one theory must weakly (incompletely, strictly) reduce to the core of the other. Second, every intended application of the first theory must stand in the reduction relation to an intended application of the second theory (weak reduction) or correspond to an intended application of the second in the sense that both applications have enrichments which stand in the reduction relation to each other (incomplete and strict reduction). Using the abbreviations "$EK_T(E)$" for "E is an expanded core of the theory T," "$K_T(K)$" for "K is the core of the theory T," and "$App_T(I)$" for "I is the domain of intended applications of the theory T," these concepts may be defined as follows:

If $T = \langle K, I \rangle$ and $T' = \langle K', I' \rangle$ are theories, then $WERD(\rho, T, T')$ ("ρ *weakly reduces T to T'*") iff

$K_T(K) \wedge App_T(I) \wedge WRED(\rho, K, K')$
$$\wedge \wedge x(x \in I \rightarrow \vee x'(x' \in I' \wedge \langle x, x' \rangle \in \rho)).$$

$(I)ERD(\rho, T, T')$ ("ρ *strictly (incompletely) reduces T to T'*") iff

$K_T(K) \wedge (I)RED(\rho, K, K') \wedge App_T(I) \wedge App_{T'}(I') \rightarrow \langle I, I' \rangle \in \bar{\rho}$
$$\wedge \wedge x[x \in I \rightarrow \vee x' \vee y \vee y'(x' \in I' \wedge y \in M_p \wedge y' \in M'_p$$
$$\wedge\ x = r(y) \wedge x' = r'(y') \wedge \langle x, x' \rangle \in \rho)].$$

Of all the concepts introduced here, the three most important are the strict reduction relation between expanded cores, the reduction relation ρ^* induced by it, and the strict reduction relation between theories. That the last of these is in turn more important than the other two can be recognized by considering the *dynamic situation*. This reduction concept dealing with theories enables us to speak of the reduction of a theory (rigid body mechanics, thermodynamics) to another (classical particle mechanics, statistical mechanics), *although these theories undergo development in the course of time*, e.g., through the discovery of new or the rejection of old laws, or the addition of new constraints. This is possible because the reduction concepts for theories are based on the three reduction concepts for *plain* cores, *not* on the corresponding reductions for *expanded* cores.

Part II
Theory Dynamics: The Course of 'Normal Science' and the Dislodging of Theories During 'Scientific Revolutions'

10 T. S. Kuhn's Conception of Science: An Intuitive Sketch of His Ideas

Nothing is easier than to caricature a philosophical position or a philosophical theory. It is not uncommon that even the most careful serious efforts produce nothing more than a caricature. And then, too, that which is new, a novel way of looking at things coupled with unfamiliar conceptual tools to produce the bare outline of a fully unorthodox theory, tends to defy adequate description.

So it is with the kind of thinking developed by T. S. Kuhn in his book, *The Structure of Scientific Revolutions*. Our first task will be to sketch Kuhn's basic ideas. But this sketch will be neither complete, nor perfectly lucid, nor objective and neutral. Instead it will be drawn in a certain sense from *his theory as reflected in the mind of his critics*, without, however, directly doing violence to his thesis. It may be supposed that this sketch is very like the one Kuhn's work calls forth in impartial critical readers. In the next chapter some of the sharp critical reactions to Kuhn's ideas will be presented— critical reactions all of which *prima facie* seem to hit home.

In later chapters this picture will be modified on the basis of Sneed's reconstruction of the nonstatement view of theories. This modification of our sketch of Kuhn's view will not be puny. Indeed, it will be *so radical as to constitute an almost complete revamp of our 'primary sketch' of Kuhn's conception*. This revision will not transpire in one fell swoop. Instead, certain parts of the original sketch will gradually crumble in light of a new way of looking at things, taking *with them* the corresponding critique. In the end a *totally new picture* will emerge. *Nor* can this picture lay claim to *completeness*; for the psychological–sociological aspect is not considered in full. Nevertheless, it is hoped that all the key concepts important for an adequate understanding of Kuhn's theory will be explicated to the point where the reader can effortlessly fill in the remaining details when reading Kuhn's book. The most important thing is to provide *a reconstruction of these key concepts which fully disperses the appearance of irrationality, absurdity, and eccentricity one so easily tends to see in Kuhn's work.*

Kuhn's book is presumably the most important documentation of what, depending on one's philosophical orientation, is felt to be *rebellion against the philosophy of science* or, alternatively, *revolution within the philosophy of science.* Watkin's catchphrase comparison of the positions of various philosophers on the subject of the "development of the sciences," which Lakatos then extended to include Kuhn, offers a good introduction to the kind of thinking which appears to await us here.

According to D. Hume, all nonmathematical scientific disciplines rely on *inductive generalizations.* The inductive process is, though, in Hume's estimation *not a rational process* in the sense that inductive inference cannot be rationally justified. Subsequent 'inductivist philosophers,' especially Carnap, attempted to remedy this supposed shortcoming concerning rationality. According to them, inductive reasoning, too, follows logical rules, the rules of *inductive logic.* In this view as opposed to Hume's one can think of inductive reasoning as *rational reasoning.* Not, however, Popper. According to him there is no such thing as an inductive process—neither inductive methods of 'discovery' nor of 'justification.' Nevertheless, scientific testing is rational in the sense that it can be rationally reconstructed in the language of deductive logic alone as the *deductive method of strict testing.*

Where does Kuhn fit in here? The rejection of inductivism and careful attention to developments in the history of sciences ally him with Popper. But he deviates from Popper in decisive points concerning the view he takes of that history. In Kuhn's view of science there seems to be nothing corresponding to the method of strict testing, of falsification and corroboration.

Thus, the question, "How does exact science develop historically?" is answered (schematically) in four ways:

(1) Hume says that it develops *inductively* and *nonrationally*;
(2) Carnap's idea is that it develops *inductively* and *rationally*;
(3) Popper's answer is the dual counterpart of Hume's, namely, that it follows a *noninductive, rational* course;
(4) Kuhn's view deviates from all of these. A comparison of his conception with the other three seems to indicate that he thinks the course of science is *noninductive* and *nonrational.*

136

One thing, now, seems to unite all the representatives of 'rational' philosophy. They believe they must immediately and energetically protest an answer like (4). "That *cannot* be right! The history of science *cannot* have unfolded as, e.g., the history of religions or of political ideologies. Science *is* distinguished by the fact that it offers *reasons*, that it attempts to convince with *arguments* rather than seduce with propaganda, that changes of conviction follow *insight* rather than conversion experiences, etc."

One might imagine that Kuhn would react to such reproaches as did Wittgenstein concerning a different matter, namely, with "don't think, look!" with "see how it really was with science!" whereby he has in the back of his mind: "maybe you'll then be prepared to give up your *rationalistic clichés.*"

In the final analysis, however, there appears to be lurking in Kuhn's conception a consequence which from the standpoint of the philosophers of science could not be more radical. It is a consequence which although strongly suggested by Kuhn's investigations was first explicitly uttered by P. Feyerabend, namely, "The philosophy or metatheory of science ought to be dropped." This is a simple consequence of a thesis which seems to be without precedent but which many believe must be read into Kuhn's work. The thesis is sometimes called Kuhn's *irrationalism*. This name is, however, quite misleading, because it makes one think of an irrational philosophical position on Kuhn's part. But there have always been irrational philosophies. And presumably the accusation of irrationality against philosophies has been leveled even more often. What is new, radical, and unprecedented in Kuhn's position seems, however, to be his apparent insistence that *the development of the various scientific disciplines, in particular of the so-called exact natural sciences, not only can be interpreted as a completely 'irrational' process, but must be so interpreted.*

But now we have gotten ahead of ourselves. For the moment it suffices to know that Kuhn himself never uses the expression "irrational," and claims only to seek a much humbler goal: namely, to show that scientific progress does not consist of a successive 'accretion of knowledge.' Here we reach the point where the 'rationalist' might impatiently ask just how the development of the sciences does proceed. To which Kuhn would retort: "*which* sciences?" This reply would, however, not be aimed at a difference between various disciplines. It concerns instead the difference between *various forms of pursuing science*. According to him there are two such forms: *normal science* and *extraordinary* or *revolutionary science*. In order to grasp this distinction, one must free oneself of an assumption made more or less routinely by the 'rationalist' and the 'empiricist' alike when asking the above question.

This assumption could be called the idea of a *linear accumulation of knowledge*. As witnessed by countless references in the forewords and introductions to textbooks, this idea is regarded as a correct interpretation of the historical development of the various disciplines by the representatives of the natural sciences themselves. According to this idea, scientific development consists of a gradual growth of knowledge accompanied by a successive elimination of unscientific ballast. This growth is thought to have width as well as depth. New facts are always being discovered and better, more precise instruments devised with which to measure and describe them. On the other hand, logical connections between law-like regularities already discovered are established and these regularities are imbedded into theories. That this process proceeds no faster than it does is attributed only partly to the limitations of human inventiveness and perceptiveness. To a considerable extent prejudice and unscientific elements in the early stages of scientific practice are held responsible. Only gradually does science succeed in freeing itself from that 'mixture of error, superstition, and myth' inhibiting more rapid progress.

Indeed, it is not denied that occasionally theories come to be regarded as obsolete and are replaced by new ones. But this is never to be interpreted as a genuine revolution inasmuch as the old theory is seen not to be completely false, but rather a marginal case of the new theory. Thus the dislodging of one theory by another accords entirely with the notion that 'science is gradually nearing the truth about nature.' The theory which dislodges another has come closer to the truth than the old one which, relative to its replacement, is still always 'approximately right.'

Kuhn confronts this picture with a totally different conception, in support of which he adduces a legion of historical examples. He distinguishes between *normal science*, which always transpires within the framework of some traditional paradigm and concentrates on '*puzzle solving*,' and *extraordinary science*, which manifests itself in 'tradition destroying intrusions into the tradition-bound activity of normal science.' Extraordinary science appears only when normal scientific enterprise is faced with a crisis occasioned by the frequent appearance of anomalies which cannot be dealt with by the traditional methods. We then get a *scientific revolution* in the course of which the paradigm changes and with it the problems and standards of the discipline involved.

According to Kuhn it would be false to think only of *contemporary* forms of scientific endeavor as normal science while simply relegating outmoded views to the ranks of the myths. If one chooses this course, one must admit that myths are 'generated by the same methods and believed for the same reasons' which today lead to scientific knowledge. The other possibility is to regard such 'outmoded views' as science too. But then one cannot help admitting that there are sciences containing beliefs fully incompatible with contemporary ones.

Confronted with these alternatives, the historian must opt for the second. For, besides the reason just given, contemporary science enjoys no special advantage over these other sciences with respect to the danger of one day being shunted aside. As we will see, this choice has far-reaching consequences. In particular, the conviction that scientific development is a growth process must be discarded.

Examples of sciences which, with the exception of the last one named, differ from the contemporary version are: Aristotelean physics, Ptolemaic astronomy, the physics of Newton's *Principia*, Newton's optics, Franklin's theory of electricity, phlogistic chemistry, and the Copenhagen interpretation of quantum physics.

All of these cases of normal science were preceded by a state of affairs in which no uniform interpretation of known phenomena existed. Indeed, various persons found themselves confronted with the same *realm* of phenomena, but not with the same *phenomena*, and they described and interpreted these in different ways. These initial deviations disappeared for the most part as soon as one theory along with its paradigm prevailed. The above examples are also examples of different paradigms. These are more than just theories. They are generally acknowledged scientific achievements which for a certain time provided models and solutions for a community of specialists. The paradigm determines not only which theories and laws hold, but also which problems and methods of solution are acknowledged as scientific. Even the way in which a scientist of a certain tradition sees a certain phenomenon is determined by the paradigm: "when Aristotle and Galileo looked at swinging stones, the first saw constrained fall, the second a pendulum."[1]

The paradigm lays down a mission. Fulfilling it is the task of *normal science*. The success of a paradigm manifests itself at first only in isolated, imperfect examples. This initial success is, however, enough to let it prevail over competing paradigms. But otherwise the paradigm gives only a promise of success, the realization of which must be achieved by normal science.[2]

The task of normal science can be divided into a nontheoretical and a theoretical part. The nontheoretical activity includes the *gathering of experimental data*, and indeed of three kinds: first, that which is thought to be important for and revealing of the nature of things from the standpoint of the chosen paradigm; second, that which may be compared with the predictions of the paradigmatic theory; and third, that which serves to render the theory precise and to remove such obscureness as still infected it in the beginning.[3] These experimental tasks are accompanied in normal science by analogous tasks at the theoretical level: namely, additional manipulations designed to make a theory suitable for predicting; reciprocal adjustments between theory and facts through idealizations and the development of physical methods of approximation; and numerical adaptations of concepts and theorems of the theory.

---

[1] Cf. [Revolutions], p. 121.

[2] Cf. *op. cit.*, p. 24f.

[3] For examples from various areas of science cf. *op. cit.*, p. 25ff.

As a collective name for the activities of normal science Kuhn uses the expression "*puzzle solving*." The successful scientist in this context is the one who becomes an expert in solving experimental, conceptual, or mathematical puzzles.

It is no accident that Kuhn almost always speaks of paradigms, seldom of theories or laws. One is tempted to use an expression of K. Jaspers and say that a paradigm in Kuhn's sense is something *all-embracing*—relative, namely, to all the laws, theories, and rules which one is able to give. Only a small part of what he calls a paradigm is exhibited by explicitly formulated rules: "Normal science is a highly determined activity, but it need not be entirely determined by rules."[4] If scientists belong to the same tradition, they concur in the *identification of the paradigm* without having to be of one mind concerning the complete *interpretation* and *rational* realization of this paradigm; indeed, without even having attempted such a realization.[5] Their concurrence means in particular, though, that they are unanimous as to what may be regarded as a *legitimate problem* and as an *acceptable* solution to it.

In this way paradigms regulate scientific endeavors more perfectly than rules, which might be abstracted from them, ever could. For this there are various reasons.[6] First, it is *very difficult even to recognize the rules* governing a given normal scientific tradition. The difficulty here is similar to the one described by Wittgenstein of saying what is common to all games. Second, one must free himself of the idea that scientists learn concepts, laws, and theories *in abstracto. It is always by means of concrete application that they learn the use of these 'conceptual tools.'* The learning process which the scientist undergoes and which accompanies him through his entire scientific career is, thus, comparable with the learning process involved in the 'finger exercises' of a pianist, whose development is not just a matter of sitting at his desk and studying music theory. Third, *the need for rules comes up only with the appearance of suspicions about the reliability of the paradigm.* And this happens only in a crisis situation at the beginning of and during a scientific revolution. Only the periods directly preceding the introduction of new paradigms are regularly accompanied by debates over valid methods, problems, and solutions, periods, that is, in which paradigms are first attacked and then replaced.

But what of the *testing of hypotheses* during a period of normal science? The above reference to the fact that normal science, among other things, uses the paradigm theory to make predictions, indicates a close affinity to Popper's notion of the 'strict testing' of theories. Is it not inevitable that falsifying data be found among the experiences of the normal scientist?

[4] *Op. cit.*, p. 42.

[5] Cf. *op. cit.*, p. 44.

[6] Cf. *op. cit.*, p. 46ff.

Kuhn disputes the existence of such experiences.[7] Indeed, paradigms are periodically rejected. But this never happens because of 'recalcitrant data ' which defies the paradigm theory; it happens *because the paradigm is dislodged by a new one in the course of a scientific revolution.*

But then, what happens when the scientist is not able to dispose of the problems which appear to be *counterexamples* to his theory? Kuhn does not deny that in such cases a theory may be rejected. But this rejection takes a completely different form than the one envisioned by falsificationism. In particular, it is not a process within the confines of science itself. It consists, namely, solely in the *compulsion to change professions:* "... rejection of science in favor of another occupation is, I think, the only sort of paradigm rejection to which counterinstances by themselves can lead."[8] By way of clarification Kuhn quotes the proverb, "it's a poor carpenter that blames his tools." *This serves to describe exactly the attitude of the normal scientist.* If he cannot dispose of a puzzle having the form of falsifying data in Popper's sense, then *this discredits the scientist alone, not the theory he uses.* Therefore normal science must see to it that theory and fact are brought into ever better accord—a task which it actually accomplishes for a certain span of time.

All scientific theories are confronted with puzzles at any time. If, following Popper, these are seen as refutations of the theory, then the historian is forced to the paradoxical conclusion that *all theories stand refuted at all times.*

The reader can now easily understand at least one of the charges leveled by Kuhn's opponents: namely, that *he imputes to 'normal' scientists a high degree of irrational behavior.* Normal scientists never examine their paradigm critically, in particular the paradigmatic theory. They simply use the theory uncritically as an instrument for puzzle solving.

Normal science could, according to Kuhn, be rightly throught of as a *cumulative enterprise.* But this accumulation of knowledge takes place only at the cost of novelty: "Normal science does not aim at novelties of fact or theory and, when successful, finds none."[9]

If, then, the whole problem of confirmation and testing seems to be banned from the realm of normal science, it remains to be asked whether this lack of rationality is made up for by those processes which Kuhn counts as extraordinary science. The result of his analysis is still more astonishing: *a clearly negative answer* to this question.

When falsifying data is not acknowledged in 'normal' scientific circles, when it is not regarded as counterinstances but as puzzles which the scientist with the help of his instrument, the paradigm theory, must solve, how can something like a scientific upheaval come about?

[7] Cf. especially *op. cit.,* p. 146ff., where Kuhn explicitly refers to Popper.

[8] *Op. cit.,* p. 79.

[9] [Revolutions], p. 52.

It would be fully incorrect to suppose that perhaps Kuhn assumes that for the revolutionary phase of science a number of critical minds raise themselves above the 'obtuseness of everyday science,' see the difficulties for what they are, namely, *refutations of hypotheses,* and on the basis of this insight seek to draft new theories. Incorrect, because Kuhn's answer is that when a theory once reaches the status of a paradigm it can never be repealed by 'experience.' It can only *be dislodged by another theory,* by ' another candidate prepared to take its place.' Metaphorically speaking, it is not the comparison of a theory with nature that can lead a scientist to reject this theory; it is the struggle between competing theories which leads to rejections. Rejecting a theory always means rejecting it *in favor of another theory:* "No process yet disclosed by the historical study of scientific development at all resembles the methodological stereotype of falsification by direct comparison with nature. ... The decision to reject one paradigm is always simultaneously a decision to accept another."[10]

How, then, does it happen that new paradigms appear and challenge the old? A key factor in understanding this phenomenon is the recognition of certain dynamic processes associated with an increase in the frequency with which puzzles appear and their development into so-called *anomalies.* Included here are especially what has been called the "discovery of new facts."

> Kuhn points out a great danger adhering to the description of such phenomena, a danger to which historians often fall victim. His remarks about it are also interesting in that they indicate another *important point of contact between his way of thinking and Wittgenstein's.* Kuhn points out, namely, that the usual talk about discoveries is totally misleading because it is patterned after talk (itself questionable) about seeing.[11] One is all too ready to suppose that discovering, like seeing, or better yet, *touching an object,* is a process which can be unambiguously attributed to a *certain individual* at a *certain point of time.* Using 'the discovery of oxygen' as an example, he shows how mistaken, indeed how absurd, this way of talking about discoveries is. One of the reasons he gives is the following: discovering consists not only of knowing *that* something is, but also knowing *what* it is. In the case of scientific discovery, however, an answer to the question "*what* is it?" requires not merely some everyday notion, but *a definite theory with whose help the phenomenon in question is interpreted.* For example, we would not hesitate to give Priestly credit for discovering oxygen if we too still believed that oxygen is nothing other than dephlogistigated air. Since we no longer subscribe to this belief, should we, therefore, give the credit to Lavoisier? That would be justified had his 'discovery' induced a change in chemical theory. But a long time *before* his work played any part in the discovery of the new gas, Lavoisier was convinced that 'something was wrong with the phlogiston theory,' and

---

[10] *Op. cit.,* p. 77.

[11] Cf. [Revolutions], pp. 53–58, especially p. 55.

that burning bodies absorb some part of the atmosphere. On the other hand, Lavoisier originally thought he had, in oxygen, identified "air itself entire." And he was convinced to the very end that the gas oxygen was formed by a combination of oxygen as the 'atomic principle of acidity' with the substance of heat, 'caloric.' Should the discovery of oxygen thus be dated sometime after the theory of caloric was relinquished? But caloric was still believed in as late as 1860, 66 years after Lavoisier's death and ca. 83 years after his 'discovery of the new gas,' i.e., at a time when oxygen had long been a 'standard substance.'

The conclusion to be drawn from historical investigations of this kind is simply that *such phrases as* "oxygen was discovered then or then by this one or that one" *should not be used at all.* They constitute a misleading use of language tending to generate a wholly false impression of scientific dynamics. Through the use of such phrases one loses the ability to recognize and understand the essential intertwining of observations with concept formation, of data compilation with theory construction, and more easily falls victim to such thought patterns as "here the facts, there the theories serving to interpret and explain these facts."

Thus, according to Kuhn 'new discoveries' involve more or less complicated processes which cannot be unambiguously localized with respect to persons or dates. Such discoveries have a conflicting effect. Since, according to Kuhn, all scientists are initially trapped in their paradigms like a clam in its shell, the old paradigm often renders them *oblivious* to new discoveries; for the old paradigm is the only available means of interpretation. On the other hand, such discoveries are a source of new puzzles and put the scientist standing in the tradition of normal science *on the lookout for anomalies* not fitting into the paradigm theory.

The discovery of x-rays offers an historical example, which by the way, according to Kuhn, is also a classic example of a 'discovery per chance' — something which, according to him, occurs much more often historically than 'the standards of impersonal scientific reporting' would let us know.[12] The discovery was made in the course of a normal investigation of cathode rays which Roentgen interrupted because a screen began to glow. *The screen should not have glowed*—not, that is, according to the prevailing paradigm theory. In this respect Roentgen's discovery is like Lavoisier's, whose experiments also yielded unexpected results in terms of the contemporary phlogiston paradigm.

There is not necessarily an essential difference between that which Kuhn calls a "scientific puzzle" and that which he calls an "anomaly." But there is at least a difference of degree with respect to the effect on the scientist. For instance, an unsolved problem which at first 'is only felt to be annoying' can as a result of the further development of the science become an anomaly

[12] Cf. [Revolutions], p. 57.

and cause a crisis (e.g., the problem of weight relations in eighteenth-century chemistry). Or a puzzle becomes an anomaly because its solution is for practical reasons felt to be especially urgent. The frustrated applications in question plunge the theory into a crisis (e.g., the task of producing an exact calendar within the framework of Ptolemaic astronomy). An intrinsic difference could at best be spoken of when the given difficulty casts doubts on *fundamental* assumptions of the theory (e.g., the problem of ether waves in the Maxwellian theory of electromagnetism).

Anomalies can, thus, cause a more or less pronounced uneasiness in scientists depending on the importance of the assumptions questioned and the degree of divergence from the expectations generated by the traditional theory. When the anomalies stubbornly defy all interpretations which the paradigm allows, and when they begin to pile up, normal science lapses into a *crisis*. This word is the summary expression for *a collective uncertainty among the ranks of tradition oriented scientists*. It stems from the *persistent inability* to deal with the anomalies as puzzles of normal science by taking them to their expected solution within the framework of this science. Diverging versions of the theory, subsequently recognizable as *ad hoc* adaptations, begin to spread and the rules of the normal science gradually lose their grip.

But even this feeling of uncertainty, be it ever so strong, is never by itself reason to discard the paradigm. As we have seen there always are, according to Kuhn, difficulties concerning the 'dovetailing of theory and nature.' Most of these are at some time or another disposed of, often in an unforeseen way. Thus many scientists, even in times of crisis, will not damn the paradigm which led them into it, but lull themselves at first with the belief that one day a solution will still appear within the framework of the paradigm theory. For others the anomalies have already become more than just bothersome knots for normal research activities. They lose confidence and begin to look around for alternatives.

This signals the end of a period of tradition-oriented research, of working within the confines of normal science. A new phase of *extraordinary science* and *extraordinary research* is beginning. More and more new formulations and versions are probed. There is a willingness 'to try anything.' Open expressions of discontent are heard. Foundational discussions commence, and refuge is sought in philosophy. *All of this is symptomatic of the transition from normal to extraordinary research.*[13]

In this way scientific revolutions cast their shadows ahead of themselves. Finally the new paradigm appears, neither gradually nor as the result of the intensive cooperative effort of research teams. The new idea appears suddenly: "... the new paradigm ... emerges all at once, sometimes in the middle of the night, in the mind of a man deeply immersed in the crisis."[14]

---

[13] Cf. [Revolutions], pp. 89–91.

[14] *Op. cit.*, p. 90.

And then the upheaval can get under way, the dislodging of an old paradigm by a new. Here we have the positive complement to the previous negative assertion that anomalies and crisis alone are not enough to fell a paradigm. This can only be done by the 'tradition-breaking counterpart to the ruling tradition of normal science,' the *new paradigm* which carries the day.

Thus, *neither* during a period of normal science *nor* in a phase of extraordinary research is a paradigm eliminated by falsification. In the former it is *not even* questioned; in the latter it is not 'recalcitrant data,' but *another theory* which undermines it. It is this second point which induces Kuhn to draw on political terminology concerning this form of upheaval. Such terminology serves to emphasize the *noncumulative character of the development of science*. "Political revolutions are inaugurated by a growing sense, often restricted to a segment of the political community, that existing institutions have ceased to meet adequately the problems posed by an environment that they have in part created. In much the same way, scientific revolutions are inaugurated by a growing sense, again often restricted to a narrow subdivision of the scientific community, that an existing paradigm has ceased to function adequately in the exploration of an aspect of nature to which that paradigm itself had previously led the way."[15]

Rationalists and empiricists alike will tend to say: "And here the analogy stops. *Installing* a new theory is entirely different from installing a new political form. That which is *better founded*, has the *better arguments* going for it, and *best stands the test of experience* will prevail in the end." But Kuhn will have none of this.

Such things as empirical tests or empirical checks could only referee objectively between different paradigms if there were such a thing as a *neutral observational language* in relation to the competing theories. The *existence of a theoretically neutral observational language is, however,* for Kuhn, as for Hanson,[16] who originally formulated the thesis of the 'theory-ladenness of all observational data,' *an illusion*. When a new theory is accepted, not only the phenomena are 'rethought,' but all descriptive expressions are *newly interpreted* too. Known definitions and explanations are either explicitly replaced by new ones, or, where this is not the case, the background knowledge is so greatly altered that the old expressions receive new meanings even without such explicit revision. To those scholars who have changed paradigms it seems as if they have transferred to another planet. Familiar things appear in an entirely different light, and previously unknown things crowd around. The entire conceptual network through which they looked at the world has shifted. It is no exaggeration to say that *with a paradigm change the world itself changes*.[17]

[15] *Op. cit.*, p. 92.

[16] Cf. N. R. Hanson, *Patterns of Discovery*, p. 19.

[17] Cf. [Revolutions], especially p. 102 and p. 111.

If, thus, the '*empiricists*' argument folds, perhaps the '*rationalist*' will have better luck by pointing out that there is nevertheless an inter-subjectively understood language in which arguments and counterarguments can be formulated. But according to Kuhn this is but another dogma taking its place beside the *dogma of a neutral observational language*, namely, the *dogma of a common intersubjective language*. In paradigm conflicts not only the consensus of observation among scientists collapses, the common denominator of the spoken word meets its end too. *There exists no common scientific language bridging the gap between competing paradigms.* One does indeed find debates between representatives of various schools. But from antiquity on two things can always be observed as characteristic of such debates: first, the participants *talk right past one another* when it comes to comparing the merits of the various paradigms, and second, *circular argumentation* prevails in which it is shown that each paradigm satisfies the criteria it prescribes for itself while failing to satisfy some criteria dictated by the competition.[18] Since, moreover, different paradigms solve, in part, different problems, it inevitably comes to a squabble over *which problems and solutions are most important*. And, as with competing norms, the question can only be decided on the basis of criteria lying outside normal science.

Here we meet a second parallel between political revolutions and scientific upheavals which provides additional justification for regarding the latter as revolutions. "Political revolutions aim to change political institutions in ways that those institutions themselves prohibit."[19] As the crisis deepens, more and more people commit themselves to a concrete program for re-building society within an entirely new framework of institutions. Thus, society splits into parties struggling against each other, one trying to defend the old order, one attempting to construct a new order. And since no higher institutional authority for the arbitration of differences is recognized, "... the parties to a revolutionary conflict must finally resort to the techniques of mass persuasion, often including force."[20] The analogy to scientific upheavals is, according to Kuhn, as follows. The choice between competing paradigms, like the choice between competing political institutions, is "... a choice between incompatible modes of community life."[21] And as antagonistic political camps acknowledge no suprainstitutional authority for reconciling conflicts, so the evaluative processes of normal science must fail in the presence of paradigm conflicts, since they are themselves dependent on a paradigm which in time of crisis enjoys *no* general acknowledgement. This explains the circular nature of the argumentation in paradigm debates mentioned above, and its purely persuasive character.

[18] Cf., for example, *op. cit.*, pp. 109–110.

[19] *Op. cit.*, p. 93.

[20] *Op. cit.*, p. 93.

[21] *Op. cit.*, p. 94.

146

Occasionally, however, it is argued that in contrast to victories in the political arena, a new theory, after it has dislodged another, retains this theory as a marginal case; thus, e.g., Newtonian dynamics constitutes a marginal case of relativistic dynamics. At the only place in his book where Kuhn offers even so much as a sketch of a formal argument,[22] he attempts to show that there can be no talk of a derivation of Newtonian from relativistic dynamics. This is because the fundamental notions of *position, time,* and *mass* have changed—only the names remain the same.

When one theory dislodges another, the two cannot be logically compatible with each other; in most cases they are not even *commensurable,* i.e., *not comparable* due to the fundamental difference in their conceptual apparatus.[23] Therefore, one could not even do Kuhn justice by invoking the image of Hegelian dialectics and alleging that the new theory represents a sort of 'synthesis' in which the former is somehow 'preserved' or ' accommodated.' No, the relationship between the two is that of abrupt polarity.

For us this point is of utmost importance. *If Kuhn's thesis of the incommensurability between dislodging and dislodged theories is right, then no rational arguments can decide between the two.*

But if neither empirical tests nor rational arguments decide the issue, how can the ascendancy of a new paradigm be explained? The first thing to notice here is that it is mostly young people or newcomers to a discipline who come up with new theories. And in any case it must be people who have a *belief* in the new theory, and *commit* themselves to it with the fervor of converts. Such a commitment is necessary because with the initial appearance of a paradigm the new theory is *always confronted with still more problems* than even the old, crisis-ridden theory. Without the sustaining power of belief such a commitment would not be possible.[24] Adopting a new paradigm is comparable to a *conversion,* not a mere change in theoretical opinions. And the means of converting others to the same belief are not arguments, but, even as with political revolutions, *persuasion* and *propaganda.* The converts have experienced something in their thinking and perceiving comparable to what psychologists call a gestalt switch: "Just because it is a transition between incommensurables, the transition between competing paradigms cannot be made a step at a time, forced by logic and neutral experience. Like a gestalt switch it must occur all at once ... or not at all."[25] Those who have taken the plunge often resort to phrases like "the scales fell from my eyes." Talk of gestalt switch is, however, somewhat misleading

---

[22] Cf. *op. cit.,* p. 101.

[23] Cf. especially the remarks following the critique of the supposed derivation of Newtonian from relativistic dynamics, *op. cit.,* p. 103.

[24] Cf. especially *op. cit.,* p. 157 and 158.

[25] [Revolutions], p. 150.

according to Kuhn. In a visual gestalt switch the subject can go from one image to another and *back again* (e.g., see the drawing first as a rabbit's head, then as a duck's head, then again as a rabbit's head, etc.), while a scientist switching paradigms does *not* retain the freedom of switching back and forth between different ways of seeing things. He simply *sees* something new not seen by those adhering to the old paradigm.

As already mentioned, it is mostly young people who bring new paradigms into the world. And it is young people who are most inclined to champion new causes with religious fervor, to thump the propaganda drums. What about those not prepared to let themselves be converted, especially scientists of the older generation who, in most instances, can give a good reason for resisting: namely, why believe in something new when it involves still more difficulties than the old? And when they, as is sometimes the case, can give no reason, then it is simply habitual modes of thinking that make their conversion impossible. Here nature lends change a helping hand through that biological phenomenon we call *death*. On p. 151 Kuhn quotes M. Planck who, looking back on his scientific career, remarks sorrowfully: "A new scientific truth does not usually establish itself by convincing its opponents who then declare themselves enlightened, but rather because its opponents gradually die off and the new generation is familiar with the truth from the beginning."[26]

"Familiar with the truth"—that raises still another question. To what extent do scientific revolutions mean scientific *progress*? Kuhn seems to speak most clearly on this question where he says: "Revolutions close with a total victory for one of the two opposing camps. Will that group ever say that the result of its victory has been something less than progress? That would be rather like admitting that they had been wrong and their opponents right."[27] For the members of the victorious party the outcome of the revolution *is* progress. Moreover, this group is also in the favorable position of being able to make sure that future members of the scientific community see things its way.

Thus, it must be sufficiently clear that even in extraordinary research and times of scientific revolution the rational component by no means dominates according to Kuhn, nor even represents a decisive factor in understanding such epochs. These phases of science are also described in terms which make the scientific personality an irrational one. For it is not in terms of *neutral observation, strict testing, data corroboration or inductive confirmation, and convincing argument* that we are to describe the revolutionary process by which one theory dislodges another, but rather in terms of

---

[26] M. Planck, [Autobiographie], p. 22: "Eine neue wissenschaftliche Wahrheit pflegt sich nicht in der Weise durchzusetzen, daß ihre Gegner überzeugt werden und sich als belehrt erklären, sondern viel mehr dadurch, daß die Gegner allmählich aussterben und daß die heranwachsende Generation von vornherein mit der Wahrheit vertraut ist."

[27] *Op. cit.*, p. 166.

belief, the commitment to something new, persuasion, propaganda, conversion experiences, gestalt switch, and death.

Without, as I hope, having been unfair to Kuhn, this sketch does accent those aspects of his analysis which make the reactions of his critics understandable. Anyone raised in 'more or less rational philosophical tradition' will be moved to protest, and Kuhn's critics can reckon with a very positive echo at least from such philosophers.

11 Some Criticisms of Kuhn

11.1 Preliminaries

Kuhn's ideas have purposely been sketched so as to cast a clear light on the radical consequences they suggest—consequences some of which he explicitly draws, some of which are implicitly contained in his writing, and all of which elicit protest.

The *thesis of the futility of all metatheories of science* (not explicitly alleged) could be regarded as the most provocative consequence emerging from his work. If someone today proposed engaging a team of experts to find out with which banks the present king of France had his capital invested, this project would rightly be deemed senseless. It rests on the false assumption that there is currently a king of France. By analogy it appears that if Kuhn is right, then all metatheories and philosophies of science rest on a false presupposition. They may deviate ever so widely in their ideas of scientific standards, criteria, and forms of argument; in *one* thing they doubtlessly concur: namely, that science, in particular 'exact natural science,' is a *rational* enterprise—no matter how "rational" may ultimately be explicated. But Kuhn's view amounts to a denial of this fundamental presupposition; at least this is the impression shared by most critics.

Kuhn's reaction to such accusations as 'irrationalism' or relativism, which he allegedly represents, are noteworthy. He neither denies nor admits them. Instead he emphasizes that he does not understand them, that the use of such terms by his critics must be based on misunderstanding.[28] Perhaps this indicates that in Kuhn's view his critics apply *inadequate criteria of rationality*. Since, where science is concerned, he regards himself as a historian and not a logician, it can scarcely be held against him that he does not elaborate this point with sufficient clarity. In any case we want to keep this

---

[28] Cf. especially [My Critics], p. 259ff. Kuhn's reply to such charges is naturally much more detailed than the global formulation above indicates. In the present context, though, we can overlook these details.

possibility in mind. We will take it up again after hearing all the counter-arguments and pursue it in subsequent chapters. It turns out that Sneed's conceptual apparatus, especially his precise formulation of the nonstatement view of theories, permits us to reconstruct some of Kuhn's ideas in a way which relieves them of the *appearance of irrationality*.

Since we have such a reconstruction in mind, it seems opportune to make preliminary comments on the following criticisms as we present them. In this way the reader will be gradually prepared for the subsequent reconstructions and will have no great trouble establishing their connection with the following text.

11.2 Immanent criticisms: Shapere and Scheffler

In his review [Kuhn], D. Shapere sharply criticizes in particular Kuhn's paradigm concept. He censures the lack of clarity in the concept as well as the contradictory way in which Kuhn describes the supposedly free access we have to a paradigm.

If one surveys all that Kuhn has to say about paradigms, one gets the unsettling impression that a paradigm encompasses a gigantic collection of seemingly heterogeneous components. Among these are *laws, theories, models, standards, criteria, methods*—some codified, but mostly unwritten, because according to Kuhn an explicit formulation is usually first attempted in a time of crisis—and also more or less *vague intuitions, as well as metaphysical beliefs and prejudices*. Shapere rightly wonders[29] whether Kuhn's thesis, which attributes the conformity among representatives of a dominating scientific climate to the effect of the prevailing paradigm, is really the result of a thorough historical study, or whether it does not simply rely on the tremendous scope of the expression "paradigm." It may be asked whether the use of "paradigm" as a common appellation for such a wealth of activities and functions does not dull the perception of differences between them instead of sharpening it.

Shapere finds Kuhn's remarks about *recognizing* paradigms as such no less confusing. In [Revolutions], p. 44, Kuhn maintains that a paradigm is open to 'direct inspection' and that the identification of paradigms is not difficult for the historian. On the other hand, he emphasizes, for example, on p. 11 and p. 44, that explicitly formulated rules were almost always rejected by some members of the group of scientists investigated, and that a paradigm must be regarded as something which *precedes* the various concepts, laws, theories, and viewpoints drawn from it. If, Shapere ironically remarks, verbalizing, i.e., adequately formulating a paradigm, presents such monstrous difficulties, then one must doubt whether paradigms are

---

[29] [Kuhn], p. 385.

really so directly open to inspection, or one must be astounded at Kuhn's powers of perception.

Shapere comes to the critical conclusion that the differences between paradigms are either a matter of different formulations and verbalizations of one and the same paradigm, or at best a matter of gradual differences. Hence, the difference between scientific revolution and normal science is also at best a gradual difference, such things as expressions of dissatisfaction, the development of competing formulations, and foundational discussions accompany the *entire course* of science.[30]

Shapere's critical comments about the paradigm notion are justified to the extent that one must really ask if Kuhn was well advised to use this word. Later, in Section 13.3 we will distinguish (at least) three entirely different factors in the Kuhnian paradigm concept. First there are *psychological, mental processes, and functions*, which can be the subject of research psychology but not of a metascientific analysis aiming at rational reconstruction. Second, there are those components for which the 'problem of verbalization' disappears because they can be exactly and precisely described, namely, *the components of the mathematical structure of a theory*. Third, there is *the set of intended applications I* of a theory. Only for this third factor will we establish a connection with the Wittgensteinian notion of paradigm. Thus it seems that of the original intended meaning of "paradigm" there remains only a tiny, indeed, an infinitesimal part. But this tiny bit will be enough to let Kuhn's notion of normal science appear in an entirely new light. *The behavior of the members of a normal scientific tradition will lose its apparent irrationality.* (For a somewhat more detailed, but nevertheless preliminary sketch, cf. Section 11.5.)

As far as Shapere's conclusion that the Kuhnian polarity represents only a gradual difference is concerned, we will *not* take the critical position it implies. This, however, is only because we will limit ourselves to something quite special: namely, to the second class of components just enumerated, cast in terms of Sneed's conceptual apparatus, not Kuhn's formulation. In very rough anticipation of the subsequent discussion one can say that we will, in contrast to Shapere's surmise and in accord with Kuhn's line of thought, not arrive at a merely gradual, but rather an '*essential*' difference. This is because we—at least where physical theories are concerned—construe the holding of one and the same theory in the course of 'normal science' as the *retention of one and the same core*, while the shifting convictions of the scientists of a normal scientific epoch find their expression in *various proposals for expanding this stable core*. We will only speak of a theory being dislodged when a theory with one particular core is *replaced by a theory with a different core*.

Still another of Shapere's criticisms should be mentioned briefly. Concerning Kuhn's thesis that with a change of paradigm the *concepts*, i.e.,

[30] *Op. cit.*, p. 388.

the *meanings of the primary terms*, change too, he charges that Kuhn offers no analysis of the concept of meaning and that, therefore, his thesis remains an unprovable allegation.[31] We will deal with this point briefly in Chapter 17, but it occupies no great place in our discussion. For if meaning is taken here in the sense of *intension*, the matter belongs to the philosophy of language, not the philosophy of science. Should something else be meant, then it is imperative to provide a precise foundation for the discussion. For how should the presence of 'meaning changes' be *proved* so long as no exact criteria of constancy or change have been formulated? As we will see, in the case of certain precisely definable changes in connection with *theoretical concepts* one can actually speak of a shift in meaning if one takes as a criterion the *truth conditions* for sentences in which such concepts occur. Briefly, we think that this Kuhnian thesis can be partly exonerated, though not on the basis of his intuitive conceptual apparatus. It requires the support of a reconstruction using, among others, concepts such as that of a *constraint* as well as the *theoretical–nontheoretical* dichotomy.[32]

I. Scheffler advances a different immanent criticism involving Kuhn's method of argumentation, not his conceptual basis.[33] He points to the obvious self-contradiction involved in denying the existence of theoretically or paradigmatically neutral facts and then referring *to historical facts* to support this thesis. Thus Kuhn supports his thesis with exactly what it claims should be impossible. Or at least he must maintain that a historian is capable of achieving what is in principle impossible for the natural scientist.

Should Kuhn's view, which is attacked here, really amount to an allegation of impossibility, i.e., a claim of the form "communication between the representatives of different paradigms is impossible," this criticism would surely have to be accepted. But it pays to take Kuhn's thoughts here as observations which, despite exaggerated formulations, must always be relativized to a given theory. Using the terminology of Part I the idea could then be formulated roughly as follows: "One cannot with the help of the mathematical structure of a theory compare this structure with a different one. Yet, in times of crisis this is exactly what is always attempted by the scientists concerned." In order to make a comparison, *both* structures must be made the *object* of an investigation, which, of course, is no trouble at all. Here we find one of the few places where the philosopher of science can draw attention to a mistake in the reasoning of the scientist, thus assuming a *normative function*.

[31] Cf. especially [Kuhn], p. 390.

[32] In [Scientific Change], Shapere offers a more detailed exposition of the connection between theory change and meaning shift in his discussion of Feyerabend's criticism of philosophical empiricism. Feyerabend stresses the thesis that every change in a theory must involve a change in meaning of the terms occurring in this theory even more than Kuhn.

[33] Cf. [Subjectivity], p. 21f., p. 52f., p. 74; and [Vision], p. 366f.

11.3 Epistemological criticisms: Shapere, Scheffler, Popper

Shapere points out a number of places where Kuhn makes statements about what *must* hold for science and its development.[34] But how is it possible to *substantiate* statements of this sort when, as the result of historical studies, we only know *what actually happened in the past*? The answer is simple enough. It cannot be done. And Kuhn could only claim to have determined what must be on the basis of knowing what was, if he embraces an extremely broad philosophical essentialism according to which historical facts constitute the basis for *beholding the essence* of that which is given.[35] Thus the statements criticized by Shapere must be regarded either as carelessly formulated hypothetical assumptions or mental lapses.

Two of Kuhn's theses are subjected to penetrating criticism by Scheffler in [Subjectivity]. The first is that there are *no objective, theory-neutral observations*; the second, that between proponents of various 'paradigms' there is *not even a common scientific language*.

Because a detailed discussion of these two questions would force us to adopt an extremely high level of epistemological abstraction, only a few remarks will be made about each. First, it must again be noted that Kuhn's methods can yield at best historical facts, not proofs of nonexistence. Moreover, concerning the first question one could again point to a self-contradiction. For, according to Kuhn, a theory must appear *better than* its competition if it is to be chosen,[36] and a new theory *must achieve much*, if not all, of what the theory it dislodges was able to do. Such statements would be hard to understand, or even senseless, if they did not contain a tacit appeal to 'intertheoretical,' observable phenomena which the theories claim to explain or predict.

Since considerations of this kind are always in imminent danger of being regarded as hair-splitting, it should be pointed out that Kuhn's thought contains a *grain of truth*. This point will come up again in a systematic context where it becomes clearer. It seems appropriate to mention it now, though, because this partially valid line of thought is paired with an *error* common to thinkers like Hanson, Toulmin, and Feyerabend as well as Kuhn. It is true, namely, that a description of the facts 'relevant' for a theory often (perhaps even always in theoretical physics) requires using a theory. *But this latter theory is, of course, not identical with the former.* In the somewhat abstract terminology of the first chapter: in order to describe a partial

---

[34] Shapere, [Kuhn], p. 385f. Such places may be found, for example, in Kuhn, [Revolutions], at the bottom of p. 16, at the top of p. 79, at the middle of p. 87, and at the top of p. 146.

[35] There are actually occasional hints that Kuhn does believe in something like this; e.g., in [Revolutions], at the bottom of p. 112.

[36] [Revolutions], pp. 15 and 16.

possible model for the mathematical structure of a theory, one will as a rule need in turn a theory. This is, however, a 'lower-order' theory than the one whose mathematical structure is being referred to.

But it is not possible that something becomes 'a relevant fact for a theory' *solely under the assumption that this same theory holds*? The answer is "yes," and it should be added that this highly curious state of affairs produces an extremely difficult problem. It is nothing less than what in Part I was called the problem of theoretical terms, whose solution we have already discussed in considerable detail.

As far as the second point is concerned, Scheffler has in principle shown how the difficulty is to be dealt with.[37] Naturally the *internal criteria* of a theory determining the problems and solutions of this theory must fail when it comes to comparing it with another. For this one needs *external criteria*. These must be formulated at the *metatheoretical level* at which internal criteria are not used, but themselves analyzed. There can be no doubt that this transition is possible in principle. The contents of Chapter 7ff., as well as the continuation of the analysis begun there and its application to Kuhn's work in Chapter 13ff. could serve as proof of this possibility. 'Internal criteria' would serve for comparing different expansions of the core of one particular theory held by those using the criteria. 'External criteria' can only be applied when cores themselves are being analyzed as in Part I and in all those passages to follow where the cores of arbitrary unspecified theories are discussed. The various reduction concepts of Chapter 9 may be regarded as examples of such external criteria.

The situation here is in principle the same as when representatives of various philosophical persuasions enter into debate. Here too, a rational discussion can be initiated by first discussing criteria for the use of the philosophical language in a *metalanguage understood by both parties*.[38]

Should the 'paradigm discussions' in the history of the natural sciences really have transpired in the way Kuhn maintains, this could be seen as *an implicit stimulation for metatheoretical investigations*. In any case the hope that analyses like those found in this book might help to overcome the desolate state of affairs described by Kuhn does not seem to be entirely unfounded.

There are strong indications that Kuhn intended no mere summation of historical observation, but instead a *philosophical thesis* with his claim that proponents of various paradigms can find no common language. This thesis coincides with what Popper called "the myth of the framework" in [Dangers][39] and considered to be an element of philosophical relativism.

This thesis and its possible variants will also be ignored here because

---

[37] Cf. especially [Subjectivity], p. 84ff. and [Vision], p. 368, point (8).

[38] Concerning this point cf. Bar-Hillel, [Philosophical Discussion], p. 258ff.

[39] [Dangers], p. 56.

Kuhn's ideas about normal science and scientific revolutions can be critically reconstructed without entering into the discussion of philosophical foundations necessary for dealing with relativism.

11.4 Criticism of the analysis of normal science and scientific revolutions: Watkins, Popper, Lakatos

As might be expected, the sharpest critical reaction concerns Kuhn's picture of the dynamics of science, for this view seems to be incompatible with the idea that science is a *rational* undertaking leading to *genuine progress.*

Popper admits that Kuhn's distinction between normal science and extraordinary research is an important one. But for him the attitude of the normal scientist is pitiful. It is the attitude of a quite uncritical professional who adopts current doctrine like current fashions, never questions it, and demands of his students the same uncritical stance. "In my view the 'normal' scientist, as Kuhn describes him, is a person one ought to be sorry for."[40] He has been poorly educated. For scientific institutions ought to foster and encourage critical thinking. Popper sees, therefore, a great danger in the training which produces normal scientists. It amounts to nothing less than substituting indoctrination in a dogmatic mentality for teachings which serve to make the fledgling scientist familiar with problems.

Watkins, too, turns emphatically on normal science; especially against the idea that it *tests no theories*, but *only the cleverness of the experimenter at puzzle solving*, as Kuhn emphasizes in accord with the above sketch on p. 5 of [Psychology]. In the face of a mentality which knows no strict testing and thus no falsification either, he urges *permanent revolution* as a motto for science.[41]

Subsequently we will see why these and similar criticisms—which incidentally are not so much criticisms of Kuhn as of the *behavior he reports*—are unsatisfactory.

Still more energetic are the protests precipitated by Kuhn's remarks about scientific revolutions. The three most important must well be the accusations of *vagueness*, of *contradictoriness*, and of a *rationality gap*.

Re *vagueness*: The catchwords 'empirically testable' and 'good for puzzle solving' at first appear to indicate merely the different but equal criteria espoused by Popper and Kuhn, respectively, for delineating science from nonscience. Watkins points out,[42] however, that it is not quite as simple as that. Kuhn emphasizes that many of the theories mentioned by Popper were not tested before being rejected, but that "... none of these was replaced

---

[40] [Dangers], p. 52.

[41] J. W. N. Watkins, [Normal], p. 28.

[42] [Normal], p. 30.

before it had ceased adequately to support a puzzle-solving tradition."[43] Watkins remarks how extraordinarily vague this notion of adequate support for a puzzle-solving tradition is. The difference between support and non-support is at best gradual. Kuhn is not able to indicate where the line between a tolerable and an intolerable level of anomalies lies. In contrast to the notion of falsification, the *critical level* at which a change of paradigm is justified is missing here.

Re *contradictoriness*: Watkins,[44] like Scheffler before him,[45] points out that Kuhn's incommensurability thesis contradicts his other thesis according to which competing theories are incompatible. If paradigms are incomparable, then it remains unclear how they can be thought to compete with each other, to be rival alternatives. To take Watkins' example, if one regards a biblical myth as incomparable with Darwinism, both can peacefully coexist.

Re *rationality gap*: Nearly all of Kuhn's critics share the feeling that his description of scientific revolutions contains a decisive lacuna. One no longer understands, assuming one wants to take him seriously, what *scientific progress* is; that is, one must interpret it and its cognates in terms of power politics: the victors are by definition the progressives. Kuhn seems to fail completely to account for that which Popper expresses as follows: "In science (and only in science) can we say that we have made genuine progress: that we know more than we did before."[46] A good part of Lakatos' efforts in [Research Programmes] aim at closing this rationality gap. We will later attempt a precise reconstruction of some of the most important of Lakatos' ideas (cf. Section 16.4). As it turns out, the notion of a research programme, which goes back to Popper ([Dangers], p. 55), proves to be less important than an intuitive idea which Lakatos attempts to incorporate into the notion of 'sophisticated falsificationism.'

11.5 Summary and initial comments

In the following Chapters we will be occupied with a critical reconstruction of some of Kuhn's fundamental ideas using Sneed's conceptual apparatus as introduced and partly modified in Part I. Thus, we implicitly regard these ideas as important enough to warrant a reconstruction. And this in turn means that the criticisms introduced in Section 11.4, although partly justified, appear to us unsatisfactory as a whole. The reasons for this may best be summarized by anticipating some basic facets of the subsequent reconstruction after considering a certain principle.

[43] [Psychology], p. 10.

[44] [Normal], p. 36f.

[45] [Subjectivity], p. 82f., and [Vision], p. 367f.

[46] [Dangers], p. 57.

156

Our first concern must be not to overestimate the value of those aspects of Kuhn's work which can safely be ignored when analyzing 'theory dynamics.' Among these are most of the points mentioned in Sections 11.2 and 11.3. It may well be that Kuhn believes in something like a philosophically untenable historical relativism. It also may well be, as we saw, that he himself, on pain of being inconsistent, must believe in the possibility of intersubjective observation much more strongly than he admits; that he underestimates the possibility and power of metatheoretical reflection; and that he draws somewhat hasty conclusions from what-was to what-must-be.

For anyone earnestly reflecting on the subject, the radical divergence between the *static* and the *dynamic* aspect of science must become a source of deep disturbance. It is an oversimplification to think that metascientific analysis can yield only *instantaneous photographs of manifoldly idealized structure cross sections*, while the investigation of the *dynamic aspects* of science must be reserved for the psychology and sociology of research. *Is it then conceivable that these two ways of considering things lead to incompatible results?*

Were a historian of mathematics to claim that in the history of this discipline he was unable to find any logical reasoning, not even the most rudimentary attempts, one would rightly reply that he must be blind. The discoveries of modern logic are precisely the result of comparing traditional syllogistic with *actual mathematical reasoning* and thus recognizing the limitations of the former. According to a widely held opinion, *proofs* in logic and mathematics correspond to *empirical testing* in the natural sciences. Thus it becomes a matter of serious concern when a competent historian of these latter disciplines finds not merely that empirical testing of theories is a scarce item, but that *not one single* process as yet uncovered by historical research has *any resemblance* at all to the 'methodological stereotype' of falsification of a theory by comparison with our experience of nature.[47]

Indeed we have here, as with our imaginary mathematical historian, the alternative of claiming that Kuhn must be blind—at least as far as the aspects of testing and corroboration are concerned. But that can hardly be done in good conscience considering that Kuhn, as attested to by his numerous historical examples and references, has immersed himself in different forms of scientific thinking and arguing better than most historians or philosophers of science before him.

Kuhn's findings should not simply make us shake our heads in disgust as the 'Popperians' do when confronted with the irrationality, dogmatic narrow-mindedness, and uncritical attitude of 'normal scientists.' Perhaps the philosopher of science should look for the trouble in himself instead of others and admit that *there are grounds for supposing that to date something has totally gone astray in our reflections on theories.*

[47] The exact wording of this passage from the first paragraph of [Revolutions], Chapter 8, is quoted in Chapter 10.

Empirical sciences do *develop* in one way in which mathematical disciplines do not. Confirmation, falsification, and the dislodging of theories have no logical, mathematical analogue. For this reason a metascientific analysis *must also* turn its attention to the dynamic aspect. Logical analysis and historical, psychological research are two different methods of tackling this subject. And when their results clash, the logician, too, must be prepared to make fundamental revisions. Is, in the final analysis, no 'immunization strategy' needed to protect theories from falsification because they *are* from the very beginning immune to refutation by contrary experience?

11.5.1 Normal science and paradigms

We will now, on the basis of Sneed's apparatus, attempt to approximate Kuhn's notion of normal science with the help of the *concept of holding a theory*. The macrological concepts of Chapter 7 will play a deciding role here.

The concept of holding a theory makes precise the idea that a person or group of persons *hold fast to one particular theory although their theoretical convictions, suppositions, and hypothesis are constantly changing*. The *apparent* contradiction between the stability of the theory and simultaneous instability of these beliefs is disposed of by anchoring the 'theoretical aspect' of holding a theory in the *core*, i.e., in a mathematical structure, and not in a system of statements. The hypotheses, on the other hand, changing from time to time and person to person, manifest themselves in sentences. The traditional way of thinking would regard them as classes of sentences. But according to the conception developed in Part I, each 'system of hypothetical suppositions' finds its expression *in a single cohesive statement—the central empirical claim of the theory*—or in its propositional counterpart, a *strong theory proposition*. It is the *cores* of theories that remain stable in normal science. What constantly changes are, among other things, the provisional attempts to use *core expansions* for formulating central empirical claims.

Popper's horror at the mentality of the normal scientist is unfounded. The normal scientist is no more a narrow-minded dogmatist than he is someone engaged in extraordinary research. While the latter aims at contributing to the development of new theories by constructing *new cores*, the tradition-bound scientist hangs on to a core *as his tool*, and works on hypothetical core expansions with respect to which he is always ready to revise his stance. A dogmatist is one who also *hangs onto the hypotheses* at all costs and wants to move others to do the same.

As a mathematical structure, a theory is immune to falsification because it just is not the sort of entity of which it can sensibly be said that it is refuted, anymore than it is sensible to say, e.g., that the group concept is empirically refuted.

If this reconstruction attempt is right in principle, then we may justifiably conclude that the discussion between Kuhn and his 'rationalistic' opponents is similar to the paradigm debates he describes in that *the parties*

to it are continually talking right past each other in a really fantastic way.
For the automatic point of departure for *all* of Kuhn's opponents is the
statement view according to which theories are systems or classes of sentences
or sentence-like entities. The theory concept which Kuhn has in mind when
describing normal science, on the other hand, can only be satisfactorily
explicated on the basis of the nonstatement view. Kuhn himself may possibly
have contributed to the confusion by conceding his 'Popperian opponents'
too much in the course of logical discussions, e.g., that a theory must be
"testable in principle."[48]

Holding a theory does indeed involve working with a mathematical
structure, but it *does not* stop there. Already in Chapter 7, the set of intended
applications *I* was taken as part of a theory without, however, having been
further analyzed. What most critics seem to have completely overlooked is
that in contrast to formal logic this set *I* is, as a rule, not extensionally, but
only *intensionally* given, and that this even holds for the domains of individuals of the elements of *I*. This is where the paradigm notion can be put to
work. The sets in question are usually determined only *by a paradigmatic
example*. This has far-reaching consequences: the still to be formulated
rule of autodetermination, according to which the scope of application of a
theory is not antecedently given but is determined by the theory itself,
displays a superficial resemblance to a 'method of autoverification,' but
implies nothing irrational *although it considerably increases the immunity
of the theory against recalcitrant data*.

These hints as to how the notion of normal science may be freed of the
odium of irrationality must suffice for now.

11.5.2 Scientific revolutions

Here we have to differentiate. Where criticisms in which Kuhn is accused
of having failed to provide a sharp criterion for choosing a new theory are
concerned (cf. Watkins' objection in [Normal], p. 30, mentioned above)
we will again be defending Kuhn's view. One can, though, do nothing
more than instill *insight* and *understanding* as to why the formulation of
precise rules is precluded here.

On the other hand, those critics pointing to a rationality gap as the consequence of Kuhn's incommensurability thesis are right. If one rejects as
absurd such progress notions of 'power politics' as "in science, too, the
victorious are the progressives," one is forced to the conclusion that within
the framework of Kuhn's thought there is no room for a concept of scientific
progress. Paradoxically, though, this rationality gap plagues Kuhn only
because *he falls back into his adversaries' way of thinking*. Using the reduction
concepts of Chapter 9 it can be said what it means for the dislodging theory
to be superior to the dislodged. Thus, one can also differentiate between a

---

[48] [Reply], p. 248.

reasonable and an *unreasonable* change of theory. Instead of embracing Kuhn's conclusion that the theories involved cannot be compared because the sentences of the one cannot be derived from those of the other and vice versa, one must conclude that a reduction concept resting on 'deduction relations between classes of sentences' is unsuitable for comparing theories.

11.5.3 Testing, confirmation, corroboration

Problems belonging to this group Kuhn either minimizes or ignores. This is at least partly due to the fact that such problems play an insignificant role, if any, in theory dislodgement and none at all involving the theories held by scientists of a tradition-bound 'normal' epoch. But mainly it is due to the fact that the expression "puzzle solving" covers a host of various activities *including* the proposing, improving, and rejecting of hypotheses. 'Puzzle solving' involves not only such things as improving methods for determining natural constants or explaining phenomena which have as yet resisted explanation. It also includes, for example, *proposing special force laws* for certain applications of a theory, improving them, and *rejecting them* if they fail. In general, we can say that anything having to do with changes in core expansions (not affecting the core itself) or changes in the set of intended applications may be subsumed under the activities of the normal scientist. Using the macrological concept of theory proposition, we will later introduce a uniform, perspicuous formulation of all forms of *'normal scientific progress'* and also of *'normal scientific setback'* (refutation by experience).

It appears that Kuhn even infected his opponents with his negligence. In particular, Lakatos' newly coined falsification concept, which bears the imprint of the Kuhnian challenge, has scarcely any similarity at all to the Popperian concept of the same name (cf. Section 16.4).

Actually, all of these problems concerning confirmation and testing raise their heads again as soon as the testing and confirmation of hypotheses, i.e., not theories, but theory *propositions*, are considered. Since neither the problems of confirmation for deterministic nor for statistical hypotheses belong to the themes dealt with in this book, they will only be touched upon in the chapter dealing with *holism*. But it should be noted here that several important aspects of holism are adopted as an immediate consequence of Sneed's continuation of Ramsey's approach and not first in relation to a reconstruction of Kuhn's ideas.

12 A Stronger Concept of Physical Theory; Holding a Theory in the Sneedian Sense

12.1 The Sneedian concept of a physical theory

The contents of Part II up to this point tend to foster a false conclusion which might be described as follows: "*the dynamic aspect of theory construction*, the genesis, growth, and decline of theories, *is closed to metascientific analysis*. There is no such thing as the 'logic of scientific discovery.' The philosopher of science must vacate these premises in favor of the psychologist, the sociologist, and the historian. The catchword must be the 'sociology and history of scientific discovery' instead of the 'logic of scientific discovery.' Since, for many, progress and growth appear to be the most interesting aspect of human knowledge, metascientific inquiry is thus disqualified from the investigation of one of its more fascinating and attractive aspects.

Actually the contents of Chapters 10 and 11 do urge such a conclusion. So far as T. S. Kuhn makes metascientific claims, these appear to lead to untenable, exaggerated theses according to which research processes are a highly irrational enterprise. On the other hand, since it is difficult to deny that he has a number of important things to say, it seems to be an unavoidable conclusion that indeed his *philosophical and epistemological* theses are false, but that he has made considerable contributions concerning the truth about the dynamics of theory construction—not in his capacity as philosopher, but *as historian and sociologist*.

The following chapters should serve to show that, and why, such a view is false by attempting a systematic analysis of *theory dynamics* which makes extensive use of Sneed's conceptual apparatus.

The most surprising result is the *metamorphosis in the Kuhnian version of the 'philosophy of science.'* His key statements will lose much of their apparent abstruseness. The suspicion of neoobscurantism will prove to be unfounded.

In the rest of Part II we will have to rely on pragmatic concepts even more heavily. The fundamental aim is a precise explication of the notion of *a person holding a theory*. 'Imbuing rationality' to Kuhn's conception of science will in large part be served by disposing of the *apparent contradiction* between the facts that *a person (or group of persons) holds a certain theory and nevertheless constantly changes his (their) opinion respecting this theory*. This we will regard as a contribution toward clarifying Kuhn's notion of ' normal science.' There will also be some remarks about 'revolutionary ' changes, under which two things may be understood: first, there is the *transition from pretheory to theory*; second, the *dislodging* of a theory having a certain basic mathematical structure and a certain 'paradigm' *by another one* with a different basic mathematical structure and 'paradigm.'

First we must recall that the details of the analyses in Part I were for the most part concerned with the logical-mathematical conceptual apparatus. The statements concerning the set I of intended applications were sparse. Even for a tenable physical theory it was merely required that $I \subseteq M_{pp}$ hold (i.e., that each intended application be a partial possible model of the theory). This will now be remedied by adding some conditions concerning the set I. These represent, then, necessary conditions for a *physical* theory. Two preliminary remarks, (A) and (B), should serve to clarify why this discussion has been postponed until now.

(A) In themselves these additional stipulations have no direct bearing on the problem of theory dynamics. In principle they could just as well have been introduced in Chapter 7. They were not introduced there because they would have been superfluous for the explications aimed at there. These were, we remember, a concept of *theory proposition*, permitting a precise model-theoretic characterization of the content of the central empirical claim of a theory, and a concept of *theory*, permitting the formulation of precise criteria for equivalence and reduction. For these two purposes the conceptual apparatus there was fully sufficient.

(B) Some of the additional conditions affecting the nature of I are not very exact. Moreover, subsequent developments will give a strong pragmatic thrust to the characterization of the set I. At the present stage of research it is impossible for pragmatic concepts to attain the level of precision usually expected of semantic, syntactic, and set-theoretic concepts. The qualification "at the present stage of research" should be understood in the sense that a future *systematic pragmatics* might be able to overcome this deficiency. In any case this is a second reason for *not* introducing these conditions in Part I. In the context of the analyses there it would have amounted to an unnecessary asymmetry of precision. The relatively exact concepts really needed there would have been burdened with a ballast of not only superfluous, but far less precise concepts.

> The realization that, contrary to the original hopes of many of its proponents, the metatheory of science must time and again resort to pragmatic concepts is presumably responsible for the widely held opinion that precise definition is, in this discipline, a hopeless, unfruitful project. Yet, even discounting the possibility of a future systematization of pragmatics just mentioned, this sort of a resignation is unfounded, mainly because the nonpragmatic aspects of metascientific problems are open to precise treatment. True, this claim will rightly be judged on the basis of the success the treatment achieves. And the following exposition will lay claim to just such a success: the clarification and resultant 'demythologizing' of holism as well as the exact exposition of

Sneed's and Kuhn's 'nonstatement view' of theories would have remained entirely impossible without the model-theoretic work in Part I.

The discussion of Kuhn's ideas to date as reported in Chapters 10 and 11 bears witness to the urgent necessity for such a clarification. For *without* it the opposed parties remain irreconcilable as shown by the criticisms of Kuhn and his replies to them. *Either* both critique and reply are conducted at an intuitive, metaphoric level, *or* the critique is more exactly formulated presupposing at least that notions like "theory," "normal science," "observational language," and "paradigm" can be rendered sufficiently precise. In the first case the exchange can be continued indefinitely without reaching any conclusion because both critique and reply are subject to a multitude of interpretations (e.g., Lakatos' criticism and Kuhn's reply; for the latter cf. especially [Growth], pp. 239–240). In the second case the critique usually misses the point because it tacitly incorporates the traditional, i.e., the *hitherto known* attempts at precision which prove to be inadequate. Kuhn's replies are then for the most part likewise unsatisfactory, because he forgoes explication of his key notions creating the impression that he acquiesces in the presuppositions of his critics (e.g., the criticism of I. Scheffler and Kuhn's replies).

Sneed lists three necessary conditions which the second member *I* of a theory $\langle K, I \rangle$ has to satisfy in order to be considered a *theory of physics*.

(1) The first condition is that the elements of *I* must be *physical systems*. This notion is sufficiently broad—one could also say sufficiently inexact—to allow a very large number of entities to qualify as intended applications of a theory of physics, i.e., as that "about which the theory is talking."

An important *formal* aspect should not, however, be overlooked. Sneed's requirement implies that physical systems can *never be mere domains of individuals*. They must always be objects *which are described in a certain way*, namely, *by means of nontheoretical functions* rather than qualitatively. In our minitheory, for example, the systems in question are ordered pairs, each consisting of a domain of individuals and a nontheoretical function. In the case of particle mechanics an application consists of individuals *whose position is measured by a position function* while their other properties are ignored as being irrelevant. Thus, a theory always talks about *individuals-cum-nontheoretical-functions*.

Which conditions are *sufficient* to qualify something as a physical system is as yet an unresolved problem. In our day, when the problem of evolution is conceived of as a problem concerning the 'evolution of matter,' i.e., as the problem of an exact scientific description of the transition from macromolecule to the first living cell, one can no longer appeal to a theory of a stratified world in order to characterize physical objects. But even the more humble belief of such pioneer philosophers of science as N. R. Campbell, namely, that physical objects could be 'ontologically distinguished' by characterizing them as objects having relational properties *which can be metricized*, must be discarded in today's world. Against it speaks the fact that

163

quantitative concepts are with ever increasing frequency being successfully applied in the social sciences and psychology, i.e., in sciences certainly not investigating 'physical systems.' For the time being a scientist must rely on his intuition and experience in deciding what a physical system is.

(2) As was exhaustively discussed in connection with refining the Ramsey method, specifically the transition from (II) to (III$_b$), the role of constraints consists of establishing certain kinds of cross-connections or bonds between the various applications of the theory. These bonds are such that from known values of nontheoretical functions in certain applications unknown values in other applications may be inferred. In this case the individual domains of the applications, i.e., of the partial possible models involved, must overlap. It makes good sense to place a minimal requirement on such bonds, namely, that the individual domains of any two applications be linked by a chain of individual domains of partial possible models in such a way that the intersection of any two successive domains in the chain is not empty.

Let $\mathfrak{D}$ be the class of individual domains of the elements I and assume that for any $A, B \in \mathfrak{D}$ there exists a sequence $D_1, D_2, \ldots, D_n$ of elements of $\mathfrak{D}$ such that $D_1 = A$, $D_n = B$, and $D_i \cap D_{i+1} \neq \varnothing$ for all $i = 1, 2, \ldots, n - 1$. We will then say that *A is linked with B.*

(3) As a last condition Sneed requires the attribute of *homogeneity*. The intuitive idea here is that *various* partial possible models can be 'combined' or 'put together' to produce a new and larger possible application of the theory. This idea actually does seem to be quite important. Unfortunately, however, its precise definition presents considerable difficulty.

> To illustrate, suppose I to contain only partial possible models of a mathematical formulation of hydromechanics. Some elements of I are, e.g., systems of fluids flowing through pipes. Other elements of I are electrical lines. While parts of systems of the first kind can be combined with parts of other systems of the *same kind* to produce a system *of this kind*, and likewise in the second case, we *cannot* combine parts of a system of fluids with parts of an electrical system and obtain a system of either the one kind or the other, the reason being that homogeneity is *lacking*.
>
> But things are somewhat more complicated than this example suggests, which is why an exact explication of the homogeneity concept promises not to be so simple. For instance, why should parts of fluid systems not prove to be parts of electrical systems *too*? Plainly any theoretician would shrink from formulating constraints connecting such heterogeneous possible models. Perhaps he would say that the properties which an object has as part of an electrical system need 'have nothing to do' with those it possesses as a component of a system of fluids.

Sneed conjectures that the homogeneity stipulation tacitly *appeals to a theory underlying the theory being considered.* In the case of classical particle mechanics a *theory of length measurement* would, for example, constitute such an underlying theory for the nontheoretical position function. (Should several nontheoretical functions occur in the theory under consideration, there might accordingly be several such underlying theories.) The question of how such an underlying theory may be characterized precisely takes us, however, beyond our present scope. Such a theory is *no longer a theory of physics*. It is (in part or entirely) a *qualitative theory*, i.e., a theory which does not, or not *only*, describe quantitative attributes with the help of functions, but has *only*, or *also*, axioms concerning nonquantitative attributes. (For a more detailed discussion of various further difficulties cf. Sneed, [Mathematical Physics], pp. 257–260.)

Using the three properties just introduced, of which as yet only the second is precisely characterized (and that only in the sense of a not entirely unproblematic *minimal* condition which will often be too weak), we can strengthen the initial theory concept. For reasons already given we will work with the concept of a weak theory; i.e., we take a theory to be an ordered pair consisting of a core K and a set I of possible intended applications.

D26 X *is a Sneedian-type theory of physics* only if there exists a K and an I such that

(1) $X = \langle K, I \rangle$;
(2) $K = \langle M_p, M_{pp}, r, M, C \rangle$ is a core for a theory of mathematical physics;
(3) $I \subseteqq M_{pp}$;
(4) each element of I is a *physical system*;
(5) if $\mathfrak{D}$ is a class containing exactly the individual domains of the elements of I, then for any two elements D_i and D_j of $\mathfrak{D}$, D_i *is linked with* D_j;
(6) I is a *homogeneous* set of physical systems.

12.2 What does "a person holds a theory of physics" mean in the context of the 'nonstatement view' of theories?

When we ask a question like what it means that a person or group of persons, e.g., a research team, *has a theory*, *accepts a theory*, or *holds a theory*, we are undoubtedly turning to a *pragmatic context*. Pragmatic circumstances have already been explicitly incorporated into the theoretical–nontheoretical dichotomy, and, as future research may show, perhaps implicitly into stipulations (4) and (6) of the last definition too. Nevertheless it must be said that the concept of physical theory just introduced is, in an exactly specifiable sense, *not* a pragmatic concept, in contrast to the Kuhnian theory concept to be introduced in Chapter 15. It is not pragmatic in the sense that when X is a theory in accord with D26, it makes no difference 'how scientists or other persons relate to it.' *X* can be thought to be right. It can be accepted provisionally ('until refuted') for certain purposes—be this only for 'purposes of strict testing in the Popperian sense.' It can be the object of critical study. It can even be regarded as false or so absurd as not to merit 'serious critical consideration.' All these are examples of various pragmatic contexts.

At this point one is reminded of Spinoza's dictum *omnis determinatio est negatio*. On the basis of the 'statement view' of theories the answer would have to be quite different, than on the basis of the theory concept D26. Consider briefly what, roughly, would have to be said according to the traditional conception.

Since according to this conception a theory must be regarded as a class of sentences, *that which* a person holds is just such a class. As a *rational* person one cannot entertain an unfounded belief in the elements of this class. He must have *good reasons* for his convictions. As an expert in his field it is not even enough to have *just any* good reason; they must be good reasons *of a very particular kind*. When a scientist uses a theory from a neighboring discipline, the fact that all his colleagues from this discipline 'believe in this theory' undoubtedly constitutes a good reason for doing so too. But regardless of who these authorities may be, such a belief would surely be toppled by Bacon's *idola theatri* criterion if this reason was really the one given as justification for believing in the theory. The special reasons must be *the same ones* on which the authorities themselves rely. These are reasons characterized by phrases like "the theory is solidly confirmed by the available empirical data," "the theory has stood the test of experience" or "the theory is well supported by the facts."

A big disadvantage to the view sketched in the last paragraph becomes immediately apparent when one considers matters from a historical perspective. One must interpret each shift in conviction concerning the theory *as a change in the theory itself*. There is no room left for the idea that *during a period of time scientists' convictions are continually changing although these scientists hold the same theory for the entire period.*

Perhaps one should be more cautious and say that on the basis of the traditional view of theories as sets of sentences there is no room for a *natural* interpretation of this idea. One could try for example to distinguish, in relation to the whole system, *subclasses* or *subsystems*, as *subtheories*, from *fundamental laws* so that it could be said: "this and this subtheory was changed, but the fundamental laws were retained." We need not pursue this line of thought further. For reasons given in Part I, *the entire empirical content* of a theory is exhibited by the *central empirical claim of the theory*, i.e., by a simple cohesive claim of the form (III_b), (V), or (VI). And *these* sentences will, *and must*, change in the course of time when convictions concerning the theory change, although we will nevertheless want to maintain that *the theory itself has not changed.*

The conceptual apparatus of Part I permits us to give such ideas *a completely natural interpretation*. Beliefs concerning a theory can change in at least three respects *without changes in the theory itself*: (1) *new applications* for the theory may be discovered; (2) *new laws* may be postulated for certain, established applications; (3) some applications may be placed under *additional constraints*. Corresponding to these three ways of 'augmenting conviction' are three possibilities for 'diminishing' it: namely, by eliminating certain possible applications from the class of intended applications of the theory, by rejecting special laws, and by rejecting additional constraints.[49] The bedrock under the shifting beliefs is that basic component of the mathematical structure of a theory which we have called the *core*.

There is, however, still a difficulty here. We not only want to say that the *core* remains the same, but that the *theory* $\langle K, I \rangle$ consisting of a core *and a set of possible intended applications I* remains the same. To this end we assume that a '*typical group*' of intended applications remains constant over the course of time. A detailed discussion of this last point must be postponed for now. The concept of a Kuhnian theory, to be introduced in Chapter 15, contains two important additional conditions. First, there are detailed specifications concerning the 'typical group' of intended applications remaining constant over the course of time. Dealing with this point requires an explicit *paradigm* concept. Second, there is an additional assumption about the '*historical origins*' of a theory which finds its expression in a ' first successful application of the theory.' The first of these additional conditions will serve to mitigate the initial vagueness of the 'typical group of *I*,' at least as far as the definition of paradigm allows.

In order to ensure a standard reference concerning the empirical content of a physical theory, the *central empirical claim* of a theory will hitherto always be understood as a sentence of form (VI). That the theory remains constant while the beliefs of the theoreticians shift can now be succinctly expressed as follows: *A theory in the Sneedian sense remains constant, but is used at various times to assert different central empirical claims* (or the strong theory propositions corresponding to them).

This idea can be regarded as the essence of 'holding a theory.' Only we must formulate it more clearly. As we know, on the basis of the considerations

---

[49] The rejection of *general* constraints, on the other hand, should *not* be included here. If, for example, at one time or another we began to work with a mass function *which was not an extensive quantity*, one would presumably not maintain that classical mechanics had indeed been retained with 'the addition of the new discovery that the mass function was not an extensive quantity.' One is much more apt to talk of a *new theory* having taken the place of the old one.

Presumably one can only distinguish between *special* laws and *special* constraints from the *logical* view, because *de facto* changes of type (2) and (3) almost always appear concurrently. (Cf. the example with Hooke's law in Section 6.2. The values of K and d are in each instance regarded as 'constant properties' of the spring connecting both particles, i.e., understood to be constraints.)

in Section 7.3, there is exactly one strong theory proposition corresponding to every claim of a theory, namely, the proposition which it expresses. When a theory in the present sense remains constant, so does in particular its core while the *expansions* of the core along with the claims of the theory vary.

If a physical theory consists of the pair $\langle K, I \rangle$ and $E_1, E_2, \ldots, E_i, \ldots$ are the various expansions of K used at various times $t_1, t_2, \ldots, t_i, \ldots$ for making claims of form (VI), the foregoing can, using the application operation $\mathbb{A}_e$, be described *without any reference to linguistic entities* as follows: *the theory $\langle K, I \rangle$ remains unchanged; the theory propositions $I \in \mathbb{A}_e(E_i)$ constructed with its help and thought to be true vary with the time t_i.*

Suppose for a moment that we lived in an 'epistemically perfect world.' This is *not* a world in which everything knowable is actually known (i.e., not 'the best of all possible epistemic worlds'). It is a world *in which scientific progress proceeds in the way that we wish it would*. This ideal would be realized when nothing believed at a certain time would have to be rejected later. A theory is *successively refined* by conjoining more and more new laws and additional constraints permitting the formulation of ever stronger statements. The *empirical content* of claims of form (VI) increases. In the propositional (nonlinguistic) idiom this means that the theory propositions $I \in \mathbb{A}_e(E_i)$ believed over the course of time satisfy the condition:

$$\mathbb{A}_e(E_1) \supseteq \mathbb{A}_e(E_2) \supseteq \cdots \supseteq \mathbb{A}_e(E_i) \supseteq \cdots.$$

In *our* world things aren't always so neat. *Physicists can make mistakes.* If an error occurs in restricting the expanded core E_i, in use at time t_i, to yield expanded core E_{i+1} at time t_{i+1}, it may turn out that $I \notin \mathbb{A}_e(E_{i+1})$ despite $I \in \mathbb{A}_e(E_i)$. This sort of error may, to mention only the most important case, be discovered by *falsification* of one or more special laws used in restricting E_i to E_{i+1}.

All of these remarks continue to hold when we subsequently strengthen the concept of a Sneedian theory to that of a Kuhnian theory by adding further conditions as already indicated. If the reader is prepared to accept this for a moment, he will also see, so far as he has been able to follow the discussion, *exactly how Popper's falsificationism can be reconciled with T. S. Kuhn's conception of science*. Falsification, namely, concerns only *special laws*; hence, the theoretician is only forced to retract the attempted restriction of an E_i to E_{i+1}. He can indeed continue to believe $I \in \mathbb{A}_e(E_i)$, must, however, at the same time acknowledge $I \notin \mathbb{A}_e(E_{i+1})$. *The theory $\langle K, I \rangle$ is in no way affected by this sort of failure on the part of the theoretician. Continued belief in the theory on the part of the scientist despite this failure is in no way irrational*, contrary to the *prima facie* impression.

Let us return now to the task of explicating the notion "holding a theory." A first, necessary condition, if a person is to hold a theory $\langle K, I \rangle$, is that this person believe certain propositions $I \in \mathbb{A}_e(E)$ for expansions E of K. For each time span t under consideration, E_t will be understood as the *strongest* expansion which the person possesses for formulating such a proposition. Thus this proposition runs $I \in \mathbb{A}_e(E_t)$. This is the strongest (strong) theory proposition which a person can assert at time t.

The convictions of this person should not be unreasonable. Since we are, however, not going to discuss confirmation problems in the present context, the 'certain kind of good reasons' a person must have for believing a proposition of the form $I \in \mathbb{A}_e(E)$ (or a claim) will be expressed simply by the phrase "the proposition $I \in \mathbb{A}_e(E)$ is *supported by the observable data* available to the person." The relation of support by observable data will remain *undefined*.

The following remarks should help, though, to prevent any misunderstanding concerning this relation.

> *Remark 1.* Leaving this concept undefined here is, of course, perfectly compatible with the fact that we regard it as an important concept *in need of explication.*

> *Remark 2.* Nothing is implied as to whether the concept should ultimately be introduced as 'qualitative' or 'quantitative,' 'inductivisitic' or 'deductivistic,' or neither 'inductivistic' nor 'deductivisitic.'

> *Remark 3.* The possibility of incorporating such a stipulation into the present as well as the subsequent 'Kuhnian' concept of holding a theory shows that there are no grounds for suspecting, as is occasionally done, that Kuhn's conception of science represents a neo-obscurantism or, at the very least, a flagrant contradiction of every form of empiricism be it ever so liberal. In any case such complaints are unfounded under the assumption that the route to a rational reconstruction of a fundamental Kuhnian idea being taken here is 'in principle accepted.'

D27   *A person p holds, in the Sneedian sense, the physical theory $T = \langle K, I \rangle$ at time t* (abbreviated $H_S(p, \langle K, I \rangle, t)$) iff

(1) $\langle K, I \rangle$ is a Sneedian-type theory of physics (cf. D26);
(2) there exists an expansion E_t of K such that p believes $I \in \mathbb{A}_e(E_t)$ at time t. E_t is the strongest such expansion of K in the sense that $\wedge E[(E$ is an expansion of K such that p believes $I \in \mathbb{A}_e(E)$ at t and p has observable data supporting this proposition) $\rightarrow E_t \subseteq E]$;
(3) p has observable data supporting the proposition $I \in \mathbb{A}_e(E_t)$;
(4) p believes at time t that there is an expansion E of K such that
   (a) $I \in \mathbb{A}_e(E)$;
   (b) $\mathbb{A}_e(E) \subset \mathbb{A}_e(E_t)$.

(1) says that the weak concept of physical theory is being used. (2) guarantees that *p* believes at least one of the theory propositions that can be constructed with the help of the theory *T.* The additional stipulation in (2) guarantees that of all the theory propositions which *p* believes, $I \in \mathbb{A}_e(E_t)$ has the *strongest factual content.* (3) lays down the minimal condition concerning empirical support which was mentioned without being explicated. The fourth stipulation could be said to contain *p's belief in progress.* This belief finds its expression in *p's* conviction that his theory will be strengthened in the future.

To (4) it might be objected that it ought to be a physicist's prerogative to believe that this theory cannot be nontrivially restricted any further and still yield true claims. In this extreme case of 'maximal belief' we surely cannot deny that the physicist holds the theory! While this and similar objections must certainly be conceded in certain contexts, it is the *goal of the explication* which justifies this stipulation here. What we are after is a clarification of progress in *normal science* (or *normal scientific progress*) in contradistinction to '*scientific revolutions.*' The fourth stipulation in D27 should serve to incorporate an essential aspect of the *belief in normal progress,* i.e., of the *belief in progress without scientific revolutions.* Part of this belief is the conviction that *while retaining the conceptual fundament of the theory,* i.e., the *core* of the theory, it will in the course of time be possible to increase the precision of the statements about the physical systems to which the theory is applied. One could also say the conviction that in the future we will always be able to better explain the behavior of the individuals belonging to these systems.

---

13   What Is a Paradigm?

13.1 Wittgenstein's concept of paradigm; Wittgenstein's game example

The unbiased reader of T. S. Kuhn's book, [Revolutions], who is also somewhat acquainted with Wittgenstein's philosophy will at first get the impression that Kuhn's concept of a paradigm has little or nothing in common with Wittgenstein's. On the other hand, in the fifth chapter of this book Kuhn refers specifically to Wittgenstein, in particular to Wittgenstein's discussion of the word "game" in Section 66ff. of the *Philosophical Investiga-*

tions. This indicates that there must be some sort of connection. Ferreting it out is, however, no easy task.

We will proceed methodically, first taking a closer look at Wittgenstein's example. Then we will consider how much of this can be applied to Kuhn's notion. It turns out that Kuhn's analogy represents *only a half-truth. Only a single component* of his notion of paradigm, which is much more complex than Wittgenstein's, can be compared to the latter, and Wittgenstein's remarks about ' *family resemblances*,' etc., are *only* applicable to this one component. This component for which the analogy holds is exactly what we called *the set of I intended applications of a theory.* The remaining components of Kuhn's notion of paradigm can for the most part be subjected to exact rational reconstruction. Since there is no 'vagueness' adhering to these components like that attached to the notion of game, the analogy to Wittgenstein's notion of paradigm atrophies where they are concerned.

The activities called "games" were used by Wittgenstein to undermine the belief that where *one* concept is given, *one* property, too, must exist which is common to all and only those things falling under this concept. Between the activities called "games" there are only occasional, overlapping, crisscross resemblances bereft of continuity as is the case between members of a family. Hence the designation "family resemblance."

Let us analyze this more closely. In attempting to isolate the notion of game one will first try to *list typical cases.* During an initial 'period of uncertainty' this list will be modified by additions and subtractions. New experiences, personal and otherwise, gleaned, for example, from observations made while traveling or from reading travelogues and histories will serve to extend this list. Some activities originally included will be dropped after closer inspection because, for instance, of their magical-religious significance, the seriousness of the consequences they produce, or the legal-economic 'implications' involved. The uncertain phase can, however, only be terminated in one direction, so to speak. After preliminary considerations a '*minimal list*' will be arrived at. More and more new games can be added to it on the basis of new knowledge, but one will refuse to reduce it further. Let S be the extension of "game," and S_0 the minimal list. This list S_0, satisfying the condition $S_0 \subseteqq S$, will be called the *list of paradigms for game.* The method based on specifying such a list will be called *the method of paradigmatic examples.* Concerning the relationship of S_0 to S the following five conditions hold:

(1) S_0 is *effectively extensionally given*; i.e., the elements of this set are enumerated in a list.

(2) It is decided never to delete an element from S_0, i.e., never to deny an element of this set the attribute of being a game.

(3) The elements of S_0 can have common properties. In the present case, for instance, this holds for the property of *being a human activity.* (Which,

incidentally, shows that it is not correct to assume one can find no 'continuity' between paradigmatic examples as Wittgenstein's remarks would seem to suggest. The crucial point is that these properties, if known, represent only necessary, not sufficient conditions for inclusion in the class of games.) These properties are *at best necessary*, but *not sufficient* for belonging to S. In general, the elements of a list of paradigmatic examples can have one or more, even infinitely many properties in common. But no matter how many there are and how many of these we regard as necessary conditions for membership in the larger class, *we cannot derive a sufficient condition for membership from them.*

(4) A sufficient condition for membership in S involves an *ineradicable vagueness*. If an individual not belonging to S_0 is to be considered a member of S, it must share a 'considerable' or 'significant' number of properties with all, or 'nearly all,' elements of S_0.

(5) The sense in which the vagueness mentioned in (4) is ineradicable—even when "nearly all" is unambiguously specified per convention—can be *precisely* given (which goes a step further than Wittgenstein). *For every single element* of $S - S_0$ one must indeed be able to give a list of properties which this element has in common with all or 'nearly all' individuals in S_0. As opposed to this, however, one can present no finite list of properties ensuring membership in S. We can go a step further and say that *there is not even a finite list of lists of properties such that membership in S is guaranteed for an individual possessing all the properties enumerated in one of these lists.* Speaking in terms of set theory: not even a finite class of sets of properties is sufficient to guarantee membership in S for objects not already in S_0. Thus we have here a combination of *precision concerning a necessary condition* with *a lack of precision concerning a sufficient condition* for membership in S.

> On this basis, Wittgenstein's remark at the end of Section 67 of the *Philosophical Investigations* is incorrect. He postulates someone who argues: "Thus there is something common to all these constructions—namely the disjunction of all their common properties," and himself replies: "You are only playing with words here. One might as well say something runs through the whole thread—namely the continuous overlapping of those fibers." Apart from the fact that it is debatable whether or not a (real!) disjunction of common properties represents a mere play with words, one could say that Wittgenstein *concedes too much* with his reply: namely, that there exists a finite disjunction. He could have been more radical and replied roughly as follows: "Even if I let you get away with calling the continuous overlapping of fibers 'something running through the whole thread,' your comparison fails. You suppose, namely, that *the thread is composed of a finite number of fibers.* But there is no comparable finite class of sets of properties ensuring membership in S."

13.2 The adaptation of Wittgenstein's paradigm concept to the domain of applications of a physical theory: the basic set I_0 of paradigmatic intended applications

Let $T = \langle K, I \rangle$ be a weak theory. In order to pin down one important aspect of Kuhn's paradigm concept we will, *in analogy to Wittgenstein's example*, take up the idea of *characterizing the set I of intended applications by means of a basic set of paradigms*. I corresponds, thus, to S of the last section and the set I_0 to S_0.

In the next chapter we will, following Sneed, make a systematic survey of the ways of introducing the set I as well as the members of its elements. The case where I is *intensionally* rather than extensionally *specified* will prove to be particularly important. But this alone does not serve to establish a connection with the paradigm concept. For as is well known, the usual method of determining a set intensionally consists in specifying a property possessed by exactly the elements of the set. Assume now that we require our set I of intended applications of a theory to be determined in this way.

Such a demand has two disadvantages: it meets with a *great*, perhaps in most cases *insurmountable difficulty*, and it has a *fatal consequence*. The difficulty lies in the fact that as a rule physicists simply are not able to name a property both *necessary and sufficient* for membership in I. In particular, one must bear in mind that they do not have 'time to consider' this problem; i.e., they are not prepared to make a lengthy, detailed search for this defining property. The theory should serve for making empirical claims. In terms of our reconstruction this means that after having proposed a theory the physicist must be able to give the *central empirical claim of this theory*. Since, however, this claim can only be formulated after the intended application is known, the claim cannot even be formulated under our assumption.

Still more telling is the second disadvantage. Assume for a moment that the physicist has a property defining I. As soon, then, as he is confronted with an element of I, i.e., a physical system (partial possible model) which his theory T is supposed to explain, but in fact does *not*, he must *discard the theory as empirically falsified*. Here we have arrived at one of those junctures where the '*deep difference of opinion*' Kuhn so often emphasizes between himself and Popper, as well as Popper's followers, begins.

Seen from the vantage point of Popper's brand of rationalism, this consequence represents no disadvantage at all. *As a rational person* a scientist should be prepared to make this sacrifice. The degree of inclination against rejecting that which has been empirically refuted is, in this view, a good barometer for the degree of irrationality in the personality of the scientist. Kuhn's claim that *this sort of falsification has never appeared in the history of science* fails to impress his 'rationalistic opponents' according to whom it

173

indicates at best how far the *flesh and blood* scientist falls short of the rational-istic ideal.

This conflict between 'real' and 'ideal' is by no means the last word, though. The situation can be interpreted in a way which vindicates Kuhn without having to limit the vindication to historical facts. What we mean is that the historically documented behavior of physicists can be reconstrued *as rational behavior*. Thus, given the choice between the alternatives presented by Popper and Kuhn, we will opt for Kuhn's. Not because we prefer 'un-reasonable' history to reason in the 'contest between reason and history,' but for the simple reason that the reconstruction of Kuhn's view is *the more adequate*. And indeed more adequate in the sense that it is compatible with historical fact *and* open to rational reconstruction (which Kuhn himself, however, neglected). The opposing view can also be rationally reconstructed, is, however, historically ill-fitted.

The reason that Popper's conception fits poorly with historical fact can perhaps be most succinctly described as follows: *no physicist seems ever to have let himself in for the risk of falsification which would result from explicitly defining a property necessary and sufficient for membership in I*. To hold this against the physicists is, seen from Kuhn's angle, to espouse an *exaggerated* rather than a sensible *rationalism*.

Thus, we will assume that I is intensionally characterized in formal analogy to the pattern set by Wittgenstein's intensional description of "game." The scientist has then explicitly extensionally presented I_0 (by means of a list) *as the set of paradigmatic examples*. Further, he knows that $I_0 \subseteq I$. He also accepts the kind of inevitable 'vagueness' associated with the paradigmatic determination of a set described in Section 13.1 (4) and (5). With this vagueness, however, he purchases a tremendous advantage: namely, *his theory is immunized against the sort of falsification just described*. This advantage is so extraordinarily great because Kuhn is presumably right in assuming that *without this immunity every theory at any time must be regarded as refuted*—at least if one has retained a realistic eye for *human limitations* in the area of theory construction to date.

This immunity does *not* extend to the paradigmatic examples. Should certain elements of I_0 stubbornly resist explanation by T, T would have to be dropped in the end. (Later we will have more to say about the '*period of grace for the theory*' implied by 'stubborn resistance.') When, on the other hand, an element of $I - I_0$ stubbornly resists the theory, *the theoretician can decide to drop this element from the set of intended applications*.

It is absolutely necessary to understand clearly that *this immunity has nothing to do with irrationality*. Thus, it by no means falls under Popper's notion of an immunization *strategy* via *ad hoc* conventions. Even when one is not prepared to acknowledge the second disadvantage of the method of specifying a property mentioned above (is, thus, prepared to accept what we called an 'exaggerated rationalism'), there still could be no talk of a strategy, because, for the first reason mentioned, the physicist usually *can* do nothing other than introduce I via a set I_0 of paradigmatic examples. This is true in particular of classical particle mechanics. The same paradigmatic examples still hold for it as were already acknowledged to be applications of his theory in Newton's own time: namely, the solar system and various subsystems of it (Earth–moon, Jupiter and its moons), several comets, free-falling bodies near the Earth's surface, tides, and pendulums.

We can now easily discern a modification that will have to be made in D27 if we want to incorporate Kuhn's notion of a paradigmatic characterization of the intended applications into the concept of holding a theory. Concerning the strongest expansion E_t introduced in D27 (2), it must be required that the person p believes $I_0 \in \mathbb{A}_e(E_t)$ at time t.

What held for games not belonging to the set of paradigmatic examples now holds in perfect analogy for the physical systems belonging to $I - I_0$. The elements of this difference set must have certain *resemblances* to the paradigm examples, i.e., to the elements of I_0. Such resemblances can also encourage the physicist to be on the lookout for ever new applications of his theory, or more precisely, ever new physical systems which can be taken as possible applications, and, as he hopes, eventually applications of his theory. But again there is not only no list of properties *sufficient* for ensuring membership in I; there is not even a finite *class of* property lists such that the possession of exactly the properties from one of these finite number of lists will guarantee membership in I. Not even the number of properties sufficient for such membership can be exactly determined.

As in the case of games there is here, too, a certain vagueness adhering to the stipulation of 'what really belongs to I.' But, as we had to point out that there is nothing irrational about immunity, we must here, too, expressly emphasize that *this vagueness does not mean that the assignment of elements to I is purely a matter of whim.*

Let us see why this is so. To this end we will separate the newly 'observed' physical systems[50] into two types: the *unproblematic* and the *problematic*. To the first type belong those systems about which there is no trouble deciding whether or not they belong to I. The second type consists of those systems about which we are not sure. Only when a physicist settles such a case by an *ad hoc* decision would the objection "vagueness implies caprice" be justified. This, however, he will not do. He will instead *investigate further*. And indeed these further investigations will not only involve the new potential candidates for I, they will *also* include *the paradigm examples*. It could be that such 'two-track' investigations uncover *new properties* which had as yet attracted no attention, but whose consideration now permits the same clear decision to be reached as in cases of the first type. In other words,

[50] It should not be forgotten that, logically speaking, physical systems do not consist of individuals alone, but of individuals-*cum-nontheoretical-functions* which serve to render the empirical descriptions of these individuals in a quantitative language.

further investigations have the effect of transforming what *prima facie* appeared to be a problematic case into an unproblematic one. The first type absorbs the second.

It is, of course, conceivable that this procedure does not always work. A physicist *could* become convinced that further empirical investigations of the question of membership in *I* are useless. *At most* such cases would require an arbitrary decision. Hence *at most* it would be correct to maintain that *the set I_0 of paradigm examples produces several sets $I_1, I_2, \ldots$ of intended applications instead of one unambiguously determined set.* These sets would result from the decisions involving the unclear marginal cases just mentioned.

But 'unclear marginal cases' need not necessarily lead to this sort of resignation. What other possibility is there besides an arbitrary decision? The somewhat startling answer is that if the scientist is convinced that further empirical investigations are useless, *he can let the theory itself decide about membership in I.* We have already seen that in the case of intensional characterization by means of paradigm examples physical systems can be deleted from *I* if they stubbornly resist application of the theory.

Although we have no *strict proof* that the combination of these two methods—new 'two-track' empirical investigations and use of the theory itself in deciding unclear cases—will always succeed, Kuhn and Sneed are presumably right in supposing that they always function where physics is concerned. If so, we obtain the important consequence that *despite mere paradigmatic determination of the set of intended applications by means of a set of examples I_0, a single set I of real applications will be found.*

Furthermore, we have seen that *using a theory as a means for determining its own applications* involves no antirational moment. The suspicion of auto-verification, were it to appear here, would be groundless. More exactly, we must say that it is the first member of a theory $T = \langle K, I \rangle$ and its expansions which have, under the circumstances outlined here, a decisive influence on the final selection of *I*. Talk of autoverification is thus groundless, because cores and expanded cores are simply not the kind of entities of which "verified" or "falsified" can be sensibly predicated.

Before completing the remarks about Kuhn's paradigm concept, we will summarize the three results obtained so far. They are especially important because all three help to make it plain that indeed certain of Kuhn's views ' sound irrational' when one assumes a traditional stance, but that in truth there is nothing irrational about them.

(1) Characterizing the intended applications with the help of a list of paradigms involves in principle an unavoidable potential vagueness. But *this vagueness does not imply arbitrariness in decisions about membership in I.*

(2) The nonextensional description of the domain of applications of a theory *renders the theory immune to falsification.* Indeed, this immunity means *reduced risks* for the theoretical physicist, but is *no symptom of unreasonable, irrational behavior.*

(3) The fact that *a theory itself serves as a means for determining its own applications* does *not* mean that refuge is being sought in an *obscure method of autoverification*. On the contrary, this procedure is methodologically flawless and has, furthermore, the positive effect of minimizing, if not eliminating, the vagueness adhering to the method of paradigmatic examples. Besides, it offers the only possibility for combining the method of paradigmatic examples with the delineation of *exactly one* set of intended applications.

13.3 Kuhn's paradigm concept

Section 13.2 should have served to build a bridge between the Kuhnian and Wittgensteinian notions of "paradigm"—*but no more than this*. It would undoubtedly be a mistake *to identify* Kuhn's notion with the idea of determining a class of intended applications of a theory by a set of paradigm examples. The outline in Chapter 10 as well as the criticisms of Chapter 11 have certainly shown that Kuhn has something *essentially more comprehensive* in mind. This is presumably also the reason that there did not, at first, seem to be any connection between Kuhn's notion and Wittgenstein's.

Kuhn's notion can be split up into at least three fully heterogeneous classes of components. Two factors are decisive for this division: (1) what is, and what is not, amenable to precise rational reconstruction, and (2) what does, and what does not, belong to the field of the philosophy of science.

*Class I: Possible objects of precise
logical-metascientific reconstruction*

Here we must differentiate between the topics treated in this volume and those not included among its themes.

(1) The paradigm of a theory as Kuhn understands it includes part of the mathematical structure of this physical theory, indeed, that part remaining *unchanged* during the vicissitudes of 'normal scientific progress.' Since expanded cores are constantly changing (e.g., through the introduction and rejection of special laws and additional constraints), this leaves only two components of the mathematical fine structure as parts of the paradigm: *frames* and *cores*. Since this point is discussed in detail in Chapters 14–16, we will pursue it no further here.

(2) Theory dynamics should not be equated with scientific dynamics. There are changes in empirical sciences which do not affect the basic structure of a theory, at least not directly. Such are, for instance, the observation of new sorts of phenomena, the discovery of confirming or of negative data for hypothetically assumed special laws and additional constraints, or the appearance of new scientific explanations produced with the help of laws and theories already available. The problems arising here must be systematically investigated by a theory of confirmation eventually supplemented by a theory of the rules for accepting and rejecting hypotheses (test theory).

There are many indications that various of Kuhn's statements concerning paradigms belong to this group. One example would be the idea that a 'paradigm' is only declared invalid when there is some other candidate ready to take its place. It appears to me that a part of the reconstructable background for this and similar ideas consists of the assumption that, at least in the case of 'revolutionary progress,' only *a concept of confirmation making explicit reference to rival alternatives* will be useful. (This corresponds to the thesis I have propounded in [Statistik], Part III: namely, that only a comparative support concept referring to rival alternative hypotheses is useful for judging statistical hypotheses.)

Class II: The set I of intended applications determined by paradigmatic examples

Concerning this point everything essential has already been said in Section 13.2. It is *only this* class which justifies Kuhn's appeal to *Wittgenstein*. From the very beginning we have conceived the weak theory concept $T = \langle K, I \rangle$ so that its first member falls into Class I, its second into Class II. (The latter holds, of course, only if the set I is determined according to the method described in 4.b. The next Section offers a systematic survey of all *conceivable* methods.)

Class III: Those components of Kuhnian paradigms whose study belongs to the psychology and sociology, not the metatheory of science

A cursory glance at Kuhn's work, [Revolutions], gives the impression that most of his statements about paradigms concern *this* aspect. Not so. Consider, for instance, the 'psychologistically depicted' characteristic of paradigms brought into play at the beginning of Chapter 3 in [Revolutions]: namely, the *promise of success* whose realization is the task of normal science. While this surely has its psychological–sociological aspect *too*, some of what Kuhn means by it, indeed a thoroughly essential aspect, can be expressed in the logically precise language of the conceptual world of Class I. That proposing a new paradigm brings with it a promise of success can, within the framework of a rational reconstruction, be translated into the assertion that a theoretician presenting a frame and a core for a theory *prophesies successful expansions of the core.* And the statement asserting that the task of realizing the promised success falls to normal science can be translated into the claim that *the success of normal scientific endeavor consists in perfecting suitable expanded cores.*

Some caution was exercised above in claiming that Kuhn's paradigm concept included *at least* these three classes of components. Detailed investigation as well as future progress in the metatheory of science could distinguish still *further components.* It is, for example, not entirely clear whether

Kuhn's statements in Chapter 3 *et passim* concerning the compilation of data and experimentation in normal science can be exhaustively divided into sociological and confirmational aspects. It could, for example, turn out that a tenable *theory of experiment* can only be developed within the context of an as yet nonexistent *systematic pragmatics*. In fact there are already any number of signs indicating that the philosophy of science will in the future need more than the logical (syntactic, semantic, and set-theoretic) conceptual inventory it has as yet used. (For such indications in the context of explanation and of confirmation, cf. the last sections of Stegmüller [Erklärung], Chapter 1, and Part IV of [Statistik].)

Or consider Kuhn's views according to which a paradigm cannot be adequately described with words, nor equated with rules, concepts, theories, and points of view; according to which it can be grasped and identified without allowing itself to be fully interpreted and rationally reconstructed. It is not yet clear to me whether all of these involve only the psychologically comprehensible intuitive backdrop of frames, cores, their expansions, and their intuitive implications, or whether they have to do with the *metaphysical background* of physical theories, which he also mentions at various places. Should this latter be the case, Kuhn's paradigm concept would, counting the possibility mentioned in the last paragraph, involve not less than five fully heterogeneous components.

In addition much of what has been said about the concepts included in subclass (1) of Class I will need to be revised and supplemented. Part I is only the beginning for the 'nonstatement view.' The reconstruction of complex physical theories will presumably require further refinements in the methods for dealing with the mathematical structure of a theory. This will surely be the case, for example, within the *probabalistic context of quantum physics* no matter how the final explication of the statistical probability concept turns out. Likewise, the exact analysis of what we called *theory hierarchies* will presumably disclose new aspects.

In view of the fact that at least three—maybe even five or more—' disparate' notions fall under that which Kuhn calls a "paradigm," it is not surprising that critics have found this notion in part *incomprehensible*, in part *contradictory*, although a closer analysis reveals that neither is the case. One can certainly ask, though, if it was practical of Kuhn to employ this term. But we do not want to enter into a 'literary' discussion. The hints given here were intended merely as an aid for the reader of Kuhn's work. With their help it should be possible, when studying this work, in each case to decide from the context what is meant, whether it is something which can be rendered precise or not, and whether (how) it stands in relation to the corresponding notion of Wittgenstein. Kuhn's *general* remarks about paradigms will, however, *always* cause certain *difficulties of interpretation*. For if that which has been said here is right, *there are then no general statements about paradigms having both precision and interest, or both interest and content.*

A certain additional confusion arises inasmuch as Kuhn, despite his reference to Wittgenstein, uses the expression "paradigm" very differently than Wittgenstein in at least one respect. Compare, for example, the two notions "game" and "*Newtonian physics.*" Wittgenstein would be inclined to say: "The notion of game is determined by paradigmatic examples. And besides, there are at best family resemblances between the activities called 'games'." Applying this to the second notion, we arrive at a statement of the following sort: "The notion of Newtonian physics is delineated by paradigmatic examples (of the activities of such persons as call themselves Newtonian physicists). And besides there are at best family resemblances between the activities of Newtonian physicists". Kuhn, however, also employs phrases like: "Newtonian physics is a paradigm." That would correspond with respect to the first notion to: "Game is a paradigm"—*something which Wittgenstein would never have said.* The simplest way to resolve the difficulty here is by regarding the phrase "Newtonian physics is a paradigm" *as a linguistic abbreviation* for the more awkward characterization just given.

That Kuhn decided upon this somewhat unusual manner of speaking is understandable when one remembers that he wanted to avoid expressions like "Newtonian theory" because today we are all too accustomed to using the expression "theory" in the sense of "*codified* theory."

Our usage differs from Kuhn's in that we always and unmistakably speak of *the set of paradigmatic examples.* Besides, we couldn't even apply the notion of paradigm to the second example of the next to last paragraph. For we have decided never to use this notion to characterize an 'entire theory' (in the presystematic sense), but rather only *to distinguish certain kinds of conditions for 'intended applications' of theories.*

Finally, it should be pointed out that all the remarks made in this section are in one essential respect incomplete. They must be supplemented, and where necessary modified, by the Kuhnian concepts of a theory and holding a theory developed in Chapter 15.

14 Systematic Survey of the Possibilities for Describing the Intended Applications of a Theory; The Immunity of a Theory Against Potential Falsification

14.1 Extensional and intensional descriptions of the set I

As in Section 13.2 we will differentiate between extensional and intensional descriptions. Since the use of these expressions might arouse the suspicion that a special 'theory of the intensional meaning of linguistic expressions' is being presupposed here which has long been the subject of a complicated discussion, a few remarks are in order. They are intended solely to emphasize the *harmlessness* of this classification.

We will understand the *extensional description* of a set to be a list in which the individuals belonging to the set are explicitly named. All other kinds of descriptions we will call *intensional* descriptions. "Intensional" is, thus, simply another word for "nonextensional."

In order to ascertain which sort of description is given in a particular instance, it must be *clear what object is being described*. That the method of paradigmatic examples described in Section 13.2 was labeled *intensional* could only astonish someone who had not paid careful attention to what the *object* to be described was and what was used *as the means of* describing it. The object being described was the set I. The set I_0 of paradigm examples served as the means for making the description. This latter is, of course, in any case *extensionally* described; i.e., the list of its elements is explicitly given. The reason for nevertheless speaking of an intensional description of *the set I* lies in the fact that membership in $I - I_0$ was made dependent on the presence of certain properties. Likewise, the vagueness, mentioned earlier, connected with the specification of these properties involves at most this difference set. Concerning membership in the set I_0 itself there is no vagueness of any kind.

A systematic survey of the possible descriptions requires that we distinguish *three* different sorts of entities. The first is *the set I as a whole*. If we pick out an element of I, i.e., a physical system (partial possible model), we are still confronted with two further sorts of objects, the *domain of individuals* and the 'empirical' *functions*. Thus, the question of whether a description is extensional or intensional must be separately asked of the individuals and of the functions. *One* logically possible combination can, however, be ruled out immediately: namely, an intensional description of the individual domain together with an extensional description of the functions defined on it. This is because the extensional description of a function includes the extensional description of its domain *which* in this case *is identical with the individual domain*. Thus we arrive at table of logical possibilities for descriptions similar to Sneed's:[51]

(1) *Extensional description of I*:
   (a) purely extensional description of each element of I; i.e., an extensional description of D and of $f_1, \ldots, f_n$ for each element of I;
   (b) partial intensional description of certain[52] elements of I; i.e., for certain elements of I: D and $f_1, \ldots, f_j$ are extensionally, $f_{j+1}, \ldots, f_n$ intensionally described $(0 \leq j \leq n - 1)$;[53]
   (c) complete intensional description of certain elements of I; i.e., for these elements D and $f_1, \ldots, f_n$ will be intensionally described.
(2) *Intensional description of I*:
   (a) analogous to (1)(a);
   (b) analogous to (1)(b);
   (c) analogous to (1)(c).

For the discussion of all these types we will assume the same pragmatic situation. This is most easily done via D27. Let p be a person holding in the Sneedian sense a theory $\langle K, I \rangle$. How does this bear on the question of *how I is given to this person*?

Class of type (1)

The *subtype* (a) is the least interesting of all. Person p is acquainted with all those physical systems to which the theory should apply; i.e., he can enumerate all of these systems. Further, he can enumerate all the individuals occurring in each of these systems. Finally, he even has available a complete list of the values of all nontheoretical functions. In this case who needs a theory? It has neither prognostic nor explanatory value. For no matter what it is like, it is *in any case superfluous*, since *all* values of *all* nontheoretical functions are, per assumption, already given independently of it. When, nevertheless, theoretical functions are used, the *only* justification would be that they permit a *syntactic simplification*. The theoretical functions are

---

[51] Sneed, [Mathematical Physics], p. 274.

[52] "certain" means here "at least one, possibly all."

[53] $j = 0$ means that *only* the individual domain is extensionally described.

without exception Ramsey-eliminable.[54] The core K of the theory contains then either no theoretical functions at all, or at most such whose use could only be defended by appealing to a simplification in the description of what could have also been described with nontheoretical functions. *Presumably such a case has never made its appearance in the exact natural sciences.*

The *subtype* (b) is the first interesting case, albeit here, too, the elements of I are listed as are the individuals of the domains of each element of I. Consider an element of I for which some functions are only described intensionally. The crucial point is that we do not know the values of these functions for all individuals. Here it makes sense to seek expansions for the core containing newly postulated laws permitting us to predict values for these nontheoretical functions. For the first time theoretical laws and general as well as special constraints for theoretical functions become really important. *The person p will at all times t try to arrive at the strongest theory proposition $I_t \in \mathbb{A}_e(E_t)$ compatible with the available empirical data.*[55] He will arrive at this proposition by seeking the *smallest* class $\mathbb{A}_e(E)$ combining compatibility with the data and maximum prognostic power with respect to the as yet unknown values of the nontheoretical functions.

Not all attempts will be crowned with success. Some of the special laws postulated can be *empirically refuted*. In this case the tentative claim (or the corresponding theory proposition) is also refuted. If the general constraints C involve only the *theoretical* functions and the special laws are *theoretical* laws too, p will, in the case of a conflict, retain the constraints, which belong to the core, and give up the laws. In spite of such falsification a person can remain doubly optimistic. He can *retain the theory $\langle K, I \rangle$ itself* and he can *retain the conviction that a successful nonempty expansion E of K will yet appear. No* empirical data can offer a rational person *conclusive* grounds for giving up the theory. It cannot even constitute grounds for giving up the conviction that a nonempty, i.e., genuine, expansion of the theory compatible with the empirical data is possible. This circumstance is not, however, what *supports* the optimism. It is only a reason for not letting

---

[54] We must not overlook the fact that our person here may well have knowledge of empirical laws. These laws connect values of nontheoretical functions. As with all empirical knowledge, here too this knowledge is, of course, of a hypothetical nature. The simplification just mentioned would concern these empirical law-like regularities. It appears that with the exception of Ramsey almost all philosophers of science did for a long time believe that the purpose of theoretical functions consisted *solely* in making syntactic simplifications. Should this be true, this first subtype would at least be of historical interest. It could also inspire a cynical remark to the effect that—excepting Ramsey—the analysis of theoretical functions had suffered under the choice of an extremely uninteresting and trivial marginal case 'as paradigm.'

[55] Sneed, *op. cit.*, p. 277f., makes a detailed analysis involving two possible cases, one where the constraints are only on *nontheoretical* functions, one where they are only on *theoretical* functions. This brings the important role of *general constraints on theoretical functions* clearly into focus. The analysis yields the surmise that all 'real' physical theories contain only constraints on the *theoretical* functions.

an otherwise justified optimism be shaken. This 'other justification' lies in the knowledge that the conceptual apparatus we have called the core K of the theory has repeatedly proved itself 'applicable' to the physical systems belonging to I; i.e., claims (theory propositions) formulated with the help of this apparatus have in the past repeatedly been successful.

> The falsification concept just mentioned is, of course, meant to include the *well-known qualifications* emphasized by Popper and his disciples: falsification is relative to accepted observational data, and also to a context including some unchallenged background knowledge itself containing hypothetical laws (*ceteris paribus* clause).

The *subtype* (*c*) differs from the previous one in that it affords more predictions; "more" not only in a quantitative, but also in a *qualitative* sense. It permits *new kinds of prognosis*—prognosis no longer concerned only with the values of nontheoretical functions for certain individuals, but with the number of individuals in the physical systems of I under consideration. A concrete example would be the discovery of a new planet in the solar system. (This aspect is ignored in philosophical conceptions where existence hypotheses are thought to be metaphysical claims.)

Still another *qualitative* difference appears when compared to (1)(*b*). It concerns an 'immunity of the theory' which has already been discussed in Section 13.2 'at a higher level.' Should it turn out that constraints—be they on theoretical or nontheoretical functions—cannot be met, one can decide '*to throw*' *those individuals causing the trouble out of the domain.* When, as in the present case, the domain is not given per list, its membership being determined instead by the specification of a *property*, one can, rather than acknowledge an empirical falsification, *seek the error elsewhere.* The person p can admit having erred in attributing the (defining) property to the 'recalcitrant' individuals. It would be unfair and unfounded to call such behavior irrational. (In Section 13.2 the situation lay at a 'higher level' in the sense that it was a matter of *which physical systems* were to be elements of the set I of intended applications of a theory, whereas now the question concerns the objects which are to be elements of the domain of a concrete physical system (partial possible model).)

> Sneed discerns still a third qualitative difference: the possibility of *new, more congenial methods* for measuring theoretical functions. The idea behind this is to simplify the calculations in question by *seeking out new individuals.* A closer look at his analysis reveals that the realization of this project involves finding *further suitable elements of I*, i.e., further physical systems qualifying as partial possible models. The search for such physical systems, however, makes sense only if the elements belonging to I are not already listed. But such a list is presupposed for the subtype (1) (*c*). Hence it would have been more appropriate had Sneed saved the analysis at the middle of p. 281 of [Mathematical Physics] for the subtype (*c*) of the *intensional* description of I.

Class of type (2)

Although it is conceivable that cases of type (1)(*b*) and (1)(*c*) appear, the really interesting cases of physics all belong to class (2). This undoubtedly holds for Newton's theory. Neither in his time nor since was the idea ever prevalent that the given examples of the application of his theory represented *the only* possible applications.

Nevertheless, the above remarks concerning (1)(*b*) and (1)(*c*) are not wasted because they can be applied to the set of paradigm examples of Section 13.2. In other words, if one substitutes the set I_0 of Section 13.2 for the set I, both of these special cases of (1) are relevant. For despite the intensional characterization of I, its special subset I_0 is explicitly extensionally specified. One can even go a step further. As we are about to see, there exists for *all* the subtypes of class (2) an extensionally specified subset of I to which the remarks concerning class (1) apply just as they apply to the subclass I_0 of paradigms.

For this reason all types belonging to (2) have a certain formal similarity making it superfluous to deal with them separately. It should, though, be mentioned that subtype (*a*) is neither precluded, as might appear to be the case *prima facie*, nor *so* trivial as its counterpart (1)(*a*). We would be dealing with a (2)(*a*) type when I is indeed described intensionally but by chance a list of the individuals and function values were available for every physical system discovered to be an element of I. That this case is less trivial than (1)(*a*) is due to the fact that this time *the search for new partial possible models* makes sense and the efficiency of the theoretical apparatus—albeit still humble—might increase.

In order to verify the above claim we will assume that a person p holds a theory $\langle K, I \rangle$ in the Sneedian sense at time t (cf. D27). Further, we recall a direct consequence of earlier definitions. If, namely, for an expansion E of the core K the theory proposition $I \in \mathbb{A}_e(E)$ is true, then for every subset $H \subset I$ the proposition $H \in \mathbb{A}_e(E)$ is also true.

Now let I_t be the union of all sets I^* of which p possesses an extensional description and believes $I^* \subseteq I$ at time t. Thus I_t contains all individuals whose membership in I could be ascertained by the person p at time t on the basis of lists. I_t *is the set mentioned above*. Further, one can say that *if $\langle K, I_t \rangle$ is a Sneedian-type theory of physics, then the person p holds this theory in the Sneedian sense at time t.*

Concerning this last statement a few words of explanation are in order. Due to the consequences from earlier definitions just mentioned, we assume p believes $I_t \in \mathbb{A}_e(E_t)$ at t for the strongest expansion E_t (in the sense of D27 (2)). Further we may assume that p is convinced he will find an expansion E with which he can assert a still stronger proposition of this kind about I_t. The phrase "we may assume" means that we suppose that p *believes in certain* logical consequences of those propositions in which he believes under the stipulations of D27.

The condition "if $\langle K, I_t \rangle$ is a Sneedian-type theory of physics" must be added on account of the first, 'Platonic' stipulation of D27. It is not stipulated there that *p believes* $\langle K, I \rangle$ *to be a Sneedian-type theory of physics*, but that $\langle K, I \rangle$ *be* a Sneedian-type theory of physics (in the sense of D26).

If we now ask what kind of intensional description *I* should get, the answer is: exactly the one treated in detail in Section 13.2. From a systematic point of view it would have been practical to save that exposition until now (which could of course be repeated). Since, however, the logical connection between the Wittgensteinian and Kuhnian paradigm concepts is more difficult to comprehend than the present systematic classification, it appeared advisable, for extrasystematic reasons, to consider the paradigmatic subset I_0 of *I* first.

Furthermore, it is hoped that readers raised in the tradition of 'critical rationalism' will in the meantime have shaken off any 'immunity shock' which might have resulted from the argument there showing a theory's immunity to possible empirical falsification. We have again encountered an analogous situation at a lower level in the case of (1)(c).

The possible rational reactions of a person *p* can now be characterized using the generalized set I_t just introduced. We assume *p* holds the theory $\langle K, I \rangle$ but has discovered to his regret that the proposition $I_t \in \mathbb{A}_e(E_t)$ for the strongest expansion E_t of *K* at *t* is false. *p* then stands before the following alternative:

(A) *p gives up his belief in the truth of* $I \in \mathbb{A}_e(E_t)$. Intuitively this means *p* admits to some mistake in the construction of the core expansion E_t. On account of the 'relative immunity of constraints as compared with laws' described earlier, *p* will as a rule seek to locate the cause of the trouble in the special laws he postulated. Thus he will *drop special laws incorporated into E_t*, and try to replace the discarded expansion E_t *with another core expansion E_t'* such that $I \in \mathbb{A}_e(E_t')$ accords with the data. This formulation already implies that *p does not drop the theory itself.*

(B) *p continues to believe that* $I \in \mathbb{A}_e(E_t)$ *holds.* Because he has already convinced himself that $I_t \in \mathbb{A}_e(E_t)$ is false, he must admit having made a mistake in assuming $I_t \subseteq I$. This means that *p* will decide to delete certain physical systems which he initially held to be apt candidates for an application of his theory from its set of intended applications *I*. This is the point already discussed in Section 13.2 (with I_0 instead of I_t). When, for instance, classical particle mechanics ran into trouble with optical phenomena— Newton thought it would be applicable to them—it was *not* concluded that *classical particle mechanics was refuted*. The reaction was rather that *light did not consist of particles*. This could be considered a typical example of taking the second alternative.

Of course, in principle there also remains the third possibility of rejecting the theory in favor of another. This would correspond to what Kuhn calls *revolutionary progress* in science. The two alternatives just introduced may be regarded as attempts at describing as accurately as possible what we, along with Kuhn, can call *development or progress in normal science.* This account is of particular import because Kuhn has above all been *accused* of imputing irrational behavior to 'normal science.'

As opposed to this it has been shown here that in the face of recalcitrant experiential data either a decision of type (A) or of type (B) guarantees the immunity of the theory itself and that this immunity is in all cases compatible with behavior on the part of p which can be regarded as strictly rational.

These last remarks must be taken *cum grano salis* They anticipate, namely, *the concept of the Kuhnian sense of holding a physical theory.* This concept is in several respects considerably *stronger* than the concept introduced in D27 and *will not be discussed until later.*

Corresponding to these two reactions to 'negative instances' are *two possibilities for progress within the confines of 'normal science,'* i.e., *for progress under one and the same theory.* The *first* possibility has already made its appearance in connection with the extensional characterization of *I*. It is the successive discovery of expansions $E_1, E_2, \ldots, E_i, \ldots$ of K such that $\mathbb{A}_e(E_1) \supset \mathbb{A}_e(E_2) \supset \cdots \supset \mathbb{A}_e(E_i) \cdots$ for which the increasingly stronger statements $I_t \in \mathbb{A}_e(E_i)$ are found to be true. The *second* possibility, viable only when *I* is intensionally characterized, consists of discovering ever new elements of *I*, i.e., of discoveries of the following kind: if t_j is later than t_i, then $I_{t_i} \subset I_{t_j}$.

We have already said that a systematic discussion of the three subtypes of (2) is not necessary. It is enough to note in closing that the peculiarities pointed out in connection with the subtypes (*b*) and (*c*) of the extensional description of *I* also apply to their counterparts under (2). In particular, when, as in the case of (2)(*c*), *everything* is intensionally characterized, it is possible in the face of recalcitrant experience to exclude individuals from a given domain *as well as* entire physical systems from *I* provided they do not belong to the set of paradigm examples.

14.2 Remarks about an imaginary example of I. Lakatos

In laying the groundwork for his characterization of the difference between 'naive' and 'sophisticated' falsificationism, Lakatos invents a story about 'planatory misbehavior' in [Research Programmes], p. 100f. This story is intended to illustrate that, contrary to the view of 'naive falsificationism,' even acknowledged and admired scientific theories fail to ban observed facts. First we will relate Lakatos' story and then interpret it in a somewhat different way. This difference is not intended as a polemic against Lakatos' interpretation; it is meant to illuminate a certain aspect of what in Section 14.1 we called the complete intensional description.

The 'hero' of this story is a pre-Einsteinian physicist. He has used a theory N consisting of Newtonian mechanics including the law of gravity along with accepted initial conditions A to calculate the path of a newly discovered planet p. The theory N does not allow for deviations from this path. Thus it must stand *refuted* should it be discovered that the actual path of p clearly does deviate from the one calculated. Exactly this happens. But lo and behold our Newtonian physicist does *not* react as expected. Instead he postulates *a not yet discovered planet p' which is disturbing the path of p* to explain the observed deviation. He calculates the mass, path, etc., of this hypothetical planet p' and commissions an experimental astronomer to test his hypothesis. No luck—not even the strongest telescopes can find p'. The astronomer applies for funds to build a much stronger telescope than any currently available. Should p' be discovered the Newtonian theory can book a considerable success. Still no luck—the planet *cannot* be found. Must the physicist now *give up* the theory N? *By no means.* He has a new hypothesis: a cloud of cosmic dust is hiding the planet from us. He calculates the position and properties of this cloud and applies for funds to build a satellite to check out his calculations. Should the instruments of the satellite indicate the existence of the hypothetical cloud, one would again take occasion to celebrate a great victory for the Newtonian theory. The cloud of cosmic dust *cannot*, however, be found. But does the Newtonian at last give up and admit that his theory has *not stood* the test? No. He presumes there is a magnetic field in the area disturbing the instrument package of the satellite. So another satellite is sent up to check out this possibility. Finding this field would mean a sensational victory for the Newtonian. *No* field is found. Will not ' Newtonian science' finally be considered refuted? *No again.* Perhaps still more experiments will be tried. And when all have produced negative results the whole matter will be relegated to the archives where it can collect dust without attracting further notice.

One listens to this story with mixed feelings. On the one hand the repeated recourse to *ad hoc* hypotheses *appears* to constitute a kind of irrational behavior. On the other hand it *appears* one can somehow approve of the physicist who loses patience, not with his theory, but with particular developments which he then bans to the archives, perhaps with the epitaph "It's beginning to bore me anyway."

Note first that in our terminology it is not a *theory* at all which is being discussed here, but merely a very special law which could be discarded without leaving any trace of effect on the core of the theory. Within the Sneedian reconstruction of the Newtonian theory the formulation of this law would require a fourfold specialization of the primary predicate.

Technical details may be found in Sneed, [Mathematical Physics], pp. 140–141. The predicate characterizing classical particle mechanics must first be specialized to the concept of Newtonian classical particle mechanics.

Further specializations lead then to distance forces, inverse-square forces, and gravitational forces. Expressing the set-theoretic predicate describing the law in question in the natural idiom requires quite a mouthful: "is a distance, inverse-square, gravitational, Newtonian, classical particle mechanics." The reader can extract this concept effortlessly from the sketch in Sections 6.1 and 6.4.

For our present purposes, though, this point may be considered unimportant since, of course, the problem of empirical testing could be limited *to this special law*. The important point concerns the question of the individuals in the given domain. We are dealing with a typical case of type (2)(*c*). As far as *I* is concerned that has already been made clear. But it is not a question here of this 'higher level' involving the set *I* of intended applications (where (1)(*c*) would have done just as well). Its a matter of the subtype, and we can rest assured that it is a case of subtype (*c*), since the stipulation of the property "is a planet" plainly constitutes an *intensional*, not an explicit extensional description of the individuals of this particular application of classical particle mechanics. A planet is something similar to Mercury, Venus, Earth, Mars, Jupiter, etc., moving in such and such a course around the sun. Thus, the question of membership in this domain is open in the sense described in Section 14.1, i.e., in the sense in which the theory itself becomes the decisive factor. Until now we have only considered the possibility of 'throwing something out of the domain' (individuals at the level of application; physical systems one step higher at the level of *the set I* of applications). But the situation can also be reversed. Perhaps the 'stubborn resistance of experience to the theory' can only be broken by adding new individuals to the domain. We have before us a special case of this kind. To reports that the disturbing planet *p'* has *not* been empirically discovered the ' Newtonian physicist' could therefore reply "but I *have* already discovered it." The special way in which he has applied his theory is, under the circumstances described, tantamount to a *process for discovering individuals belonging to the domain*—in this case planets.[56]

The test theoretician will presumably protest that the pragmatic context has been changed whereby no little bit of 'intellectual skulduggery' has been brought into play. First a law should be tested. But then suddenly the test method becomes a '*method of discovering individuals.*' We must now try to *make clear that, and why, such a reaction would be totally uncalled for*. In order to be able even to describe the alleged test situation one must be able to proceed on the assumption that an exact *list* of the planets is given. But *one cannot make such an assumption*. (*Did Newton ever maintain that there were less than 6300 planets*? And if he had alleged something of the sort it

---

[56] Of course this does not serve to contest the fact that it is desirable to ascertain the existence of individuals through several 'independent methods.' The imaginary example describes a case in which this wish—unfortunately—is not fulfilled.

would have been unfounded and could not have been taken seriously.) We mean such an assumption would rest on a 'metaphysical' fiction in the worst sense of the word. Taking again the example of "game," it is as if someone were to concede to Wittgenstein that the notion of game could be delineated solely by the method of paradigmatic examples only to suddenly exclaim: "Let's assume now that we have a list of all games." Wittgenstein would rightly reply: "*You obviously fail to understand the method of paradigmatic examples.*"

Reflecting on Lakatos' imaginary situation might possibly contribute to a better understanding of our position concerning the immunity of a theory to 'recalcitrant data.' The behavior of our *imaginary* Newtonian is *no more* '*irrational*' than that of the *real* Newtonian who one day proclaimed: "Light does not consist of particles." There are but two formal differences: in one case it is a matter of 'inclusion,' in the other of 'exclusion,' and in this latter case the level is one step higher (i.e., the first case is concerned with whether an object is an element of the domain of a certain particular element of I, whereas the second case is concerned with whether something is an element of I).

> Since in the present context we only wanted to illustrate the use of a theory for 'finding a new individual' in an intensionally given domain, the above remarks were not very precise. An exact analysis could only be given within the framework of a detailed treatment of Newtonian classical particle mechanics. Point (1) of Section 5.1 offers a brief glimpse. Indeed, the Ramsey method appeared there *in its original form* (II). But in our present context this makes no difference, since the other applications of classical particle mechanics play no part. The concrete example there involved the discovery of the planet Neptune in 1846. It was assumed that a well-confirmed claim of form (II) was available for the predicate, say N, mentioned above whose natural language wording is extremely awkward.
>
> The formal structure involved in 'finding a new individual' is then roughly the following: "Since (II) is well confirmed, but it is impossible to enrich the paths of the planets known prior to 1846 so as to obtain a model for N, there must be an as yet unobserved planet." Size, path, and other properties of this planet are revealed by the fact that its addition to the domain (set of planets) must serve to create a model for N out of the otherwise unsuitable enrichments.

190

15 A Pragmatically Restricted, Intuitively Richer Theory Concept; The Kuhnian Sense of Holding a Theory

15.1 The pragmatic elements of Kuhn's theory concept

The remarks in Section 13.2 and Chapter 14 dealing with the intensional characterization of I by means of a set I_0 of paradigmatic examples were of a purely *semantic* nature. For Kuhn's theory concept it is essential that the set I_0 also have *pragmatic significance* for the theory whose range of application it paradigmatically characterizes. We want to clarify the nature of these pragmatic components and incorporate them into the theory concept as well as a corresponding concept of holding a theory. We will indeed be able to draw upon the concepts defined in D26 and D27, but will need, besides I_0, still other extralogical notions.

> In order to define the Kuhnian theory concept we will need to depart still further from Sneed's procedure. He tried to parallel his previous procedure in the sense that he also gave this stronger theory concept a purely logical characterization and first incorporated pragmatic aspects into the concept of holding a theory. But the goal cannot be reached in this way. In the new theory concept he requires essentially nothing more than adding $I_0 \subseteq I$ to the stipulations of D26. Since, however, no additional pragmatic requirements are made of I_0, *any subset of I* can be taken, and the resulting theory concept *only appears* stronger.

The basic idea here can best be illustrated with an abstract example designed so that according to definition D27 two persons hold *the same* theory while in accord with Kuhn's intentions they hold *different* theories.[57] Thus we have physicists who in the sense of D27 hold the physical theory $\langle K, I \rangle$. We will even assume that both expand the core K in exactly the same way and apply this expansion to the same set I.

"What can still be different here?" one might ask. The answer is that the *historical origin* could in each case be different. In one instance this starting point was a set of paradigm examples I_0, in the other a different set I_0^*.[58]

---

[57] Sneed draws the contrast in a similar fashion. Cf. *op. cit.*, p. 293.

[58] In order to make the contrast as drastic as possible, we can assume the two sets to be disjunct. But in order to avoid an unnecessary complication, we will also assume that *both physicists themselves* (and not their predecessors) started from the respective sets I_0 and I_0^*.

On the basis of our earlier conceptual apparatus we must characterize the situation as follows: "Both physicists hold *the same theory*. They even use the same expanded core to assert the same theory proposition.[59] The sole difference is that *by chance the theory had different origins in each case*. The physicists did not start with the same set of paradigm examples." Over and against this the Kuhnian view would argue: "Because the two physicists start from entirely different sets of paradigm examples, they have also started *with entirely different theories*. Common to both is only that *by pure chance they arrived at the same result*."

If this last interpretation is taken seriously, it is most appropriate to incorporate the paradigm concept itself into the theory concept.

> Sneed's interpretation goes a step further in that he assumes the embryonic theory also includes *a special core expansion E_0*. In this we will not follow him. For E_0 is either a *genuine* expansion containing certain special laws and additional constraints, or it is an *'empty expansion'* which could be defined by identifying the class L of laws with the unit class $\{M\}$. In the first case we would then have to incorporate *these special stipulations*, which perhaps have been rejected this long time, into the theory. This does not seem very plausible. In the other case the expansion does not warrant being mentioned.

On the other hand, it appears that the germinal idea contained in the fictitious example above must be further developed and its explication built into the theory concept. To this end we must try to determine which components are *invariant* according to Kuhn's conception and which can *change* within the same theory. The invariants include two parts. The first consists of that mathematical part of the theory structure which must remain constant if we are to speak of *the same* theory. This part is comprised of the *frame* and the *core K*. It is enough to mention K since it includes the frame as a part. *This component can be characterized purely logically*. The second part consists of the *set of paradigmatic examples I_0. According to Kuhn the retention of just this set I_0 is essential for the identity of the theory through the course of time*. Since, however, only *a definite belief in the applicability of the theory to I_0* can serve to make the retention of I_0 manifest, the concept of belief itself necessarily finds its way into the Kuhnian theory concept. What can change in the course of time also consists of a component which can be characterized by purely logical means and one which can only be pragmatically described. The first is comprised of the various core expansions E_i, the latter of the physical systems thought to be in $I - I_0$. Again it is *the belief in the mutability of $I - I_0$* which must somehow be incorporated into the theory concept.

Two further pragmatic stipulations are needed to capture the following two ideas. There must have been a *person* or *group of persons* who first

---

[59] We can even go a step further and assume that both formulate the same central empirical claim.

started K and I_0 on their way. By their action they have already decided which parts of the theory will be variable and which invariable with *the passage of time.*

Thus it appears that one needs a total of four extralogical concepts to formulate the concept of a Kuhnian-type theory: *person, belief* or *conviction, set of paradigm examples,* and *course of time.* Finally, one will also need both the earlier (weaker) concepts of theory (D26) and of holding a theory (D27). In this way all the pragmatic aspects of the Sneedian sense of holding a theory find their way *into the Kuhnian theory concept* itself—not first into his concept of holding a theory.

15.2 Theory and holding a theory in the Kuhnian sense

After the preliminaries of Section 15.1 we can now begin with the explication proper. The previous concepts of a theory and of holding a theory have a cosmetic flaw. They refer to the 'Platonic' entity I of 'true' intended applications. This notion does not fit well into a satisfactory reconstruction of Kuhn's ideas. In contrast to Sneed we will free ourselves of this Platonism by requiring I to be an *open*, not a closed set. The only initial demand made of it is that it contain the set of paradigm examples; i.e., that $I_0 \subseteq I$. (This additional stipulation is explicitly built into D29.) Additions to the initial set I_0 are subsequently regulated by the rule of autodetermination.

> Another alternative would be to drop the reference to a set I altogether. In its place one could work with the class $\bar{A} = \bar{R}(\mathscr{P}(M) \cap C)$ of sets of intended applications determined by the core.

As a first step it will prove convenient to introduce the auxiliary concept "set of intended applications of a theory assumed by a person p at time t."[60]

D28 I_t^p is *the set of applications of the physical theory $T = \langle K, I \rangle$ assumed by the person p at time t* iff

(1) p holds in the Sneedian sense the theory T at time t (cf. D27);
(2) p believes $I_t^p \subseteq I$;
(3) there exists an expansion E_t of K such that p believes at t that E_t is successfully applicable to I_t^p; i.e., p believes the theory proposition $I_t^p \in \mathbb{A}_e(E_t)$ at t;
(4) for all $X \subseteq I$: if there exists an expansion E_t^* of K and p believes $X \in \mathbb{A}_e(E_t^*)$ at t, then $X \subseteq I_t^p$.

(Stipulation (4) guarantees that I_t^p is the *maximal* set of intended applications known to p at t.)

---

[60] This definition was suggested to me by my student, C. U. Moulines.

The concept I_t^p is incorporated into the concept of a Kuhnian-type theory in the following way: for all persons p and times t the set of paradigm examples I_0 must be contained as a subset in all such sets I_t^p.

D29   *X is a Kuhnian-type theory of physics* iff there exist a K, an I, and an I_0 such that

(1) $X = \langle K, I, I_0 \rangle$;

(2) $K = \langle M_p, M_{pp}, r, M, C \rangle$ is a core for a theory of mathematical physics;

(3) (a) $\vee p_0 \vee t_0 \vee E_0$ (the person p_0 chose at t_0 the set I_0 as the set of paradigm examples for I and for the first time successfully applied the expansion E_0 of K to I_0[61]);

   (b) $I_0 \subseteq I \subseteq M_{pp}$;

   (c) $\wedge p \wedge t$ (if I_t^p is the set of intended applications of the physical theory $T = \langle K, I \rangle$ assumed by p at t (in the sense of D28), then p believes $I_0 \subseteq I_t^p$ at t);

(4) every element of I is a physical system;

(5) if $\mathfrak{D}$ is a class containing as elements exactly the domains of the elements of I, then for any two elements D_i and D_j of $\mathfrak{D}$: D_i is linked with D_j;

(6) I is a homogeneous set of physical systems.

The three stipulations (4)–(6) of this definition are identical with stipulations (3)–(5) of D26. Thus, in these three respects the new theory concept corresponds word for word to the weaker concept of a Sneedian-type theory. New are *the explicit reference to the set of paradigm examples I_0 and the demands made of it*: namely, that it be specified by the 'theory's inventor' and that this inventor succeed in applying the theory to it for the first time.[62] Thus, the idea contained in the phrase "retention of the set of paradigm examples in the course of time" is explicitly built into the concept of a Kuhnian-type theory.

D30   *A person p holds, in the Kuhnian sense, a physical theory $T = \langle K, I \rangle$ at time t* iff

(1) $\langle K, I, I_0 \rangle$ is a Kuhnian-type theory of physics;

(2) there exists an expansion E_t of K such that p believes $I \in \mathbb{A}_e(E_t)$

---

[61] E_0 can be an empty expansion. Thus the stipulation is extremely liberal. If the theory in question is, e.g., classical particle mechanics and p_0 were Newton, it would be enough that he simply advanced the core of the theory. One could consider strengthening this stipulation by requiring that the 'theory's creator' know of a strong theory proposition for at least one non-trivial expansion E of the theory core K (i.e., an expansion other than the empty one).

[62] For the sake of simplicity we have omitted the obvious formal definition of "for the first time."

at t. This expansion is the strongest such expansion of K in the sense that $\wedge E$ [(E is an expansion of K such that p believes $I \in \mathbb{A}_e(E)$ at t and p has at t observable data supporting this proposition) $\to E_t \subseteq E$];

(3) p chooses I_0 as the set of paradigm examples for I;
(4) p believes at t that $\wedge t'$ (if $I_{t'}^p$ is the set of applications of the Sneedian-type theory of physics $\langle K, I \rangle$ assumed by p at t', then $I_0 \subseteq I_{t'}^p$);
(5) p has at t observable data supporting the proposition $I \in \mathbb{A}_e(E_t)$;
(6) p believes at t that there exists an expansion E of K such that
   (a) $I \in \mathbb{A}_e(E)$;
   (b) $\mathbb{A}_e(E) \subset \mathbb{A}(_e E_t)$.

Stipulations (1), (2), (5), and (6) are the same as stipulations (1)–(4) in the definition of the Sneedian sense of holding a theory (cf. D27). Stipulations (3) and (4) are new. They require that the person p himself *acknowledge I_0 to be the set of paradigm examples for I*, and that p be convinced that I_0 is a subset of every set of intended applications which *he himself* will ever assume in the future (in the sense of D28).

The new stipulations guarantee that the *historical origins* of the theory, manifest in the original selection of a set of paradigms I_0 and a core, as well as *the retention of this set of paradigms through the course of history* become integral parts of the concepts of theory and holding a theory.

> We could have called the concepts introduced in D26 and D27 the *weak* concepts of a theory of physics and holding a physical theory in contrast to those introduced in D29 and D30 which would then be regarded as the *strong* concepts of a theory of physics and holding a physical theory. We wanted, however, to avoid any possible confusion with earlier terminology. In Part I, namely, we distinguished between weak and strong theories (and theory propositions) according to whether the mathematical structure was a (nonexpanded) core or an expanded core. *Of these earlier concepts only that of a weak theory is used in Part II.*

16 Normal Science and Scientific Revolutions

16.1 The course of normal science in Kuhn's sense; The rule of autodetermination for the range of application of a theory

The pragmatic concepts introduced in D29 and D30 together with the expositional comments constitute essentially a characterization of what Kuhn calls "normal science." This is possible because holding one and the same theory is compatible *with a legion of diverging convictions.* Theory propositions, formulated with the help of suitable expansions of a core, can vary from person to person. Furthermore, it is *neither* alleged that a person p holding a theory at time t in the Kuhnian sense *will* continue to do so in the future, *nor* that he *should.* But *so far* and *so long* as a person p holding a theory at a given time continues to do so (to retain it), his thinking moves within the confines of normal science. He can, of course, one day lose his belief in the possibility of successfully applying expansions of the core K to the sets I determined by the set I_0 of paradigm examples, and turn to an entirely new theory with a new core and (or) new paradigms. If he does, however, he is no longer a 'normal scientist,' *he has become a scientific revolutionary.*

The most notable aspect about the concept of normal science is also *prima facie* the most disconcerting: namely, the *immunity of a theory against the hazards of possible empirical refutation as depicted.* Later we will have more to say about this.

The pragmatic concepts of theory and holding a theory were introduced in a way designed to illuminate their connection with as well as their difference from the weaker 'logical' concepts of D26 and D27. It might be objected, and rightly so, that this advantage was bought with the disadvantage mentioned above: namely, the set I of 'true' intended applications of a theory is an *absolute Platonic essence* which has no place at all in a reconstruction of Kuhn's conception of science.

We have already seen, though, how this shortcoming may be remedied. We regard I not as a fixed, 'immutable' set, but as *a potentially open-ended collection* generated by a process, to be precisely characterized, for enlarging I_0. One might already roughly characterize this process using the language of Section 13.2: *the theory itself is used to determine its applications.* "theory" is used here in a preexplicative sense. What is meant is that the core K and the expansions E_i, which in the course of time have been proposed for it, determine what besides the elements of I_0 are to be intended applications. Physical systems whose addition to I_0 at time t yields a set I_t such that the available data adequately supports the proposition $I_t \in \mathbb{A}_e(E_t)$ for the tentative expansion E_t will be admitted to I. Systems stubbornly resisting a successful application will be removed. We have already seen in Section 13.2 that this method does not entail 'autoverification of the theory.' On the other hand, we could speak of a *rule of autodetermination of I by means of K and an initial set of paradigms* (briefly: rule of autodetermination of I by the theory).

One could thus tentatively supplement both the definition of Kuhnian-type theory and Kuhnian theory holding with the stipulation that *the set of intended applications always be determined according to the rule of auto-determination of I by the theory*. At least for such developments as Kuhn reckons to the practice of 'normal science' —i.e., as long as *no theory confrontations* are involved—this rule might be incorporated. In this way these concepts would take on an even more realistic hue. In particular, the last 'Platonic remnant' is banned from the theory concept.

Kuhn's critics have been especially disturbed by the *stability and immunity of theories* implied by the use of this rule, which makes it appear practically impossible to disqualify a theory on the basis of 'empirical counter-examples.' And Kuhn's assurance, that a theory (a 'paradigm' in his terminology) is only then rejected when another is available, tends to strengthen this impression.

Actually, claims like this last one do exaggerate, at least when no qualifications are added. Two typical situations can be described in which one would practically be forced to give up the theory *regardless of whether an alternative is available or not*. And a third situation can be described in which it is at least debatable whether the theory must go or not.

The *unlimited* application of the rule of autodetermination must well be based on a thesis to the effect that we dare not have any *a priori* expectations concerning the things to which a theory should be truly applicable. For then no disappointed expectations of this sort could result in letting the theory fall. But this unlimited application of the rule is certainly a pipe dream. *The rule has an absolute limit in the paradigm examples themselves.* If it fails with respect to these, it *must* be rejected on pain of a total collapse of meaning for "the theory's realm of application."

> The question of whether or not a theory can always be 'rescued' with the help of suitable auxiliary hypotheses or other 'immunization strategies' must be excluded here. Its discussion would lead us too far afield. Normally it is discussed in the context of confirmation and testing. But it is not a problem for scientific *metatheory* at all; it is a problem for scientific *morals*. Every scientific activity involves a pragmatic context which must be regulated at the outset, be it through ever so many 'arbitrary decisions' obligating the participants to each other. When, for example, it has been agreed *to accept* a statistical hypothesis *for the purposes of a certain investigation*, one must respect *this*

197

decision as long as one is working on *this* investigation. If the hypothesis is used to make a prediction, for example, and testing this prediction indicates that something extremely improbable has happened, a participant in the investigation is *not* being *irrational*, but *delinquent* if on the basis of this result he changes his mind, breaks with the hypothesis, and thereby with the initial agreement. Likewise, breaking a contract or promise does not usually imply lack of rationality but rather lack of morality.

One thing must be admitted though even for these marginal cases—an admission that once again moves us close to Kuhn's view. The notion of *stubborn resistance to a theory* is presumably not amenable to precise logical articulation. Hence, there always remains a *certain* arbitrariness when it comes to deciding whether or not a theory has been successful with respect to a paradigm example.

To understand this one must recall that only the core K is fixed by the theory; the task upon which success or failure depends consists of trying *to find a suitable expansion E. The number of possibilities for such an expansion is, however, potentially infinite*! Since they cannot be effectively checked out, *any statement asserting the failure of the theory rests in the final analysis on the decision to give up the search for a new expansion as a 'practically hopeless undertaking.'* Despite this element of arbitrariness in any such negative decision about a theory, one can give no convincing reason why this 'realization of practical hopelessness' *cannot*, or *should* not come *before* someone has thought out a new theory to replace the old one. The appeal to the fact that in the history of natural science 'it has never been so' is no argument. On the other hand, an allegation to the effect that a theory must from a certain time on be regarded as irrevocably refuted *cannot* be substantiated either. In this situation one can do no more than seek to *understand* the actual behavior of scientists (cf. Section 16.3).

These considerations also afford a basis for commenting on Kuhn's remarks in [Revolutions], p. 43f., where he says that the success of a paradigm is, in the beginning, largely a *promise of success* the realization of which comprises normal science. And what happens when this success does not materialize? "The theory has failed" is the typical answer. After what has just been said, though, it is easy to see that this is a *non sequitur* even when the 'promise' concerns elements of the set of paradigm examples *taken in our sense*. We need only again specialize Kuhn's paradigm concept to its rationally reconstructable component; i.e., we read "core" instead of "paradigm." The realization consists, then, in finding suitable expansions. If none have been found up to a certain time, one can at best presume, *not*, however, infer that there are none. *In this way it can be said exactly in what sense the promise of success is not to be refuted.*

In passing, it might also be mentioned that even the *sharp* delineation of the set of paradigm examples hitherto assumed could be questioned. Perhaps even here there are *borderline cases* which one would be prepared to drop from I_0 if the theory were successfully applicable to all other elements of I_0 except this one. For a long time the *tides* represented a problematic case for Newton's theory. To a certain degree they have remained so right up to the present. We must remember that D. Bernoulli's equilibrium theory, the first serious theory in this area, appeared more than fifty years after the 'discovery of the tide-producing forces by Newton' and even then failed completely in many respects; that the inertia of water could first be accommodated by P. S. Laplace's *dynamic theory* nearly one hundred years after Newton's discovery; that it was about two hundred years before the Coriolis force found its way into S. S. Hough's *dynamic theory*; that first in this century did A. T. Doodson succeed in calculating the tide-producing forces postulated by Newton. When one considers these and other stages in the wearisome struggle with the problem of tides, which the contemporary physicist passes off with the remark that the complicated shape of the oceans presented considerable mathematical difficulties, it appears at least *conceivable* that the experts could have lost their patience and turned to an entirely new non-Newtonian treatment of the tide problem *without*, however, dropping this theory as a suitable theory for the rest of the 'paradigmatic cases.'

A second interesting situation which could precipitate the fall of a theory is mentioned by Sneed on p. 291 in [Mathematical Physics]. In order to depict it we will assume that the method of autodetermination is used according to the following rule as a *sufficient condition for belonging to I*: "Each physical system x such that the core K can be successfully applied to the set $I_0 \cup \{x\}$[63] is *eo ipso* an element of *I*." We may now find that of two physical systems, x_1 and x_2, *each* can *by itself* be added to the elements of I_0 so as to yield a successful application of K, but *not both together*. Thus K is successfully applicable to $I_0 \cup \{x_1\}$ as well as to $I_0 \cup \{x_2\}$, but not to $I_0 \cup \{x_1\} \cup \{x_2\}$. Here, incidentally, we again see a special effect of constraints; for they alone make such a situation possible. Intuitively, this result might be interpreted as follows: the set of intended applications of the theory can be extended beyond the set of paradigm examples *in two incompatible ways*. Since the theory can then develop 'in two mutually exclusive directions' between which the above rule is unable to discriminate, demanding the inclusion of *both, we are forced to let the theory fall*. But again it is important to note why it would be grossly misleading to regard this as *falsification*. It obtains, namely, *only relative to the rule presumed to be assumed in the strong version formulated above.*

A third type of situation arises when the method of autodetermination is employed *to obtain a necessary condition for membership in I*. In this case a physical system is acknowledged to be an element of *I* only if K can be successfully applied to the set consisting of it plus I_0. Note that whether, and to what extent, it 'resembles' the elements of I_0 makes absolutely no

---

[63] Anytime we speak of a successful application of K to a set Q we mean, of course, that an expansion E of K has been found such that the proposition $Q \in \mathbb{A}_e(E)$ is supported by the empirical data.

difference here. It is primarily *this use* of the autodetermination method for formulating a *necessary condition* for membership in *I* which will elicit protest from 'rationalistic' critics.

As a concrete example, consider the case of Brownian motion. Suppose, for the sake of illustration, that classical particle mechanics completely failed to explain these quivering motions of small particles suspended in a liquid. Consider now how two stereotypes would presumably react to this situation, one being the traditional 'rationalist' (be he of Popperian persuasions, be he of a non-Popperian 'inductivistic' cut), and the other a 'proponent of the autodetermination method' radically championing the Kuhnian position.

The traditional rationalist would argue roughly as follows: "if we really did suppose this fictitious situation to be true, intellectual integrity would demand that we regard classical particle mechanics as falsified ('deductivistic' interpretation) or extremely improbable ('inductivistic' interpretation). Any rationally justifiable test theory, i.e., any theory with rationally founded rules for acceptance and rejection, would, therefore, demand that classical particle mechanics be rejected."

The ideal proponent of the autodetermination method (in the sense of this third type of case) would of course arrive at an entirely different conclusion, roughly: "this failure of classical particle mechanics only proves that Brownian motion falls outside the set of intended applications of classical particle mechanics." The subsequent protest of his rationalistic antagonist over this 'arbitrary decree' would leave him fully unruffled. For what lies at the basis of this *allegation* of arbitrariness but some notion to the effect that Brownian motion *is after all* motion of small particles and must, therefore, belong to the set of intended applications of classical particle mechanics *quite independent of what this theory can do*. But this notion, this foundation of rationalistic protest, it could be argued, plainly bears the mark of a *subjective feeling*: namely, the feeling that there is sufficient similarity between Brownian motion and particle motion to force one to subsume the former under the latter. The appeal to such feelings, which the proponent of the autodetermination method regards as *fully irrational*, is *explicitly excluded* in the above rule employing this method as a necessary condition for membership in *I*. To support the claim that his position is not only rational but *historically accurate* as well, our 'Kuhnian' could point to the analogous situation, already mentioned, concerning the Newtonian emission theory of light. When Newton's supposition that optical phenomena were to be interpreted as particle motion in the sense of particle mechanics proved wrong, no one entertained doubts about particle mechanics on this account. Instead they concluded that light did not consist of particles. And what is the formal difference between our fictitious example and this historical one? The 'autodeterminist' would say: "*there is none*, when one leaves out that appeal to subjective feelings of similarity and dissimilarity."

As we postulated three situations in which a theory *might* be rejected we labeled this third type *debatable*. We mean, of course, that only on the basis of such stereotyped positions as we have just described will one *always* arrive at a clear-cut decision.[64] A somewhat *more realistic* analysis, without such idealizations, will presumably arrive at more discriminating judgments. In *many* cases one will work with the autodetermination rule. In *some* cases, however, where a theory fails with respect to a physical system bearing an ' otherwise preponderant similarity' to elements of I_0 the theory itself will be blamed. Within the confines of what Kuhn calls normal science such cases will certainly be rare exceptions.

Hopefully the ideas sketched in the foregoing paragraphs have contributed to a clearer, more differentiated picture of the previously established immunity of a theory to 'recalcitrant data.' We have learned to see *just how limited the possibilities of giving up a theory during a period of normal science in Kuhn's sense are*, i.e., during a period in which a theory is held in the sense of D30. Even in the extreme marginal cases just considered, anything like *compulsory rejection of the theory* is always *relative to* the decision to adopt certain methodological rules the rationality and utility of which can be seriously questioned.

If one wants an easy-to-remember formula for the basic attitude of scientists whose research falls within a period of normal science, i.e., who in the Kuhnian sense hold a theory, the following might be recommended, which after the foregoing discussion *should no longer be misleading*:

In dubio pro theoria

But slogans are always misleading. Therefore, it is perhaps not entirely superfluous to recall our starting point and *our way of dealing with the notions it involved*. We were chiefly concerned with explaining *the sense in which one can speak of the constantly changing convictions of scientists within a certain period of time during which they hold one and the same theory*. The concept "holding a theory in the Kuhnian sense" was intended to explicate this basic idea. It is extremely important not to forget all that must be included in this ' shifting of beliefs.' Not only the discovery of new phenomena, the inclusion in and exclusion from *I* of physical systems, the improvement of experimental methods, etc., belong to 'realizing the promise of success' in which normal science according to Kuhn manifests itself; *the changes also includes the assumption and rejection of new additional constraints and special laws.* For what is called accepting and rejecting laws *in the traditional idiom* finds, within the framework of our conceptual apparatus, its expression in the *variability of expanded cores*. The successive restrictions and liberalizations of expanded cores leave, however, the core *K*, *whose* expansions they are, completely untouched, hence also the 'abstract' (weak) theory concept of

---

[64] Cf. Sneed's interesting remarks on this subject, *op. cit.*, p. 292.

Part I and both of the intuitively and pragmatically strengthened concepts of a Sneedian-type and a Kuhnian-type theory. Only the *strong* theories of Part I and the corresponding *strong theory propositions* (the propositional counterparts of theory claims) are subject to change in 'normal science.' That is also why we are justified in subsuming such processes under the notion of *theory dynamics*, not merely the dynamics of belief or conviction.

16.2 The first kind of scientific revolution: The transition from pretheory to theory; Three different concepts of "theoretical"

Kuhn's theses about scientific revolutions must now be specialized and differentiated following Sneed's procedure. The specialization again consists of limiting considerations to *physical* theories alone. The differentiation involves the following distinction:

(1) The *initial appearance* of a physical theory 'explaining a piece of reality ' for which hitherto no theory, or at least no physical theory, existed.
(2) The *rejection* of a current theory—i.e., a theory scientists have held in the Kuhnian sense for a certain period of time—*in favor of another.*

The reader should first be warned, though, that revolutionary theory dynamics represents a phenomenon where metascientific analysis runs up against a 'natural barrier.' Many aspects of this phenomenon which are of interest to a historical observer either defy exact description or would infuse into it strong hypothetical components for which a historian, but not an analyst, can answer. On the other hand, much of what can be described precisely will not appear especially interesting. Thus it will be difficult to attain results that are both *correct* and *exact* as well as *interesting and important.*

Not all that can be said about this theme will be said here. Aspects involving the problem of testing and confirmation will be surveyed in the next chapter under the title "Holism." In the present section we will only tackle the first theme concerning the *initial appearance of theories.*

One of the most exciting and at the same time puzzling events in the course of the 'evolution of the universe' is the emergence of beings who not only possess a cerebrum and a 'consciousness,' but who also succeeded in freeing themselves from the pressures of a life ruled by instinct to the extent that 'impersonal' curiosity and 'a striving for objective knowledge,' already observed and described by Aristotle, rose within them. Scientific theories constitute the 'highest' and 'purest' form of this desubjectivized aspiration. Physical theories which are not built on the basis of others or which do not replace others we will call *primary theories.* Our first question must be whether anything of metascientific relevance can be said about the appearance of primary theories.

In any case it would be somewhat hasty to take the position that with regard to primary theories the still traceable historical beginnings *alone* constitute the object of historical studies and that those beginnings of knowledge lying still further back must be the subject of a special division of the theory of evolution. The philosopher must resign himself to the idea that the origins of knowledge are irretrievably lost in the mists of time.

Consider now the following speculative question: would it have been possible *in principle* for someone to have developed the Newtonian theory one thousand years before Newton's time? The answer *appears* to depend only on how "possible in principle" is to be understood. Thus it must run: "if by possibility, *logical* possibility is meant, then the answer is plainly positive. If, on the other hand, possibility is understood in some plausible sense of *real, psychological* possibility, the answer is negative, since supposing this achievement to have been realized at such an early date without the preliminary work of people like Kepler, Galileo, etc., involves a false psychological hypothesis about human capabilities."

This sort of answer is, however, inadequate. And it is very important to understand *why* this is so. The answer to the question concerning the real possibility by no means depends *solely* on the psychological problem of what mental achievements a human being is capable. No, the question itself rests on a false presupposition. An adequate reaction to it would be to *expose the source of error in this presupposition*.

To this end we will refer back to the model-theoretic characterization of the core K of this (or some other) theory. Although K contains *all* the essential factors for the theory, there is a tendency to think of only three of them explicitly: the set M_p of those entities to which the 'axioms proper' are applied, namely, the *possible models*; the basic mathematical structure determined by the axiom system and extensionally represented by the *set M of models*; and the *set C of constraints* linking the theoretical functions 'across' the various possible applications and subjecting them to more or less strong limitations.

But what about the '*conceivable models*' M_{pp} from which the set I of intended applications is extracted as a subset? Concerning these entities we easily lapse into a 'naive realism' and revert to an idea which may be aptly, if ever so vaguely, described as follows: "the elements of M_{pp}, i.e., the partial possible models, are '*things lying about out there in the world*' of which those must be sorted out that the theory is capable of explaining."

That this idea rests on a mistaken intuition becomes clear when one recalls that partial possible models are not merely individual domains, but *physical systems*, i.e., sets of individuals *together with certain numerical functions* having real-number values for the individuals. This indicates that a certain kind of 'theoretical treatment' must have already taken place if one is to even speak intelligibly about a set of intended applications. At this juncture one must pick up an idea advanced by several authors, in particular Kuhn

and Feyerabend: namely, that *in order to judge whether a physical theory is
(even 'conceivably') applicable to something, one needs still another theory.*

> *Remark.* This thought often appears in another context, pointing up the
> 'theory-ladenness of the observational language' and warning of the fiction
> that in the 'observational language' facts are described 'independent of
> any theory.' This aspect has already been discussed in Chapter 1.
>   Occasionally such ideas also appear in connection with *holistic theses*
> (cf. Chapter 17). Such contexts must be clearly distinguished from those in
> which the problem of *theoretical terms* is being discussed. T-theoretical de-
> scriptions of facts are formulated in the language of *the same* theory *for which*
> the facts are relevant. The present question of whether or not one needs a
> further theory to decide if something is an application of a theory *does not*,
> of course, *refer to the same theory* both times but *to a different theory.* Con-
> fusion often ensues because authors do not pay attention to the fact that
> in discussions belonging to this present context the reference is to some *other*
> theory than the one whose application is being discussed.

This idea becomes somewhat more obvious when one considers exactly
what the given functions are used for: namely, to formulate *descriptions of
facts in a quantitative language.* The thesis could thus be paraphrased as
follows: "the task of a physical theory is primarily to explain *metrically
determined facts,* not 'pure, uninterpreted facts' —whatever that might be.
Since quantitative descriptions can be given only with the help of functors and
the use of functors is possible only within the framework of a theory, the
question of whether or not a fact X is a fact for the theory T depends on how
the fact X has been determined by *another* theory T^*." The recourse to
another theory immediately creates the impression of an infinite regress.

In order to clear things up here and remove as much of the vagueness as
possible from various parts of the paraphrase such as "fact for," we will
distinguish three cases. Let the given theory be called T. It does not need to
be precisely reconstructed. Using our previous symbolism the partial possible models of this theory may again be exhibited as an ordered $(n + 1)$-tuple
$\langle D, f_1, \ldots, f_n \rangle$, where the functions f_i defined on D are T-*nontheoretical*.
The three cases may now be easily distinguished by answering the question
of how value $f_i(x)$ for a given $x \in D$ may be obtained:

(1) There already is a *physical* theory T^* such that f_i is a T^*-theoretical
    function and the determination of $f_i(x)$ is a matter of calculation within
    T^*.
(2) As in the last case, there is a theory on which the calculation of the value
    rests. But this theory is *not a physical* theory.
(3) There is still no theory at hand, only a 'pretheoretical conception.'

The ideal case is (1), and it is also amenable to precise analysis. However,
for a reason which will soon become apparent, such an analysis lies beyond
the power of our present conceptual apparatus. Physical theories as a rule

are introduced not independently of one another but *in a certain order*. Let *T* be a theory (e.g., thermodynamics) which immediately follows *T** (e.g., classical particle mechanics) in this order. In this case all *T**-nontheoretical functions will indeed also be *T*-nontheoretical. On the other hand, *some, or even all, T-nontheoretical functions can be T*-theoretical*. (This relation would presumably constitute part of the precise definition of "immediately following in the order.") An example would be the thermodynamic non-theoretical function *pressure*, whose value in classical particle mechanics is calculated with the *CPM*-theoretical function *force*.

An exact analysis precisely formulating the essential aspects of the *theory hierarchy* being hinted at here is a task for the future. For the moment we are concerned only with elucidating the idea that the facts for one theory may be dependent upon some other theory, were both theories are *physical* theories. We will encounter an analogous situation in (2), where the given theory is, e.g., a measurement theory.[65]

The question of how the 'observable data' to be explained by the given theory *T* can assume the form of partial possible models for *T* consisting of 'quantitatively determined facts' has now been answered. *Some other physical theory* provides the means for a numerical description of these facts. Technically speaking, in order to ascertain if $\langle D, f_1, \ldots, f_n \rangle \in I$, one must be able, for all $x \in D$, to ascertain the values $f_i(x)$ of the *T*-nontheoretical functions. This is done by means of a theory *T** in relation to which the f_i are theoretical.[66]

The next step in constructing the primary theory *T* consists in *completing the core K of T*. Usually an *instrumentalist view* is favored here. According to it 'any conceivable theoretical function' and any constraint whatever on theoretical functions can be incorporated into the core as long as they repre-sent optimal contributions to two goals: first, to the creation of the *simplest mathematical structure possible*; second, to the *easiest possible method for calculating* the values of the nontheoretical functions. One could regard this view figuratively as the 'Martian approach to theory construction.' It is as if

[65] The reasons why a theory of measurement is not a physical theory will be given there.

[66] The question of how one can be sure that the nontheoretical functions of one theory are *the same* as the theoretical functions of another is examined more closely by Sneed in [Mathe-matical Physics], p. 252. He distinguishes two ways of interpreting the question. According to the first—it might be called the *metatheoretical* because it concerns the work of the philosophers of science—absolute certainty is not attainable. Instead it is an *empirical* matter concerning the theories to be reconstructed. According to the second, 'theoretical' interpretation, it is a matter of how the *theoretician himself* discerns the identity. And this question may be trivially answered by pointing out that this depends in turn on *how the theoretician describes his intended applications whereby an identification is established*. Here, too, the problem of knowing whether or not a certain list of ordered pairs consisting of individuals and function values *really represents the function described* can still crop up. But this is a purely practical problem which, as Sneed points out, is not essentially different from the difficulty involved in learning whether some particular person is John's oldest boy when one already knows that John's oldest boy has red hair.

beings from a distant planet were to land on Earth and teach us the use of a
new theory without taking any prescientific or extrascientific human
experience into consideration, which to be sure is not available to them. It is,
of course, just possible that talented scientists would finally grasp the theory
and learn to use it. But it is unrealistic to suppose that our theories arose
under these two 'instrumentalistic leitmotifs' alone. A detailed discussion
of this point is best reserved for case (3) since the problem of the '*historical
anchoring of theoretical concepts in specific mundane human experience*,' as it
might be called, is a cardinal question concerning the relationship between
theory and pretheory.

Case (2) concerns the emergence of primary theories which cannot look
to other physical theories for support. Such theories we will call *initial
physical theories*. This case is historically more interesting but metatheoretically more difficult to deal with. The difficulty is that although the intended
applications of an initial physical theory must be described in *numerical form*,
we cannot rely on the help of any available physical theory in dealing with the
question of just how the 'raw experiential data' is to be converted into
quantitative form. A rational reconstruction must rely in this case on one or
more theories of measurement (or metrizations) enabling us to introduce the
desired functions. If we limit ourselves to the most important instance, that
of *extensive* quantities, an *extensive* system $\langle B, R, o \rangle$ is required[67] which
can be expanded by means of an isomorphism or homomorphism correlator
h to an *extensive scale system* $\langle B, R, o, h \rangle$. While the introduction of the
function h does take care of the metrization problem, it requires in turn
the construction of an extensive system. And for this, as is detailed in Chapter
1 of Stegmüller, [Theoretische Begriffe], it is by no means enough to propose
some likely conventions and introduce clever definitions; numerous *empirical
hypotheses must be proposed and tested*. The reason that such a 'basic metric
theory' cannot be considered a *physical* theory is that according to our
definition a physical theory may contain *only numerical functions*, but no
qualitative predicates. *All* descriptions within the framework of a physical
theory are in quantitative language. An extensive system involves, however, a
nonmetric relation R and a *nonmetric combination operation o*.

For the sake of an example let us assume that the function to be introduced
is the *length function*. The theory of length manifest in the extensive scale
system will be called L. Here, at a 'lower level,' we find in principle a repe-
tition of everything we found at a 'higher level' for physical theories. We
have introduced the set-theoretic predicate "x is an extensive system," and
are seeking models for it. These models may overlap, indeed, in a nontrivial
way; i.e., the union of the domains of two such models may *not* yield the
domain of a model. Taken together these models comprise the partial possible

---

[67] The axioms characterizing such a system are given in Stegmüller, [Statistik], p. 406. Cf. also
Sneed, [Mathematical Physics], p. 18f. and p. 86ff.

models for the set-theoretic predicate "*x* is an extensive scale system." The *empirical claim of the theory* of length can then essentially be reduced to the claim that by the addition of a function *h* it is possible to enrich all of these partial possible models so as *to obtain models for the predicate* "*is an extensive scale system*."

In this way, however, the function *h* attains exactly the same status as the *T*-theoretical functions of a physical theory *T*. The only difference is that the theory *L* is not a *physical theory* in our sense. We have, though, in Section 3.2.9 made it sufficiently clear that the criterion for theoreticity can be carried over to nonphysical theories (indeed even to nonmetric concepts—which makes no difference here since *h* itself represents a function). *Calling length an L-theoretical quantity is, therefore, justified.*

Thus we can distinguish *two concepts of T-theoretical in the strong sense: T-theoretical in a physical sense and T-theoretical in a nonphysical sense.* We speak here of the strong sense of "theoretical" because in both cases Sneed's criterion for theoreticity is being used. (The *weak notion of* "*theoretical*," first mentioned in Stegmüller, [Theoretische Begriffe], Chapter 4, will be discussed under case (3).)

The central question of case (2) was "*where do initial physical theories get the numerical descriptions of 'things lying about the world' necessary for determining their applications?*" The answer now is analogous to the answer for case (1): namely, the numerical descriptions are produced with the help of functions which are *T*-nontheoretical with respect to the initial physical theory *T* but, nevertheless, *theoretical in respect of a metric theory 'underlying' T*. Thus again, the decisive 'numerical preliminaries' are taken care of *by some other theory*. Only this time this other theory is, contrary to case (1), not a physical theory.

Classical particle mechanics offers a good illustration of *both* cases. The functions *force* and *mass* are *CPM*-theoretical; the *position* function is, however, *CPM*-nontheoretical. Since classical particle mechanics is an initial theory in our sense of the word, this last function is not identical with a theoretical function of a *physical* theory. It is, however, *L-theoretical* when *L* is understood to be the theory of length measurement.

Let us now return to our original question of whether Newton could have formulated his theory a thousand years earlier. Presupposing *only* his genius as physicist and mathematician *and nothing more*, the answer is *no*. The formulation of such a theory requires not only *special* preliminary work like that of Kepler and Galileo; it also requires *the painstaking detail work of several centuries of transforming qualitative phenomena into quantitative data*. A positive answer to our question would thus entail the assumption that Newton, *in addition to* his scientific genius, also possessed the superhuman mental powers required to do the work of all those *centuries* by himself.

We will now turn to some metatheoretically interesting aspects of case (3). Again we can make use of the theory of length just mentioned or, more general still, a theory of extensive quantities. This can be regarded as an *initial non-physical theory proceeding out of a pretheoretical stage of thought.* Concerning this theory questions analogous to those confronting the numerical non-theoretical functions of a physical or metric theory can be raised about the *nonnumerical* notions used, e.g., the relation *R* and combination operation o. Here, too, it must be admitted that it would be an irresponsible simplification to say these notions are 'a part of our everyday thinking.'

Consider for a moment such *everyday* notions as "is shorter than" or "is at least as long as." In order for any reconstructable theory of such *pretheoretical* notions to arrive at a relation *R* and a combinative operation o fulfilling the axioms for extensive systems and making possible the introduction of a numerical function leading to an extensive scale system, *extraordinarily strong idealizations* are required. In particular, these idealizations must allow us to interpret the theory of length in such a way that all known empirical methods for determining the truth value of *R*-sentences deal with *one and the same* property. Further, they must meet certain mathematical requirements which may remove the systematic concept quite far, at least in a psychological sense, from its everyday base as, for example, requiring the position function to be *twice differentiable with respect to time.* (The phrase "at least in a psychological sense" may be understood roughly to mean that for someone not at all acquainted with exact theories, the 'distance' between the everyday notions he uses to describe motion and a twice differentiable position function appears greater than the difference between this position function and the functions of *mass* and *force*.)

It is easy to see that we are dealing here with exactly the same problems which in Stegmüller, [Theoretische Begriffe], Chapter 4, Sections 1–3, were given as a motive for adopting 'theoretical' concepts which cannot be 'reduced to the observational language.' We will label such concepts *theoretical in the weak sense.*

For the first time we can now establish a connection between the conception developed in this book and the one called the dual-level conception of scientific language in [Theoretische Begriffe]. Moreover, we can also see the reason for the ambivalent feeling that this dual-level conception is *in certain respects adequate while in others it offers a much too primitive picture of the structure of modern science.* In principle the dual-level conception represents an adequate tool for the philosopher of science interested in *describing initial primary theories and their relationship to the prescientific basis in everyday thinking and speaking.* The idealizations and conceptual identifications going into these theories *constitute that part of the theoretical conceptual network projecting out of the 'experiential' or 'observational' plane.* The members of this network are the *theoretical terms* or *theoretical concepts in the weak sense.*

For *mature science*, which has left the initial theory stage, this picture is no longer appropriate. Here we are working with *theories containing T-*

theoretical terms in the strong (Sneedian) sense. And we must not forget that this is by no means just a 'gradual difference.' It is *something so radically new as to force a complete revision of our thinking about theories.* It was the insight that modern physical theories work with theoretical functions *in the strong sense* that produced the problem of theoretical terms, whose solution in turn lead to the 'nonstatement view' of theories. *The concept of theoretical terms in the strong sense forces us to stop thinking of theories as classes of sentences in favor of thinking of them as complex mathematical structures supplemented* (only as a rule) *by paradigmatically determined sets of intended applications and used at any time only to assert a single cohesive sentence, the central empirical claim of the theory* (or its propositional counterpart, *a strong theory proposition $I \in \mathbb{A}_e(E)$*).

The reasons given in [Theoretische Begriffe], Chapter 4, Sections 1–3, for deserting early empiricism still hold. *But they are not enough.* In retrospect it may be said that it was shown there that even for the *most primitive* forms of theories early empiricism's 'single-level model' does not fit the bill because theoretical terms in the weak sense occur even in these theories. Just how a *mature* theory is to be analyzed is outlined in Chapters 5–8, 12, and 15, where we do not want to forget that when we are dealing with *qualitative* primary theories we must rely on an intuitive notion of "theory" not covered by the explications in Chapter 7.

Axiomatic theories of measurement have already been referred to twice. They offer the best rational reconstructions currently available of the introduction of quantitative functions leading to various types of scales. It should, however, be said that they practically always ignore *one* aspect of quantitative systems. They do indeed give most exacting accounts of the conditions qualitative relations must satisfy in order to permit the introduction of quantities. But this says absolutely nothing about whether or not the metric systems involved are '*useful and interesting.*' This extraordinarily important point has two aspects. One looks 'backward' toward the intuitive origins, the other 'forward' toward the theory of which empirical progress and success is expected. The first might be called the aspect of *familiarity*, the second that of *fruitfulness*. The concept of *acceleration* in classical mechanics departed not only from familiar ideas about motion; it also represented a relatively 'unfamiliar' concept in relation to the 'theoretical–classical' methods of describing motion which essentially were *purely geometric*. The double aspect of having 'something to do' with familiar notions and nevertheless playing an important part in a successful theory is perhaps a distinguishing characteristic of this concept.

The concept of acceleration presents, incidentally, a good opportunity for critically comparing the theoretical niveau of the natural sciences with the systematic social sciences. In monetary theory the notion of the *circulation rate* of money plays a central role. Complementing it, one can also precisely define the notion of *circulation acceleration*. The difference could be of considerable practical significance. But, as is well known, it always takes some decades before theoretical developments in national economy are taken seriously by the practitioners. In the equilibrium and employment theory of J. M. Keynes, developed in the 1930's and just recently acknowledged by practitioners, the creation of money plays a decisive part as a means of maintaining full employment. It might be that Keynes has erred here insofar as his method for creating full employment is not only, as he thought, coupled with a certain mild, constant inflation *rate*, but rather with a constant inflation *acceleration* whose disastrous side effects could more than outweigh the positive effect of the methods for maintaining the employment level.

The remark about acceleration offers an opportunity to take a final critical shot at the 'instrumentalist interpretation' of theoretical concepts mentioned at the outset. According to this interpretation the core of a theory may be completed by incorporating any theoretical function so long as 'it does the theory good service.' In [Mathematical Physics], p. 297ff., Sneed argues that something has been overlooked here. It could be called the *desire to harmonize theoretical explanation and intuitive understanding as far as possible*. These efforts distinguish our mechanics from a 'Martian mechanics.' With this desire a specific *human* element finds its way not into *all* theoretical concepts, but certainly into the theoretical concepts of *primary* physical *theories* such as classical particle mechanics. Seen from this perspective, older philosophies of nature postulating, for example, a subjective experience of force as the source of a real understanding of the basic concepts of mechanics, prove to be neither so 'outmoded' nor, indeed, ' silly.' Thus *mass* as 'the resistance of a body to being set in motion ' involves something which everyone has experienced in countless instances, be it, for example, a situation in which he just manages to edge a table along, or a situation in which he does not succeed in moving a piano. Likewise, he has repeatedly experienced the subjective strain of exerting a force on something and still uses the word "force" constantly although he may never have heard of such a thing as mechanics. But *when* he then studies classical particle mechanics and sees how it explains special types of motion, he feels a certain satisfaction and is inclined to say: "Aha! That behaves just *as I expected*; that I *understand*."

The quite human desire for *comprehension* and *understandable explanations* enables us to grasp *metatheoretically* the connection between pretheoretic ideas and the T-theoretical concepts of a primary theory T; for example, the historical continuity between 'pretheoretic reflections on the phenomena of motion' and the 'explanations of moving masses with the help of *CPM*-theoretical concepts.'

This last point should not, however, be overestimated. In the first place it concerns only *primary theories*, not theories 'appearing later in the theory hierarchy.' The concept *entropy*, and most certainly a concept like *isospin*, have no pretheoretical counterpart. In the second place one should not be tempted to think that the intuitive precursors of his T-theoretical concepts are a millstone around the neck of the 'primary theoretician.' He has a great deal of latitude in '*the abundant use of mathematical idealizations*' such as continuity, differentiation, and integration, and in *construing the connection between the theoretical and nontheoretical functions*. Newton's second law, the central component of the core of classical particle mechanics, can be seen as an attempt to bring the concepts being used to deal with motion into an 'orderly constellation per nomothetical injunction.' Finally, it may be expected that the connection of pretheoretical attributes to *nontheoretical* functions is, all in all, much stronger than to *theoretical* functions. The nontheoretical functions are but idealized forms representing those properties ' to which we have direct empirical access.' We have, on the other hand, no direct access to the values of *theoretical* functions despite the connection afforded by a historical continuity with a pretheoretical basis. This is again a consequence of the way *theoretical functions* are handled.

That there must actually be 'more latitude' concerning theoretical functions than nontheoretical becomes especially clear when one considers the course of normal science. Different expansions E_t and $E_{t'}$ of the same core at different times t and t' will, as a rule, yield *different* values of the theoretical functions for certain individuals in the domain. Hence it can be said that *the extensions of the theoretical functions are constantly changing* in that form of dynamics where the theory remains constant while beliefs change.[68] Only in the special case of 'linear' development leading to successive restrictions, i.e., where $\mathbb{A}_e(E_1) \supset \mathbb{A}_e(E_2) \supset \cdots \supset \mathbb{A}_e(E_i) \supset \cdots$, can it be said that *the same* theoretical function is becoming more and more precise.

Some will perhaps feel that the influence of specific intuitive ideas on the theoretical concepts of a primary theory mentioned above is incompatible with this last observation. But harmony may be restored here by further observing that *the pretheoretical notions are potently reflected in the constraints imposed on the theoretical functions*. Thus, for example, weight was regarded as an *internal* property of bodies in the pre-Newtonian era when it had not yet been distinguished from inertial resistance. The same holds for force. In constructing the theory this is taken into account by incorporating the constraint $\langle \approx, = \rangle$. Likewise, the constraint requiring mass to be an extensive quantity may be regarded as the expression of pretheoretical ideas about 'material quantity.' We have seen that *these general constraints can be, and are, held on to tenaciously.* When a core expansion E of a theory $\langle K, I \rangle$ is used to formulate the strongest possible theory proposition $I \in \mathbb{A}_e(E)$, and this empirical claim runs afoul of experience, *it is the theoretical laws that are held responsible, not the constraints. The theoretical laws are*

---

[68] As is easily seen, the same thing holds when the membership in I changes.

sacrificed rather than the constraints imposed on the theoretical functions. Were someone in such a conflict situation to propose, for example, giving up the idea that mass is an extensive quantity rather than giving up some special theoretical law about mass, the reaction would presumably run: "he wants us to come up with an entirely new theory!"

16.3 The second kind of scientific revolution: The dislodging of one theory by another

Up to this point we have analyzed two types of dynamic process: the initial appearance of a theory and the course of normal science. The first can *always* be regarded as *scientific progress*, the second, only in certain cases depending on *the two possibilities for normal scientific growth*. These are the discovery of new elements of I (i.e., $I_t \subset I_{t'}$ for $t < t'$) and restriction by means of successful core expansions (i.e., $\mathbb{A}_e(E_{t'}) \subset \mathbb{A}_e(E_t)$ for $t < t'$) making possible ever stronger empirical claims and theory propositions. These two cases represent those forms of scientific growth in which *the convictions of scientists are continually shifting under the mantle of one and the same theory.*

A third type of progress consists of scientific revolution in the narrow sense *in which an already available theory is rejected in favor of a newly conceived substitute.* In [Revolutions], p. 97, Kuhn observes that in principle there are only three conceivable contexts in which a new theory can appear. In the first, there is already a theory available which explains the empirical phenomena satisfactorily. In the second there is a theory which 'hints at' the nature of these phenomena, but a lot of details remain to be cleared up by a further articulation of this theory. In the third we find an accumulation of 'anomalies' stubbornly resisting explanation by the currently available theory.[69] Kuhn then adds that *only the last situation really accommodates the advent of a new theory.* In the other two there is either no motive for seeking a new theory or, if proposed, no reason to adopt it.

These remarks concerning the first two situations can be precisely articulated within the framework of our conceptual apparatus. The first involves normal scientific growth as depicted in the next to last paragraph. Here there is actually no reason to cast about, since the successful applications of the available theory are on the increase and special problems have been successfully solved by suitable expansions of the core. The second can be identified with those cases where a core and a set of paradigm examples are on hand, but normal scientific progress has yet to be realized. This is normal science in the 'promise phase.' And as long as it has not been ascertained whether or not the promise will fulfill itself, there is again no reason to seek a new theory

---

[69] Where we speak of theories here, Kuhn speaks of 'paradigms.' His terminology is misleading, because the present context concerns the *mathematical structure* of the theory, not the paradigmatically determined set of intended applications.

which in the beginning can *also* offer nothing but a similar *promise* of success.

Thus, it actually appears that only the third situation, the repeated failure of the available theory, need be taken seriously. If, nevertheless, many critics of Kuhn's view here again find an appeal to irrationality, there are two reasons. First, Kuhn does *link* the rejection of a theory *to the acceptance of a new one*. Second, his thinking *does appear to exclude a precise articulation of the circumstances under which this sort of transition must take place.*

Again it is easy to see that on the basis of the 'statement view' the charge of irrationality seems to be justified, but that for the 'nonstatement view' it is either empty, or at best reduces to those *possible* criticisms mentioned in Section 16.1. To believe in the elements of an empirically falsified class of sentences appears at best less irrational than clinging to a demonstrably inconsistent mathematical theory in the sense that the 'basis of falsification' could itself contain false claims. When, on the other hand, a person holds a theory in the Kuhnian sense (D30), there can, as we saw, at no time be convincing empirical reasons for letting this theory fall. It *was successful.* It *has proved itself* in the formulation of central empirical claims (VI) or, alternatively, the assertion of theory propositions. Should normal scientific progress grind to a halt, nothing can prevent the scientist from regarding this stagnation as a *temporary setback* which will be taken care of by the return of 'better times' like 'the good old days' when he or his predecessors successfully applied the theory.

We know why such a reaction is absolutely in no sense 'irrational.' Even *when the scientist explicitly admits his hypothetical assumption to be wrong*, he need *not* give up the theory he holds. For we must carefully distinguish between *holding a theory* and the *empirical claims of form* (VI) or strong *theory propositions hypothetically assumed* by the person holding the theory. It is only the propositions, not the theory, which may prove false. The nonempirical component of the latter consists of a mathematical structure K which in the past has rendered good service in dealing with a part of the empirical components (the paradigm applications of I_0 and perhaps even an extension I_t of I_0). Why should it not, despite certain setbacks, continue to do so in the future?

"It is a poor carpenter who blames his tools." Both this proverb, quoted by Kuhn ([Revolutions], p. 80), and his remark (*op. cit.*, p. 79) that *the only kind of rejection to which counterinstances can lead is rejection of science in favor of another occupation* can be readily interpreted here. We must merely assume that we are speaking of a 'normal' scientist lacking what it takes to induce a scientific revolution. The proverb could then be supplemented by the phrase "and to create *new* tools it takes more than a carpenter." The carpenter himself will first try to improve the tools that have worked well until now and, failing this, look for new and better inventions. And when despite considerable effort he can *neither* improve the old *nor* find the new, *what remains but to get out of the field*?

213

One thing is certain: as the 'failure frequency of a theory,' i.e., the frequency of unsuccessful attempts to produce a proposition $I_t \in \mathbb{A}_e(E_t)$, increases for him and his colleagues, the situation becomes increasingly uncomfortable for a scientist. And with growing dissatisfaction, the readiness to try a new theory, as far as one is available, grows too. A crisis situation such as this makes it *understandable why it is no mere historical accident that the decision to drop a theory is always a decision in favor of a new theory* as Kuhn so forcefully emphasizes. A theory—contrary to a true or false theory proposition or empirical claim—is a complicated implement which one tries out to see 'how far one can get with it.' One can *understand* that such an implement will not be thrown away as long as nothing better is at hand. One can, we said, understand; but one *cannot* produce *logical grounds* for this attitude, simply because there is nothing more here to be logically grounded. It is also no 'historical accident' that anyone would rather have a house with holes in the roof than no house at all, or that a shipwrecked sailor would rather have a broken oar than none at all. In each of these cases we have feasible *psychological explanations* for the behavior involved. But we would shake our heads in dismay should it be demanded of us *to prove that humans must, or indeed should, always behave that way.*

Thus, one cannot expect more in our case either. Classical particle mechanics proved itself again and again when it came to predicting or explaining the motions of *middle-sized* bodies with *moderate velocities*. With electrically charged bodies at extremely high velocities it ran into trouble. Nevertheless it is *understandable* that one continued to work with it until a new mathematical structure, the theory of relativity, was discovered which proved successful in all areas where the old was successful and gave good reason to expect success in dealing with those phenomena where the old had failed.

Unfortunately, this defence of Kuhn's conception must be followed up by *two substantial criticisms*. His exposition of this sort of scientific revolution, which we will call *the dislodging of a theory by a substitute theory*, contains an exaggeration and a mistake.

Indeed, a *most reckless exaggeration* is contained in the allegation that with this new interpretation of theory dynamics the problem of confirmation simply disappears so that the distinction (originally Reichenbach's) between the contexts of discovery and of justification becomes meaningless. The error made by the proponents of the 'statement view' finds its partner here. That there *must* be a mistake somewhere should be obvious enough when one recalls that the 'nonstatement view' of theories should not lead to the absurd proposition that physicists make no empirical claims at all. According to our reconstruction, the empirical content of a physical theory is contained in one single, cohesive statement which is, therefore, *especially rich in content* and *sensitive to empirical testing*. It is only where *the theory itself* is concerned that the problem of confirmation disappears—something overlooked by Kuhn's adversaries. Concerning the *central empirical claim* and its propositional content, *the strong theory proposition*, the problem of confirmation holds *undiminished* as before—something to which the 'Kuhnians' are apparently blind. In the final analysis the success or failure of a theory is decided exclusively by the question of *whether or not theory propositions* $I_t \in \mathbb{A}_e(E_t)$ *'stand the test of experience.'* Should *statistical laws* be included in the class L of laws of the expanded core E_t (or even, as in quantum mechanics, occur in the component M of the core K itself), the corroboration problem falls under the jurisdiction of *statistical support and testing theory.* If, on the other hand, the core laws in M as well as the special laws in L are *deterministic*, we will be confronted with a revival of the 'inductivist' – 'deductivist' quarrel. And *the problem must be solved*—indeed via a precise explication of the confirmation concept—*if one wants to arrive at a rational criterion for judging the nonstatistical Ramsey–Sneed claims of a theory.* Those 'Kuhnians' who think the traditional discussion of these questions is a lot of rubbish are due for a rude awakening.

While the refusal to acknowledge confirmation problems entails merely an exaggeration, there is a logical error in Kuhn's vigorously propounded *thesis that a theory and its successor are not only incompatible, but incommensurable.* It is, however, not easy to locate this error. But once discovered it is (again!) quite understandable how Kuhn and his followers made it. The many details proffered by Kuhn buried the error on the one hand while strengthening on the other his critic's impression—*this time rightly so*—that the dislodging of theories by new ones must according to him be interpreted as an entirely irrational process. We need only remember statements to the effect that any argument in favor of a paradigm (i.e., in favor of a theory $\langle K, I_0 \rangle$) is basically *circular*, that the proponents of various theories can *not communicate* due to the lack of a neutral metalanguage, that the strife between competing theories is similar to *religious* or *political struggles* between incompatible ways of life in a community, that, therefore, the conflict is not resolved by arguments, i.e., in a rational way, but rather by propaganda, persuasion, and even the gradual 'dying out' of the 'old guard.'

Two points in Kuhn's conception remain unexplained. First, how it is that the older, dislodged theory had been *successful*. Second, how we come to speak of *progress* in the case of scientific upheavals. The term "progress," one might suppose, must be *exclusively* reserved for the two forms of development indigenous to the course of normal science as described. Dislodging a theory could *only* be thought of as an upheaval.

The constructive nucleus of I. Lakatos' criticisms of Kuhn's conception in [Research Programmes] can be interpreted as *singling out these two rationality gaps and trying to close them with the notion of a research programme.* We will first adopt Sneed's conception, which would *seem* to be quite different. In Section 16.4 we will, however, show how Lakatos' theory can be reconstructed so as to coincide with this conception in the essential points.

The relation which must obtain between dislodged and dislodging theories, should the relative success of the old and the superiority of the new both be accounted for, may be very briefly formulated:

The dislodged theory is reducible to the dislodging theory.

Both Kuhn and, in a like manner, Feyerabend seem to have explicitly denied this. [Revolutions], p. 101, is presumably the only place in Kuhn's work where something like the *outlines of a logical argument* are given. Kuhn details there the reasons why Newtonian dynamics may *not* be said to be *deducible* from relativistic dynamics. This argument is a joke. Kuhn uses the metatheoretic 'paradigm' of his opponents to support the incommensurability thesis. For the 'statement view,' reduction problems can only turn on one thing: namely, the 'inference relations between classes of sentences.' *However, instead of arguing from noninferability to nonreducibility, we will argue that an adequate concept of reduction cannot be defined in terms of inference.*

We have here, one could say, a typical instance of *someone exceeding his competence.* An analogy should serve to make clear what is meant. Were an expert on the history of mathematics to allege that a constructive proof of the consistency of number theory is impossible, ergo "G. Gentzen cannot really have produced such a proof," one would rightly retort that he is not competent to judge such matters. He should study metamathematics and point out the alleged error or nonconstructive step in Gentzen's proof. Likewise it can be said here that the question of whether or not one theory is reducible to another is not a matter to be decided by the historian of science, not even one with a novel metascientific conception. The task of explicating a suitable reduction concept is a logical one, and indeed, as we saw, an *exceptionally tough* one. It must be left to competent experts. A bit of musing about 'the noninferability of certain sentences from others' is absolutely insufficient.

E. W. Adams indicated how the problem must be approached in [Rigid Body Mechanics]. His notion of reduction is considerably more complex and subtle than the one to which Kuhn appeals at the place mentioned above. But that, and why, even Adams' concept is not enough was shown in Chapter 9. He, Adams, worked exclusively with a *simple* basic mathematical structure (the "characteristic property" in his terminology) defined by the set-theoretic predicate of the axiomatic theory. The Sneedian conception, which also takes into consideration the *difference between theoretical and nontheoretical functions,* the *multiplicity of intended applications,* and *special laws* in addition to general ones, leads, as we saw in Chapter 9, to a further, indeed very penetrating refinement in the structure of the reduction concept. For the moment it is only important to realize that with the help of this concept *both rationality gaps can be closed.* It enables us to understand how a dislodged theory could prove successful in certain situations, but also how the

216

dislodging theory can be successful in the same *as well as still other, new situations* and can be 'progressive' in this sense.

Finally we would like to point out what might be called the *Kantian aspect of revolutionary theory dynamics.* We can assume at the outset at least a *formal analogy* between the reconstruction of the relationship of 'theory and experience' offered here and Kant's theory. Kant, too, postulates a basic conceptual apparatus, the system of 'concepts of pure reason,' which together with the 'metaphysical foundations of experience' deduced from it is not affected by changes in the realm of experience. There is, however, one essential difference. For Kant the *a priori* apparatus was externally fixed, and not potentially subject to change. *His* a priori *was absolute, not temporally relativized. Theoretically there should be but one way to pursue science.* Many of Kant's followers and admirers have regretted this rigidity in his conception of the *a priori* and have propounded a sort of temporal relativization or flexibility—most decisively perhaps E. Cassirer. That the idea of 'liberalizing Kant's theoretical philosophy' had almost no effect at all on the philosophy of science is understandable considering that modern philosophy of science derives from modern *empiricism,* and *no* version of modern empiricism had any idea at all of what to do with even a 'relativized ' Kantian conception. According to empiricist views *anything* done by a theoretician must answer before the tribunal of experience. *Nothing* is immune to empirical control.

Neither does the Kuhnian view of the development of science immediately suggest an analogy to a liberalized Kantian conception. But this lies entirely in the complexity of Kuhn's paradigm concept. When the expression "paradigm" is appropriately limited, namely, to the set I of intended applications of a theory characterized by paradigmatic examples, we have something which is specifically *not* a priori—not even in a temporally relativized sense, but something 'empirical' that changes as ('normal scientific ') experience accumulates. Thus, if one wants to apply Kant's basic intuition to our present case, one cannot look to the second member I of a theory $T = \langle K, I \rangle$—which in this context could well be considered the *empirical* component of a theory—one must consider the first member K, which may be regarded as *the a priori component of a theory* in a sense that as long as someone holds *this* theory *this* component remains unchanged. It *is* immune to the storms plaguing the world of experience and need not first be immunized by 'conventionalistic tricks.' As something *relatively* a priori the core of a theory remains sovereign over 'struggles for the favors of experience ' which transpire in 'nether regions.' In terms of the conception offered here, these latter are the rivalries between central empirical claims or theory propositions, which in a fortunate case can take the form of a 'linear normal scientific development': namely, from a proposition $I_t \in \mathbb{A}_e(E)$ to an *empirically stronger* proposition $I_{t'} \in \mathbb{A}_e(E)$ with $I_t \subset I_{t'}$ or to $I_t \in \mathbb{A}_e(E^*)$ with $\mathbb{A}_e(E^*) \subset \mathbb{A}_e(E)$.

While this combination of changes at the empirical level coupled with a constant core K is characteristic of the course of normal science, one can discern in the onset of a crisis and the resulting scientific revolution a shift of the 'power struggle' from the empirical to the *a priori* level. *Empirical rivalries give way to* a priori *skirmishes*. And the victor in this contest is— despite all the beguiling talk of Kuhn and Feyerabend—not he who concocts the best propaganda for the scientific mob, or any other, but he who accomplishes all that his predecessor did and then some. And since the victor can *also* accomplish *the same things*, the image of dislodgement is again in one sense quite misleading (as is *always* the case with figurative comparisons in one way or another). In order to grasp the real relationship between the *a priori* components of a theory and those of its substitute, one must again take leave of metaphorical thinking and rely on the conceptual instrument provided by the precise *reduction concepts* of Chapter 9.

However, before doing so, the image may still serve to clarify the distinction between the *relative* and the absolute *a priori*. The reason that we may *only* speak of a relative *a priori* is that *no* core, be it ever so sophisticated and yield it ever so many successful expansions, can be guaranteed never to get caught in an *a priori* conflict with some future alternative and go down before it because this opponent can 'deal with anomalies which it cannot.'

Above we explicitly spoke only of a *formal* analogy to Kant's theoretical philosophy. Even the 'temporally relativized version of the *a priori*' should not disguise the fact that in terms of content fundamental differences remain. One can convince oneself of this most quickly by glancing at the set-theoretic apparatus of Chapter 7. When we exhibit an expanded core à la Sneed as an 8-tuple $\langle M_p, M_{pp}, r, M, C, L, C_L, \alpha \rangle$, the line between the relative '*a priori* ' and the 'empirical' components falls between the fifth and sixth members. The nonempirical invariant in normal science is the core $K = \langle M_p, M_{pp}, r, M, C \rangle$. The 'empirical component' consists of the remaining three members L, C_L, and α, plus, for each point of time, the set I_t fulfilling the condition $I_0 \subseteqq I_t$ in case of a paradigmatic determination. The 'vicissitudes of experience' affect, thus, the members of the quadruple $\langle L, C_L, I_t, \alpha \rangle$. ($\alpha$ is included since this relation assigns the *special* laws of L to *special* applications for which they are hypothetically supposed to hold. Thus the extension of α can vary with a change either in the class L or the intended applications.) The 'relatively *a priori*' core K contains three components *which have no intuitive counterpart in Kant's thinking*: the *theoretical-nontheoretical*[70] distinction, the *constraints*, and the *distinction of several, partly overlapping intended applications* needed for the concept of constraint.

Kant claimed that his theory reconciled rationalism and empiricism, the *a priori* and the empirical components in the scientific process. The

---

[70] It is obvious that the division into 'relatively *a priori*' and 'empirical' parts made here does *not* allow us to equate the difference between theoretical and nontheoretical functions with a difference between *a priori* and *a posteriori* conceptual components.

reconstruction of Kuhnian theory dynamics with Sneed's conceptual apparatus is perhaps a better candidate for this job.

16.3.1 Figurative synopsis

A mature physical theory, being one which has superseded not only the pretheoretical but also the nonphysical qualitative stages and is, therefore, at least an initial physical theory, offers quite a different picture than that of a 'system of sentences connected by deductive and inductive relations.' It is an unusual thing with an inert center and organically growing and changing extremities. The center consists of a more or less complicated but relatively stable *mathematical structure* which may be subdivided into various fine structures. The instable parts are first grasped by tracing their dynamic life cycle 'from the cradle to the grave.' A temporally instantaneous cross section is not enough. Unlike earthly creatures, its basic constitution or intellectual substance, the core, is also its ironclad skeleton already given to it in the cradle. The flux of organic parts, on the other hand, is not predetermined. The kind, number, and development of these parts is determined by how, and with what success, the theory is used by its creators to systemize experience, i.e., to systematically describe, explain, and predict. The growth of the organic superstructure proceeds in an amoeba-like fashion. Unlike earthly organisms, developed organs, the 'laws' and the 'constraints' connecting them, can retrogress when 'recalcitrant experience' so demands to make room for the growth of new organs of similar type. As a relative *a priori* the basic constitution is on the other hand *not* exposed to the storms of experience; it is invulnerable to empirical wounds. Only the organic hull is afflicted by injuries including amputation, but even then only in a way which does not hinder its *overall growth*, its 'normal scientific growth.' This picture changes only then when the empirical afflictions begin to pile up. But in this case, too, it is not alleged 'falsifying experience' which seals the fate of the old theory; it is a new theory with a new basic intellectual constitution which in a conflict of *a prioris* dethrones its predecessor. Yet its beginnings are not entirely new. Some of the old is spared, which of course does not mean that the cradle of the new theory must be big enough to accommodate the coffin of the old. Via palingenesis and metempsychosis the spirit of the old is reincarnated in the body of the new, where it inspires not only the realization of new creative achievements but bequeathes all of its own achievements on the new theory. The transition is not 'mere change,' it is 'genuine revolutionary progress.' Since the success of the normal scientific growth of a theory depends not only on its adaptability to 'objective reality,' but this adaptability *also* decides the outcome of *a priori* duels between theories, both normal scientific and revolutionary progress represent no 'mere shifts in belief,' but genuine *growth* of knowledge according to objective standards.

16.4 'Research programmes' and 'sophisticated falsificationism' according to I. Lakatos: Two alternatives for closing the rationality gap in Kuhn's rendition of theory dislodgement

Our critical discussion in Section 16.3 served to point out a *rationality gap* in Kuhn's conception of the dislodging of one theory by another. It is easy to underestimate the significance of this gap. In order to grasp it we will first clarify in what respect there is a gap at all. This is best done by means of a comparison with both of the other types of 'theory dynamics.' Within the course of normal science there are, as we have seen, progressive developments and setbacks. Here we can say precisely what may be called "progress" and what may be called a "setback." Roughly speaking, *normal scientific progress* consists of either a genuine expansion of the intended applications of a theory held by someone, or a successful application of a 'restricted' expansion of the theory core K, i.e., an expansion with additional special laws and (or) constraints. In our macrological idiom both forms of normal scientific progress could be succinctly described as follows: "a proposition $I \in \mathbb{A}_e(E)$ has been found which, regarding content, is stronger than any of its predecessors and is empirically supported." The dual counterpart to this is *normal scientific setback* expressed either by the exclusion of physical systems from the set of intended applications or by the rejection of a core expansion. No explicit notion of progress was introduced to cover the case where theories appear for the first time. But here we can in *any* case speak of progress in relation to the previous 'theory-less' situation. For by definition a theory is born when the core or one of its expansions has been *successfully* applied at least once. And *this* success certainly represents progress when compared to a situation where no theory at all is held, hence no 'success' is given either.

These two kinds of progress cannot be augmented by a third kind within the framework of Kuhn's conception of the dislodging of one theory by another. His incommensurability thesis precludes a logical comparison between the original theory and the dislodging theory *thus making it impossible to talk of progress*. At best we can speak of *change*. Intuitively this is an unsatisfactory result—both from a logical and an historical point of view. From a *logical* point of view it should at least be *conceivable* that theory dislodgement means 'progress.' From an *historical* point of view it can hardly be denied that in fact certain theory dislodgements 'did bring progress.' *This* progress must be elucidated, not denied.

How is it that Kuhn's theory yields this strange consequence rendering talk of 'revolutionary progress' of this type impossible? A comparison with our solution to the 'rationality gap' in Section 16.3 throws some light on the subject. We were able to say that the superiority of the new theory lay in the fact that it not only 'solved problems which the old one could not,' but was also successful wherever the old one had been successful *because the old one is reducible to the new one.* In doing so we appealed to Adams' reduction concept as expanded and refined by Sneed. This reduction concept was not available to Kuhn, *forcing him to resort to* 'inference relations between sentences' ([Revolutions], p. 101ff.). The reflections stemming from this basis supported his incommensurability claim.

Now we certainly might run across cases where the dislodging of a theory is *mistakenly* thought to represent progress when in fact it does not. This would be this case when it was mistakenly believed that the old theory is reducible to the new one. We in no way wish to deny the existence of such cases of *'revolutionary setback'* as it might be called in analogy to normal scientific setback. (If and when this has actually happened could only be ascertained by a combination of logical and historical studies.) The crucial point is that *we are in a position to differentiate sharply between cases of theory dislodgement with and theory dislodgement without progress while the Kuhnian conceptual apparatus allows for no such differentiation at all.*

In Section 16.3 we mentioned that Lakatos, too, has observed this rationality gap in Kuhn's views. In bridging it we nevertheless adopted Sneed's apparatus which, we said, *appears* to have no connection with Lakatos' methods. We will now try to show that this is actually *no more* than an appearance, that at least Lakatos' comments concerning this point can be precisely articulated so as to yield the same conclusion, namely, reduction.

First, two brief remarks: (1) Lakatos' writings contain an abundance of systematic starts and detailed historical studies. Of these we will only concern ourselves with two: *a certain aspect of his concept of a research programme* and his *new formulation of the falsification concept.* Thus we are by no means promising to deliver a precise articulation of all those points which he himself held to be important. In particular the 'methodological aspect,' which he prized so greatly, will not be considered here. (2) Where Lakatos introduced new concepts he did so on an intuitive basis at the bottom of which implicitly lay the 'statement view.' In 'translating' into the language of our concepts we will assign his theory concept *one of two different concepts* depending on context. This is a consequence of the fact that that which the statement view calls "theory" must sometimes be construed within the nonstatement view as a *theory* and sometimes as a *theory proposition.*

The *concept of a research programme* will serve to show that this translation is not merely arbitrary. The objects under consideration here are not single 'theories' in Lakatos' sense, but entire *sequences of* 'theories.' As Lakatos himself pointed out,[71] the 'continuity' welding the members of such a sequence together into a research programme reminds one of Kuhn's

[71] [Research Programmes], p. 132.

conception of normal science. When we consider this remark we see that we are forced to construe such a sequence as a sequence of *claims* or *propositions, not* a sequence of theories in our sense. Within the framework of our reconstruction it is characteristic of the course of normal science in Kuhn's sense that the theory remain *constant* while only convictions change. And these are formulated with the help of central empirical claims or their propositional counterparts. For the sake of simplicity we will work only with strong theory propositions instead of linguistic entities. We must, however, *also* refer to a theory, or more exactly, to the *holding of a theory*, since every strong theory proposition contains expansions of the core of a theory as well as sets of partial possible models of *this* theory. In the present context it makes no difference whether we take the weaker concept of holding a theory in the sense of D27 or the pragmatically restricted Kuhnian concept in the sense of D30.

> Since Lakatos would presumably not like to make all too great a concession to the special ideas of Kuhn, one can expect to remain better in tune with his views if one works with the *weaker*, or Sneedian, concept of holding a theory (assuming, of course, that he would in general find the present conceptual framework an acceptable vehicle for a precise articulation of his concepts).

More precisely, we will assume that a person or a group of persons p hold one and the same theory $T = \langle K, I \rangle$ during a period of time which is to be regarded as a sequence of discrete times $t_1, t_2, \ldots, t_i, \ldots$. *Thus person (group) and theory are fixed.* The core expansions of which we will be speaking are, therefore, always expansions of this one core K. Furthermore, the intended applications assumed should in each instance be subsets of I.

As members of a sequence representing a research programme we will take strong theory propositions of the form $I_{t_i} \in \mathbb{A}_e(E_{t_i})$. A sequence of n members $\phi_1, \phi_2, \ldots, \phi_n$ will be symbolized by $\langle \phi_i \rangle_{i \in \mathbb{N}_n}$, where $\mathbb{N}_n$ stands for the set of natural numbers smaller than or equal to n.

Lakatos says that a research programme embodies *theoretical progress* when each 'step' increases empirical content.[72] We can articulate this notion without any trouble by direct reference to both forms of normal scientific progress (cf. Section 16.3, first paragraph).

In this concept of theoretical progress the epistemic component is still unaccounted for. This can be taken care of by requiring progress to represent *empirical* progress as well. The simplest way of expressing this idea consists of requiring that each step of the program be corroborated. For the sake of terminological continuity with previous definitions we will again use the *undefined* notion of support.[73]

---

[72] *Op. cit.*, p. 134. The predication of an empirical content is by the way a further independent motive for us to construe the members of the sequence as theory *propositions* and not as *theories*.

[73] Concerning this last point Lakatos' views are ambiguous. Alternative possibilities will be indicated later.

D31 Let p hold (in the Sneedian, Kuhnian, or a third sense still to be defined) a theory $T = \langle K, I \rangle$ for a time span S consisting of discrete times $t_1, t_2, \ldots, t_n$. We then say: *p holds an n-member theoretically and empirically progressive research programme in the sense of normal science* iff there exists a sequence $\langle I_{t_i} \in \mathbb{A}_e(E_{t_i}) \rangle_{i \in \mathbb{N}_n}$ of strong theory propositions such that each E_{t_i} is an expansion of K and for every $i \in \mathbb{N}_n$: $I_{t_i} \subseteq I$ and p believes in the ith member of the sequence at t_i and

(1) for every $k < n$ either

(a) $I_{t_k} \subset I_{t_{k+1}}$

or

(b) $\mathbb{A}_e(E_{t_{k+1}}) \subset \mathbb{A}_e(E_{t_k})$
or both;

(2) for every k, $1 \leqq k \leqq n$, p has observable data supporting (1)(a) or (1)(b) as the case may be.

If (2) is left out we get the concept of a *theoretical* research programme. (2) is formulated such that each step entails an 'excess corroboration' in Lakatos' sense.

> *Remark.* The simultaneous reference to belief (conviction) on one hand and confirming data on the other could be simplified by introducing a concept of knowing: "p knows X at t" would be an abbreviation for "at t p believes that X and p has at t observable data supporting X." This applies to the definitions D27 and D30, too.

So defined, the descriptive concept of a research programme does *not* exceed the confines of Kuhn's conception as reconstructed in Chapter 15 and Sections 16.1–16.3. A glance at stipulations (1)(a) and (b) informs us that we have here nothing other than a '*rectilinear*' *development of normal science in Kuhn's sense undisturbed by setbacks.*

Lakatos also hints at some liberalizations. On p. 134, for example, he requires only that the various members of the sequence be *retrospectively* corroborated. This, he adds, permits a programme to be compatible with "*prima facie* 'refutations'." If we may interpret this as meaning that the various members of the sequence can be *toppled*, i.e., that at certain times *unsuccessful core expansions* may appear, this would in effect make the expressions "research programme" and "normal science" *synonymous*. Naturally this last observation holds only for the *descriptive* interpretation of the expression "research programme," which is the only one being considered here. The question of normative decision directives, to which Lakatos would like to see his research programmes coupled, is an entirely different story.

If the notion of 'normal scientific' research programme thus does not transcend the framework of holding a theory in the Kuhnian or a weaker sense, it is an entirely different matter where the *notion of progress* as developed *on the basis of 'sophisticated falsificationism' is concerned*. The fact that Lakatos introduced the new falsification concept as a relation concept strongly suggests that we, too, interpret this concept *as a relation between theories* in our sense, not merely theory propositions. Furthermore, since it is a relation which obtains if, and only if, a *theory dislodgement* in our sense obtains, we find ourselves outside the province of 'normal science' and must turn to 'revolutionary science.'

Lakatos gives three conditions characterizing the new notion of falsification. From the context it is clear that compared with Popper's original falsification concept the fundamentally new aspect of this notion is the fact that it is conceived of *as a relation between theories*. Due to its pragmatic components it will be advisable to let the concept refer explicitly to a person (group) and time. The relation to be defined *Fals*(T, p, t_0, T') can thus be read as "the theory T is falsified for p at t_0 by the theory T'." We begin with the second condition which is the most important in the present context. It requires that T' 'explain the previous success of T'.[74] If we recall the remarks of Section 16.3 and the notions precisely articulated in Chapter 7, it is not difficult to see that *this condition in the new falsification concept means essentially that T be reducible to T'*.[75] First we will try to define this component by itself. The explicandum will be called *weak falsification*.

Two auxiliary notions will be introduced. Using the predicate "$EK_T(X)$" for "X is an expanded core of the theory T" (cf. Chapter 7), let the five-place relation "I is the set of applications known to p at time t for the expanded core E_t of the theory T" be defined as (for the sake of brevity we also use the expression "knows" introduced in the remark above):

App(I, p, t, E_t, T) iff $EK_T(E_t) \wedge I \neq \varnothing \wedge p$ knows at t that $I \in \mathbb{A}_e(E_t)$.

We still need to restrict this notion to the *maximal* set of applications of the core known to p at t.

Max App (I, p, t, E_t, T) iff App$(I, p, t, E_t, T) \wedge$
$$\wedge I'[\text{App}(I', p, t, E_t, T) \rightarrow I' \subseteq I].$$

D32 Fals$_w(T, p, t_0, T')$ iff T and T' are theories and

$$\wedge I \wedge E_{t_0}\{\text{Max App}(I, p, t_0, E_{t_0}, T) \rightarrow \vee I' \vee E'_{t_0} \vee \rho$$

$$[\text{Max App}(I', p, t_0, E'_{t_0}, T') \wedge rd(\rho, M_p, M'_p) \wedge \langle I, I' \rangle \in \bar{\sigma}_\rho$$

$$\wedge p \text{ knows at } t, \text{ that } \text{RED}(\rho, E_{t_0}, E'_{t_0})]\}.$$

---

[74] Lakatos, [Research Programmes], p. 116.

[75] I would like to thank C. U. Moulines for the suggestion of explicating the condition quoted in the previous footnote by means of the reduction concept.

ρ is the *reduction relation* of Chapter 9, "RED" is the predicate for *strict theoretical reduction*, and σ_ρ is the *empirical reduction* induced by this strict theoretical reduction ρ.

That the theory T is falsified for p at t_0 in the weak sense can be expressed as

$$\vee\, T'\; \mathrm{Fals}_w(T, p, t_0, T').$$

For a moment it may seem strange that in contrast to Popper's falsification concept this one makes no explicit reference to *empirical data*. Such data is, however, mentioned in the definiens due to the stipulation that *p knows that* every expansion of the core of T is reducible in the strict theoretical sense to a suitable expansion of the core of T'.

The other two stipulations which Lakatos incorporates into the new falsification concept require that the 'falsifying' theory T' possess more content than T in the sense that it allows for the prediction of *new* facts,[76] and that some of this extra content of T' be corroborated.[77] These two notions *cannot* be precisely articulated in analogy to D31 since there we were dealing with theory *propositions* while now we are working with the *theories themselves*. We can, however, fit Lakatos' basic ideas into the macrological ' language of reduction relations' quite smoothly. We require, namely, *that there be partial possible models which may be subsumed under the ' falsifying' theory T' but not under the 'falsified' theory T, and that p know of this*. The intuitive notion of subsumption used here can be readily expressed by means of the application operation $\lambda_x A_e(x)$: "y is subsumable under T" means, for example, the same as "there is an expansion E of the core T such that $y \in A_e(E)$."

Thus we arrive at the following definition of "the theory T is falsified in the *strong sense* for p at t_0 by the theory T'" (that part of the definition stemming from D32 must be written out again because the new definition differs from the previous one only in the appearance of additional conjunction members in the last part):

D33 $\quad \mathrm{Fals}_{st}\,(T, p, t_0, T')$ iff T and T' are theories and

$$\wedge I\, \wedge E_{t_0}\{\mathrm{Max\ App}(I, p, t_0, E_{t_0}, T) \to \vee I'\; \vee E'_{t_0}\; \vee \rho$$
$$[\mathrm{Max\ App}(I', p, t_0, E'_{t_0}, T') \wedge rd(\rho, M_p, M'_p) \wedge \langle I, I'\rangle \in \bar{\sigma}_\rho$$
$$\wedge\, p \text{ knows that } \mathrm{RED}(\rho, E_{t_0}, E'_{t_0}) \wedge p \text{ knows that } \Phi]\};$$

---

[76] Cf. *op. cit.*, p. 116.

[77] Cf. *op. cit.*, p. 116.

where ϕ is an abbreviation for:

$$\vee\, I'\ \vee x'\{x' \in I'\ \wedge\ I' \subseteq M_{pp}\ \wedge\ I' \in \mathbb{A}_e(E'_{t_0})\ \wedge\ \neg\, \vee x\, \vee I$$
$$\vee\, E[x \in I\ \wedge\ EK_T(E)\ \wedge\ \langle x, x' \rangle \in \sigma_\rho\ \wedge\ I \subseteq M_{pp}\ \wedge\ I \in \mathbb{A}_e(E_{t_0})]\}.^{78}$$

x' is the *novel fact* of which Lakatos speaks. ϕ says roughly the following: "there exists a set of partial possible models I' of T' to which a core expansion (namely, E'_{t_0}) of T' is correctly applied and this I' contains an element x' for which there exists no element (partial possible model) x of a set I of partial possible models of T such that $\langle x, x' \rangle$ belongs to the empirical reduction relation induced by ρ and I belongs to the set of correct applications of a core expansion E_{t_0} of T."

Assume now a case of theory dislodgement in the sense of Section 16.3. Let T be the dislodged, T' the substitute theory. We can then add the condition:

> *For all persons p and all times t at which p holds T', the theory*
> *T is falsified for p at t by the theory T'.*

If one accepts this additional condition the rationality gap which we criticized in Kuhn's version of theory dislodgement disappears. Since the decisive new component in the refined falsification concept consists of the reduction concept of Chapter 9, our previous claim is also substantiated: *closing Kuhn's rationality gap à la Lakatos may be reconstructed so as to be essentially the same as Sneed's solution.* There is a difference only insofar as this time *the idea of a corroborated increase in the capabilities of the new theory* is *also* explicitly built in by a suitable additional condition. This could provide a reason for giving the nod to Kuhn's idea as improved with the help of the concept introduced in D33. It incorporates all essentials in one 'progressive revolutionary change': namely, that *the new theory is able to do everything which the old one could,* that *the new theory is able to do more than the old* (i.e., has applications for which there are no corresponding applications of the old), and finally that *one is aware of both these facts.*

Within the framework of Lakatos' thinking it is, however, not at all necessary to take the new falsification concept as a basis *for achieving this special end.* One could just as well start by defining the notions of *theoretical and empirical progress* introduced at p. 118 of [Research Programmes], and then replace the above requirement by stipulating that *in the case of theory dislodgement there must be empirical progress.* The following indicates how this may be done, whereby we also include an epistemic relativization and give both definitions simultaneously by adding the restriction for empirical progress in parentheses. (Actually the two concepts differ in only one place where "believes" is replaced by "knows.")

---

[78] Some parts of the definition, e.g., "$I \in M_{pp}$," could be left out since they are already implied by other parts. They are included only for the sake of greater suggestivity.

D34 *T′ is for p at t theoretically (empirically) more progressive than T* iff

$$\wedge E_{t_0}\{EK_T(E_{t_0}) \rightarrow \vee E'_{t_0} \vee I' \vee \rho[EK_{T'}(E'_{t_0}) \wedge I' \in \mathbb{A}_e(E'_{t_0}) \wedge$$

p believes (knows) at time *t* that

(*a*) $\mathrm{RED}(\rho, E_{t_0}, E'_{t_0})$

and

(*b*) $\neg \vee I(I \in \mathbb{A}_e(E_{t_0}) \wedge \langle I, I' \rangle \in \bar{\sigma}_\rho)]\}$.

The use of this empirical progress concept to close the rationality gap also amounts 'essentially' to using the reduction concept.

When in Section 13.2 we first spoke of the immunity of theories for 'normal science' in Kuhn's sense, we said that from its perspective the opponents of the view embrace not a critical, but an *exaggerated* or even *extravagant* rationalism. Subsequent considerations, especially those in Section 16.3, *appeared* to back up Kuhn. In Section 16.3, though, we were forced to acknowledge that Kuhn's analysis of theory dislodgement did actually show an inadmissible gap which, however, could be closed by making substantial use of the reduction concept. Thus we must differentiate. If under "rationalistic criticism" one understands the polemic against the immunity of theories in the course of normal science as previously described, this criticism is in fact *not justified*. If, though, under "rationalistic criticism" nothing more is meant than the criticism of the rationality gap in Kuhn's description of scientific revolutions and an attempt to close it in a satisfactory manner, the criticism is *fully justified*. Since *most* 'rationalistic critics' —for the most part implicitly—find fault with *both*, most criticisms will be *partly justified, partly not*. The discussion in Chapter 15 and Sections 13.2 and 16.1 indicates exactly what is not justified in such criticisms; the discussion in Section 16.2 as well as the present section serves to determine exactly in what respect the critics are right.

Even if one should choose the second of the above alternatives for closing the rationality gap à la Lakatos, a precise version of the falsification concept within the framework of 'sophisticated falsificationism' is not superfluous. It, together with the other concepts, certainly helps to *dispel an eventual illusion*: namely, the illusion *that with 'sophisticated falsificationism' the whole question of confirmation disappears*.

This is, of course, no question at all. In all the above definitions containing the phrase "knows that" *an adequate concept of confirmation is presupposed*. Exactly the same holds here as was said in Section 16.3 of Kuhn. He also tacitly presupposes such a concept because in the course of normal science theory propositions are only held to be well or poorly confirmed *on the basis of empirical findings* and *accepted or rejected* on the basis of these judgements. Presumably a deductive confirmation concept like Popper's concept of corroboration offers a satisfactory explication as long as no statistical hypotheses are involved.

I should like once more to point out the multiple confusion involved in the "deductivistic–inductivistic" polarization as I have already done in [Induktion]. First, one often arrives at a different result depending on whether one takes the *intuitive point of departure* or starts with *the explicit definition* of the notion. Furthermore, the intuitive basis is often difficult to assess. Nicod's confirmation criterion as reconstructed by Hempel offers an example. Is Nicod's concept deductivistic or inductivistic? It is certain that Nicod used *expressions* like "induction," "probability of a hypothesis," etc. But such notions do not find their way into the technical definition. And Nicod, who died years before *Logik der Forschung* was published, can scarcely be blamed for *not using Popper's terminology*. Perhaps he would have aligned himself with 'Popper's deductivism' as concerns the corroboration concept had he had the chance to study this book. There are presumably two reasons why Hempel's criterion, formulated in the language of *deductive* logic, is nevertheless often counted in the inductivistic trend. First, Hempel began by formulating and discussing Nicod's criterion *which was habitually being called inductivistic*. Second, in his *Inductive Logic* Carnap—erroneously(!)—held Hempel's criterion to be the qualitative analogue to his own concept of degree of confirmation. The real quantitative counterpart is Carnap's concept of *relevance*. What if Carnap had quite reasonably continued to label Hempel's concept a qualitative confirmation concept and also chose this same label for his quantitative counterpart, the relevance concept? *Would he under these circumstances have become a deductivist?*

The confusion adhering to the usual polarization has several roots, some of which lie in the vagueness of the intuitive basis, some in the kind of reference point used for interpreting explications. When, for example, a quantitative theory is called *inductivistic* only if it works with a concept of *hypothesis probability* satisfying the Kolmogorov axioms, one should not then regard *all other* confirmation concepts as deductivistic, but only those which are actually formulated *in the language of deductive logic alone*. An immediate consequence is, thus, that the "deductivistic–inductivistic" polarity does *not* represent *an exhaustive alternative*. When one takes the likelihood concept as the key notion in a support concept for statistical hypotheses, as is the case in [Statistik], Part III, the theory must be said to be *neither deductivistic nor inductivistic*.

We can now sum up our results. The reconstruction of the *descriptive* content of various of Lakatos' ideas yields:

(1) nothing essentially new concerning normal science (*'research programmes in the sense of normal science'*) vis-à-vis Kuhn, but, depending on the articulation, something the same as, or similar to, the notion of holding

in the Kuhnian sense a theory or the special case of "normal scientific progress without setbacks";

(2) two alternatives for closing the rationality gap left by Kuhn's exposition of theory dislodgement: one via a *'sophisticated' relational concept of the falsification of one theory by another*, the other via a concept of *empirical progress*. For all variants the confirmation question remains *open* or is *assumed to be settled*. (The interpretation of the methodological rules as *normative directives for scientists* is not considered here. According to Lakatos these instruct the scientist which 'paths of research' to avoid or pursue.[79] This normative aspect will be briefly discussed in Chapter 19.)

A remark about Lakatos' *use of the word* "*falsification*." Various reasons speak against applying this expression to the notion proposed by Lakatos for which we have tried to define a weak (D32) and a strong (D33) version:

(1) The transition from what Lakatos calls *dogmatic falsificationism* to that which he labels *naive falsificationism* involves only that one relinquish the assumption of an 'absolutely certain rejection basis.' This has no effect upon Popper's notion of falsification as far as its being a relation between data and hypothesis is concerned. The transition to Lakatos' notion of falsification, on the other hand, subjects this expression to *an extraordinarily strong shift in meaning*. A glance at both definitions and a bit of reflection on their intuitive background confirms this. The new concepts are *substantially more complex* than the old and *structurally different*—they no longer involve *a relation between hypotheses and data*, but a *relation between theories*.

(2) The falsification concept was thought to be a '*negative counterpart*' *to the notion of corroboration* and the latter a 'positive correlate' to the former. Such a correspondence disappears here. It can no longer even be said that the new concept represents something essentially negative, for the 'negative' aspect concerning the old theory is balanced by a '*positive*' *aspect concerning the new theory*.

(3) Not only is the new falsification concept not a 'negative counterpart' to that of corroboration; it presupposes this notion (or some other 'deductive confirmation concept'). (As we saw, the 'traditional confirmation problem' does not somehow disappear; it is only shifted from theories to theory propositions or the empirical claims of theories.) Lakatos, too, presupposes an explication of this notion, as is shown by the definitions.

These reasons, together with the fact that Lakatos intended his falsification concept as a precise articulation of the notion 'that the new theory can do all that the old one could and then some,' suggest a change in terminology. Instead of reading "the theory T is falsified for p at t_0 by the theory T'" in the weak case (D32), we could substitute "*the theory T is outmoded for p at t_0 by the theory T'*"; and likewise "*the theory T is outmoded for p at t_0 by the more powerful theory T'*" could be used in the strong case (D33). The greater power is to be understood here as predictive or explanatory.

[79] Cf. [Research Programmes], p. 132

16.5 Theory dynamics and the dynamics of science

That sciences "develop" is a triviality that does not tell us much. Such an observation first begins to be informative when we realize that development means something entirely different for empirical sciences than it does for mathematical disciplines. *A major shortcoming of the philosophy of empiricism to date is not to have attempted an analysis of the characteristic features of development in the empirical sciences.* It limited itself to 'snapshots' of the structure of empirical science, supposing that these would reveal all the essentials. It is true that some insight into this structure must precede an understanding of theory dynamics. But once again Aristotle's observation that what is nearest to the nature of things is furthest from us proves itself. It is no accident that Kuhn *only intuitively grasped* the structure of physical theories in making important, valid contributions to the interpretation of the dynamic process of science from the historical side, while only later did Sneed discover the best explanation as yet of the structures underlying this process. Nothing could better demonstrate the necessity of backstopping historical investigations of science with metascientific analysis. And nothing could better accentuate the extraordinary importance of rational reconstruction as a means of gaining genuine understanding than *this historical development within the philosophy of science itself.*

But it is also no accident that empiricist philosophers, among others, sensed an obscurantism behind Kuhn's ideas which is incompatible with any rational interpretation of empirical sciences. The intellectual groundwork was lacking which would have brought the new structures to light by means of which it could have been seen that an apparently 'irrational process' was, on the contrary, *quite rational.* One was all too used to the metamathematical analogy according to which theories are *infinite classes of sentences* and the *entire structure* reduces to *logical relations* between the elements of these classes.

That the lack of an analysis of the *dynamic aspect* of empirical science represents a real shortcoming becomes abundantly clear when one answers our original question on the basis of all that has been considered since then. The rationally reconstructable dynamic aspect of the empirical sciences has absolutely no similarity with the rationally reconstructable dynamic aspect of mathematical disciplines. As long as this is not realized, one cannot claim to have understood empirical science *as empirical science.* Indeed, one could also try to construct the mathematical analogies to 'normal' and 'revolutionary' science. Likewise, one could distinguish a pretheoretical stage of practical calculation from a theoretical. But the 'normal discipline' here would consist, for example, of such things as finding simpler proofs for known theorems, deducing new theorems in established theories, or contriving a new axiomatization for a theory. The counterpart to the fundamental characteristic of normal science first articulated by Kuhn is, however, completely missing: namely, that *a group of scientists hold one and the same theory although their convictions concerning this theory are continually changing.* Likewise, *the analogue to the immunity of theories against possible empirical refutation is missing too.* (It would have to be an immunity against logical refutation—something not to be found.) Normal scientific progress in mathematics would amount to a linear, accumulative increase in knowledge; the normal scientific progress of an empirical theory is neither linear nor necessarily accumulative. Likewise for the 'revolutionary stage.' New mathematical theories are *added* to those previously known. There is *no analogue to the phenomenon of theory dislodgement.* (One could, indeed, also speak of one theory 'dislodging another' in mathematics. The expression would, however, take on other meanings. For example, one theory *is used instead of another as the fundament* for a further discipline; e.g., measure theory instead of combinatorial theory as the basis for the probability calculus.)

17 Initial Steps Toward Demythologizing Holism

17.1 The 'Duhem–Quine thesis'; Its amplification by Kuhn and Feyerabend

We use the term 'Duhem–Quine thesis' here in the same sense that Lakatos did in [Research Programmes], p. 184ff. As far as I know, it was introduced there for the first time. After a preliminary intuitive sketch we will try to formulate the thesis in two key statements. A substantial amplification of the thesis, stemming from ideas advanced by Kuhn and Feyerabend, will then be formulated in a third, and finally in a fourth key statement closely connected with it. Together this could all be subsumed under the notion of *modern holism.* Should one want to distinguish the Duhem–Quine thesis from the amplified version mentioned, one could refer to the conjunction of the first two key statements as *moderate holism* and the conjunction of all four as *strict holism.*

A glance at the usual expositions gives the impression that moderate holism is something which can only be presented in a fuzzy metaphorical way. And then the third key statement appears to assert something so unreasonable that it is no wonder that philosophers feeling themselves committed to a rational mode of thought are convinced they must combat this ' mythological picture of science.'

In Section 17.2 the holistic view will be critically discussed. In contrast to the traditional 'rationalistic' criticisms, this discussion will surface as a

231

new *interpretation*, not as a *repudiation*. This new interpretation will infuse a precise meaning into the holistic thesis, although various possibilities for deviating occasionally come up. In the end it will turn out that each particular interpretation of the key statements of holism yields *a position* which can not only be clearly formulated but even *rationally grounded*. It is this rational reconstruction consisting of *interpretation and justification* which we call the demythologizing of holism. Thus, we are seeking to clarify what *in particular* lies behind 'holistic views.' "In particular" is used here in the same sense as when we say Aristotle made the first attempt to find out what *in particular* we mean when we use expressions like "hence" or "therefore." There is, of course, one essential difference: whereas Aristotle was concerned with clearing up one aspect of human theorizing itself, we are only trying to clear up one aspect of *metatheoretical statements about theorizing*.

The first three key statements, to which the entire subsequent discussion refers, are, with the exception of minor changes, formulated in this form by Sneed in [Mathematical Physics], p. 90. (Unfortunately, the problem of holism appears entirely out of context there. In that chapter Sneed is still discussing the question of how the Ramsey formulation of a theory may be emended.) The reconstruction, whose analogue could scarcely be realized on the basis of the traditional idea of theories as sentence classes, will rely essentially on the 'nonstatement view.' The two key notions are the concept of the *central empirical claim* of a theory (in the sense of Section 5.7) and the corresponding concept of *strong theory proposition* (cf. Section 7.3).

The fundamental proposition of holism was first formulated by P. Duhem. According to it each theory is indeed confronted with experience—thus far it is compatible with at least a liberal empiricism—but it is not *particular* statements which can be subjected to empirical test; it is always, and only, the *theory as a whole*. More recently W. V. Quine has picked up this idea, elucidating and qualifying the thesis especially in [Two Dogmas], Section 6, and the introduction to [Methods]. These represent the frame of reference for the next three paragraphs.

We do indeed compare our system of statements about the external world with experience. But as a whole it is "underdetermined by experience," since *entirely different* sentence systems are compatible with *the same* experience. A check of the *whole system* is, however, possible, because the goal of science is to predict future experience with the help of past experience. And future experience can actually turn out other than predicted. This by no means, however, allows us to make single statements of the system responsible for a prognostic failure. At first we can only draw a weak conclusion: "When such predictions of experience turn out wrong, the system has to be changed somehow. But we retain a wide latitude of choice as to which statements of the system to preserve and which ones to revise."[80]

---

[80] Quine, [Methods], p. 2.

This freedom of choice, it might be added, constitutes an important difference between *logical argumentation* and *empirical testing*.[81] In a mathematical proof *certain sentences* are proved or refuted. Likewise, in metatheoretical argumentation *certain sentences* are shown, for example, to be undecidable (neither provable nor refutable), or *special axioms* to be either superfluous, i.e., deducible from the rest of the axiom system, or not (e.g., the parallel postulate of Euclidean geometry, or the axiom of choice in axiomatic set theory). Empirical testing can, on the contrary, only affect the *entire* system of affirmations: "our statements about external reality face the tribunal of sense experience not individually but as a corporate body."[82] What consequences should be drawn here?

In [Research Programmes], p. 184ff., Lakatos outlines two possible interpretations of Quine's version of holism: a weak and a strong one.[83] The *weak interpretation* denies the possibility of empirically *refuting* a special component (a *certain* statement) of the theoretical system. The *strong interpretation* denies the possibility of *rationally* choosing from among the infinitely many alternatives for realigning the system with experience. According to Lakatos *the weak thesis is trivially correct*—for each test is actually a challenge to our total knowledge—*the strong thesis, on the other hand, may be countered with rational arguments.* Indeed, both *naive falsificationism* as propounded by Popper and *sophisticated falsificationism*, as Lakatos calls his 'theory of *research programmes*,' which develops Popper's ideas, offer the possibility of rationally overturning this thesis. According to naive falsificationism the inconsistency must be remedied as follows: from the totality of our affirmations we select a *theory* to be tested (figuratively, a *nut*) and a set of *accepted basic statements* (figuratively, a *hammer*); the remaining claims of the entire system serve as *uncontested background knowledge* (figuratively, *an anvil*). The strict method of testing consists now of 'tempering' the hammer and anvil to the point where they together can crack the nut. This is Popper's negative *experimentum crucis*. Sophisticated falsificationism, on the other hand, relinquishes the idea of a decisive experiment and allows for changing any component in the scientific system. Sharply distinguishing this position from holism in the strong interpretation is, nevertheless, the circumstance that such a change is only allowed when it

---

[81] Quine himself includes the system of logical and mathematical sentences in his holistic view. But since this rests on his special theory about the relationship of logic, mathematics, and experience which is not (or at least not expressly) shared by other 'holists,' we will in the present context ignore this specific feature of his view.

[82] Quine, *op. cit.*, p. 19.

[83] This distinction is *not* the same as the one between moderate and strict holism drawn in the first paragraph of this chapter. These latter expressions were actually chosen in order to avoid confusion with Lakatos' terminology. Strict holism will be discussed later. The weak as well as the strong interpretation of holism in Lakatos' sense both refer exclusively to *moderate holism* in our terminology.

fits into a *progressive research programme* permitting the successful prognosis of new facts. Lakatos theory of research programmes will not be pursued any further here for two reasons. First, we have already attempted to articulate some of its aspects. Second, *we will take an entirely different approach to the ' problem of holism.'* Instead of *combatting* the (apparently) irrational strong thesis by formulating methodological rules, we will attempt to articulate this thesis in such a way that *it loses the appearance of irrationality.* Lakatos' criticism, and presumably all 'rationalistic criticisms,' presuppose the 'statement view' as a matter of course. Lakatos' theory of research programmes can *also* be regarded as an attempt *to replace* the figurative-mythological characterization of holism *with a system of clear rules*, but remains, however, well within the confines of the traditional 'statement view.' In Section 17.2 a *more radical* approach to the problem will be taken via a precise interpretation of the key holistic theses from the standpoint of the 'nonstatement view.'

But let us return again to Quine. It is somewhat inaccurate to maintain that he denies 'any rational choice among the alternatives.' Instead he makes a series of expository remarks which it cannot be denied remain figurative and vague. He observes first that where predictions are falsified the choice of what should be retained is made according to a "vague scheme of priorities."[84] In principle, one can indeed retain any sentence as correct so far as one is prepared to make sufficient practical changes elsewhere in the system. Likewise, one can, *in principle*, decide not to exempt any sentence from possible revision.[85] Actually, though, sentences "on the periphery of our experience" will be "guarded pretty jealously" as long as possible.[86] These are sentences like "my pen is in my hand," or "the thermometer shows just 80°F." Another, in a certain sense opposing priority demands that the more fundamental a law is the less it is contemplated changing it.[87] Both priorities stem from our natural desire to disturb the whole system as little as possible.[88] But this second priority allows for many graduations: "Our system of statements has such a thick cushion of indeterminacy, in relation to experience, that vast domains of law can easily be held immune to revision on principle."[89] "Our conservative preference for those revisions which disturb the system least," and which finds its expression in these two priorities, is "opposed by a significant contrary force, a force for simplification."[90] Quine's further remarks indicate that he regards considerations of simplicity as the most important force behind revolutions in physics.

[84] [Methods], p. 19.

[85] [Two Dogmas], p. 43.

[86] [Methods], p. 19.

[87] [Two Dogmas], p. 44.

[88] [Methods], p. 20.

[89] *Ibid.*

[90] [Methods], p. 21.

Taken literally these remarks seem to indicate a gigantic gulf between metamathematics and the metatheory or philosophy of science. Strict reasoning is possible in the former, the latter must be content with a metaphor-laden description of scientific processes relying on feelings and natural tendencies: namely, our *natural bent* to change as little as possible; our *subjective feel* for what lies on the 'periphery of experience,' what on the other hand is central to the system, and for the levels of laws; and finally, the *natural inclination* to simplicity opposing the first tendency. And since the priorities and tendencies can get embroiled in conflicts with one another, still another decision must be made on the basis of *feelings and tendencies*.

As already indicated, it is not our intention to 'replace' the holistic view with something better, thereby 'surpassing' it. Instead we hope to give it the modicum of precise articulation needed to dispel the impression that it is a position which can be talked about only in terms of more or less fuzzy metaphors and which continually appeals to our subjective impressions of what is 'peripheral,' what is 'central,' what is better in the sense of ' simpler,' etc. Where the theses involve *confirmation problems*, these will indeed be mentioned but not discussed because they do not belong to the present context. In this sense the subsequent interpretation remains incomplete.

The first two key statements of moderate holism may now be explicitly formulated:

(*I*) *A theory is accepted or rejected as a whole, not piecemeal by assuming or rejecting its single components (statements).*

(*II*) *There is no such thing as the rejection of a theory on the basis of an experimentum crucis.*

Strict holism is characterized by an additional thesis appearing to go considerably further than the early holists contemplated. First we will formulate this thesis and then expand on it with the help of a quote from Kuhn's work.

(*III*) *One cannot sharply distinguish between the empirical content or empirical claims of a theory and the empirical data supporting them.*

What is meant by this thesis? In [Revolutions], p. 141, Kuhn emphasizes that theories do indeed 'fit facts,' that this is, however, only possible because information which did not even exist for the preceding 'paradigms' is ' transformed into facts.' "... theories too do not evolve piecemeal to fit facts that were there all the time. Rather they emerge together with the facts they fit from a revolutionary reformulation of the preceding scientific tradition."[91] One can hardly be blamed were he to lay aside Kuhn's book at this point.[92] Hegel is at one time supposed to have rejoined to a critic's

[91] *Op. cit.*, p. 141.

[92] In fact I myself *did* shelve it at the first reading because it precipitated in me the picture about to be described.

accusation that his philosophy did not jive with experience: "so much the worse for experience." With this episode and Kuhn's lines in mind one can ask oneself how theoretical physicists are to be distinguished from Hegel. An appeal to Kuhn urges the following comparison: while Hegel let it go at the arrogant remark quoted, physicists, as 'super-Hegelian counterfeiters,' busy themselves 'hammering theories and facts into shape' until they fit each other. Can thus, one must ask oneself, *any rational interpretation* at all still be given to thesis *(III)*?

17.2 Discussion and critical reconstruction of strict holism

We will begin with *thesis (I)*. Were we to utilize only the analysis of Chapter 5, the interpretation would have to be that a theory does not even consist of a *class* of sentences, but *of one single cohesive sentence*, the Ramsey–Sneed sentence (which for the sake of simplicity and unambiguity will again be assumed to have the strongest form (VI)). Thus, if *we* were to think of a theory as something 'linguistic' at all, we would have *an exact, fitting interpretation* of the first thesis. We would not even have to stop with the linguistic interpretation. We could in every instance replace the central empirical claim with its propositional counterpart, a strong theory proposition $I_t \in \mathbb{A}_e(E_t)$.

Yet, as we already know, we cannot make it quite so easy for ourselves. Both concepts of holding a theory were introduced precisely for the purpose of being able to say that the theory remains constant while convictions change. Thus we must differentiate further. Assuming the set *I* to be determined according to the method of paradigmatic examples, we can interpret the first key sentence somewhat schematically as follows:

A theory $T = \langle K, I \rangle$ consists of a fundamental mathematical structure K as well as a set I of intended applications characterized only by a set I_0 of paradigm examples and, thus, by and large open. The acceptance of such a theory is an *all-or-nothing decision* in the sense that we decide to apply the mathematical formalism to at least the paradigm examples. This decision in favor of a theory partly determines its future course, but is compatible with two forms of *growth for the theory*. First, the theory may become *applicable to new phenomena*. Second, with the acceptance of the theory T absolutely nothing has been determined concerning the *possibilities of amplifying the fundamental mathematical structure K so as to produce expanded cores E_i*. The acceptance of a theory is also compatible with growth in this respect, in particular, with the discovery of new special laws and additional constraints. The all-or-nothing decision in favor of a theory is even compatible with *occasional setbacks*—be it the removal of 'recalcitrant physical systems' from the set of intended applications or the subsequent abandonment of special laws once hypothetically assumed.

Consider both types of growth in relation to a central empirical claim (VI). The addition *of new* applications for the theory would mean that the individual constant a must be replaced by a different one, a^*, designating a larger set of partial possible models. Notice that this change in sentence (VI) also affects those entities to which the sentence had previously applied because the constraints on theoretical functions occurring in the sentence concern all the elements of a^*, so that even the elements previously contained in a must again be checked to see if all the constraints continue to hold. The sentence (VI) indeed retains the same structure, but the domain of the existential quantifier is enlarged. The second form of growth, involving the discovery of new laws as well as additional constraints, would find its expression in the appearance of further restrictions $S^{n+1}, \ldots, S^p$ of the primary predicate S as well as more constraints $C_{k+1}, \ldots, C_r$ in the sentence (VI). Thus, here, even the structure of the central empirical claim changes. *Retention of a theory is thus compatible with changes in the meaning of the central empirical claim of two different dimensions.*

If we regard key statement (*I*) as an aphoristic rendition of the contents of the last two paragraphs, we can see that *the first key thesis of holism is correct, given this rational reconstruction.*

We said above that this interpretation of the first key statement was somewhat schematic. This was because it relies on the notion of holding a theory, so that all the details involved in this concept would have to be considered. Among other things one would have to decide whether he wanted to use the 'weaker' (Sneedian) concept or the 'stronger' (Kuhnian) one.

Attention should be drawn to still another point. The growth processes and setbacks of 'normal science' are decided by testing and confirmation, not of 'the theory,' but of *special assumptions about the theory*. Since we are not going to enter into a detailed discussion of confirmation in this volume, the question of just what form they have can remain open. Even the question of their *exact metatheoretical reconstruction* can remain open here. The first holistic thesis is not affected in any way by whether one takes an 'inductivistic' or a 'deductivistic' position concerning this problem complex. Concerning the theory itself, though, one notices that since traditional confirmation and testing theories are applicable only to *sentences* or *propositions*, while theories are neither sentence-like nor propositional entities, *it cannot even be said of a theory that it is well or poorly confirmed.*

The first of these observations could be tacked onto the reconstruction of the key statement (*I*). One could then say that *the first holistic thesis is indifferent to the different varieties of inductivism as well as to the issue of inductivism versus deductivism.*

The second observation leads directly to the interpretation of *key statement (II).* The most radical exegesis which could be given within the framework of our conceptual edifice runs: *A theory is just not the type of entity of*

*which it can sensibly be said that it is well or poorly confirmed, and thus neither
can it be sensibly said that it is discarded on the basis of experiments.*

There can be two grounds for rejecting this key thesis. The first stems
from the fact that normally "theory" is understood as something else;
namely, a more or less complex empirical hypothesis—in our terminology:
a certain particular central empirical claim or its propositional counterpart.
If "theory" is so understood, *then naturally the second holistic thesis is false.*
The progress of normal science consists of a continuous succession of
central empirical claims, formulated with the help of a theory and instigated
entirely and alone by new empirical discoveries, or, if you prefer, *by critical
testing.*

But even when one takes the theory concept in our sense, this second thesis,
so interpreted, tends to meet with resistance. This point has already been
dealt with in connection with the discussion of Kuhn's notions of normal
and revolutionary science. We might, however, add that even when one feels
forced to insist on a rationality gap in Kuhn's 'paradigm change,' *its existence is no tragedy.* Again one need only keep clearly in mind what holding a
theory 'essentially' consists of: namely, having a mathematical formalism
along with the hope of 'being able to apply it successfully in the world.'
To what it may be applied remains at first quite open because the set of
intended applications is determined only by paradigm examples. *How* it
may be applied is also to a large extent open since *the given mathematical*
apparatus includes only the core K. It is only necessary that there be *some*
expansions providing the conceptual apparatus for formulating empirical
claims like (VI). An *experimentum crucis* or decisive experiment can at most
force a scientist to give up a *certain* claim of form (VI) (or what amounts to
the same thing, to relinquish the belief in a *certain* strong theory proposition
$I_t \in \mathbb{A}_e(E_t)$). This is fully compatible with the conviction that the goal will yet
be achieved with *some other expansions of the same core K*; i.e., that some
other central claims (theory propositions) will be found which are correct
and which have a stronger content than those representing previous successful
applications of the theory (cf. stipulations (4) of D27 and (6) of D30 in
which the 'scientist's belief in progress' is articulated). Failures and setbacks are foreseen. Progress in normal science need not be free of them.
There is a rationality gap only insofar as it is scarcely possible to estimate
precisely the *number* of failures and *types* of setbacks needed to force a
scientist to give up his hope of again attaining success with the mathematical
formalism available to him. In the case of *theory dislodgement*, on the
other hand, the rationality gap closes as was shown in Section 16.3. For
here we require, besides a successful nontrivial application of the new theory,
a *reduction* of the old to the new.

(Remember that *due to his particular formulation* Kuhn does have a rationality gap here, too, since he unnecessarily denies this reducibility.)

The third key holistic thesis can also be given a 'harmless' interpretation by referring to the description of facts with the help of T-theoretical functions. The enigmatic aspect of these concepts is that *there can be no facts involving T-theoretical functions which are completely independent of at least a hypothetically accepted empirical claim of form (VI)*. But, as Sneed rightly points out, there is nothing irrational in this. Kuhn's rather curious formulations *only create the impression* that 'theoreticians mold the facts to fit the theory.' The problem involved here is basically the same as that which in Section 3.1 was called *the problem of theoretical terms*—only the formulation is different. Assimilating this problem as far as possible to the language of the Kuhnian passage quoted above, it might be formulated as follows: "*How is it possible to describe facts supporting a theory with the help of concepts which can only be understood if the theory is true?*" The answer contains nothing inscrutable. But neither is it trivial. It consists of repeating the reasons against viewing the empirical claims of theories as sentences of form (I) together with the reasons for exhibiting the empirical content of a theory by means of a sentence of form (VI).

> For the interpretation of statement (*III*) one might also think of looking to the idea discussed in Section 16.2: namely, 'that a fact for one theory may be determined by another theory.' We have not pursued this line of thought further because (*III*) emerged from an interpretation of the passage quoted from Kuhn in which *the reference to one and the same theory is essential*. Thus, recourse to the distinguishing feature of T-theoretical functions remained our only chance to rationally interpret the thesis.
>
> Nothing, of course, stands in the way of taking the notion of the 'theory-ladenness of facts' *as a fifth key holistic thesis in its own right*.

The third key holistic thesis is closely connected with a further point often underscored by Feyerabend. It might be called *the thesis of the dependence of theoretical terms on the content of the theory*. Due to its importance we want to treat this thesis as a distinct part of strict holism:

(*IV*) *A change in the range of application of a theory entails a change in the meaning of the theoretical terms of this theory.*

When in the present context we speak of "sense" or "meaning," it should not be assumed that the proponents of holism want to see these expressions understood in a special *intensionalistic* way. (Else they would have to be referred to the philosophy and theory of language, where they would have to deal in particular with Quine's linguistic theses.) In fact (*IV*) can be interpreted in a way involving only the extensional notion of *truth condition*.[93] To this end consider the kind of normal scientific progress where the set of intended applications is enlarged: $I_t \subset I_{t'}$. The claim (VI) contains then at t' an individual constant $\mathfrak{a}^*$ designating the larger set $I_{t'}$, while the corresponding claim at t contains a constant designating the *smaller* set I_t.

[93] Cf. Sneed, [Mathematical Physics], p. 93.

Through this addition the truth conditions for the claim (VI) *have changed.* (Analogously a decrease in the set would change them too.) The *constraints* are again responsible. The limitations they impose on the T-theoretical functions depend on how the domains $D_1, D_2, D_3, \ldots$ of the particular partial possible models designated by α in (VI) overlap. And these intersections change with the addition or subtraction of such domains D_i. If one now also stipulates that the meaning of theoretical terms depends on the truth conditions for the claims in which they occur, one obtains a precise appropriate interpretation of the key thesis *(IV)*: *A change in the 'range' of a theory entails a change in the truth conditions of the empirical claims about the values of T-theoretical functions. This changes the meaning of the T-theoretical terms designating these functions.*

Thus we see that not only the key theses *(I)* and *(II)* of moderate holism, but even the additional theses *(III)* and *(IV)* of strict holism (and eventually the thesis *(V)* mentioned above) can be interpreted in such a way that *all of these assertions become true.*

Holism under this interpretation is altogether compatible with a '*sensible empiricism.*' Theories are not drafted for their own sake. They are intended to serve for formulating *empirical* claims of form (VI) or, respectively, strong theory propositions. And these claims can *stand* or *fall* on experience.

Perhaps the empiricist will say that this is not enough for him. To which one could reply: "Have you not then all you desire? What more could you possibly want?"

---

18 'Kuhnianism': Pseudoirrationalism and Pseudorelativism?

Even on the basis of the standard interpretation of Kuhn as depicted in Chapter 10, it is, as we saw, misleading to speak of 'Kuhnian irrationalism.' What is really meant is something entirely different: namely, that he *imputes an irrational posture* to the practitioners of the exact sciences in both tradition-bound epochs and times of transition from one theory to another. Nevertheless, for the sake of simplicity we want to use this short form for the allegation that such an insinuation obtains. Kuhn's own position within the framework of the standard interpretation would be more aptly characterized as *relativism,* as some of his critics, especially D. Shapere, have done.

If it is now asked which of these and other reproaches against Kuhn (and thinkers like Feyerabend who hold similar views) actually hold, one can only answer that *this is not really a very meaningful question* and try to *substantiate this*. When numerous objections are raised against a conception still in its intuitive infancy only to disappear for the most part after the infant has matured to 'the language of constructs,' should one say the objections have forced such a strong departure from the intuitive conception that it is no longer a matter of reconstruction of *this* conception? Or should one say the reconstruction shows many objections to have been ill-advised in view of the precisely articulated conception? Obviously the tendency to one or the other of these answers depends on whether one is more inclined to venomous criticism or well intentioned interpretation.

Instead of passing global judgement we will try to tabulate those of Kuhn's most important theses which have met with more or less sharp criticism and indicate, in the light of our foregoing discussion, the fitting reaction. As before the following comments are limited to *physical* theories.

Kuhn's theses	*Comment and possible interpretation*
(1) The members of a scientific tradition hold a common paradigm.	(1*) All who hold a theory use the same set of paradigm examples of intended applications.
(2) In normal science theories are not tested.	(2*) A theory is not the sort of entity of which it can be said that it is verified or falsified (nonstatement view of theories).
(3) Initially the success of a paradigm is largely a promise of success.	(3*) Holding a theory includes a belief in progress: namely, that the formulation of empirical claims using the theory will be successful.
(4) Normal scientific practice consists of puzzle solving within the framework of one and the same paradigm. Puzzles can become anomalies and these in turn, crises. But anomalies and crises alone are not enough to topple a paradigm.	(4*) Normal scientific practice consists of successfully expanding the core of a given theory and (perhaps) enlarging the set of intended applications of the theory. Ever so many unsuccessful attempts at expanding a core do not prove that future attempts must also be unsuccessful.

241

Kuhn's theses	*Comment and possible interpretation*
(5) Normal science is not totally bound by rules.	(5*) Rules do not determine how the core of a theory held by a scientist may be successfully expanded.
(6) Normal science is an accumulative enterprise.	(6*) The notion of normal scientific progress, i.e., of progress while holding one and the same theory, can be precisely formulated.
(7) Reproaches to the effect that the normal scientist as an uncritical dogmatist behaves irrationally are unfounded.	(7*) = (7) because it is correct.
(8) Problems of confirmation and corroboration disappear.	(8*) An unjustifiable exaggeration. Correct is: (*a*) these problems do not exist for the theory which one holds. (*b*) Nevertheless, again and again in the course of normal science empirical hypotheses (central empirical claims, strong theory propositions) must be tested. The normal scientific practice of puzzle solving *also* includes such testing.
(9) "I do ... take Sir Karl's notion of the asymmetry of falsification and confirmation very seriously indeed."[94]	(9*) Needless concession to the opposition which, moreover, contradicts (8).
(10) There are no theory neutral observations.	(10*) Vague and ambiguous; can be interpreted either as:
	(10$_1^*$) (*a*) the descriptions of the partial possible models of a theory ('physical systems to which the theory may be applied')

---

[94] Kuhn, [My Critics], p. 248.

Kuhn's theses	Comment and possible interpretation
	presuppose some *other* theory;
	(b) the descriptions of the possible models of a theory T even presuppose *this theory T* itself. This leads to the problem of T-theoretical terms;
	or as
	(10_2^*) the usual separation of observational and theoretical language is dubious. Besides, the dual-level conception offers no adequate means for solving the problem of theoretical terms.
(11) A theory is rejected or accepted as a whole, not piecemeal.	(11*) Correct in the sense of the holistic thesis (I) reconstructed in Chapter 17.
(12) No theory is rejected on the basis of an *experimentum crucis*.	(12*) Correct in the sense of the holistic thesis (II) as reconstructed in Chapter 17.
(13) A sharp distinction between the empirical claims (content) of a theory and the empirical data supporting them is not possible.	(13*) Correct in the sense of the holistic thesis (III) as reconstructed in Chapter 17.
(14) A change in a theory entails a change in the meaning of the expressions contained in it.	(14*) Either (a) inappropriate foray into the philosophy of language; or (b) when limited to *theoretical terms* correct in the sense of the holistic thesis (IV) as reconstructed in Chapter 17.

243

Kuhn's theses	Comment and possible interpretation
(15) "Failure to achieve a solution discredits only the scientist and not the theory."	(15*) A specialist in the normal scientific tradition who holds a theory, but fails to apply it successfully, and then blames the theory for this failure, actually is behaving 'like a poor carpenter who blames his tools.' For the theory is not a proposition (or class of propositions) in which one believes, but a tool to be used.
(16) "To reject one paradigm without simultaneously substituting another is to reject science itself."	(16*) He who holds a theory and rejects it due to a lack of success must change his profession if he cannot find or invent another theory.
(17) A paradigm is never rejected because of recalcitrant experience but first "when an alternate candidate is available to take its place."	(17*) A presumably correct empirical (historical, psychological, or sociological) hypothesis when "paradigm" is replaced by "theory of physics."
(18) There is no logical explanation for (17).	(18*) Correct in the sense that one *cannot find logical reasons* for the fact that there is no theory rejection other than dislodgement by another theory. But one can discern an *elementary psychological reason* for this phenomenon. It is roughly expressed in the platitude: "a leaky roof is better than none at all."
(19) Exponents of different paradigms are not capable of establishing logical contact with one another. They either talk right past one another or use circular arguments.	(19*) A historical-psychological hypothesis basing itself on historical facts and the trivial logical circumstance that when someone holds a theory he cannot use *this*

Kuhn's theses	Comment and possible interpretation
	theory as the neutral framework for comparing it with some other theory.
(20) Different paradigms cannot be compared with each other.	(20*) One must distinguish between (*a*) the correct statement: "theories with different cores cannot be compared at the object–theoretical level" and (*b*) the incorrect statement: "theories with different cores cannot be compared at the metatheoretical level." What is possible for Kuhn at the 'historical' metalevel is also possible at the 'logical' metalevel.
(21) A theory is incommensurable with the theory it dislodges in the course of a scientific revolution.	(21*) This is false.
(22) A theory dislodged in the course of a scientific revolution cannot be reduced to the theory dislodging it.	(22*) This is only the case if one is using a 'micrological' reduction concept. (It then says that the concepts of the one theory cannot be defined by those of the other and its theorems cannot be deduced from it.) From the macrological standpoint it is false.
(23) Revolutionary scientific change is noncumulative since there is no criterion for progress available.	(23*) The first half is true, the second false. The change which takes place when a theory is dislodged is 'noncumulative' in the sense that the core of the substitute theory is not obtained by

245

Kuhn's theses	Comment and possible interpretation
	improving the core of the dislodged theory. Nevertheless with the help of the macrological reduction concept we can differentiate between theory dislodgement *with* and *without* progress.
(24) Anomalies and crises are not resolved gradually by reflection but by a relatively sudden event comparable to a gestalt shift.	(24*) Presumably a correct psychological description of ' what goes on in the mind of a person' who discovers a new theory. Whether or not it is correct is metascientifically irrelevant.

This last point is the only example given here of Kuhn's many theses concerning the psychology of research. Being compatible with it they do indeed dovetail with the logical interpretation but have no direct relevance for it.

The discussion in Chapter 13 of the Kuhnian paradigm concept, not being amenable to brief summary, was not repeated here.

Of special significance are, besides the '*demythologizing of holism,*' the *rational interpretation of the behavior of 'normal' scientists* made possible by the nonstatement view and *the argument showing that the phenomenon of theory dislodgement need not lead to relativism.* The dynamics of normal scientific change include the special case of '*accumulative' normal scientific progress.* Revolutionary theory dynamics include the special case of '*noncumulative' theory dislodgement which nevertheless represents progress in the sense that the theory being dislodged is reducible to the theory dislodging it.*

> We are not, of course, suggesting that the reduction concepts sketched in Chapter 9 are sufficient, even in principle, for apprehending all types of ' progressive theory dynamics.' Since research in this area is just getting under way, one must presume that future investigations will reveal the necessity of numerous additions and modifications.

Against the view that Kuhn's treatment of the phenomenon of theory dislodgement contains a rationality gap it might be objected that Kuhn's conception is not as coarse as we make it out to be. Actually, should one decide to 'put the best construction on everything,' one could interpret Kuhn's view as *presenting a challenge to the philosophy of science*: namely, to introduce a concept of the growth of knowledge with whose help the two apparently incompatible aspects of 'revolutionary' dynamics, *incommensurability* and *progress*, can be reconciled. We could then no longer maintain that Kuhn's exposition of theory dislodgement is *faulty*. We would have to limit ourselves to the observation that he has pointed out a desideratum. A concept of scientific progress is needed which allows for his incommensurability thesis and which is not teleological, in contrast to Popper's ' teleological' notion of ever-increasing approximation to truth.

It seems appropriate to conclude by adding a few expository remarks designed to take the sting out of the accusation implicitly contained in the emphasis placed on a rationality gap and lend a friendlier tone to the discussion of this one point in which we appeared to dissociate ourselves completely from Kuhn.

To start with, the remark that Kuhn's account of the phenomenon of theory dislodgement contains a rationality gap was *not* meant as a logically founded statement, but only as a sort of 'expression of inconceivability.' When someone asserts that *A* and *B* are incommensurable, the introduction of a 'meaningful' concept of *B*'s progress vis-à-vis *A* appears *inconceivable*. The inconceivability leaves only one apparent escape route: follow Hegel and *identify world history with world justice*—those who actually prevail *are* the more progressive. Kuhn himself seems to have fallen victim to this temptation, at least in the passage from p. 166 of [Revolutions] quoted earlier.

Now one could, however, attempt to disarm the inconceivability presumption itself by asking in what sense exactly *incommensurability* is thought to exist. Since *A* and *B* are theories, one naturally thinks right away of their *internal construction*. And all of Kuhn's relevant remarks as well as those of Feyerabend indicate that *just this* was meant. But a comparison of internal structure is *not the only possible way to compare two theories. Even theories with 'totally incommensurable' internal structures can be compared with respect to their achievement capacities.* Kuhn himself draws *such* comparisons when, for example, he asserts that a new paradigm is capable of 'solving puzzles' which the old one could not handle. And it was just this sort of comparison concerning the 'external achievement capacity,' not the 'internal structure,' that, among other things, motivated the introduction of the Adams–Sneed type of reduction concept in Chapter 9. Seen from this angle various earlier statements must be revised or watered down. Instead of alleging Kuhn's version of theory dynamics to be faulty, we must acknowledge that it contains an implicit challenge to explicate more precisely what he has said metaphorically about greater achievement capacity despite total difference of internal structure. We can then assume the position that the said reduction concepts represent a promising beginning for a successful explication, although certainly not the last word.

The last five pages of Kuhn's book could be cited as additional evidence that things really *ought* to be seen from this angle. Above all the comparison of his conception with Darwin's theory makes it clear *what* he is *aiming at*, and especially *what* he is *against*. His concluding remarks are intended to explain why his theory must appear as offensive to contemporaries as did Darwin's theory. In both cases the reason lay in the *nonteleological approach*. The idea that Man evolved from lower species was not, so Kuhn remarks, the really new aspect of Darwin's theory. There was already plenty of evidence supporting this idea. The most significant, and at the same time most bothersome, aspect of his theory was his entirely novel insistence that evolution could *not* be interpreted as a goal-directed process in which the successive stages of development represent *a more perfect realization of a plan present from the very beginning.*[95]

Kuhn wants to *apply this aspect of Darwinian theory to the development of the natural sciences*. The development of science, or scientific progress as it is often called, should no longer be interpreted as a *goal-directed evolutionary process*, as a development leading to the complete, objective, only true interpretation and explanation of nature, whereby scientific achievement is to be measured in terms of the degree to which it contributes to attaining this goal. Evolution-from-what-we-do-know should take the place of evolution-toward-what-we-wish-to-know.

Our reconstruction also complies with this desideratum. One might even see this as the chief difference to the Popperian interpretation of scientific evolution. Popper's idea of an *ever-closer approximation to truth* represents a species of the *teleological* view of progress. On the other hand, our resolution of the 'rationality gap' in Kuhn's analysis of theory dislodgement presupposes nothing which requires this process to be seen as a *goal-directed* process. *The concept of theory reduction does not involve even the most indirect reference to a teleological idea.*

Moreover, this concept even accomplishes Kuhn's further analogy to biological selection: the 'increasing refinement and specialization' of the instruments we call modern scientific knowledge. The reducing theory permits more differentiation than the one reduced. Where the latter discerns but *one* thing, the former can distinguish *several* different things. The idea of a 'total difference in internal structure (core),' on which Kuhn's incommensurability thesis rests, is amenable *both* to a 'quantitative' achievement comparison of 'more or less' *as well as* to the 'qualitative' comparison of 'coarser or finer.' And especially important for us is that all these features can be precisely articulated in a rational reconstruction so that one can get a detailed look at their *conceptual construction* and is no longer dependent on images and metaphors.

Finally, let us again remember that theory *propositions*, not theories, are only *empirically tested* in certain fixed ways. We must realize that of the triad *holding a theory*, *theory dislodgement*, and *testing and corroboration*

---

[95] Cf. [Revolutions], pp. 171–172.

of hypotheses no member can be played off against the others as 'true rationality' or the 'essential characteristic of science.' They constitute a unit (albeit not a trinity) in the sense that each of them needs the other, and that the omission of any one of them narrows and distorts our picture of the *rational* components involved in the growth of knowledge.

19 Methodology of Research Programmes or Epistemological Anarchy? The Lakatos–Feyerabend Controversy

19.1 The normative aspect of methodological rules according to Lakatos

In Section 16.4 we tried to interpret some of Lakatos' ideas, partly as suggestions for subsuming certain processes belonging to the course of normal science in Kuhn's sense under the concept of research programme, partly as an attempt to close the rationality gap opened up by Kuhn's incommensurability thesis. Lakatos' thinking also has a normative aspect, as was mentioned at the end of Section 16.2 but not discussed further.

Much of what Lakatos says can best be understood as a reaction to Kuhn's challenge to that brand of 'critical rationalism' represented by Popper. He *tries to develop Popper's ideas further, and indeed in such a way that the results obtained may be used to launch a counterattack on Kuhn's conception of science.*

Just how this should serve to accentuate the normative aspect so strongly may best be seen by carefully noting that Popper's original version of 'falsificationism' can be *interpreted in three different ways.*

Popper's discourses in [L. D.], as well as in his other epistemological writings, can be interpreted first as *historical observations* or the rational reconstruction of such.[96] Second, they can be regarded as the intuitive spadework for metascientific analysis, or for the reconstruction and explication of certain concepts of the metatheory of the empirical sciences. According to this second reading, the 'formalizer's' reading, one can discern in Popper's studies *the formulation of 'metascientific research programmes'* —albeit *mostly unrealized* programmes, since both Popper and his followers have a perplexing aversion to concept explication, i.e., *an aversion to saying clearly what they really mean.*

---

[96] This is, for example, the interpretation upon which Kuhn bases his criticism of Popper. It was Popper's 'narrative tone' that urged him to adopt this interpretation. Cf. his quotation from the beginning of *The Logic of Scientific Discovery* in [Psychology], p. 4, along with the commentary.

Two brief examples illustrating this last point: Popper's notion of *corroboration* is intended to be the deductivistic 'counterpart' to the concept of inductive confirmation, whereby one usually proceeds as if one knew what "corroboration" meant. *But this is by no means the case.* As proof of this one can cite the thinking of W. Salmon, who attempted to show that under the name "corroboration" the problem of induction finds its way into deductivism.[97] Salmon's idea, which is drawn from various Popperian sources and is *prima facie* quite plausible, I have criticized elsewhere.[98] But Salmon can scarcely be blamed for his error, since the only precise clue Popper gives as to what he understands under "corroboration" seems to be confined to a single passage—quite well hidden at that—in the second paragraph of footnote 1 on p. 266 of [L. D.]. Even here there is no exact definition, but at least an indication of how an explication of this *deductive confirmation concept*, as one might label it instead of "corroboration," must run.[99]

Another catchword used by the Popper school—this time for polemical purposes—is the expression "*justificationism.*" One can scarcely imagine a more misleading label for what it is supposed to denigrate. It is at least as misleading as the phrase "critical rationalism" seen retrospectively in the light of our analyses. It insinuates that the inductivists—be they, like Salmon, from the Reichenbach camp or be they 'Carnapians'—are still seeking methods of justifying scientific hypotheses while the 'deductivists' have this long time recognized the hopelessness of such an enterprise. In truth, the 'deductivists' have a goal similar to that of the 'inductivists.' It consists (1) of *explicating the confirmation concept*, and (2) of demonstrating the *adequacy and relevance* of this confirmation concept. (It is, of course, assumed that the belief in mechanical rules leading to certain truth has only historical interest today, but can no longer be considered a tenable position, and thus need not be considered in its own right here.) Ever so many programmatic declarations, coupled with redubbing the *still to be explicated* deductive confirmation concept "corroboration," cannot disguise the fact that inductivists of all different shades have come nearer to their explication goal than the deductivists. As one difference between justificationism and deductivism (corroboration theory), they could thus rightly claim that *justificationists at least make an effort to specify what they mean while 'antijustificationistic' Popperians do not* (be it that they do not want to, or that they are not able to).

A third interpretation is the *normative methodological.* According to it Popper has attempted to formulate the rules which a rational scientist *ought* to follow.

Here, too, one could differentiate still further. For instance, in ⌊History⌋, p. 92, Lakatos distinguishes between systems of 'mechanical rules' for

---

[97] Cf. W. Salmon, [Inference], p. 26, and [Justification], p. 28.

[98] Stegmüller, [Induktion], p. 46 and p. 48f.

[99] In [Induktion], p. 32, an explication is suggested which stems from my colleague M. Käsbauer and can form the basis for the discussion of further refinements.

solving problems ("methodology" as understood in the seventeenth and eighteenth centuries) and modern methodology which develops criteria for judging *theories already at hand*. As opposed to *heuristics* which provides the scientist with rules for finding solutions to problems, the *Popperian methodology* is supposed to provide rules for judging solutions already at hand. (Cf. Lakatos, *op. cit.*, footnote 2, p. 123.)

This distinction is not, however, maintained consistently either by Popper or by Lakatos, as the following remarks show.

The basic outlines of this methodology run roughly as follows. Scientific research begins with *problems*. Problems are the result of a conflict between expectation and observation. Since there is no certain path to truth in empirical sciences, solving a problem *ought* to conform to the rules of criticism. Suggested solutions *ought* not to be supported and protected from criticism; instead they *ought* to be subjected to the severest critical scrutiny or strictest test possible. Any step which can serve to erect a protective wall around a hypothesis leads away from criticism and should be cast aside. Any step contributing to a sharper critical evaluation of the hypothesis is *welcome*. Now, hypotheses differ in breadth of content, i.e., with respect to the class of potential falsifying factors. Since broader content means greater vulnerability for the theory, the broadest possible hypothesis among those offering themselves as a solution to the problem *ought* to be chosen. Criticism has the best chance here. If it is successful, i.e., if potential falsification becomes *effective* falsification by way of an acknowledged basis, the theory *ought* to be considered dead once and for all (relative to the acknowledged basis). In particular one *ought not* try to rescue a hypothesis with *ad hoc* assumptions; i.e., one ought to reject conventionalistic immunization strategies. At a higher level two new problems arise. It must first be explained why the theory was initially successful and then why it nevertheless falls before experience. The solution of these problems consists of constructing a new theory which *ought* to satisfy the following three formal conditions: it allows for *all* the successful predictions which the old hypothesis did; it yields *additional* experientially corroborated predictions which could not be obtained with the old theory; and finally it does *not* yield the empirically refuted consequences of the old theory.

It hardly needs saying that this methodology falls completely within the orbit of the statement view as witnessed among other things by the equating of hypotheses and theories. Moreover, the view according to which problems arise from a 'conflict between expectation and experience' shows that an everyday situation is being thought of *in which there is still no complicated conceptual inventory available for formulating problems*. The decisive difference between the theory dynamics of Popper and of Kuhn (in the Sneedian reconstruction) is that in Kuhn's version the old theory is directly dislodged by the new theory while according to Popper it can only take the place of the old after the old has been falsified by experience. Popper's picture may be more appropriate for more primitive stages of thought where there is no need to distinguish between hypotheses and theories. But at least in those cases involving *a theory of mathematical physics held in the sense of D30* the Kuhnian view *alone* is appropriate. For both in the case where the theory remains the same, as well as where it changes, old hypotheses are discarded and new ones formulated. But only the reconstruction of theory dislodgement as Kuhn understands it is capable of clearly differentiating between those cases where hypothetical convictions change *while the theory remains constant* and those cases where not only convictions but the *theory as well* changes.

Yet we are not concerned here with criticizing Popper, but with paving the way for the possible interpretations of Lakatos' views. *These, too, can be interpreted in three ways.* Setting aside for the moment the historical reading, we find in the second alternative a complete parallel to Popper's case. As systematic analyses, Lakatos ideas may be seen as metascientific research programmes—"programmes," because, again, they contain only intuitive outlines. Seen in this light the exposition in Section 16.4 comprises *an attempt to successfully realize some of Lakatos' metascientific 'research programmes.'* But we must remember that paradoxically this attempt helps undermine his normative methodology. For with the Lakatos solution to the rationality gap created by the incommensurability thesis, not only the course of 'normal science,' but Kuhnian scientific revolutions as well, lose the *appearance* of irrationality.

This attempt is in any case much more appropriate than one undertaken with the help of Popper's notion of verisimilitude. For truth is at best the goal, not the means, of judging a hypothesis. On this point cf. my article [Induktion], pp. 47–48.

But no matter which closure of the Kuhnian rationality gap one prefers, *cumulative growth of knowledge and noncumulative theory dislodgement are no longer mutually exclusive alternatives.* When a dislodging theory 'takes over all the achievements of the dislodged' and adds some of its own, one can certainly speak *of the accumulation of knowledge in the revolutionary phase,* despite the 'incommensurability' of the theories (i.e., the heterogeneity of their cores).

In [Research Programmes] Lakatos seems to have thought otherwise. Like Popper, he too thought he must combat irrationalism, vanquishing it with a normative methodology. Under the pressure of Kuhn's challenge he liberalized Popper's original methodology and sought to improve it with his *methodology of research programmes.* If we understand the concept of research programme used in Section 16.4 in a normative, not a descriptive sense, the basic idea amounts to the following: it is not isolated theories which are judged but *sequences of theories.*[100] If, then, the development is successful in the end—a development creating a 'progressive problem shift' —the research programme is sanctioned, even if some members of the sequence must be rejected according to Popper's 'naive falsificationism' because they can only be saved from falsification by *ad hoc* hypotheses. When, on the other hand, the sequence produces a 'degenerative problem shift' in that it hinders research and slows up development, the research programme represented by this sequence should be dumped.

In [Against], p. 77f., Feyerabend points out an internal difficulty with this conception. It can *only* be realized *when combined with a fixed temporal limit.* If no such limit is set, one is not able to say how long one must wait to determine whether or not the development is successful. What initially looks like a degeneration can subsequently turn out to be 'progressive.' Thus it remains undetermined which case holds, and, hence, whether the program ought to be approved or discarded. On the other hand, the introduction of a fixed temporal limit is arbitrary (why not wait just a little bit longer?[101]) and obviously means only a very slight modification of 'naive falsificationism.' (*Exactly the same criteria* are used as in Popper's case, only now the phenomenon being judged is more complex.)

In [My Critics][102] Kuhn raises another presumably justifiable complaint. When that which Lakatos calls negative heuristic and positive heuristic is really to be understood as *normative* (so that the first instructs the scientist which route to avoid, the second which to take), his exposition is far too indefinite. The criteria or rules which are supposed to guide scientists in their decisions must be exactly specified. Otherwise, says Kuhn, Lakatos has "told us nothing at all."

If we think back on our reconstruction of Kuhn's normal science concept and draw into it the concept of a research programme in accord with the proceedings of Section 16.4, it should be clear that, and why, an attempt to

---

[100] We speak here of theories although we actually mean theory propositions (or, alternatively, expanded cores). Since in contrast to Section 16.4 we are for the moment interested in depicting normative methodology and not in a reconstruction of a concept of scientific progress, we will overlook the difference.

For those familiar with Lakatos' article it should be pointed out that it is not just within the framework of our reconstruction that his expression "theory" must be assigned two different meanings. Lakatos himself does not use the expression uniformly. For example, after having introduced theories at p. 118 of [Research Programmes] *as members of a sequence* of the sort called "research programme" on p. 132, he nevertheless speaks of the Einsteinian *theory* and the Newtonian *theory* at p. 124. Since it would obviously be absurd to regard these 'theories' as members of a sequence in the sense of p. 118 (what could possibly constitute a research programme including them both?), one cannot help but regard the use of the word "theory" in phrases like "Einsteinian theory" as a lapsus linguae and substitute "research programme" for it (e.g., "Newtonian *research programme*" etc.).

[101] Feyerabend cites here the historical fact that once in a while a theory flowers again after centuries of stagnation.

[102] P. 239; cf. there also the second reading of Lakatos' remarks suggested by Kuhn.

meet this Kuhnian challenge to Lakatos must remain a hopeless undertaking. Lakatos still wants to play off the 'empirically based' rejection of a theory or sequence of theories, which to him appears to be the only rational way, against the phenomenon of theory dislodgment, which to him appears irrational. But what he regards as a sequence of theories is a sequence of theory propositions all of which are formulated with the help of the same mathematical apparatus (core). Even when normal science stalls and a period of successful core expansions gives way to setbacks—when in Kuhn's terminology the anomalies begin to pile up—there is still no reason to junk the theory. *To search for the critical point at which rational grounds dictate such a move is to chase fantasies.* To *see* this one needs no more than to recall the psychological platitude, already quoted, to the effect that *one should not throw away a tool which once served well, if not exceptionally, as long as a better one is not available.*

From this vantage point one dark side of the Kuhn–Lakatos controversy can presumably be illuminated. In [Lakatos] Kuhn remarks that his and Lakatos' views have a far greater similarity than Lakatos is willing to admit. Lakatos, Kuhn feels, disproportionally plays up the differences because he, Lakatos, believes he must defend the rationality of science and fears that should he take *history* as earnestly as Kuhn he will end up with a view similar to the one he imputes to Kuhn: namely, that science is an irrational undertaking.[103]

An adequate commentary on this passage must distinguish between a positive and a negative side: positive, namely, in the sense of "pro Kuhn, contra Lakatos" and negative in the sense of "contra Kuhn, pro Lakatos." The *positive side*: There actually is a great similarity as the reconstructions in Section 16.4 have shown. A detailed articulation of Lakatos' ideas within the framework of the nonstatement view would make this similarity so striking that one could be tempted to say Lakatos had 'almost become a Kuhnian' —albeit one who, as far as possible, describes the same phenomena in a 'Popperian terminology.' Various of Lakatos' more recent statements seem to underscore this similarity explicitly, for instance, the altogether fitting remark: "Rational reconstruction of science ... cannot be comprehensive since human beings are not completely rational animals."[104]

The *negative side*: As we saw, various of Lakatos' ideas can be interpreted as aiming at a solution of the rationality gap created by Kuhn's incommensurability thesis. This point is, however, compromised by the fact that Lakatos—like various other of Kuhn's critics, e.g., Watkins—occasionally spies a rationality gap where there is none. In [History], p. 96, for example, he reproaches 'conventionalism' for being unable to *explain rationally why*, at a particular stage of development, one theoretical system is preferred to

[103] Cf. especially Kuhn's remarks in [Lakatos], pp. 139 and 143.

[104] [History], p. 102.

254

another when the relative merits of the systems are still unclear.[105] Here one can do nothing but repeat that no one is capable of giving a rational explanation *of this kind*, and this must simply be recognized. The situation is completely analogous to the case where an inventive craftsman produces a new tool. There is no rational, but at best an historic-psychological or genetic explanation as to why he created exactly this tool instead of choosing one of the many hundreds of millions of other possibilities.

> In [History] Lakatos surveys schematically the various competing methodologies of science. However, none of the titles he mentions fit the conception developed in this book. At best one could think of it as a variant of the *instrumentalism* he mentions on p. 95. But the objections raised there do not apply to this 'new' instrumentalism. It is not based on confusing truth with confirmation, nor does it overlook the possibility of something being both true and unprovable. Instead, it drops the fundamental presupposition that a theory *can* even be true or false. And this presupposition is *not* dropped because talk of truth is disqualified as 'dumb philosophical blather,' but rather *because only propositions can be true or false and a theory is neither a proposition nor does it consist of propositions.*
>
> Instrumentalism is for Lakatos a special case of conventionalism. And conventionalistic historiography in general he accuses[106] of being unable to explain *rationally* why certain 'systems of pigeonholes' are given a try instead of others. If we take 'systems of pigeonholes' to mean cores, the superiority of the 'new' instrumentalism lies not in the ability to deliver such rational explanations, but rather to explain why they are impossible.

In [History] Lakatos is also concerned with demonstrating the relevance of metascientific constructions for the history of science. This is undoubtedly an exceptionally important question which we must, however, pass over here because it belongs to a theme we are not treating: namely, the methodology of the history of science.

But this article is also relevant for our present problem since in it Lakatos waters down considerably the claim raised in [Research Programmes]. There he explicitly emphasizes that a normative methodology states rules telling scientists which paths they *ought* to pursue and which to avoid. In [Replies], however, he tries to defuse various objections brought against his views by maintaining that *his methodology is not intended to guide scientists in their current or future behavior; he is only concerned about an ex post facto evaluation of past scientific theories or research programs.* (*Today* Lakatos would presumably see the decisive difference between his conception and that of Lorenzen as lying in this explicit rejection.)

---

[105] In [History], p. 94, Lakatos does not actually speak of theoretical systems but uses the metaphorical phrase "system of pigeonholes which organizes facts into some coherent whole" tailored to conventionalism.

[106] *Op. cit.*, p. 96.

In the light of this reply various criticisms which Lakatos raises against Kuhn and Feyerabend in [History] come into focus. On p. 104, for example, he says that these two critics have confused *methodological evaluations* of theories and programmes with *heuristic advice* about what scientists should do. Thus, on the basis of this, *methodology* should be limited to the evaluation of *given* scientific achievements, while something different, namely, *heuteristic*, alone gives *advice* to the scientist. Three things must be said here:

First, this view does not accord with that of [Research Programmes]. In passages like this last one and [Replies], p. 174, he *distinguishes sharply between methodology and heuristic.* But in [Research Programmes], p. 132, he not only explicitly says that a research programme contains *methodological rules* specifying which paths of research *ought* to be taken and which left alone, but as labels for these two types of advice he adds in parentheses the words "positive heuristic" and "negative heuristic." *Thus heuristic is explicitly acknowledged to be a part of methodology,* and we are faced with the alternative of saying that Lakatos contradicts himself or of assuming he has changed his position since writing [Research Programmes]. Faced with the necessity of choosing between an ill- and a well-intended criticism we will opt for the latter and repeat our belief that Lakatos (presumably under pressure from the criticism of Kuhn and Feyerabend) revised his view in an essential point.

Second, the distinction between methodology and heuristic will not even hold up in relation to the original version of Popper's theory. Indeed, only those hypotheses already on hand should be subjected to the 'strictest possible test.' However, in case the hypotheses do not stand the test and are rejected, Popper *admonishes* scientists to seek hypotheses having the greatest possible empirical content, being thus especially vulnerable to falsification. *Lakatos himself says* expressis verbis *that this kind of methodology must be counted as heuristic* when he labels the *imperative* "devise conjectures which have more empirical content than their predecessors" as "Popper's supreme *heuristic* rule."[107]

The third and decisive point is that with this retreat to *ex post facto* evaluations nothing is gained; or even worse, with it Lakatos' *theses threaten to lose all intelligibility.* Smart, for example, while discussing these last works of Lakatos in [Science], quite reasonably asks on p. 269 *what the sense of an evaluation can possibly be, if not even a heuristic follows from it.* And in fact it is not so certain *just how evaluations and recommendations can be separated.* When, for example, someone in response to the appropriate question declares "A is a good teacher," this is, depending on the situation, a *recommendation* for interested parties to attend A's lecture series, or a *recommendation* that a university *should* hire A, or a *recommendation* to students that they *ought* to participate in A's seminars, etc.

---

[107] [Research Programmes], p. 132. Italics are mine.

To a certain extent Lakatos seems to be aware of this difficulty. He is now explicitly prepared to accept (because of the separation of evaluation and heuristic) the consequence that awareness of the degenerative character of a research programme *does not* entitle us to infer *that this research programme should not be pursued further.* It is, he remarks, fully rational *to play a risky game.*[108] Here again we encounter a new term. What is, then, a risky game (in the sense of "a risky research programme")? It must well be one that we assume will not be successful. *But how can it be rational to continue pursuing something we assume will fail?* (A gambler playing only for the thrill of it, not for the prospect of winning, is precisely what we do *not* call a rational player.) Besides, *why* does one assume that success will elude it? On the basis of divine revelation, or of an inductive conclusion enabling us to project the present 'degeneration curve' of the research programme into the future? Both would run contrary to Lakatos' metascientific convictions. But when none of this is the case, why should one not assume that this initially falling curve will climb from some future point of time on, as Feyerabend emphasizes first in [Consolations][109] and then later in [Against].[110] Smart weighs still another interpretation.[111] Perhaps Lakatos understood "risky" in the sense of "possibly risky." But then one can only say to *every* scientist (or *every* politician): "Whatever you might do, *it is possibly risky.*" One cannot avoid the conclusion that *all of this no longer makes any sense at all.*

Let us return, however, to the principal problem of a normative methodology. Our position is already indicated by the previous discussions in Part II. It is quite simple. *The specification of normative methodological rules, adherence to which should restore a lost rationality to scientific practice, is completely superfluous. The belief that such rules are needed rests on a false premise.* This false premise consists of Kuhnian 'irrationality,' as the standard interpretation likes to call it, and the 'vague and nebulous' holism propounded by Kuhn and Feyerabend. (We may recall why the first label is entirely misleading. Even if the standard interpretation were true, it would not be Kuhn's position which must be called irrational, but rather the attitude which he *ascribes* to scientists.)

Lakatos' point of departure (somwhat coarsely formulated) is the same as Popper's and many other of Kuhn's opponents. The *normal scientist* is an uncritical dogmatist who does not test his hypotheses. Anyone engaged in *extraordinary research* is a religious fanatic seeking to proselytize others by any means of persuasion and propaganda whatever. When he is successful, he perpetrates a scientific revolution. This sort of 'mob psychology,'

---

[108] [History], p. 104.

[109] P. 215.

[110] Cf. also the discussion of Feyerabend's conception in Section 19.2.

[111] [Science], p. 272.

characteristic of the behavior of the unreasonable masses pursuing science, must be replaced by rules advising the scientist what he should and should not do. Adherence to these rules will restore a *rational character* to the scientific enterprise. Moreover, they should dispose of the mythological holistic theory. The idea that only 'whole systems' can be tested must be replaced by rules instructing the scientist *which parts* of the whole he should reject under *which circumstances*.

This threefold presupposition is null and void for us. The rational reconstructions proposed in Chapters 12–17, i.e., the concepts of normal science ('holding a theory in the Kuhnian sense'), scientific revolution ('one theory dislodging another'), and holism should have dispelled the *appearance of unreasonableness* attaching to these positions and, thus, the motive for combating them. The *normal scientist* does not uncritically hold fast to hypotheses; he *uses a conceptual instrument* whose retention is compatible with changing hypothetical assumptions (nonstatement view). Moreover, the range of application of his theory is almost always only intensionally given—in most cases by paradigm examples—ensuring his theory additional immunity against recalcitrant experience (the rule of autodetermination for the range of application of a theory). Neither is *extraordinary research*, which on the basis of our interpretation consists of erecting new cores, an irrational undertaking (and indeed quite independent of the amount of persuasion and propaganda which may be involved in *spreading* the results of this research). For even if the new core at its inception offers more or less only the 'promise of success,' in the last analysis the theory's usefulness, or lack thereof, is decided by *objective success criteria* derived from the answer to the question of whether or not the new core could be successfully used for core expansions. Likewise it is possible to *compare objectively* old and new theories with the help of macrological criteria. The precise articulation of Lakatos' pertinent ideas in Section 16.4 indicated that "sophisticated falsificationism" constitutes a better metatheoretic research programme than does Popper's notion of verisimilitude, which is not suited for closing Kuhn's rationality gap.

Finally, as far as holism is concerned we tried to show in Chapter 17 that this philosophical conception, too, may be 'demythologized' and rationalized even in the strong form cited there.

Thus, in our view Lakatos' entire normative methodology is based on an empty presupposition. Accepting this view requires that one be prepared to admit that the question "what is rational scientific behavior?" poses no trivial, but rather a difficult 'metatheoretical research programme' in the course of which it may prove necessary to acknowledge that certain initially plausible rationality criteria are *too stereotyped* and must be *given up* in favor of others obtained by a more differentiated analysis.

Whether or not one is prepared to admit this is in turn closely connected with what we earlier called naive rationalism at the metalevel and extravagant rationalism at the object level. The belief that the notion of rational scientific behavior can be cleared up by a few reflections on principles is not that of critical, but rather of a *naive* rationalism. To realize this one need only apply Popper's thesis of the infinity of ignorance *to the metalevel of reflection over human knowledge as well*. Clearing up the notion of scientific rationality need not be less difficult than designing an adequate model of the atom or creating a demonstrably consistent system of mathematics. It is worth recalling here that the 'rational articulation' of various aspects of Kuhn's conception of science had to take the laborious path through the analyses of Part I.

' Extravagant rationalism' at the object level is a consequence of 'naive rationalism' at the metalevel. The conviction that one can in some simple way arrive at a clear and adequate concept of rational scientific behavior spawns, for example, such demands as the one for 'permanent revolution.' But it does not make sense to greet a student of a scientific discipline with the imperative "become a second Einstein!", which is what this demand is tantamount to. He who nevertheless takes such a position nurtures an *inhuman*, not a critical rationalism.

This polemic against a normative methodology is not intended to disguise the fact that every metascientific rational reconstruction has not only a descriptive but also a normative aspect which can at times become very prominent.[112] Nevertheless it would be most misleading to allege that the philosopher of science is striving to create norms for rational scientific behavior. It would be just as misleading as were someone to allege that Kleene's book on metamathematics contains the *norms* which an intuitionistic mathematician as well as a classical logician *ought* to follow. Deductive logic can certainly have a 'normative methodological' function here. When a mathematician, unversed in modern logic, has constructed a complicated proof and feels 'that something is wrong,' he can consult a book about mathematical logic, try to formalize his proof, and find out in this way *what he has done wrong*. The rules of logic can even take on a *heuristic* function. For after he has discovered the mistake he will perhaps tell himself he *ought* to have studied logic sooner in order to avoid such a mistake, that in this case his search for a proof would presumably have taken a different, more successful course.

Generally one will scarcely be able to say more than that clarity at the second level of rational articulation *can* be a positive factor for analogous endeavors at the first level.

---

[112] For general considerations cf. Stegmüller, [Personelle Wahrscheinlichkeit], Introduction, 1 (III). For specific examples cf. the corresponding remarks in Chapters 12–17.

19.2 Some tongue-in-cheek remarks about Feyerabend's 'counter' reformation[113]

We cannot give a detailed account of Feyerabend's conception here. It will be enough to say that it is quite similar to Kuhn's in most points that are relevant for us.

The difference between our position and Feyerabend's in relation to the normative methodology of Popper and Lakatos could be briefly depicted as follows: while we have contested the validity of the *presupposition* upon which normative methodology is based, Feyerabend attacks it because of its *consequences*.

> A detailed account and criticism of Feyerabend's view may be found in D. Shapere's article, [Scientific Change], pp. 51–85. (This article, however, appeared prior to Feyerabend's [Against].) Shapere describes first what might be called Feyerabend's variant of the incommensurability thesis, namely, the rejection of the 'consistency condition' according to which only compatible theories replace each other,[114] along with his thesis concerning the dependence of meaning on theory. (In Feyerabend's opinion this constitutes an attack on the central theses of traditional empiricism. For according to him the *consistency condition* and *meaning invariance* represent the cornerstones of this philosophical position.) Shapere then explores the internal difficulties of Feyerabend's conception.
>
> He first points out the vagueness of various key concepts. For example, Feyerabend's theory concept is just as unclear as Kuhn's notion of paradigm (p. 56). Furthermore, no indication is given of what is to be understood under meaning and meaning shift (p. 55). Since according to Feyerabend every theory 'has its own experience' and all observations are interpreted in the light of the theory, difficult questions arise: *why make observations at all*, and *on the basis of what criteria is one to decide between various theories*? After discussing three solutions proffered by Feyerabend (pp. 58–61), all of which are doomed to failure on the basis of Shapere's analysis, he finally comes (p. 65) to the conclusion that Feyerabend's interpretation of science has the consequence that *neither* a comparison of theories with experience *nor* a comparison of theories with each other is possible. Thus, Feyerabend's conception, like Kuhn's, leads to *relativism* (p. 66).
>
> Although Shapere's criticism of the three attempted solutions appears to be substantially correct, I would *not* agree with him on other points, in particular concerning the radical consequence. The reasons are similar to those given previously in connection with his criticism of Kuhn (cf. Sections

---

[113] The original reads "Feyerabends 'Gegen'-Reformation." Since the German translation of the title of Feyerabend's article, "Against Method," is "Gegen Methode," we have a play on words here which cannot be reproduced using the standard English expression "Counter Reformation."—*trans.*

[114] In [Against], Section 13, p. 81ff., Feyerabend expressly adopts the incommensurability thesis.

11.2 and 11.3). *Almost all* of Shapere's arguments are based on the statement view and, for the most part lose their force with its rejection. So far as this has not already been done (as, e.g., in Chapter 17), the reconstructions in Chapters 12–17 can also be applied *mutatis mutandis* to Feyerabend *along with the criticism of* Kuhn's *incommensurability thesis* which he also shares. At the various places where Feyerabend *argues in favor of this thesis* he, too, relies on the statement view.

As before, similar differentiations must be made concerning many details, for instance, concerning the thesis of the dependence of all observation on theory. As we remember, one must sharply distinguish here between cases where the reference is to some other theory and those where it is to the theory which is under discussion. For the description of *partial* possible models some *other* theory is used (i.e., a different theory than the one whose models are being dealt with). For the description of *possible* models one is, on the contrary, dependent on the *same* theory (and is, thus, confronted with the difficult problem of theoretical terms).

These brief remarks should not obscure the last clause in the second sentence of this section, where we expressly draw the line at *points that are relevant for us.* Feyerabend's studies contain a good deal more than these. For instance, there are interesting challenges to traditional views, like the one directed at the usual notions about the 'relationship of hypothetical theories and observation' for which there still appears to be no adequate answer.[115] At other places he deviates from Kuhn's views, for example, in the 'methodological justification of a plurality of theories,' in, that is to say, the theoretical level counterpart to the demand for a plurality of methods directed against Popper and Lakatos.[116] The first contains an implicit rejection of Kuhn's concept of normal science. Yet this involves nothing of relevance for us in the present context.

In his latest work, [Against], Feyerabend propounds the new thesis that *anarchy* is an excellent basis for epistemology and the philosophy of science.[117] Under an *anarchistic epistemology* he understands one which lays down neither 'certain, infallible rules,' nor standards for differentiating between 'objective' and 'subjective,' or between 'rational' and 'irrational.'[118] As shown in the following, this is directed primarily against a *normative methodology* which does purport to lay down unchangeable inviolable rules for scientific behavior that simultaneously act as criteria for distinguishing between *science* and *pseudoscience.* This is also the reason

[115] Cf. especially [Against], p. 48ff. On p. 52 for example, Feyerabend asks why, in the case of a conflict between a new theory and 'well-established facts,' the theory should not be used to ferret out 'ideological components' in the so-called facts instead of resolving the conflict by scrapping the theory.

[116] Cf. e.g., [Empiricism I], p. 150; [Empiricism II], p. 257f.; [Against], p. 27.

[117] *Op. cit.*, p. 17.

[118] *Op. cit.*, p. 21.

why Feyerabend expressly takes issue against critical rationalism, indeed, in Popper's original form as well as Lakatos' advanced version.[119]

> Some parts contain brilliant passages and interesting criticisms of the norma-
> tive aspect of Popper's and Lakatos' methodologies. On p. 76ff. Feyerabend
> attempts to show that a 'scientific life' in accord with the rules of critical
> rationalism would not only be *undesirable*, but *indeed impossible*. Among
> other things the incommensurability thesis plays an important part as one of
> the premises here. Therefore, we will come back to this thesis again.

Like Kuhn, Feyerabend, too, is convinced that a belief in methodology as exemplified by 'critical rationalism' runs into insurmountable difficulties *when confronted with the results of historical research*.[120] Normally the attainment of scientific clarity and empirical success has a long, unreasonable, unmethodical history.[121] Thus, the idea that the course of science can, and should, proceed according to a few hard and fast rules is "both unrealistic and vicious."[122]

In the second paragraph of Section 19.2 the basic feature common to our view and Feyerabend's as well as the difference in approach was hinted at. Feyerabend's efforts are bent chiefly to exposing the *disadvantageous consequences for science* resulting from such a normative methodology. For us the necessity for such a methodology is *based on a false premise*: a methodology whose sole purpose is to combat and overcome 'Kuhnian irrationalism' is superfluous because this alleged irrationalism is no more than a pseudoirrationalism. The situation can also be described in such a way that the common ground shared with Kuhn and Feyerabend emerges even more clearly. Were, namely, this methodology realized, it would entail a serious loss of rationality. It would eliminate *the specifically reasonable attitudes of 'normal scientists,'* i.e., of those holding a theory, as well as *the specifically reasonable attitudes of 'scientific revolutionaries,'* i.e., of those persons who design new cores and engage themselves 'propagandistically' to ensure that their new theory dislodges its crisis-ridden competitor. This loss of rationality would presumably be no less serious than *to mean the disappearance of the phenomenon science from our planet.*

The metatheory of science, conceived of as a purely normative discipline, would exhaust itself in concocting unrealistic, i.e., humanly impossible, rationality postulates while ignoring modes of rationality humanly attain-

---

[119] *Op. cit.*, pp. 72–81.

[120] *Op. cit.*, p. 22.

[121] Cf., for example, *op. cit.*, p. 25. Here, as at all other places where *success, progress,* and *scientific rationality* are spoken of, it is nevertheless apparently assumed that there are *some* criteria for distinguishing between, for example, clarity and lack thereof or empirical success and failure.

[122] *Op. cit.*, p. 91.

able. Thus, instead of contributing to an understanding of science, it would degenerate to the empty shell of a 'metatheory of science fiction.'

> The brief formulations of the next to last paragraph involve in one respect an inadmissible assimilation of the views of Kuhn and Feyerabend. Feyerabend, as we have already hinted, takes a much more skeptical view of the achievements of normal science than does Kuhn, as witnessed by his cry for permanent scientific revolution. It goes without saying that on the basis of the considerations in the foregoing chapters we must defend the precise version of Kuhn's conception of normal science developed there against Feyerabend's criticism. We will return to this below.

Our only comment here is that perhaps it would be more practical to cite reasons for disputing a fundamental metatheoretical presupposition of ' critical rationalism' than to compete with Popper and his school as futur-ologist; in other words, *to show why this school has no adequate concept of scientific rationality* instead of speculating over possible future worlds which are deontically perfect judged by the standards of Popper's method-ology.

That there is really nothing so terrible hidden behind Feyerabend's call for epistemological anarchy, which may nevertheless shock some ears, can be illustrated by the following *fact*:

(1) *Lakatos is of the opinion that Carnap was an epistemological anarchist.*

Lakatos would certainly dispute this energetically as being a false allega-tion. And, indeed, he never actually *said* such a thing. *Sentence (1) is, however, a paraphrase of something he did actually say couched in Feyerabend's termin-ology.* In [Changes][123] he does accuse "Carnap and his school" of *com-pletely ignoring* the problem of scientific method.[124] The problems of *discovery* and *scientific progress* remain untouched by Carnap and "method, *qua* logic of discovery, disappears." *Thus, Carnap is being accused of exactly what Feyerabend is proposing.* Actually, Carnap never knew of anything like a normative methodology, *and this was good.* It is not certain how he would have reacted to *current* developments characterized above all by the chal-lenges from Kuhn and Feyerabend. But it is quite certain that on the basis of what was known *in his day*, he would have said he did not believe in a logic of discovery but rather that the investigation of the dynamics of science must be left to psychologists, sociologists and historians.

Alas, it seems Feyerabend with his 'antimethod' polemics wants not only to induce a 'Counter Reformation' aimed at those striving to reform

---

[123] Cf. especially p. 326ff., including footnote 2 on p. 326.

[124] In his inductive logic, for example, Carnap actually takes methodological rules to be some-thing like *rules for applying* 'inductive conclusions.' I have criticized this approach in various places; cf., e.g., [Statistik], p. 301f., where further citations are also given.

a corrupt scientific world by establishing methodological postulates. *He
seems also to turn against any sort of rational reconstruction of the kind
sought, e.g., by Carnap and in the systematic parts of this book.* In other words,
his polemics *against method* ease over, presumably on purpose, into polemics
against rational reconstruction as we understand it, i.e., against a clearer
understanding within the framework of the second level of rational articulation.[125]

It would certainly be false to maintain that Feyerabend seeks no clarification at all. But it does in any case seem that he has confined his own
efforts to an *historical-psychological understanding*, and wants to urge all
others who are interested in science to do the same. We will scrutinize this
position from three quite different angles: first, by means of an *historical
analogy*, which indeed offers no solution to the conflict but does serve well to
clarify the *kind of polarity* involved; second, by reflecting on the *probable
motive* for Feyerabend's 'logical skepticism'; and third, by briefly considering Feyerabend's own *method of arguing*.

(1) As an *historical analogy* let us take once again the example of
Aristotelian logic. Suppose someone had, with arguments similar to
Feyerabend's, tried to convince Aristotle that it is senseless to lose oneself
with logical obstinacy in metatheoretical ruminations over what the participants in the Platonic Dialogues meant when they said "thus" and "therefore"; that it would be much more sensible, and agreeable, to approach
these episodes with literary insight and loving attention to particular details
and surprising turns in the conversations. Had Aristotle listened to such
advice, and had he had the talents of a great Greek tragedian or comedian,
he would have produced a series of fascinating dramas or hilarious comedies.
Only one thing would, I fear, have remained undone: right up to the present
day it would never have been discovered that there is such a thing as logic.

Possibly Feyerabend would remain unmoved and remark that *this
would have been no great disaster*. I would respect such an answer. But with
it the situation changes completely. What initially appeared to be an objective point of contention suddenly turns out to be something quite different:
namely, *a difference in objective*.

Feyerabend seems less bent on achieving *greater clarity concerning the
phenomenon of science* than with *increasing enjoyment of and in science*.
(This is anchored in an 'Epicurean attitude toward life' according to which
happiness, not truth, should be the prime human concern; but we want to
abstract from that here). Between these two goals, however, there need be no
conflict, at least not if one believes those old philosophers who distinguished
levels of pleasure. For there are forms of intellectual enjoyment unattainable
without prior effort. And what difference does it make if kind and quantity

---

[125] This shift already begins at p. 19 of [Against] where the crude, inadequate means of the
logician are confronted with a number of other talents with which they ought to be replaced
(albeit here again in order to explain what actually spawned progress in the past).

are variously distributed among humans? Presumably the number of those enjoying what Feyerabend has to say about science is much larger than the number of those who enjoy trekking through the systematic parts of this book. But, nevertheless, there might just be some of this last breed. And should a conflict really crop up, it could not be resolved at the theoretical level. No, everyone would have to decide for himself where his preference lies. This is a decision which I would *not* regard as a moral matter. For *far be it from me* to equate the alternative "clarity or enjoyment" with something like the Kantian "duty or inclination" or anything even faintly resembling it.

But perhaps Feyerabend is thinking of a serious *psychological problem*: namely, the *disturbing effect of the second level of rational articulation on the first*. To take an especially flagrant imaginary example, suppose all of Wittgenstein's remarks over the foundations of mathematics are right (something difficult for me to do). One would then *prima facie* also suppose that these ideas should be circulated among mathematicians. Suppose, though, these ideas so frustrate mathematicians 'raised in the Platonic tradition' as to render them incapable of any further creative achievement. What should be done in such a situation? One could, for example, recommend and heed the imperative: "Keep all young mathematicians of creative age out of libraries where Wittgenstein's *Remarks on the Foundations of Mathematics* is available!" Besides, one could draw attention to the economic institution of the division of labor.

> Feyerabend's attitude to science could be compared to the attitude of a music lover to music. Here, too, analogous problems could crop up. *X* may perhaps realize that *in a certain way his understanding of music will be enhanced* only by a systematic study of the techniques of harmony, counterpoint, and composition. Possibly *X* fears, though, that this sort of theoretical occupation with music will seriously hamper or even wreck his enjoyment of music. *X* decides, therefore, against becoming a musician.
>
> Couched in terms of our present context this analogy runs roughly: "Since I've finally decided to contribute what I can to the 'second level of rational articulation,' i.e., to a better understanding of 'what is really going on in science,' I'm forced to shelve other pursuits in favor of this one goal, *among them* the perhaps easily underestimated enjoyment of a *non*-meta-theoretical preoccupation with science, its results and evolution."

To return to our first analogy: if one does not categorically *decide* to turn one's back on all logical problems, if, that is, one does not from the very beginning shield oneself from 'everything which this awful Aristotle started,' then one must allow that striving for an explication of what physicists (or Kuhn or Feyerabend) *mean* when they speak of *theories* is just as *legitimate* an aspiration as to seek the meaning of "thus," i.e., the meaning of logical argumentation. The very least that could be held against a rejection of this aspiration would be that with it Feyerabend's tolerance principle comes into conflict with itself.

(2) The *presumed motive* for Feyerabend's rejection of logical reconstructions can be depicted in few words. It is *the dissatisfaction with the achievements to date of a logically oriented philosophy of science.* Here too, however, one should strictly differentiate between (a) criticism of the imitation of 'big brother metamathematics' by philosophers of science, and (b) a rejection of the application of logical analyses to natural sciences. In our opinion (a) is to a certain extent justified, but not (b). Should our assumption be correct, (b) would represent a somewhat hasty induction from the inadequate achievement of logical methods to date to their future inadequacy.

Here, too, the tolerance principle and the multiple feedback mentioned in the introduction may again be pointed to. In one respect striving for clarity is like striving for *self-knowledge.* This latter is not obtained by staring into one's self and finding—of course—nothing. Instead it is '*mediated*' *by a profusion of knowledge about others*, by the picture which one learns others have of him. So *here too*, someone can stand at *one* spot and seek to obtain clarity from his vantage point, e.g., as historian. Where science is concerned, tolerance does not demand rebuking anyone because he, as befits other talents and other 'interests,' stands at some *other* place and likewise seeks greater clarity.

(3) Finally, Feyerabend's *method of arguing* might be investigated. Much more frequently than Kuhn, Feyerabend brings, besides historical, arguments of principle in favor of a view. In [Against], logical arguments are presented above all in favor of the incommensurability thesis.[126] A version of the statement view is always acting *as an unquestioned premise of these arguments.*[127] Since this premise does not hold for us, we need not accept the conclusion even if we admit the correctness of the argument.

All of these reproaches need not convince Feyerabend (and probably will not). For all such considerations can always be met with the skeptical retort that a *logic* of science "might just prove to be a big illusion in the end." The only thing I am able to reply to that would be: "every scientific activity faces this danger."

As far as the theme "*rationality of science*" is concerned, it sometimes appears (especially in [Against]) as if Feyerabend *actually propounds* a view of the sort Lakatos imputes to Kuhn: namely, that the sciences are an irrational enterprise. But this appearance is deceptive. One must not forget that the 'critical rationalism,' at which his polemics are directed, is not *the* rationalism, but an 'inhumanly extravagant rationalism' as our defence of Kuhn's view has shown. That Feyerabend may have had something similar in mind is indicated by those passages where he explicitly comments on this

---

[126] Cf. Section 13 in [Against].

[127] The reader will have no difficulty spotting the statement view of theories at many places in Feyerabend's writings. The argument in support of the incommensurability thesis on p. 82 of [Against] is an example of an argument resting *completely* on the statement view.

question. He says that science is "... *the most rational enterprise that has been invented by man.*"[128] But perhaps even more than Kuhn he is confronted with the difficulty of reconciling this *rationality thesis* with other allegations *appearing to underscore the irrational character of science.* First, there is the alleged fact that "hardly any theory is consistent with the facts,"[129] second, that irrational changes represent an essential feature of the scientific enterprise,[130] and third, the incommensurability thesis which is even more prominent with him than with Kuhn.[131] The fact that in his last work [Against], Hegel and the *Hegelian dialectics* begin to occupy a central position is probably best explained as his hope that Hegelian dialectics, more exactly, dialectic as opposed to nondialectic argumentation, would overcome this contradiction, which in the light of dialectics could presumably be characterized as merely apparent.

We do not need to go into the questions of how dialectics is to be interpreted and of whether it really would take care of the difficulty. It is enough to point out that *one need not seek refuge in Hegelian dialectics in order to overcome this difficulty. The contradiction,* as we have seen, *can be eliminated without all these problems: namely, by giving up the statement view and adopting suitable explications of the concepts of holding a theory and theory dislodgement.*

> Whether or not Feyerabend would really find Hegel on his side is a question which does not belong to our systematic problems and will not be discussed here. But there is one brief consideration which could create some doubt. The light-heartedness which Feyerabend wants to inject into science and philosophy is doubtless foreign to Hegel's basic intention. For him philosophy was a terribly serious business. Presumably he would have said that Feyerabend still has to give an account of his ideas in the language of the concept and ' assume the burden of the concept.'
>
> This remark is neutral in relation to the question of whether Hegel's efforts toward achieving a conceptual pervasion of all and everything were by and large successful, or a total disaster.

As far as they are bent toward a radical criticism of normative methodologies, Feyerabend's efforts are most welcome *because his thinking contributes to erecting a barrier against the demise of the philosophy of science into a metascience of science fiction.* Unfortunately he does not consistently maintain his position.

[128] [Against], p. 80.

[129] *Op. cit.*, p. 43.

[130] *Op. cit.*, p. 80.

[131] *Op. cit.*, p. 81ff.

267

Despite his hefty polemics against various normative methodologies Feyerabend can scarcely deny his Popperian heritage in this respect.[132] His *admonition to the scientist to continuously invent new theories*, especially such as contradict well-confirmed theories, does not jive with his fundamental antimethodological position. The *call for permanent revolution*, on the basis of which Watkins criticized Kuhn's normal science concept, stems originally from Feyerabend. At least in [Empiricism I] he detects in normal science periods of stagnation, lack of ideas, and the beginnings of dogmatism and metaphysics, i.e., something *that ought to be fought and overcome*. It is surely desirable that in times of crisis as many alternative theories as possible *be available*. Nevertheless, it must be said that with his demand Feyerabend again approaches the 'inhuman aspect' of 'critical rationalism.' *It will almost always completely overtax the human capacities* of the normal scientist, who within his discipline may be a *reliable*, even a quite *creative* worker, *should he want to conform to Feyerabend's imperative*. It must be lovely, perhaps even wonderful, to establish brand new cores. *But those who attempt it should entertain no illusions about what they have let themselves in for.* Repeatedly concocting new theories makes superhuman, and thus inhuman, demands upon the *normal* person, and thus upon the *normal* scientist. At the very least Feyerabend still owes us some suggestions concerning what should be done socially and politically about the plight of those many lives ruined by the belated recognition that it is not everyone's fate to become a second Newton or a second Einstein.

We are not faced with such problems. As the precise articulation of the concept of normal science via the introduction of the concept of holding a theory in the Kuhnian sense in Section 15.4 shows, Feyerabend, like the Popperians, *overlooks one dimension of scientific rationality from his position.*

The one and only methodological imperative which a philosopher *ought* to follow runs: "Thou shalt not tell the experts what they ought to do!" Striving for rational reconstruction constitutes no contradiction here. *Efforts bent toward greater understanding via rational reconstruction have absolutely nothing to do with a know-it-all attempt to meddle in the practices of the specialist.*

Feyerabend emphasizes repeatedly that there is no such thing as the correct method. Here one could raise the same question as can be directed at Kuhn in those places where he passes from "so it was" to "so it must be"; namely, *how can one be sure of this*? Is this knowledge acquired (1) on the basis of an *inductive generalization* from the observation that *as yet* all research conducted according to methodological maxims has been unproductive, or (2) via direct insight on the order of Schelling's *intellectual intuition*, or (3) as merely a matter of having *exceeded the competence* of the

---

[132] The qualification "in this respect" is stuck in because there is an even stronger affinity to Popper's school in the disinclination toward precise formal articulation (i.e., to my way of thinking, the disinclination toward saying clearly what one means). But this is not the issue here.

historical perspective, as it presumably was in Kuhn's case? But perhaps Feyerabend intended no assertion at all; perhaps he only wanted to *sound a warning*—a warning against the consequence of such methodologies which for the most part consist of wanting to convince people to pursue a humanly unattainable kind of science. In this case, we must again limit ourselves to the remark that Feyerabend himself does not thoroughly heed his own warning. In the same way that a consistent exponent of the tolerance idea cannot tolerate intolerance, so can a consistent antimethodologist not afford to make such recommendations as Feyerabend indeed does.

As I, a 'formalizer,' see it, the story of 'Popperism' is *the story of a tragedy* capped off by Feyerabend's polemics. If taken as historical analyses Popper's fundamental theses are, by and large, refuted by Kuhn (as Lakatos indirectly admits). If, on the other hand, Popper's ideas are understood as *the intuitive precursors of precise logical articulations still to be realized*, this is a project which has at any rate not been followed up due to the (irrational?) disinclination toward 'formalization.' There remains only *normative methodology* with its unavoidable *slide into the metascience of science fiction* which is the butt of Feyerabend's ridicule. Precisely on this account Feyerabend might reply there is nothing at all about his remarks partaking of a tragedy. But this is not how our remark about capping off a tragedy was meant. We meant rather that it was a part of the 'internal structure' of this antique drama genera that a tragedy be followed by an alleviating satire.

The comments up to this point are not intended to disguise the fact that Feyerabend has pointed out many problems—problems for which I do not have the correct answer. But for me, in contrast to Feyerabend, this is not symptomatic of the inefficacy of the philosophy of science, but rather a reminder that we have here a discipline which, unlike mathematics and logic, is still in its infancy.

If one concentrates not on the motive, but on the outcome, namely, on the rejection of a methodology dictated by philosophers, it appears that our position is substantially the same as Feyerabend's. But this should not disguise the fact that as far as the means incorporated are concerned, we are light years apart. The basis of all our systematic considerations, which in turn should serve to demonstrate indirectly the capabilities of this basis, has been, as Feyerabend sees it, the "crude and laughably inadequate instruments of the logician."[133]

---

[133] [Against], p. 19.

Concluding Remarks

The questions dealt with in this book have no effect upon the kind of solutions appropriate for problems belonging to the complex "testing, confirmation, and assumption and rejection of hypotheses." Its contents would only conflict with the claim of their being the *exclusive* criterion for answering the question "rational or not?" No matter what kind of confirmation concept is thought to be adequate (deductivistic, inductivistic, or whatever), no matter how adequate rules of acceptance and rejection might be formulated, and no matter what degree of strictness an adequate empirical test must conform to, if *this* aspect of 'critical rationalism' is taken as the absolute criterion (in a critical deductivism, critical inductivism, or critical whatever) between science and pseudoscience, *all actual science becomes pseudoscience.* For none of the forms of scientific enterprise described by Kuhn satisfy such a criterion.

Normal science would be degraded to pseudoscience because in it a theory is held fast *regardless of what experience has to say.*

Scientific revolutions would be pseudoscientific processes inasmuch as they do not eliminate a theory because it has been empirically falsified, *but because it has been dislodged by another theory.*

The philosopher of science *also* has the task of contributing, via rational reconstruction, to a logical understanding of these two types of process: namely, that in which the theory remains unaltered, and that in which it changes. Had the philosophy of science nothing to offer but a 'static analysis' of an adequate corroboration concept, static confirmation and theory dynamics would remain irreconcilable.

Understanding the rational character of both types of dynamics is *not* a matter of formulating *new criteria of rationality* and proving that they are satisfied. A different way is indicated.

The first step in the rational reconstruction leads to the recognition that *a theory is not a hypothesis and neither does it consist of hypotheses* (non-statement view).

The *apparent irrationality* of the dynamics of 'normal science' disappears as soon as the *concept of holding a theory* is explicated. Those 'having a theory' in this sense combine with it varying convictions and changing hypothetical assumptions—the core remains stable, its expansions vary.

The 'negative side' of revolutionary theory dynamics, waiting for a new theory before letting the old theory fall, is also only *apparently irrational.* For the failure of a finite number of attempts to expand a core cannot imply that a successful expansion is impossible. The belief in a 'critical empirical

270

threshold' at which an as yet unsuccessful theory *must* be rejected is therefore an *irrational* belief in the existence of an impossible proof. An alleged critical rationalism which tries to persuade us to blame the core (and not the person using it) for each unsuccessful expansion displays an *inhuman* bent in the elementary sense that the success of this attempt would presumably mean, not the optimum, but the extirpation of exact sciences on our planet.

The 'internal incommensurability' of dislodging and dislodged theories due to differences in core makes the dynamic process of theory dislodgement *prima facie* 'nonaccumulative.' Thus, it appears we are forced to speak of *mere change* instead of scientific progress. This time *talk of the progress of knowledge appears* to be irrational. Yet this rationality gap, too, can be closed. Difference of core with simultaneous progress is neither to be denied, nor can it be mastered by a promising normative methodology, nor is it a phenomenon which could be triumphantly pronounced an 'irrational moment in the rational enterprise science, understandable only as dialetics.' It is much more a matter of a 'metascientific puzzle' on its way to being *solved. The solution lies in comparing achievements by means of the macrological concept of theory reduction.* One could say that where theory reduction obtains, progress obtains which is, in one sense, accumulative while in another not. The first sense concerns an achievement increase, the second the incommensurability of the cores.

As far as hypotheses are concerned, the distinction between a *discovery context* and a *justification (substantiation) context* continues to hold. Concerning *theories*, though, this distinction no longer makes sense because of their nonpropositional character.

Since the irrationality of theory dynamics is merely apparent, there is no need to invoke a *normative methodology* to overcome it. The latter can call it quits for lack of anything to regulate.

And this robs the call for *epistemological anarchy* of much of its polemic point, since the 'real' enemy has already succumbed to superfluity.

Despite various polemic jabs Part II also aims not only at criticism, but at clarification and the reconciliation of apparently incompatible positions. This last aspect probably gives the book a somewhat archaic touch. For today, following Wittgenstein and Austin, the slogan runs "the difference makes all the difference!" Leibniz, on the other hand, regarded the exposure of common ground, deeply buried under peripheral differences, as one of the tasks of a fruitful philosophy. Yet Leibniz is long gone.

Bibliography

ADAMS, E. W. [Rigid Body Mechanics], Axiomatic foundations of rigid body mechanics, unpublished dissertation, Stanford University, 1955.

ADAMS, E. W. [Foundations of Rigid Body Mechanics], The foundations of rigid body mechanics and the derivation of its laws from those of particle mechanics, in: HENKIN, L., P. SUPPES, and A. TARSKI (eds.), *The Axiomatic Method*, Amsterdam, 1959, pp. 250–265.

BAR-HILLEL, Y. [Language], *Aspects of Language*, Amsterdam–Jerusalem, 1970.

BAR-HILLEL, Y. [Philosophical Discussion], A prerequisite for a rational philosophical discussion, in: BAR-HILLEL, Y. [Language], pp. 258–262.

BAR-HILLEL, Y. [Neo-Pseudo Issue], Neorealism vs. neopositivism: A neo-pseudo issue, in: BAR-HILLEL, Y. [Language], pp. 263–272.

CARNAP, R., *Philosophical Foundations of Physics*, New York, 1966.

CRAIG, W., and VAUGHT, R. L. [Finite Axiomatizability], Finite axiomatizability using additional predicates, *Journal of Symbolic Logic, 23*: 289–308 (1958).

DUHEM, P., *The Aim and Structure of Physical Theory*, New York, 1962.

ESSLER, W. K., *Wissenschaftstheorie I, Definition und Reduktion*, Freiburg–München, 1970.

FEIGL, H., The "orthodox" view of theories: remarks in defense as well as critique, in: RADNER, M., and S. WINOKUR (eds.), *Minnesota Studies in the Philosophy of Science*, Vol. IV: *Analyses of Theories and Methods of Physics and Psychology*, Minneapolis, 1970, pp. 3–16.

FEIGL, H., Empiricism at bay? revisions and a new defense, Boston Colloquium, October 1971.

FEIGL, H., Research programmes and induction, *Boston Studies in the Philosophy of Science*, Vol. VIII, pp. 147–150 (1973).

FEYERABEND, P. K. [Theoretische Entitäten], Das Problem der Existenz theoretischer Entitäten, in: TOPITSCH, E. (ed.), *Probleme der Wissenchaftstheorie. Festschrift für Victor Kraft*, Vienna, 1960, pp. 35–72.

FEYERABEND, P. K., Problems of microphysics, in: COLODNY, R. G. (ed.), *Frontiers of Science and Philosophy*, Pittsburgh, 1962, pp. 189–283.

FEYERABEND, P. K., Explanation, reduction and empiricism, in: FEIGL, H., and G. MAXWELL (eds.), *Minnesota Studies in the Philosophy of Science*, Vol. III: *Scientific Explanation, Space and Time*, Minneapolis, 1962, pp. 28–97.

FEYERABEND, P. K. [Empiricism I], Problems of empiricism, in: COLODNY, R. G. (ed.), *Beyond the Edge of Certainty. Essays in Contemporary Science and Philosophy*, Englewood Cliffs, N.J., 1965, pp. 145–260.

FEYERABEND, P. K. [Empiricism II], Problems of empiricism, part II, in: COLODNY, R. G. (ed.), *The Nature and Function of Scientific Theory: Essays in Contemporary Science and Philosophy*, Pittsburgh, 1969, pp. 275–353.

FEYERABEND, P. K. [Empirist], Wie wird man ein braver Empirist? Ein Aufruf zur Toleranz in der Erkenntnistheorie, in: KRÜGER, L. (ed.), *Erkenntnisprobleme der Naturwissenschaften*, Köln–Berlin, 1970, pp. 302–335.

FEYERABEND, P. K. [Consolations], Consolations for the specialist, in: LAKATOS, I., and A. MUSGRAVE (eds.), *Criticism and the Growth of Knowledge*, Cambridge, 1970, pp. 197–230.

FEYERABEND, P. K. [Against], Against method, in: RADNER, N., and S. WINOKUR (eds.), *Minnesota Studies in the Philosophy of Science*, Vol. IV: *Analyses of Theories and Methods of Physics and Psychology*, Minneapolis, 1970, pp. 17–130.

FRAENKEL, A. A.. and Y. BAR-HILLEL [Set Theory], *Foundations of Set Theory*, Amsterdam, 1958.

FRITZ, K. von [Antike Wissenschaft], *Grundprobleme der Geschichte der antiken Wissenschaft*, Berlin–New York, 1971.

GILES, R., *Mathematical Foundations of Thermodynamics*, New York, 1964.

HALL, R. J., Can we use the history of science to decide between competing methodologies?, in: *Boston Studies in the Philosophy of Science*, Vol. VIII, pp. 151–159 (1972).

HANSON, N. R., *Patterns of Discovery*, Cambridge, 1958.

HATCHER, W. S. [Foundations], *Foundations of Mathematics*, Philadelphia–Toronto–London, 1968.

HEMPEL, C. G., The theoretician's dilemma, in: FEIGL, H., M. SCRIVEN, and G. MAXWELL (eds.), *Minnesota Studies in the Philosophy of Science*, Vol. II: *Concepts, Theories, and the Mind-Body Problem*, Minneapolis, 1958.

HEMPEL, C. G., On the "standard conception" of scientific theories, in: RADNER, M., and S. WINOKUR (eds.), *Minnesota Studies in the Philosophy of Science*, Vol. IV: *Analyses of Theories and Methods of Physics and Psychology*, Minneapolis, 1970, pp. 142–163.

HEMPEL, C. G. [Theoretical Terms], The meaning of theoretical terms: a critique of the standard empiricist construal, in: SUPPES, P., L. HENKIN, A. JOJA, and C. G. MOISIL (eds.), *Logic, Methodology, and Philosophy of Science IV, Proceedings of the 1971 International Congress*, Bucharest, 1971, Amsterdam.

HÜBNER, K., Rezension von T. S. KUHN, *The Structure of Scientific Revolutions*, Philosophische Rundschau, *15*: 185–195 (1968).

JAMISON, B. N. [Lagrange's Equations], An axiomatic treatment of Lagrange's equations, unpublished dissertation, Stanford University, 1956.

KOERTGE, N., For and against method, discussion of P. FEYERABEND's [Against], *The British Journal for the Philosophy of Science*, *23*: 274–285 (1972).

KOERTGE, N., Inter-theoretic criticism and the growth of science, in: *Boston Studies in the Philosophy of Science*, Vol. VIII, pp. 160–173 (1972).

KORDIG, C. R., *The Justification of Scientific Change*, Dordrecht, 1971.

KUHN, T. S., *The Copernican Revolution*, New York, 1957.

KUHN, T. S. [Revolutions], *The Structure of Scientific Revolutions*, 2nd enlarged ed., Chicago, 1970.

KUHN, T. S. [Psychology], Logic of discovery or psychology of research?, in: LAKATOS, I., and A. MUSGRAVE (eds.), *Criticism and the Growth of Knowledge*, Cambridge, 1970, pp. 1–23.

KUHN, T. S. [My Critics], Reflections on my critics, in: LAKATOS, I. and A. MUSGRAVE (eds.), *Criticism and the Growth of Knowledge*, Cambridge, 1970, pp. 231–278.

274

KUHN, T. S. [Lakatos], Notes on LAKATOS, in: *Boston Studies in the Philosophy of Science*, Vol. VIII, pp. 137–146 (1972).

LAKATOS, I. [Changes], Changes in the problem of inductive logic, in: LAKATOS, I. (ed.), *The Problem of Inductive Logic*, Amsterdam, 1968, pp. 315–417.

LAKATOS, I. [Research Programmes], Falsification and the methodology of scientific research programmes, in: LAKATOS, I., and A. MUSGRAVE (eds.), *Criticism and the Growth of Knowledge*, Cambridge, 1970, pp. 91–195.

LAKATOS, I. [History], History of science and its rational reconstruction, in: *Boston Studies in the Philosophy of Science*, Vol. VIII, pp. 91–136 (1972).

LAKATOS, I. [Replies], Replies to critics, in: *Boston Studies in the Philsophy of Science*, Vol. VIII, pp. 174–182 (1972).

LORENZEN, P., *Methodisches Denken*, Frankfurt, 1968.

MACH, E., *Die Mechanik in ihrer Entwicklung*, 1883, 9th ed., Leipzig, 1933.

MASTERMAN, M., The nature of a paradigm, in: LAKATOS, I., and A. MUSGRAVE (eds.), *Criticism and the Growth of Knowledge*, Cambridge, 1970, pp. 59–89.

MCKINSEY, J. C. C., SUGAR, A. C., and SUPPES, P. C. [Particle Mechanics], Axiomatic foundations of classical particle mechanics, *Journal of Rational Mechanics and Analysis*, *II*: 253–272 (1953).

MCKINSEY, J. C. C., and SUPPES, P., On the notion of invariance in classical mechanics, *The British Journal for the Philosophy of Science*, *5*: 290–302 (1955).

NARLIKAR, V. V., The concept and determination of mass in Newtonian mechanics, *Philosophical Magazine*, *27*: 33–36 (1939).

PENDSE, C. G., A note on the definition and determination of mass in Newtonian mechanics, *Philosophical Magazine*, *24*: 1012–1022 (1937).

PENDSE, C. G., A further note on the definition and determination of mass in Newtonian mechanics, *Philosophical Magazine*, *27*: 51–61 (1939).

PENDSE, C. G., On mass and force in Newtonian mechanics, *Philosophical Magazine*, *29*: 477–484 (1940).

PLANCK, M. [Autobiographie], *Wissenschaftliche Autobiographie*, Leipzig, 1928.

POPPER, K. R. [L.D.], *The Logic of Scientific Discovery*, London, 1959.

POPPER, K. R., *Conjectures and Refutations*, 3rd ed., London, 1969.

POPPER, K. R. [Dangers], Normal science and its dangers, in: LAKATOS, I., and A. MUSGRAVE (eds.), *Criticism and the Growth of Knowledge*, Cambridge, 1970, pp. 51–58.

POPPER, K. R., *Objective Knowledge. An Evolutionary Approach*, Oxford, 1972.

PUTNAM, H. [Not], What theories are not, in: NAGEL, E., P. SUPPES, and A. TARSKI (eds.), *Logic, Methodology and Philosophy of Science*, Stanford, 1962, pp. 240–251.

QUINE, W. V. O. [Two Dogmas], Two dogmas of empiricism, in: QUINE, W. V. O., *From a Logical Point of View*, Cambridge, Mass., 1953, pp. 20–46.

QUINE, W. V. O. [Methods], *Methods of Logic*, 3rd ed., New York, 1972.

RAMSEY, F. P., Theories, in: *The Foundations of Mathematics*, 2nd ed., Littlefield, N.J., 1960, pp. 212–236.

SALMON, W. [Inference], *The Foundations of Scientific Inference*, Pittsburgh, 1967.

SALMON, W. [Justification], The justification of inductive rules of inference, in: LAKATOS, I. (ed.), *The Problem of Inductive Logic*, Amsterdam, 1968, pp. 24–97.

SCHEFFLER, I., *The Anatomy of Inquiry*, New York, 1963.

SCHEFFLER, I. [Subjectivity], *Science and Subjectivity*, New York, 1967.

SCHEFFLER, I. [Vision], Vision and revolution: a postscript on Kuhn, *Philosophy of Science, 39*: 366–374 (1972).

SEARLE, J. R., *Speech Acts. An Essay in the Philosophy of Language*, Cambridge, 1969.

SHAPERE, D. [Kuhn], Discussion of T. S. Kuhn, *The Structure of Scientific Revolutions*, in: *Philosophical Review, 73*: 383–384 (1964).

SHAPERE, D. [Scientific Change], Meaning and scientific change, in: COLODNY, R. G. (ed.), *Mind and Cosmos*, Pittsburgh, 1966, pp. 41–85.

SIMON, H. A., The axioms of Newtonian mechanics, *Philosophical Magazine, 38*: 88–905 (1947).

SIMON, H. A., The axiomatization of classical mechanics, *Philosophy of Science, 21*: 340–343 (1954).

SIMON, H. A., Definable terms and primitives in axiom systems, in: HENKIN, L., P. SUPPES, and A. TARSKI (eds.), *The Axiomatic Method*, Amsterdam, 1959, pp. 433–453.

SIMON, H. A., The axiomatization of physical theories, *Philosophy of Science, 37*: 16–27 (1970).

SMART, J. J. [Science], Science, history and methodology, discussion of I. LAKATOS, [Research Programmes] and [History], *The British Journal for the Philosophy of Science, 23*: 266–274 (1972).

SNEED, J. D. [Mathematical Physics], *The Logical Structure of Mathematical Physics*, Dordrecht, 1971.

STEGMÜLLER, W. [Semantik], *Das Wahrheitsproblem und die Idee der Semantik*, 2nd ed., Vienna, 1968.

STEGMÜLLER, W. [Kant's Metaphysik], Gedanken über eine mögliche rationale Rekonstruktion von Kant's Metaphysik der Erfahrung, in: STEGMÜLLER, W., *Aufsätze zu Kant und Wittgenstein*, Darmstadt, 1970, pp. 1–61.

STEGMÜLLER, W. [Induktion], Das Problem der Induktion: HUME'S Herausforderung und moderne Antworten, in: LENK, H. (ed.), *Neue Aspekte der Wissenschaftstheorie*, Braunschweig, 1971, pp. 13–74.

STEGMÜLLER, W. [Erklärung], *Probleme und Resultate der Wissenschaftstheorie und Analytischen Philosophie*, Vol. I: *Wissenschaftliche Erklärung und Begründung*, Berlin–Heidelberg–New York, 1969.

STEGMÜLLER, W. [Theoretische Begriffe], *Probleme und Resultate der Wissenschaftstheorie und Analytischen Philosophie*, Vol. II/1: *Begriffsformen, Wissenschaftssprache, empirische Signifikanz und theoretische Begriffe*, Berlin–Heidelberg–New York, 1970.

STEGMÜLLER, W. [Personelle Wahrscheinlichkeit], *Probleme und Resultate der Wissenschaftstheorie und Analytischen Philosophie*, Vol. IV/1: *Personelle Wahrscheinlichkeit und Rationale Entscheidung*, Berlin–Heidelberg–New York, 1973.

STEGMÜLLER, W. [Statistik], *Probleme und Resultate der Wissenschaftstheorie und Analytischen Philosophie*, Vol. IV/2: *Statistisches Schließen—Statistische Begründung—Statistische Analyse*, Berlin–Heidelberg–New York, 1973.

STEGMÜLLER, W., Structures and dynamics of theories. Some reflections on J. D. Sneed and T. S. Kuhn, *Erkenntnis, 9*: 75–100 (1975).

STEGMÜLLER, W., Accidental ('non-substantial') theory change and theory dislodgement: to what extent logic can contribute to a better understanding of certain phenomena in the dynamics of theories, to appear in: *Erkenntnis 10* (1976).

STEGMÜLLER, W., A combined approach in the dynamics of theories. How to improve historical interpretations of theory change by applying set-theoretical structures. To appear 1976.

SUPPES, P., *Introduction to Logic*, New York, 1957.

SUPPES, P., A comparison of the meaning and uses of models in mathematics and the empirical sciences, in: SUPPES, P., *Studies in the Methodology and Foundations of Science*, Dordrecht, 1969, pp. 10–23.

SUPPES, P., Models of data, in SUPPES, P., *Studies in the Methodology and Foundations of Science*, Dordrecht, 1969, pp. 24–35.

SUPPES, P., and ZINNES, J. L. [Measurement], Basic measurement theory, in: *Handbook of Mathematical Psychology*, Vol. I, New York, 1963, pp. 1–76.

TOULMIN, S., *Foresight and Understanding*, New York, 1961.

WATKINS, J. [Normal], Against "normal science," in: LAKATOS, I., and A. MUSGRAVE (eds.), *Criticism and the Growth of Knowledge*, Cambridge, 1970, pp. 25–37.

WITTGENSTEIN, L., *Philosophische Untersuchungen*, Oxford, 1953.

Index

Index of symbols

Index of numbered definitions

Subject index

281

Author index

Library of Exact Philosophy

Editor: *Mario Bunge,* Montreal

Coeditors: *Sir Alfred Jules Ayer,* Oxford, *Herbert Feigl,* Minneapolis, *Victor Kräft,* Vienna, *Sir Karl Popper,* Penn

Springer-Verlag New York Vienna

Probleme und Resultate der Wissenschaftstheorie und Analytischen Philosophie

by W. Stegmüller

Volume 1

Wissenschaftliche Erklärung und Begründung

Corrected reprint
1974. xxxi, 812p. cloth $52.50
ISBN 0-387-06595-4

Volume 2

Theorie und Erfahrung

Part 1

Begriffsformen, Wissenschafts-sprache, empirische Signifikanz und theoretische Begriffe

Corrected reprint
1974. xv, 485p. 12 illus. cloth $31.20
ISBN 0-387-06692-6

Part 2

Theorienstrukturen und Theoriendynamik

1973. xvii, 327p. 4 illus. cloth $25.50
ISBN 0-387-06394-3

Volume 3

In preparation

Volume 4

Personelle und Statistische Wahrscheinlichkeit

Part 1

Personelle Wahrscheinlichkeit und Rationale Entscheidung

1973. xxiv, 560p. 12 illus. cloth $36.50
ISBN 0-387-05986-5

✓ Part 2

*Statistisches Schließen
—Statistische Begründung—
Statistische Analyse*

1973. xvi, 420p. 3 illus. cloth $27.90
ISBN 0-387-06040-5

Volume 5

In preparation

Also available in paper